POLITICAL SCIENCE AND HISTORY

THE MIDDLE EAST

BACKGROUND AND U.S. RELATIONS

POLITICAL SCIENCE AND HISTORY

Additional books and e-books in this series can be found
on Nova's website under the Series tab.

POLITICS AND ECONOMICS OF THE MIDDLE EAST

Additional books and e-books in this series can be found
on Nova's website under the Series tab.

POLITICAL SCIENCE AND HISTORY

THE MIDDLE EAST

BACKGROUND AND U.S. RELATIONS

DOYLE KELLER
EDITOR

Copyright © 2019 by Nova Science Publishers, Inc.

All rights reserved. No part of this book may be reproduced, stored in a retrieval system or transmitted in any form or by any means: electronic, electrostatic, magnetic, tape, mechanical photocopying, recording or otherwise without the written permission of the Publisher.

We have partnered with Copyright Clearance Center to make it easy for you to obtain permissions to reuse content from this publication. Simply navigate to this publication's page on Nova's website and locate the "Get Permission" button below the title description. This button is linked directly to the title's permission page on copyright.com. Alternatively, you can visit copyright.com and search by title, ISBN, or ISSN.

For further questions about using the service on copyright.com, please contact:
Copyright Clearance Center
Phone: +1-(978) 750-8400   Fax: +1-(978) 750-4470   E-mail: info@copyright.com.

NOTICE TO THE READER

The Publisher has taken reasonable care in the preparation of this book, but makes no expressed or implied warranty of any kind and assumes no responsibility for any errors or omissions. No liability is assumed for incidental or consequential damages in connection with or arising out of information contained in this book. The Publisher shall not be liable for any special, consequential, or exemplary damages resulting, in whole or in part, from the readers' use of, or reliance upon, this material. Any parts of this book based on government reports are so indicated and copyright is claimed for those parts to the extent applicable to compilations of such works.

Independent verification should be sought for any data, advice or recommendations contained in this book. In addition, no responsibility is assumed by the Publisher for any injury and/or damage to persons or property arising from any methods, products, instructions, ideas or otherwise contained in this publication.

This publication is designed to provide accurate and authoritative information with regard to the subject matter covered herein. It is sold with the clear understanding that the Publisher is not engaged in rendering legal or any other professional services. If legal or any other expert assistance is required, the services of a competent person should be sought. FROM A DECLARATION OF PARTICIPANTS JOINTLY ADOPTED BY A COMMITTEE OF THE AMERICAN BAR ASSOCIATION AND A COMMITTEE OF PUBLISHERS.

Additional color graphics may be available in the e-book version of this book.

Library of Congress Cataloging-in-Publication Data

ISBN: 978-1-53616-191-5

Published by Nova Science Publishers, Inc. † New York

CONTENTS

Preface		**vii**
Chapter 1	Saudi Arabia: Background and U.S. Relations (Updated) *Christopher M. Blanchard*	**1**
Chapter 2	Saudi Arabia *Christopher M. Blanchard*	**79**
Chapter 3	Iraq: Issues in the 115th Congress *Christopher M. Blanchard*	**87**
Chapter 4	Jordan: Background and U.S. Relations (Updated) *Jeremy M. Sharp*	**127**
Chapter 5	Lebanon *Carla E. Humud*	**157**
Chapter 6	Turkey: Background and U.S. Relations (Updated) *Jim Zanotti and Clayton Thomas*	**213**
Chapter 7	Iran: U.S. Economic Sanctions and the Authority to Lift Restrictions (Updated) *Dianne E. Rennack*	**277**

Index	**341**
Related Nova Publications	**355**

PREFACE

This book is a compilation of reports on the Middle East. Chapters 1 and 2 discuss the kingdom of Saudi Arabia's relations with the United States, its stability, and its future trajectory. Iraq's government declared military victory against the Islamic State organization (IS, aka ISIS/ISIL) in December 2017, but insurgent attacks by remaining IS fighters threaten Iraqis as they shift their attention toward recovery and the country's political future as reported in chapter 3. Chapter 4 provides an overview of Jordanian politics and current issues in U.S.-Jordanian relations. Chapter 5 provides an overview of Lebanon and current issues of U.S. interest. As discussed in chapter 6, Congress has actively engaged on several issues involving Turkey. Chapter 7 identifies the basis in U.S. law for sanctions imposed on Iran, and the nature of the authority to waive or lift those restrictions

Chapter 1 - The kingdom of Saudi Arabia, ruled by the Al Saud family since its founding in 1932, wields significant global influence through its administration of the birthplace of the Islamic faith and by virtue of its large oil reserves. Close U.S.-Saudi official relations have survived a series of challenges since the 1940s. In recent years, shared concerns over Sunni Islamist extremist terrorism and Iranian government policies have provided some renewed logic for continued strategic cooperation. Political upheaval and conflict in the Middle East and North Africa have created new challenges, and the Trump Administration has sought to strengthen U.S. ties to Saudi leaders as the kingdom implements a series of new domestic and foreign policy initiatives. Successive U.S. Administrations have referred to the Saudi government as an important partner, and U.S. arms sales and related security cooperation have continued with congressional oversight and amid some congressional opposition. The Trump Administration, like its recent predecessors, praises Saudi government counterterrorism efforts. Since 2009, the executive branch has notified Congress of proposed foreign military sales to Saudi Arabia of major defense articles and services with a potential aggregate value of nearly $139 billion. The United States and Saudi Arabia concluded arms sale agreements worth more than $65 billion, from FY2009 through FY2016. Since March 2015, the U.S.-trained Saudi military has used U.S.-origin weaponry, U.S. logistical assistance, and shared intelligence in support of military operations in Yemen. Legislation has been proposed in the 115th Congress to condition or disapprove of some U.S. weapons sales and condition or direct the President to end U.S. support to Saudi operations without specific authorization (H.J.Res. 102, H.J.Res. 104, S.J.Res. 40, S.J.Res. 42, S.J.Res. 54, S. J. Res. 55). In parallel to close security ties, official U.S. reports describe restrictions on human rights and religious freedom in the kingdom. Some Saudi activists advocate for limited economic and political reforms, continuing decades-long trends that have seen Saudi liberals, moderates, and conservatives advance different visions for domestic change. Saudi leaders in 2018 reversed a long-standing ban on women's right to drive, amid some arrests of women's rights advocates and critics of social liberalization. While some limited protests and arrests have occurred since unrest swept the region in 2011, clashes involving Saudi security forces have not spread beyond certain predominantly Shia areas of the oil-rich Eastern Province. Since assuming the throne in 2015, King Salman bin Abd al Aziz (age 82) has made a series of appointments and reassignments that have altered the responsibilities and relative power of leading members of the next generation of the Al Saud family, who are the grandsons of the kingdom's founder. The king's son, Crown Prince Mohammed bin Salman (age 33), is the central figure in Saudi policymaking. He has asserted control over national security forces, sidelined potential rivals, proposed and begun implementing bold economic and social changes, and arrested prominent figures accused of corruption, including some fellow royal family members. Ambitious plans for the transformation of the kingdom's economy seek to provide opportunity for young Saudis and bolster nonoil sources of revenues for the state. Abroad, the kingdom pursues a multidirectional policy and has aggressively confronted perceived threats. Saudi decisionmaking long appeared to be risk-averse and rooted in rulers' concerns for maintaining consensus among different constituencies, including factions of the royal family, business elites, and conservative religious figures. Crown Prince Mohammed bin Salman's assertive and more centralized leadership has challenged this model of governance. The change is leading Saudis and outsiders alike to reexamine their assumptions about the kingdom's future. Congress may examine these developments when considering the scope, terms, and merits of U.S.-Saudi partnership, proposed arms sales and nuclear cooperation, and security commitments.

Chapter 2 - The kingdom of Saudi Arabia, ruled by the Al Saud family since its founding in 1932, wields significant global influence through its administration of the birthplace of the Islamic faith and by virtue of its large oil reserves. Saudi leaders' domestic and foreign policy decisions are fueling calls from some U.S. leaders for a reassessment of longstanding bilateral ties. The Al Saud have sought protection, advice, technology, and armaments from the United States, along with support in developing their country's natural and human resources and in facing national security threats. U.S. leaders have valued Saudi cooperation in security and counterterrorism matters and have sought to preserve the secure, apolitical flow of the kingdom's energy resources and capital to global markets. The Trump Administration seeks to strengthen U.S.-Saudi ties as the kingdom implements new domestic and foreign policy initiatives, while some in Congress call for change.

Chapter 3 - Iraq's government declared military victory against the Islamic State organization (IS, aka ISIS/ISIL) in December 2017, but insurgent attacks by remaining IS fighters threaten Iraqis as they shift their attention toward recovery and the country's political future. Security conditions have improved since the Islamic State's control of territory was disrupted, but IS fighters are active in some areas and security conditions are fluid. Meanwhile, daunting resettlement, reconstruction, and reform needs occupy citizens and leaders. Internally displaced Iraqis are returning home in greater numbers, but stabilization and reconstruction needs in liberated areas are extensive. An estimated 1.9 million Iraqis remain as internally displaced persons (IDPs), and Iraqi authorities have identified $88 billion in reconstruction needs over the next decade. Large protests in southern Iraq during August and September 2018 highlighted some citizens' outrage with poor service delivery and corruption. National legislative elections were held in May 2018, but results were not certified until August, delaying the formal start of required steps to form the next government. Iraqi Prime Minister Haider al Abadi sought reelection, but his electoral list's third-place showing and lack of internal cohesion undermined his chances for a second term. On October 2, Iraq's Council of Representatives (COR) chose former Kurdistan Regional Government Prime Minister and former Iraqi Deputy Prime Minister Barham Salih as Iraq's President. Salih, in turn, named former Oil Minister Adel Abd al Mahdi as Prime Minister-designate and directed him to assemble a slate of cabinet officials for COR approval within 30 days. Paramilitary forces have grown stronger and more numerous since 2014, and have yet to be fully integrated into national security institutions. Some figures associated with the Popular Mobilization Forces (PMF) that were organized to fight the Islamic State participated in the 2018 election campaign and won seats in the Council of Representatives, including individuals with ties to Iran. Iraqi politicians have increasingly employed cross-sectarian political and economic narratives in an attempt to appeal to disaffected citizens, but identity-driven politics continue to influence developments. Iraq's neighbors and other outsiders, including the United States, are pursuing their respective interests in Iraq, at times in competition. The Kurdistan Region of northern Iraq (KRI) enjoys considerable administrative autonomy under the terms of Iraq's 2005 constitution, and the Kurdistan Regional Government (KRG) held legislative elections on September 30,

2018. The KRG had held a controversial advisory referendum on independence in September 2017, amplifying political tensions with the national government, which moved to reassert security control of disputed areas that had been secured by Kurdish forces after the Islamic State's mid-2014 advance. Iraqi and Kurdish security forces remain deployed across from each other along contested lines of control, while their respective leaders are engaged in negotiations over a host of sensitive issues. In general, U.S. engagement with Iraqis since 2011 has sought to reinforce Iraq's unifying tendencies and avoid divisive outcomes. At the same time, successive U.S. Administrations have sought to keep U.S. involvement and investment minimal relative to the 2003-2011 era, pursuing U.S. interests through partnership with various entities in Iraq and the development of those partners' capabilities—rather than through extensive deployment of U.S. military forces. The Trump Administration has sustained a cooperative relationship with the Iraqi government and plans to continue security training for Iraqi security forces. To date, the 115th Congress has appropriated funds for U.S. military operations against the Islamic State and for security assistance, humanitarian relief, and foreign aid for Iraq.

Chapter 4 - This chapter provides an overview of Jordanian politics and current issues in U.S.-Jordanian relations. It provides a brief discussion of Jordan's government and economy and of its cooperation with U.S. policies in the Middle East. Several issues are likely to figure in decisions by Congress and the Administration on future aid to and cooperation with Jordan. These include Jordan's continued involvement in attempting to promote Israeli-Palestinian peace and the stability of the Jordanian regime, particularly in light of ongoing conflicts in neighboring Syria and Iraq. U.S. officials may also consider potential threats to Jordan from the Islamic State organization (IS, also known as ISIL, ISIS, or the Arabic acronym *Da'esh*). Although the United States and Jordan have never been linked by a formal treaty, they have cooperated on a number of regional and international issues over the years. Jordan's small size and lack of major economic resources have made it dependent on aid from Western and various Arab sources. U.S. support, in particular, has helped Jordan address serious vulnerabilities, both internal and external. Jordan's geographic position, wedged between Israel, Syria, Iraq, and Saudi Arabia, has made it vulnerable to the strategic designs of more powerful neighbors, but has also given Jordan an important role as a buffer between these countries in their largely adversarial relations with one another. Public dissatisfaction with the economy is probably the most pressing concern for the Jordanian monarchy. Over the summer of 2018, widespread protests erupted throughout the kingdom in opposition to a draft tax bill and price hikes on fuel and electricity. Though peaceful, the protests drew immediate international attention because of their scale. Since then, the government has continued to work with the International Monetary Fund (IMF) on fiscal reforms to address a public debt that has ballooned to 96.4% of Gross Domestic Product (GDP). The United States has provided economic and military aid to Jordan since 1951 and 1957, respectively. Total bilateral U.S. aid (overseen by the Departments of State and Defense) to Jordan through FY2016 amounted to approximately $19.2 billion. On February 14, 2018, then-U.S. Secretary of State Rex W. Tillerson and Jordanian Minister of Foreign Affairs Ayman Safadi signed a new Memorandum of Understanding (or MOU) on U.S. foreign assistance to Jordan. The MOU, the third such agreement between the United and Jordan, commits the United States to provide $1.275 billion per year in bilateral foreign assistance over a five-year period for a total of $6.375 billion (FY2018-FY2022). This latest MOU represents a 27% increase in the U.S. commitment to Jordan above the previous iteration and is the first five-year MOU with the kingdom. The previous two MOU agreements had been in effect for three years. In line with the new MOU, for FY2019 President Trump is requesting $1.271 billion for Jordan, including $910.8 million in ESF, $350 million in FMF, and $3.8 million in International Military Education and Training (IMET).

Chapter 5 - Since having its boundaries drawn by France after the First World War, Lebanon has struggled to define its national identity. Its population included Christian, Sunni Muslim, and Shia Muslim communities of roughly comparable size, and with competing visions for the country. Seeking to avoid sectarian conflict, Lebanese leaders created a confessional system that allocated power among the country's religious sects according to their percentage of the population. The system continues to be based on Lebanon's last official census, which was conducted in 1932. As Lebanon's demographics have shifted over the years, Muslim communities have pushed for the political status quo, favoring Maronite Christians, to be revisited, while the latter have worked to maintain their privileges. This tension has at times manifested itself in violence, such as during the country's 15-year civil war, but also in political disputes such as disagreements over revisions to Lebanon's electoral law. To date, domestic political conflicts continue to be shaped in part by the influence of external actors, including Syria and Iran. The United States has sought to bolster forces that could serve as a counterweight to Syrian and Iranian influence in Lebanon, providing more than $1.7 billion in military assistance to Lebanon with the aim of creating a national force strong enough to counter nonstate actors and secure the country's borders. Hezbollah's armed militia is sometimes described as more effective than the Lebanese Armed Forces (LAF), and has also undertaken operations along the border to counter the infiltration of armed groups from the war in neighboring Syria. U.S. policy in Lebanon has been undermined by Iran and Syria, both of which exercise significant influence in the country, including through support for Hezbollah. The question of how best to marginalize Hezbollah and other anti-U.S. Lebanese actors without provoking civil conflict among Lebanese sectarian political forces has remained a key challenge for U.S. policymakers. U.S. assistance to Lebanon also has addressed the large-scale refugee crisis driven by the ongoing war in neighboring Syria. There are over 1 million Syrian refugees registered with the U.N. High Commissioner for Refugees (UNHCR) in Lebanon, in addition to a significant existing community of Palestinian refugees. This has given Lebanon (a country of roughly 4.3 million citizens in 2010) the highest per capita refugee population in the world. Lebanon's infrastructure has been unable to absorb the refugee population, which some government officials describe as a threat to the country's security. Since 2015, the government has taken steps to close the border to those fleeing Syria, and has implemented measures that have made it more difficult for existing refugees to remain in Lebanon legally. At the same time, Hezbollah has played an active role in the ongoing fighting in Syria. The experience gained by Hezbollah in the Syria conflict has raised questions about how the eventual return of these fighters to Lebanon could impact the country's domestic stability or affect the prospects for renewed conflict with Israel. This chapter provides an overview of Lebanon and current issues of U.S. interest. It provides background information, analyzes recent developments and key policy debates, and tracks legislation, U.S. assistance, and recent congressional action.

Chapter 6 - Turkey, a NATO ally since 1952, significantly affects a number of key U.S. national security issues in the Middle East and Europe. U.S.-Turkey relations have worsened throughout this decade over several matters, including Syria's civil war, Turkey-Israel tensions, Turkey-Russia cooperation, and various Turkish domestic developments. The United States and NATO have military personnel and key equipment deployed to various sites in Turkey, including at Incirlik air base in the southern part of the country. Bilateral ties have reached historic lows in the summer of 2018. The major flashpoint has been a Turkish criminal case against American pastor Andrew Brunson. U.S. sanctions on Turkey related to the Brunson case and responses by Turkey and international markets appear to have seriously aggravated an already precipitous drop in the value of Turkey's currency. Amid this backdrop, Congress has actively engaged on several issues involving Turkey, including the following:

- Turkey's possible S-400 air defense system acquisition from Russia.
- Turkey's efforts to acquire U.S.-origin F-35 Joint Strike Fighter aircraft and its companies' role in the international F-35 consortium's supply chain.
- Complex U.S.-Turkey interactions in Syria involving several state and non-state actors, including Russia and Iran. Over strong Turkish objections, the United States continues to partner with Syrian Kurds linked with Kurdish militants in Turkey, and Turkey's military has occupied large portions of northern Syria to minimize Kurdish control and leverage.

Preface

- Turkey's domestic situation and its effect on bilateral relations. In addition to Pastor Brunson, Turkey has detained a number of other U.S. citizens (most of them dual U.S.-Turkish citizens) and Turkish employees of the U.S. government. Turkish officials and media have connected these cases to the July 2016 coup attempt in Turkey, and to Fethullah Gulen, the U.S.-based former cleric whom Turkey's government has accused of involvement in the plot.

In the FY2019 National Defense Authorization Act (NDAA, P.L. 115-232) enacted in August 2018, Congress has required a comprehensive report from the Trump Administration on (1) U.S.- Turkey relations, (2) the potential S-400 deal and its implications for U.S./NATO activity in Turkey, (3) possible alternatives to the S-400, and (4) various scenarios for the F-35 program with or without Turkey's participation. Other proposed legislation would condition Turkey's acquisition of the F-35 on a cancellation of the S-400 deal (FY2019 State and Foreign Operations Appropriations Act, S. 3180), place sanctions on Turkish officials for their role in detaining U.S. citizens or employees (also S. 3180), and direct U.S. action at selected international financial institutions to oppose providing assistance to Turkey (Turkey International Financial Institutions Act, S. 3248). The S-400 deal might also trigger sanctions under existing law (CAATSA). The next steps in the fraught relations between the United States and Turkey will take place in the context of a Turkey in political transition and growing economic turmoil. Turkish President Recep Tayyip Erdogan, who has dominated politics in the country since 2002, won reelection to an empowered presidency in June 2018. Given Erdogan's consolidation of power, observers now question how he will govern a polarized electorate and deal with the foreign actors who can affect Turkey's financial solvency, regional security, and political influence. U.S. officials and lawmakers can refer to Turkey's complex history, geography, domestic dynamics, and international relationships in evaluating how to encourage Turkey to align its policies with U.S. interests.

Chapter 7 - On May 8, 2018, President Donald Trump signed National Security Presidential Memorandum 11, "ceasing U.S. participation in the JCPOA [Joint Comprehensive Plan of Action] and taking additional action to counter Iran's malign influence and deny Iran all paths to a nuclear weapon." The action sets in motion a reestablishment of U.S. unilateral economic sanctions that will affect U.S. businesses and include secondary sanctions that target the commerce originating in other countries that engage in trade with and investment in Iran. Prior to this juncture, the United States had led the international community in imposing economic sanctions on Iran in an effort to change the government of that country's support of acts of international terrorism, poor human rights record, weapons and missile development and acquisition, role in regional instability, and development of a nuclear program. The United States' abrogation of its participation in the JCPOA, at least in the near-term, sets the United States apart from its allies and partners in what has been for more than a decade a unified, multilateral approach to Iran's malign activities. This chapter identifies the basis in U.S. law for sanctions imposed on Iran, and the nature of the authority to waive or lift those restrictions. It comprises four tables that present legislation and executive orders that are specific to Iran and its objectionable activities in the areas of terrorism, human rights, and weapons proliferation. On July 14, 2015, the United States, China, France, Germany, the Russian Federation, the United Kingdom, European Union, and Iran agreed to a Joint Comprehensive Plan of Action to "ensure that Iran's nuclear programme will be exclusively peaceful.... " In turn, the negotiating parties and United Nations would "produce the comprehensive lifting of all U.N. Security Council sanctions as well as multilateral and national sanctions related to Iran's nuclear programme, including steps on access in areas of trade, technology, finance, and energy." On January 16, 2016, the International Atomic Energy Agency verified that Iran had implemented the measures enumerated in the JCPOA to disable and end its nuclear-related capabilities. Secretary of State Kerry confirmed the arrival of Implementation Day (defined in Annex V of the JCPOA). President Obama, the State Department, and the Department of the Treasury's Office of Foreign Assets Control initiated steps for the United States to meet its obligations under the JCPOA (Annexes II and V)—revoking a number of executive orders, delisting individuals and entities designated as Specially Designated Nationals, issuing general licenses to authorize the resumption of some trade, and exercising waivers for non-U.S. persons as allowable by various laws. President Trump's May 8 announcement indicates that the United States will, over the next three to six months, reconstruct the U.S. sanctions regime.

In: The Middle East
Editor: Doyle Keller

ISBN: 978-1-53616-191-5
© 2019 Nova Science Publishers, Inc.

Chapter 1

SAUDI ARABIA: BACKGROUND AND U.S. RELATIONS (UPDATED)[*]

Christopher M. Blanchard

ABSTRACT

The kingdom of Saudi Arabia, ruled by the Al Saud family since its founding in 1932, wields significant global influence through its administration of the birthplace of the Islamic faith and by virtue of its large oil reserves. Close U.S.-Saudi official relations have survived a series of challenges since the 1940s. In recent years, shared concerns over Sunni Islamist extremist terrorism and Iranian government policies have provided some renewed logic for continued strategic cooperation. Political upheaval and conflict in the Middle East and North Africa have created new challenges, and the Trump Administration has sought to strengthen U.S. ties to Saudi leaders as the kingdom implements a series of new domestic and foreign policy initiatives.

Successive U.S. Administrations have referred to the Saudi government as an important partner, and U.S. arms sales and related

---

[*] This is an edited, reformatted and augmented version of Congressional Research Service, Publication No. RL33533, dated September 21, 2018.

security cooperation have continued with congressional oversight and amid some congressional opposition. The Trump Administration, like its recent predecessors, praises Saudi government counterterrorism efforts. Since 2009, the executive branch has notified Congress of proposed foreign military sales to Saudi Arabia of major defense articles and services with a potential aggregate value of nearly $139 billion. The United States and Saudi Arabia concluded arms sale agreements worth more than $65 billion, from FY2009 through FY2016.

Since March 2015, the U.S.-trained Saudi military has used U.S.-origin weaponry, U.S. logistical assistance, and shared intelligence in support of military operations in Yemen. Legislation has been proposed in the 115th Congress to condition or disapprove of some U.S. weapons sales and condition or direct the President to end U.S. support to Saudi operations without specific authorization (H.J.Res. 102, H.J.Res. 104, S.J.Res. 40, S.J.Res. 42, S.J.Res. 54, S. J. Res. 55).

In parallel to close security ties, official U.S. reports describe restrictions on human rights and religious freedom in the kingdom. Some Saudi activists advocate for limited economic and political reforms, continuing decades-long trends that have seen Saudi liberals, moderates, and conservatives advance different visions for domestic change. Saudi leaders in 2018 reversed a long-standing ban on women's right to drive, amid some arrests of women's rights advocates and critics of social liberalization. While some limited protests and arrests have occurred since unrest swept the region in 2011, clashes involving Saudi security forces have not spread beyond certain predominantly Shia areas of the oil-rich Eastern Province.

Since assuming the throne in 2015, King Salman bin Abd al Aziz (age 82) has made a series of appointments and reassignments that have altered the responsibilities and relative power of leading members of the next generation of the Al Saud family, who are the grandsons of the kingdom's founder. The king's son, Crown Prince Mohammed bin Salman (age 33), is the central figure in Saudi policymaking. He has asserted control over national security forces, sidelined potential rivals, proposed and begun implementing bold economic and social changes, and arrested prominent figures accused of corruption, including some fellow royal family members. Ambitious plans for the transformation of the kingdom's economy seek to provide opportunity for young Saudis and bolster nonoil sources of revenues for the state. Abroad, the kingdom pursues a multidirectional policy and has aggressively confronted perceived threats.

Saudi decisionmaking long appeared to be risk-averse and rooted in rulers' concerns for maintaining consensus among different constituencies, including factions of the royal family, business elites, and conservative religious figures. Crown Prince Mohammed bin Salman's assertive and more centralized leadership has challenged this model of governance. The change is leading Saudis and outsiders alike to reexamine their assumptions about the kingdom's future.

Congress may examine these developments when considering the scope, terms, and merits of U.S.-Saudi partnership, proposed arms sales and nuclear cooperation, and security commitments.

OVERVIEW

The kingdom of Saudi Arabia's relations with the United States, its stability, and its future trajectory are subjects of continuing congressional interest. In particular, Saudi leadership transitions, trends in global oil prices, Saudi budget pressures and reform plans, aggressive transnational terrorist threats, assertive Saudi foreign policies, and Saudi-Iranian tensions have fueled recent congressional discussions. U.S.-Saudi security cooperation and U.S. concern for the continuing global availability of Saudi energy supplies continue to anchor official bilateral relations as they have for decades. In this context, the Trump Administration's efforts to reinvigorate U.S.-Saudi relations have drawn increased public attention and have generated debate. Previously, the Obama Administration had differed with Saudi leaders over Iran, the Iranian nuclear program, and conflicts in Syria, Iraq, and Yemen.

Amid some continuing differences on these issues, bilateral ties have been defined since 2017 by arms sale proposals, Yemen-related security cooperation, and shared concerns about Iran, Al Qaeda, and the Islamic State organization (IS, aka ISIL/ISIS or the Arabic acronym *Da'esh*). From 2012 through 2016, the Obama Administration notified Congress of proposed Foreign Military Sales to Saudi Arabia with a potential value of more than $45 billion. President Donald Trump and Saudi officials announced agreement on some of these sales and others during the President's May 2017 trip to the kingdom, as part of a package that may potentially be worth more than $110 billion. This package of previously discussed and newly proposed defense sales is intended to address Saudi needs for maritime and coastal security improvements, air force training and support, cybersecurity and communications upgrades, missile and air defenses, and enhanced border security and counterterrorism capabilities (see "Arms Sales, Security Assistance, and Training" below and Appendix B).

King Salman bin Abd al Aziz Al Saud (age 82) succeeded his late half-brother King Abdullah bin Abd al Aziz following the latter's death in January 2015. King Salman later announced dramatic changes to succession arrangements left in place by King Abdullah, surprising observers of the kingdom's politics. King Salman first replaced his half-brother Crown Prince Muqrin bin Abd al Aziz with their nephew, Prince Mohammed bin Nayef bin Abd al Aziz, who was then Interior Minister and counterterrorism chief. The king then named his own son, Prince Mohammed bin Salman bin Abd al Aziz, then 29, as Deputy Crown Prince and Defense Minister.

In June 2017, Prince Mohammed bin Nayef was relieved of his positions and Prince Mohammed bin Salman (age 33) was elevated further to the position of Crown Prince, placing him in line to succeed his father (see Figure 1, Figure 2, and "Leadership and Succession" below). Both princes are members of the generation of grandsons of the kingdom's late founder, King Abd al Aziz bin Abd al Rahman Al Saud (aka Ibn Saud). The succession changes and Crown Prince Mohammad bin Salman's efforts to assert his role as the shaper of the kingdom's national security and economic policies have resulted in an apparent consolidation of authority under one individual and sub-branch of the family that is unprecedented in the kingdom since its founding.

Shifts in Saudi foreign policy toward a more assertive posture— typified by the kingdom's military operations in neighboring Yemen and a series of regional moves intended to counteract Iranian initiatives—have accompanied the post-2015 leadership changes. Saudi leaders launched military operations in Yemen following the early 2015 ouster of Yemen's transitional government by the Zaydi Shia *Ansar Allah* (aka Houthi) movement and backers of the late former Yemeni President Ali Abdullah Saleh (see "Conflict in Yemen" below).

Saudi Arabia

Table 1. Saudi Arabia Map and Country Data

Land: Area, 2.15 million sq. km. (more than 20% the size of the United States); Boundaries, 4,431 km (—40% more than U.S.-Mexico border); Coastline, 2,640 km (more than 25% longer than U.S. west coast).

Population: 28,571,770 (July 2017 est., —30% non-nationals per 2015 U.N. data.); % < 25 years of age: 45.4%.

GDP (PPP; growth rate): $1.789 trillion; 0.1% (2017 est.).

GDP per capita, PPP: $55,300 (2017 est.).

Budget (revenues; expenditure; balance): $171.6 billion; $227.8 billion; $56.2 billion deficit, 8.3% of GDP (2017).

Projected Budget (revenues; expenditure; balance): $209 billion; $261 billion; $52 billion deficit (2018 est.).

Unemployment: 12.9% (Q1 2018 est., Saudi nationals: females 30.9%, males 7.6%, youth [20-29] 29.5%).

Oil and natural gas reserves: 266.5 billion barrels (2017 est.); 8.602 trillion cubic meters (2017 est.).

External Debt: $212.9 billion (December 2017 est.).

Foreign Exchange and Gold Reserves: —$509 billion (December 2017 est.).

Sources: CRS using State Department, Esri, and Google Maps data (all 2013), CIA *World Factbook* estimates (March 2018), and Saudi government budget data (December 2017) and General Organization for Statistics.

A U.S.-facilitated, Saudi-led coalition air campaign has conducted strikes across the country since late March 2015, coupled with a joint Saudi and Emirati ground campaign aimed at reversing Houthi gains and compelling them to negotiate with U.N.-recognized transition leaders.Concerns about Yemeni civilian deaths in Saudi airstrikes, the operation's contribution to grave humanitarian conditions, and gains by Al Qaeda and Islamic State supporters have led some Members of Congress and U.S. officials to urge all parties to seek a prompt settlement. President Obama maintained U.S. logistical support for Saudi operations in Yemen but decided in 2016 to reduce U.S. personnel support and limit certain U.S. arms transfers. President Trump has chosen to proceed with precision guided munition technology sales that the Obama Administration deferred. In September 2018, the Trump Administration certified conditions set by Congress on Saudi actions in Yemen and renewed calls for a political solution. A U.S. State Department travel advisory issued in April 2018 warns that "rebel groups operating in Yemen have fired long-range missiles into Saudi Arabia, specifically targeting populated areas and civilian infrastructure" and that "rebel forces in Yemen fire artillery at Saudi border towns and launch cross-border attacks against Saudi military personnel."[1]

U.S. support to the kingdom's operations in Yemen and Saudi use of U.S.-origin weaponry has drawn new attention to congressionally reviewed arms sales and questions of authorization. In the 114th Congress, some Members scrutinized proposed sales of thousands of guided air-to-ground munitions and tanks to Saudi Arabia in the context of concerns about the Saudi military's conduct in Yemen (see Appendix D below).

In the 115th Congress, legislation has been enacted that prohibits the obligation or expenditure of U.S. funds for in-flight refueling operations of Saudi and Saudi-led coalition aircraft that are not conducting select types of operations if certain certifications cannot be made and maintained (Section 1290 of the FY2019 National Defense Authorization Act, P.L.

---

[1] U.S. State Department, Saudi Arabia Travel Warning, November 21, 2017.

115-232, Appendix D).[2] The provision is subject to an Administration national security waiver. A similar measure would place conditions on the transfer of any air-to-ground munitions to Saudi Arabia (S.J.Res. 40), and, in June 2017, the Senate narrowly voted to reject a motion to further consider a joint resolution of disapproval (S.J.Res. 42) on proposed sales of precision guided munitions to the kingdom. The House and Senate also have considered resolutions (H.Con.Res. 81 and S.J.Res. 54) that would direct the President to end U.S. military support for Saudi operations in Yemen unless Congress specifically authorizes the continuation of such support. Inside the kingdom, arrests of Islamic State (IS) supporters have continued since 2014, as Islamic State affiliates have claimed responsibility for a series of deadly attacks against Saudi security forces and members of the kingdom's Shia minority across the country (see "The Islamic State's Campaign against the Kingdom" below). Saudi authorities report having disrupted planned IS attacks on government targets in 2017 and counted 34 terrorist attacks in 2016, including an attempted IS-claimed suicide bombing against the U.S. Consulate General in Jeddah. Saudi leaders and their IS adversaries have reiterated their hostility toward each other since 2015, with Saudi leaders proposing new transnational counterterrorism cooperation and IS leaders redeclaring war against the royal family, condemning official Saudi clerics, and urging attacks inside the kingdom (see "Terrorism Threats and Bilateral Cooperation"). The current U.S. State Department travel advisory for Saudi Arabia warns that "terrorist groups continue plotting possible attacks" and that "terrorists may attack with little or no warning."

Since 2011, significant shifts in the political and economic landscape of the Middle East have focused international attention on Saudi domestic policy issues and reinvigorated social and political debates among Saudis (see "Domestic Issues" below). These regional shifts, coupled with ongoing economic, social, and political changes in the kingdom, may make sensitive issues such as political reform, unemployment, education, human rights, corruption, religious freedom, and extremism more prominent in

---

[2] See also CRS Report R45046, *The War in Yemen: A Compilation of Legislation in the 115th Congress*, by Jeremy M. Sharp and Christopher M. Blanchard.

U.S.-Saudi relations than in the past. U.S. policy initiatives have long sought to help Saudi leaders address economic and security challenges in ways consistent with U.S. interests. Recent joint U.S.-Saudi diplomatic efforts to strengthen economic, educational, and interpersonal ties have focused on improving opportunities for the kingdom's young population. Tens of thousands of Saudi students continue to pursue higher education in the United States, although numbers have declined in response to Saudi government funding changes.

Some nongovernment observers have called for a reassessment of U.S.-Saudi relations amid the kingdom's ongoing military campaign in Yemen.[3] They cite concern about human rights conditions in the kingdom, as well as resurgent questions about the relationship between religious proselytization by some Saudis and the appeal of violent Islamist extremism. U.S. officials have called publicly for the kingdom to seek a negotiated settlement in Yemen, allow peaceful expressions of dissent at home, and help fight extremism abroad. Any more strident official U.S. criticisms of the kingdom's policies traditionally remain subjects of private diplomatic engagement rather than official public discussion.

Saudi concerns about U.S. leadership and policies in the Middle East grew during the Administrations of Presidents George W. Bush and Barack Obama, in parallel to U.S. concerns about Saudi priorities and choices. In particular, Saudi leaders at times signaled their displeasure with U.S. policy approaches to Egypt, Israel and the Palestinians, Bahrain, Iraq, Syria, and Iran. Saudi officials also opposed the changes to U.S. sovereign immunity law that were made by the 114th Congress through the Justice Against Sponsors of Terrorism Act (S. 2040, P.L. 114-222, aka JASTA) and have sought their amendment or repeal.[4]

Saudi official public responses to the Joint Comprehensive Plan of Action (JCPOA) nuclear agreement with Iran were initially relatively neutral, emphasizing elements of an agreement with Iran that Saudi Arabia

---

[3] For a summary of debates and perspectives, see, Nicolas Niarchos, "How the U.S. Is Making the War in Yemen Worse," *The New Yorker*, January 22, 2018.

[4] For background see CRS Report RL34726, *In Re Terrorist Attacks on September 11, 2001: Claims Against Saudi Defendants Under the Foreign Sovereign Immunities Act (FSIA)*, by Jennifer K. Elsea.

would support rather than expressing Saudi endorsement of the JCPOA as negotiated and agreed. King Salman eventually endorsed the JCPOA during his September 2015 visit to Washington, DC, but later called for the agreement to be reexamined and welcomed President Trump's decision to withdraw the United States from the agreement. Saudi officials have engaged in civil nuclear cooperation talks with the United States and other countries since 2017 (see "Potential U.S.-Saudi Nuclear Cooperation").

Policy differences and specific current disagreements notwithstanding, U.S. and Saudi officials have long favored continuity over dramatic strategic shifts, despite some Saudis' and Americans' calls for fundamental changes to the bilateral relationship. The Trump Administration, like its predecessors, engages the Saudi government as a strategic partner to promote regional security and global economic stability. The Saudi government appears to view the United States as an important security partner. At the end of President Trump's May 2017 visit, the U.S. and Saudi governments agreed to "a new Strategic Partnership for the 21st Century in the interest of both countries by formally announcing a Joint Strategic Vision."[5]

With a new generation of Saudi leaders assuming prominent positions in the kingdom and chaotic conditions persisting in the Middle East region, some change in U.S.-Saudi relations may prove inevitable. The Trump Administration has thus far partnered with King Salman and Crown Prince Mohammed bin Salman on their domestic policy initiatives and their approaches to Iran, Yemen, Syria, and Iraq. The success or failure of these initiatives may have considerable significance for the bilateral relationship and consequences for international security for years to come.

DOMESTIC ISSUES

Saudi Arabia is a monarchy governed in accordance with a 1992 Basic Law, and its legal system is largely rooted in the Hanbali school of Sunni

---

[5] Joint Statement between the Kingdom of Saudi Arabia and the United States of America, May 23, 2017.

Islamic law as interpreted and applied by state-appointed religious judges.[6] An appointed, 150-member national Shura Council provides limited oversight and advisory input on some government decisions, and municipal councils with both appointed and elected members serve as fora for public input into local governance.

Political decisionmaking in the kingdom long reflected a process of consensus-building among a closed elite presided over by senior members of the ruling Al Saud family. In recent years, decisionmaking appears to have become more centralized under the authority of Crown Prince Mohammed bin Salman, with the apparent blessing of the king. Members of the conservative Salafist Sunni religious establishment have long shaped government decisionmaking on social and legal issues. Some representatives of this community have endorsed swift and dramatic changes to some social policies since 2015, while others have been imprisoned for alleged foreign ties and possibly for opposing change.

The Crown Prince has presided over efforts ostensibly designed to root out corruption among elites, including prominent businessmen and members of the royal family. These efforts may also have the effect of contributing to the centralization of power. Rumored discontent among other royal family members has not manifested in demonstrable public efforts to resist or undermine the Crown Prince's agenda.[7] At present, the balances of power, interests, and influence among the rising generation of leaders in the royal family are relatively opaque and appear to be evolving.

Over time, Saudi leaders have sought to manage vocal and public demands from the country's relatively young population for improved economic opportunities, limited political participation, and improved social

---

[6] Limited civil service and commercial codes supplement the Islamic legal system, which is based on the Quran and traditions (hadith) of the Prophet Mohammed. Some court reforms have been implemented since 2011 to strengthen the training of judges and increase the consistency of judicial outcomes. See Joseph A. Kéchichian, *Legal and Political Reforms in Saudi Arabia*, New York, Routledge, 2013.

[7] Some members of the royal family reportedly have objected to some changes under the leadership of King Salman and his son, the Crown Prince, in a series of intrafamily letters reported since 2015 and during meetings of the Allegiance Council. See David Ignatius, "A Cyclone Brews over Saudi Arabia," *Washington Post*, October 13, 2015; Hugh Miles, "Saudi Royal Calls for Regime Change in Riyadh," *The Guardian* (UK) September 28, 2015; and Simon Henderson, "Meet the Next Generation of Saudi Rulers," *Foreign Policy*, November 10, 2017.

conditions. Efforts to do so have been balanced with the royal family's commitments to protect the kingdom's conservative Islamic traditions and address a host of regional and domestic security threats.

Security forces monitor and tightly limit political and social activism in a domestic security environment that has been defined since the mid-1990s by persistent terrorist threats and to a lesser extent since 2011 by anxiety about potential unrest and economic stagnation. Relations between some members of the Shia minority population (~10%-15%) and the government remain tense, amid periodic localized confrontations between security forces, demonstrators, and armed youth in the oil-rich Eastern Province. Efforts to improve sectarian relations are complicated by anti-Shia terrorism, official discrimination, and official Saudi concerns about perceived Iranian efforts to destabilize the kingdom by agitating Saudi Shia.

High prices in international oil markets amplified oil export earnings for most of the period from 2005 to 2014, generating significant fiscal surpluses and leaving the country with sizeable foreign reserves and low levels of official debt. After 2011, the government launched large social spending programs to improve housing and infrastructure, raise public sector wages, expand education, and ease the burdens of unemployment. This spending created new fiscal burdens, and state oil revenues decreased more than nonoil revenues grew from 2014 through 2017. At present, Saudi leaders are simultaneously managing ambitious and politically sensitive fiscal consolidation and economic transformation initiatives.

Leadership and Succession

King Salman and other Saudi leaders are likely to continue to face complex questions about political consent, economic performance, and social reform as they push ahead with ambitious economic and social initiatives, and as power is transferred from the sons of the kingdom's founder, King Abd al Aziz bin Abd al Rahman al Saud (aka Ibn Saud), to his grandsons. The willingness and ability of the monarchy's leaders to successfully manage their relationships with each other and with competing domestic interest groups is among the factors that will determine the country's future stability. Succession questions and intrafamily politics may have direct implications for regional stability and for U.S. national security interests.

Source: CRS. Official photos adapted from Saudi Arabian government sources.
Notes: Succession changes in April 2015 reversed a key decision taken by King Abdullah before his death—King Abdullah had named his half-brother Prince Muqrin as Deputy Crown Prince in March 2014, and Prince Muqrin briefly served as Crown Prince after King Abdullah's death. In April 2015, Saudi authorities stated that Prince

Figure 1. Saudi Leadership and Succession Changes, 2015. Changes Effective January and April 2015.

Most sources suggest that the Al Saud family has managed a recent series of leadership transition decisions without a paralyzing degree of disruptive internal dissent. Formal announcements of major changes in succession have stated that a preponderance of members of an Allegiance Council made up of senior family members has considered and endorsed transition decisions taken since its establishment during the late King Abdullah's reign. This includes decisions made prior to and in the wake of King Abdullah's death in January 2015, and in conjunction with succession changes announced in April 2015 and June 2017 (see Figure 1 and Figure 2).

King Salman first placed two members of the next generation of the Al Saud family in line to rule. This generation—grandsons of the kingdom's founder—is more numerous and has more complex intrafamily ties than those of its predecessors, making answers to current and future questions of governance and succession less certain. There exists potential for competition among members of this generation, as positions of influence in government have been distributed and redistributed among them.

Changes undertaken in 2015 (Figure 1) elevated Prince Mohammed bin Nayef and the king's son, Prince Mohammed bin Salman, to the line of succession at the expense of senior members of their fathers' generation. Prince Mohammed bin Nayef, who became Crown Prince, retained his duties as Minister of Interior and assumed leadership of a newly created Council for Political and Security Affairs. Then-Deputy Crown Prince Mohammed bin Salman became Defense Minister and the head of the Council for Economic and Development Affairs.

In June 2017 (Figure 2), Prince Mohammed bin Nayef was replaced as Crown Prince by Mohammed bin Salman and relieved of his position as Minister of Interior. Crown Prince Mohammed bin Salman's elevation puts him next in line for the throne. Given his age, he could rule for decades upon succession. In conjunction with the change, which was approved by the Allegiance Council, the kingdom's Basic Law was amended to prohibit kings from the generation of the grandsons of the founder from choosing successors from the same maternal line of the Al Saud family.

Source: CRS. Official photos adapted from Saudi Arabian government sources.

Figure 2. Saudi Leadership and Succession Changes, 2017. Changes Effective June 2017.

This amendment presumably was agreed to in order to assuage concern among members of the family about the further consolidation of power among the branch of the family from which King Salman and the new Crown Prince hail.[8]

---

[8] King Salman and the late Crown Prince Nayef were full brothers: their sons are full first cousins. Their "Sudayri" branch of the Al Saud family is named for their grandmother Hassa bint Ahmad al Sudayri—among the best known of the late King Abd al Aziz's late wives and one of three drawn from the Al Sudayri family. She was the mother of the late King Fahd bin Abd al Aziz, the late Crown Prince Sultan bin Abd al Aziz, the late Crown Prince Nayef bin Abd al Aziz, King Salman bin Abd al Aziz, Prince Ahmad bin Abd al Aziz, two other senior princes, and four daughters. Analysts of Saudi affairs have often referred to King Fahd and his younger full brothers as the "Sudayri Seven," because of their

Crown Prince Mohammed bin Salman is asserting a public national leadership role on a range of topics, generating considerable international speculation about the potential for reported rivalry or competition to harden between him and other family members. Such potential exists, and has precedent in the family's recent past, but intrafamily dynamics historically have remained largely shielded from public view until disputes have deepened to the point that consensus breaks down.

To date there has been no clear public confirmation that leading members of the royal family have reverted to the level of overt tension and competition that characterized intrafamily relations in the mid-20th century.[9] Nevertheless, some observers expressed concern and uncertainty about Crown Prince Mohammed bin Salman's November 2017 decision to detain and investigate some royal family members on corruption charges and remove the late King Abdullah's son, Prince Miteb bin Abdullah, from his position as Minister of the National Guard.[10] These moves appeared to signal a stark end to the consensus-based approach that reportedly had prevailed among senior royal family members for decades. Taken in conjunction with the Crown Prince's bold social, economic, and foreign policy agendas, these steps may meet with different responses from various family members and components of Saudi society.

---

propensity to support one another. In the future, analysis of relationships and potential competition within this branch may be of more interest than analysis that presumes Sudayri solidarity in competition with other wings of the family. For background on Saudi succession issues, see Joseph Kéchichian, *Succession in Saudi Arabia*, New York: Palgrave, 2001. For analysis of recent succession changes and Saudi law, see Chibli Mallat, "'Riyadhology' and Muhammad bin Salman's Telltale Succession," Lawfare, June 8, 2018. Muqrin stepped down as Crown Prince at his own choosing and credited then-new Crown Prince Mohammed bin Nayef with selecting King Salman's son Mohammed bin Salman to serve as Deputy Crown Prince, with the approval of a majority of the Allegiance Council.

[9] From 1958 to 1964, supporters of King Saud (the first son to succeed King Abd al Aziz) struggled for influence with supporters of Saud's brother Faisal (the following successor). Disputes over Saudi foreign policy and the management of government finances contributed to the family's decision to force King Saud from power in favor of Faisal, who served as king until he was assassinated by his nephew in 1975.

[10] See Simon Henderson, "Meet the Next Generation of Saudi Rulers," *Foreign Policy*, Nov. 10, 2017; and, Bruce Riedel, "Saudi Arabia Shifts Policy From Risk Averse to Downright Dangerous," YaleGlobal Online, Nov. 28, 2017.

Economic Reform, Fiscal Priorities, and Administrative Changes

As of 2018, Crown Prince Mohammed bin Salman presides over the kingdom's national economic transformation initiatives, and, under his father's auspices, he has directed changes to the leadership of security and administrative bodies across the Saudi government. Saudi Arabia's *Vision 2030* initiative, National Transformation Plan, and Fiscal Balance Plan (Figure 3) seek to reshape the economy and reduce government and social dependence on oil revenue.[11] Authorities have introduced some taxes, reduced energy subsidies, and taken other fiscal measures to improve the kingdom's state finances, tailoring implementation and in some cases offering temporary financial support to citizens to ease burdens at the household level.

The IMF has commended the reform goals articulated in Vision 2030 and the National Transformation Plan, which in part reflect long-standing IMF recommendations for structural reforms to encourage private sector growth and improve employment opportunities for young Saudis.[12] Historically, Saudi policymakers have faced challenges in balancing these types of reforms with concerns for the preservation of security, social stability, and cultural and religious values.

In May 2017, IMF officials stated their view that the kingdom's leaders have "scope for more gradual implementation" of planned changes in order to allow citizens to adapt and preserve fiscal resources to respond to unanticipated needs.[13] In August 2018, the IMF judged that Saudi leaders "have made good progress in implementing their reform program,"

---

[11] See, IMF Article IV Reports, 2017/2018 and, "The $2 Trillion Project to Get Saudi Arabia's Economy Off Oil," *Bloomberg Businessweek*, April 25-May 1, 2016; Ben Hubbard and Kate Kelly, "Saudi Arabia's Grand Plan to Move Beyond Oil: Big Goals, Bigger Hurdles," *New York Times*, October 25, 2017; Ahmed Al Omran, "Saudi Arabia's sleepy city offers prince a cautionary tale," *Financial Times* (UK), May 27, 2018; Al Omran, "Record numbers of foreign workers leave Saudi Arabia," *Financial Times* (UK), July 10, 2018; and, Rory Jones, "In Rare Step, Saudi's Sovereign-Wealth Fund Raises $11 Billion Loan," *Wall Street Journal*, September 17, 2018.

[12] Ibid.

[13] IMF Press Release 17/178, IMF Staff Completes 2017 Article IV Mission to Saudi Arabia, May 17, 2017.

and emphasized their view that the kingdom should maintain the current pace of implementation and avoid the temptation of expansionary government spending, despite increases in oil prices since 2017.[14] The Saudi government's fiscal consolidation plans (Figure 3) seek to balance the kingdom's budget by 2023, an adjustment from earlier plans to achieve balance by 2020.

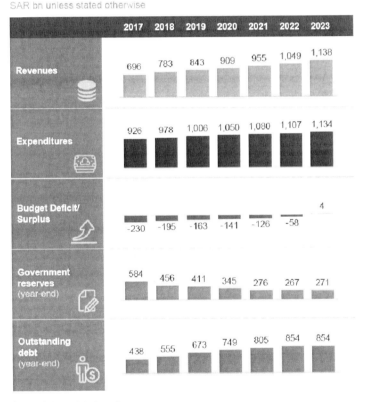

Source: Saudi Arabian government, Vision 2030: Fiscal Balance Program, 2018.
Note: The Saudi riyal is pegged to the U.S. dollar at a rate of 1 USD to 3.75 SAR.

Figure 3. Saudi Arabian Government Fiscal Projections Fiscal Balance Program Update 2018.

---

[14] IMF Country Report No. 18/263, Staff Report for the 2018 Article IV Consultation, June 28, 2018.

The kingdom's fiscal position reversed from one of repeated surpluses from 2005 through 2013 to one of actual and projected deficits in 2014. This change was rooted in lower global market prices for crude oil and major Saudi spending initiatives introduced to meet domestic economic and social demands. From 2011 to 2015, the kingdom approved a series of record-high annual budgets and expanded financial support for citizens, possibly due to government concerns that a failure to meet popular economic needs could lead to demands for political change.

When oil prices turned sharply lower between mid-2014 and mid-2017, Saudi officials turned to borrowing and deficit spending of accumulated reserves while reducing oil production levels in a bid to support global market price increases. From 2014 through 2017, Saudi officials drew more than $235 billion from state reserves and national government debt increased from 5.8% of GDP to 17.2%, as new domestic and international bonds were issued to help meet revenue needs.[15] Higher oil prices since mid-2017 have eased the kingdom's immediate fiscal burden, though IMF staff recommend that the kingdom plan for a range of oil revenue scenarios and maintain fiscal discipline.[16]

According to the IMF, Saudi officials plan to continue public stimulus spending, coupled with administrative and legal changes to encourage private sector and nonoil sources of economic growth and government revenue. They continue to review and revise state support to consumers and industry in the form of energy and utility subsidies, with some changes having already come into effect. Reviews of public land holdings are ongoing, and the kingdom has implemented a value-added tax (VAT) system. Officials also have reorganized and consolidated several important economic ministries in a bid to streamline operations, reduce costs, and support the implementation of planned reforms. Cuts to public sector salaries and bonuses were implemented in late 2016, but reversed in 2017 in response to improved fiscal performance.

---

[15] IMF Country Report No. 18/263, June 2018. Bloomberg estimated in September 2018 that the kingdom has issued $50 billion in bonds since the end of 2016. Archana Narayanan and Allan Lopez, "Saudi Arabia Raises $2 Billion in Islamic Bond Sale," *Bloomberg* September 12, 2018.

[16] IMF Country Report No. 18/263, June 2018.

> **U.S. Support in Educating the Next Generation of Saudis**
>
> The kingdom's investments in education are an acknowledgement of the challenges related to preparing the large Saudi youth population (~45% under 25 years of age) to compete and prosper in coming decades. The late King Abdullah initiated a state-sponsored scholarship program responsible for sending thousands of young Saudis abroad for undergraduate and graduate education. The number of Saudi students pursuing higher education in the United States increased ten-fold from 2000 to 2015, and exceeded 58,000 according to Saudi figures in March 2018.[17] In 2016, the kingdom announced plans to reduce funding for some overseas students, and the number of Saudi students enrolled in some U.S. universities has declined as scholarship program requirements and funding commitments have changed.[18]
>
> The growth in the number of Saudi students enrolled in U.S. colleges and universities that occurred after the mid-2000s may have cumulative economic, social, and political effects on Saudi society in future decades. This includes the possibility that a more educated and economically engaged youth population could make new social and/or political reform demands of Saudi leaders. The 2017 State Department Country Reports on Terrorism states that "The United States continued to support Saudi Arabia in reforms it is undertaking by: facilitating Saudi nationals' study in the United States and promoting educational exchanges," among other steps.

Human Rights, Gender Issues, and Minority Relations

Human Rights Concerns

According to the U.S. State Department's 2017 report on human rights in Saudi Arabia, Saudi law provides that "the State shall protect human rights in accordance with Islamic sharia."[19] Saudi law does not provide for freedom of assembly, expression, religion, the press, or association; rather, the government strictly limits each of these. The kingdom remains an absolute monarchy, and its citizens do not choose their government through election. Political parties are prohibited, as are any groups deemed to be in opposition to the government. A Specialized Criminal Court presides over trials of suspects in terrorism cases, including cases involving individuals accused of violating restrictions on political activity

---

[17] Habib Toumi, "About 60,000 Saudi students studying in US," Gulf News (Bahrain), March 21, 2018.

[18] Elizabeth Redden, "Saudi Enrollment Declines," *Inside Higher Ed*, July 18, 2016.

[19] State Department Bureau of Democracy, Human Rights and Labor, Country Reports on Human Rights Practices for 2017.

and public expression contained in counterterrorism and cybercrimes laws adopted since 2008. A government Human Rights Commission (HRC) is responsible for monitoring human rights conditions, fielding complaints, referring cases of violations for criminal investigation, and interacting with foreign entities on issues of human rights concern.

While Saudi authorities have created new space for some social and entertainment activities in recent years, they also have moved to further restrict the activities of groups and individuals advocating for political change and campaigning on behalf of individuals detained for political or security reasons, including advocates for the rights of terrorism suspects. Some young Saudis who have produced social media videos criticizing the government and socioeconomic conditions in the kingdom also have reportedly been arrested. In September 2018 Saudi prosecutors announced plans to prosecute for cybercrime individuals who produce or distribute content that "mocks, provokes or disrupts public order, religious values and public morals."[20]

King Salman, like the late King Abdullah, has moved to restrict and redefine some of the responsibilities and powers of the Commission for the Promotion of Virtue and Prevention of Vice (CPVPV), often referred to by non-Saudis as "religious police," in response to some public concerns. A government-endorsed entity, the CPVPV assumed a prominent public role in enforcing standards of religious observance and gender segregation norms for decades. In April 2016, the government formally stripped the CPVPV of certain arrest powers, required its personnel to meet certain educational standards, and instructed them to improve their treatment of citizens. The commission remains in operation, in cooperation with security forces, and its role in society, while less visible, remains a subject of debate.[21] Periodic incidents involving CPVPV personnel and the government's moves to embrace certain types of entertainment and social

---

[20] Arab News (Jeddah), "Saudi Arabia to penalize individuals who create or promote social media content that disrupts public order," September 5, 2018.

[21] The State Department's 2017 report on human rights said, "evidence available at year's end indicated that CPVPV officers were less visibly present and active after implementation of the new strictures."

gatherings shape related discussion and debate among Saudi citizens and public figures.

Critics of the kingdom's record on human issues have highlighted the fact that since the 1990s, authorities have periodically detained, fined, or arrested individuals associated with protests or public advocacy campaigns. This includes some advocates for Saudi women's rights that the government has recently moved to recognize, such as rights to drive automobiles, travel freely, or to enjoy fewer guardianship-related legal restrictions (see "Women's Rights Issues" below). Since 2016, Saudi officials have more frequently described their motives for detentions and investigations in gender-related and other human rights cases as being based on concerns about activists' relations with foreign third parties. Saudi authorities broadly reject most international calls for specific action on human rights-related cases, which they perceive to be attempts to subvert Saudi sovereignty or undermine the kingdom's judicial procedures.

Arrests and public punishments of human rights advocates have attracted increased international attention to contentious social and human rights issues in recent years, and, in February 2017, Human Rights Watch issued a report reviewing what it described as a "stepped up" campaign against activists.[22] Cases discussed in international media include the following:

- In March 2013, Saudi authorities convicted two prominent human rights activists and advocates for detainee rights, Mohammed al Qahtani and Abdullah al Hamid, on a range of charges, including "breaking allegiance" to the king.[23]
- In January 2015, Saudi blogger Raif Badawi began receiving public flogging punishments following his conviction for

---

[22] Human Rights Watch, "Saudi Arabia: Intensified Repression of Writers, Activists," February 6, 2017.

[23] According to Amnesty International, the defendants were convicted on charges including "breaking allegiance to and disobeying the ruler, questioning the integrity of officials, seeking to disrupt security and inciting disorder by calling for demonstrations, disseminating false information to foreign groups and forming an unlicensed organization." Amnesty International, "Saudi Arabia punishes two activists for voicing opinion," March 11, 2013.

"insulting Islam," a charge levied in response to Badawi's establishment of a website critical of certain Saudi religious figures and practices.[24]

- Badawi's sister Samar also is a human rights advocate—Saudi authorities questioned her in January 2016 and released her, reportedly calling her back for questioning in February 2017, and then detaining her in July 2018.[25]

The Badawis' cases have complicated Saudi Arabia's bilateral relationships with Canada and some European governments pressing for their release. In August 2018, Saudi Arabia expelled Canada's ambassador to the kingdom and recalled its ambassador from Ottawa after the Canadian embassy called for the release of Raif and Samar Badawi and other jailed activists.[26] Saudi authorities further suspended plans to invest in Canada and recalled Saudi students.

The Saudi government particularly objected to Canada's call for the "immediate release" of detained individuals, describing it as "blatant interference in the kingdom's domestic affairs, against basic international norms and all international protocols" and a "major, unacceptable affront to the kingdom's laws and judicial process, as well as a violation of the kingdom's sovereignty."[27] U.S. State Department spokeswoman Heather Nauert called on Canada and Saudi Arabia to resolve their dispute diplomatically and encouraged the Saudi government "to address and respect due process and also publicize information on some of its legal cases."[28]

---

[24] Raif Badawi was sentenced in May 2014 to 1,000 lashes (to be administered in 20 sessions of 50 lashes) and 10 years in prison. After the first session, his subsequent punishments were delayed for medical reasons. According to the State Department's 2017 Human Rights Report, Raif Badawi remained in prison in Jeddah at year's end.

[25] Ben Hubbard, "Saudi Arabia Frees Samar Badawi, Human Rights Activist, After Questioning," *New York Times*, January 13, 2016. Her former husband is a prominent human rights activist and lawyer who also was jailed in 2014 on a range of charges related to his advocacy. See Human Rights Watch, "Saudi Arabia: 15-Year Sentence for Prominent Activist," July 7, 2014.

[26] Amanda Coletta and Kareem Fahim, Saudi Arabia expels Canadian ambassador after Ottawa criticizes arrests of Saudi activists, August 6, 2018.

[27] Saudi Ministry of Foreign Affairs, Statement, August 6, 2018.

[28] State Department Press Briefing, August 7, 2018.

In parallel, press reports and human rights advocates have noted the detention of several religious figures who are presumed to be critical of the government and recent social reforms, and, in some cases, who are accused by Saudi authorities of linkages with the Muslim Brotherhood.[29] This includes prominent conservative religious figures such as Salman al Awda, Safar al Hawali, Ali al Omari, Nasir al Umar, Awad al Qarni, and Abd al Aziz al Fawzan. Several have been harsh critics of U.S. policy in the past, and some, like Awda and Hawali, were associated with the Islamist "awakening" (*sahwa*) movement of the 1990s.

Saudi prosecutors have announced their intention to seek the death penalty against some of the detainees for their involvement with the International Union of Muslim Scholars, which the kingdom considers a terrorist organization because of its ties to neighboring Qatar (see "Qatar and Intra-Gulf Cooperation Council (GCC) Tensions" below). Public backlash in the kingdom and beyond could be considerable in light of the transnational media visibility that several of the accused have long enjoyed and their large, global social media followings.[30]

Women's Rights Issues

Many women's rights issues in Saudi Arabia remain subject to domestic debate and international scrutiny. Saudi women face restrictions on travel and employment, and male guardianship rules and practices continue to restrict women's social and personal autonomy.[31] The most recent (2017) U.S. State Department report on human rights in Saudi Arabia notes that "women continued to face significant discrimination under law and custom, and many remained uninformed about their

---

[29] Ben Hubbard, "Saudi Prince, Asserting Power, Brings Clerics to Heel," *New York Times*, November 5, 2017.

[30] For a critical account, see Yasmine Farouk, "The Penalties of a Death," Carnegie Middle East Center, *Diwan*, September 17, 2018.

[31] For an overview on the guardianship system and related activism, see Nora Doaiji, "Saudi Women's Online Activism: One Year of the 'I Am My Own Guardian' Campaign," Arab Gulf States Institute in Washington, October 2017; and, Margaret Coker, "How Guardianship Laws Still Control Saudi Women," *New York* Times, June 22, 2018.

rights."[32] The report states that, despite conditions in which "gender discrimination excluded women from many aspects of public life ... women slowly but increasingly participated in political life, albeit at a disadvantage."

The late King Abdullah recognized women's right to vote and stand as candidates in 2015 municipal council elections and expanded the size of the national Shura Council to include 30 women. The third nationwide municipal council elections were held in December 2015, and expanded the elected membership to two-thirds, lowered the voter registration age to 18 from 21, and were the first in which Saudi women could vote and stand as candidates. Female candidates won 21 of the 2,106 seats, and 17 were appointed to seats.[33]

In April 2017, King Salman ordered government agencies to review guardianship rules that restrict women's access to government services and to remove those that lack a basis in Islamic law, as interpreted by the kingdom's judicial establishment.[34] The guardianship rules remain under review. In September 2017, the government directed ministries to prepare regulations to recognize women's rights to drive, and in June 2018, Saudi women began driving with state approval. These moves, while controversial in the kingdom, have been seen by some outsiders as signs that managed, limited political and social reforms involving gender issues are possible. The implemented and proposed changes nevertheless have been accompanied by the detention of some of their most prominent female proponents.[35] Saudi authorities allege the detainees have inappropriate ties to foreign entities.

---

[32] State Department Country Reports on Human Rights Practices for 2017, Saudi Arabia. The report attributes the differences in status among men and women in political life to "guardianship laws requiring a male guardian's permission for legal decisions, restrictions on women candidates' contact with male voters in the 2015 elections, and the ban on women driving, which the government announced would be lifted in 2018."

[33] National Public Radio, "Saudi Women React to Election Results," December 20, 2015; and, "After Historic Elections in Saudi Arabia, What's The Future for Women?" December 22, 2015.

[34] Human Rights Watch, Saudi Arabia: 'Unofficial' Guardianship Rules Banned, May 9, 2017.

[35] Women's rights activists Loujain Hathloul and Maysa al Amoudi were detained at the Saudi-UAE border in December 2014 for attempting to drive and publicizing their efforts and detention using social media. Their cases were referred to the Specialized Criminal Court (also referred to as the terrorism court), where cases involving those accused of

Minority Relations and Security

Saudi Arabia's Shia Muslim minority communities have historically faced discrimination and periodic violence, although outreach by government authorities and attempts at integration and inclusion have improved intercommunal relations in some instances.[36] Since 2014, IS terrorist attacks against Shia minority communities, low-level unrest in some Shia communities in the oil-rich Eastern Province (see Ash Sharqiyah in Table 1 above), and small protests by students and families of Sunni security and political detainees have created strains on order and stability.

Saudi authorities continue to pursue a list of young Shia individuals wanted in connection with ongoing protests and clashes with security forces in the Eastern Province. These clashes intensified in the wake of the 2016 execution of outspoken Shia cleric Nimr al Nimr, with arson attacks targeting public buildings in some Shia-populated areas and shooting attacks having killed and injured Saudi security personnel. Nimr had been charged with incitement to treason and alleged involvement with individuals responsible for attacks on security forces.[37]

In line with the firm approach evident in Nimr's 2014 death sentence, Saudi courts have handed down lengthy jail terms and travel bans for Shia protestors and activists accused of participating in protests and attacking

---

"undermining social cohesion" are tried. Both were released in February 2015. Hathloul was detained again in May 2018. Samar Badawi, Hatoon al Fassi, and Nassima al Sada were similarly detained. See Ben Hubbard, "Saudi Arabia Agrees to Let Women Drive," *New York Times*, September 26, 2017; Kareem Fahim and Loveday Morris, "Saudi Arabia Detains Womens Rights Advocates Who Challenged Driving Ban," *Washington Post*, May 18, 2018; and, Margherita Stancati, "Saudi Arabia Detains More Women's Rights Activists," *Wall Street Journal*, August 1, 2018.

[36] Kristin Smith Diwan, "Saudi Nationalism Raises Hopes of Greater Shia Inclusion," Arab Gulf States Institute in Washington, May 3, 2018.

[37] While Nimr had studied in Iran and Syria and used public sermons and statements as vehicles for acidic criticism of the Saudi royal family's rule, a review of his available statements and sermons suggests that he did not explicitly advocate in public for the use of violence by Saudi Shia or for the adoption of Iranian-style theocratic government. Nevertheless, his rhetoric was taken as crossing several Saudi red lines in questioning the legitimacy of the Saudi royal family's rule and in calling for mass protests and civil disobedience. The Saudi government stated its view of his activity as treasonous without reference to sectarian differences, and described his sentence as the result of due process, even as it struggled to convince some international observers that the execution was just, warranted, or wise given the current regional security environment.

security force personnel over the last several years. Islamic State-linked anti-Shia terrorist attacks (see below) and continuing views among some Saudi Shia of the state as being discriminatory and encouraging of anti-Shia extremism contribute to tensions.

In May 2017, Saudi security forces traded fire with armed individuals in Nimr's home village of Al Awamiya, and one Saudi soldier was killed. Explosions and gunfire have periodically killed and injured Saudi security officers in and around Awamiyah and Qatif since mid-2017. Saudi security operations and clashes with armed locals resulted in the destruction of areas of Al Awamiya in August 2017, and government-sponsored reconstruction efforts are now underway.[38]

U.S. travel advisories warn U.S. citizens to avoid these areas of the Eastern Province because of related tensions and the potential for renewed violence.

International Religious Freedom: Country of Particular Concern Designation

Saudi Arabia has been designated since 2004 as a country of particular concern under the International Religious Freedom Act of 1998 (P.L. 105-292, as amended) for having engaged in or tolerated particularly severe violations of religious freedom. Saudi law does not provide freedom of religion. The country's official religion is Islam, and the Quran and Sunna (traditions) of the Prophet Mohammed serve as the country's foundational legal sources. In November 2017, authorities revised the counterterrorism law to criminalize "the promotion of atheistic ideologies in any form," "any attempt to cast doubt on the fundamentals of Islam," publications that "contradict the provisions of Islamic law," and other acts deemed contrary to sharia, including non-Islamic public worship, public display of non-Islamic religious symbols, conversion by a Muslim to another religion, and proselytizing by a non-Muslim.[39] On January 3, 2018, the State Department renewed this designation and deemed the waiver of accompanying sanctions as required in the important national interest of the United States pursuant to Section 407 of the act.

---

[38] BBC, "Awamiya: Inside Saudi Shia town devastated by demolitions and fighting," August 16, 2017; and, Saudi Gazette, "Work on Awamiya development in full swing," August 4, 2018.

[39] State Department Bureau of Democracy, Human Rights and Labor, International Religious Freedom Report for 2017.

TERRORISM THREATS AND BILATERAL COOPERATION

The Saudi Arabian government states that it views Al Qaeda, Al Qaeda affiliates, the Islamic State (aka ISIS/ISIL or the Arabic acronym *Da'esh*), other Salafist-jihadist groups, and their supporters as direct threats to Saudi national security. The U.S. government has described the Saudi government as "a strong partner in regional security and counterterrorism efforts,"[40] and has reported that the Saudi government has taken increased action since 2014 to prevent Saudis from travelling abroad in support of extremist groups or otherwise supporting armed extremists. In 2016, the Saudi Ministry of Interior reported that there were "2,093 Saudis fighting with terrorist organizations in conflict zones, including ISIS, with more than 70 percent of them in Syria."[41]

Saudi and U.S. officials agree that the Islamic State and Al Qaeda in the Arabian Peninsula (AQAP)—based in Yemen and led by Saudi nationals—pose continuing terrorist threats to the kingdom. From 2014 through 2017, the aggressive expansion of the Islamic State in neighboring Iraq and in Syria and the group's attacks inside Saudi Arabia created alarm in the kingdom. Following the January 2016 execution by the Saudi government of dozens of convicted AQAP suspects, including some prominent ideologues, Al Qaeda leader Ayman al Zawahiri released a statement condemning the Kingdom and calling for revenge. Some observers, including some Members of Congress, have expressed concern about the apparent strengthening of AQAP during the course of the ongoing conflict in Yemen.[42]

Persistent terrorist threats appear to be one factor that has led the Saudi government to seek stronger partnerships with the United States. Since

---

[40] State Department Bureau of Near Eastern Affairs, Fact Sheet: U.S. Relations with Saudi Arabia, February 2, 2017.

[41] U.S. State Department Bureau of Counterterrorism, Country Reports on Terrorism 2016, August 2017. A report by the private consultancy The Soufan Group cites a 2016 Saudi Ministry of Interior estimate that more than 3,200 Saudi foreign fighters had travelled abroad, with 760 having returned home, and more than 7,000 Saudi nationals had been "stop listed" by Turkish interior security officials. See, Richard Barrett, *Beyond the Caliphate: Foreign Fighters and the Threat of Returnees*, The Soufan Group, October 2017.

[42] See, for example, Letter from 55 House Members to President Donald Trump, April 10, 2017.

2017, Saudi officials have announced plans to contribute to stabilization efforts in Syria and have reengaged with Iraqi leaders in line with U.S. preferences.[43] Saudi leaders also seek support from their regional neighbors and from the United States to confront what they describe as efforts by Iran and their Hezbollah allies to destabilize Yemen through support for the *Ansar Allah*/Houthi movement (see "Conflict in Yemen" below).

The Islamic State's Campaign against the Kingdom

Since 2014, IS supporters have claimed responsibility for several attacks inside the kingdom, including attacks on security officers and Shia civilians.[44] Claims for the attacks have come on behalf of members of IS-affiliated "provinces" (*wilayah*) named for the central Najd region and the western Hijaz region of the Arabian Peninsula.[45] In June 2015, an IS-affiliated Saudi suicide bomber blew himself up in a Kuwaiti mosque, killing more than two dozen people and wounding hundreds.[46] On January 29, 2016, attackers struck a Shia mosque in Al Ahsa, killing two people and wounding seven others. An IS-claimed attack in April 2016 west of Riyadh killed a senior Saudi police official, and in July 2016, a series of three IS-linked suicide bombings targeted the U.S. Consulate General in Jeddah, the Prophet's Mosque in Medina, and a Shia mosque in the Eastern Province. Saudi officials have arrested more than 1,600 suspected IS

---

[43] Embassy of Saudi Arabia, "Kingdom of Saudi Arabia Contributes $100 Million for Syria's Stabilization Efforts," August 16, 2018.

[44] Attacks include shootings of police officers, suicide bombing attacks on Shiite mosques in the Eastern Province, a suicide bombing at a prison checkpoint, an attack on Saudi security personnel in a mosque in the southwestern city of Abha, a shooting attack on a Shia meeting place in the Eastern Province, and a bombing attack targeting Ismaili Shia in the southern city of Najran.

[45] Statement attributed to Wilayah al Hijaz, Twitter, August 6, 2015.

[46] Ahmed Al Omran, "Saudi Brothers Suspected of Links to Kuwait Mosque Bombing Arrested," *Wall Street Journal*, July 7, 2015.

supporters (including more than 400 in July 2015) and claim to have foiled several planned attacks.[47]

The Islamic State arguably poses a unique political threat to Saudi Arabia in addition to the tangible security threats that its supporters have demonstrated through recent attacks. IS leaders claim to have established a caliphate to which all pious Sunni Muslims owe allegiance, and they directly challenge the legitimacy of the Al Saud family, who have long described themselves as the custodians of Islam's holiest sites and rulers of a state uniquely built on and devoted to the propagation of Salafist interpretations of Sunni Islam.[48] The Saudi government's use of state-backed clerics to denounce the Islamic State signals Saudi rulers' antipathy toward the group, but IS figures dismiss these clerics as apostates and "palace scholars."

IS leader Abu Bakr al Baghdadi has aggressively challenged Saudi leaders' credentials as defenders of Islam and implementers of Salafist Sunni principles, calling them "the slaves of the Crusaders and allies of the Jews" and accusing them of abandoning Sunni Palestinians, Syrians, Iraqis, and others.[49] Islamic State propaganda also has included features claiming to justify the assassination of several prominent Saudi clerics and exhorting

---

[47] Ahmed Al Omran, "Saudi Arabia Arrests 431 People With Suspected Islamic State Links," *Wall Street Journal*, July 18, 2015; Isa al Shamani, "Forty-Six Saudi Women are with DA'ISH in Syria; 1,375 Individuals Accused of being Members of the Organization," *Al Hayah* (London), September 3, 2015; Reuters, Saudi Arabia says arrests 17 Islamic State attack plotters, September 19, 2016; Reuters, "Saudi Arabia arrests 46 militant suspects involved in Medina attack," April 30, 2017; and, Reuters, "Islamic State claims responsibility for Saudi checkpoint attack," July 12, 2018.

[48] Al Qaeda leaders have long criticized Saudi leaders and pledged support for leaders of the Taliban movement, but largely have refrained from establishing their own rival proto-state entities.

[49] Baghdadi Statement, "Go Ye Forth Lightly or Heavily," Twitter, May 14, 2015. In a series of videos released in mid-December 2015, Islamic State-controlled "provinces" launched a coordinated media campaign condemning the Al Saud family as apostate tyrants, promising attacks in the kingdom, and encouraging IS supporters to rise up and overthrow the Saudi government. The videos promised to free prisoners held in Saudi jails and condemned the Al Saud for protecting Shia in the kingdom and for cooperating with the United States and others in military operations targeting Muslims. Themes, terms, threats, and promises were largely consistent among the December 2015 videos, which were released by most of the self-declared IS "provinces" in Iraq and Syria as well as "provinces" in Yemen, Libya, and Egypt.

its followers to do so.[50] In August 2018, IS leader Al Baghdadi challenged supporters in the Arabian Peninsula to rise up, reject the influence of Saudi state-aligned scholars, and resist what he described as Saudi leaders' plans to Westernize the kingdom "in a systematic campaign" to make believers "into infidels."[51]

Some analysts have examined the similarities and differences between the kingdom's official "Wahhabist" brand of Sunni Islam and the ideology espoused by the Islamic State.[52] IS ideologues draw on the writings of Mohammed Ibn Abd al Wahhab and other clerics who have played a historic role in Saudi Arabia's official religious establishment, but pro-IS ideologues differ from official Saudi clerics in their hostility toward the Al Saud family and on other matters.

IS critiques of the Al Saud and state-aligned religious scholars may have resonance among some Saudis who disagree with the government's policies or some who have volunteered to fight in conflicts involving other Muslims over the last three decades.[53] Saudi leaders argue that it is the Islamic State that lacks legitimacy, and some Saudi observers compare the group's ideology to that of other violent, deviant groups from the past and present.[54]

Terrorist Financing and Material Support: Concerns and Responses

According to U.S. government reports, financial support for terrorism from Saudi individuals remains a threat to the kingdom and the

---

[50] Islamic State propaganda has argued "...the palace scholars of the Saudi regime ...are at the forefront of this effort to dissuade Muslims from *jihad* and from upholding the *Shari'ah*, averting them from the path of Allah." See "Kill the Imams of *Kufr*," Dabiq Magazine, Issue 13, January 2016.

[51] Baghdadi statement, "But Give Glad Tidings to Those Who Patiently Persevere," August 22, 2018.

[52] For a detailed look at this question, see Cole Bunzel, *The Kingdom and the Caliphate: Duel of the Islamic States*, Carnegie Endowment for International Peace, February 18, 2016.

[53] Thomas Hegghammer, *Jihad in Saudi Arabia: Violence and Pan-Islømism since 1979*, Cambridge University Press, 2010.

[54] See Nawaf Obaid and Saud Al-Sarhan, "The Saudis Can Crush ISIS," *New York Times*, September 8, 2014.

international community, even though the Saudi government has "reaffirmed its commitment to countering terrorist financing in the Kingdom and the Gulf region."[55] Official U.S. views of Saudi counterterrorism policy have evolved since the terrorist attacks of September 11, 2001 (see Appendix C), and the U.S. government now credits its Saudi counterparts with taking terrorism threats seriously and praises Saudi cooperation in several cooperative initiatives. Saudi Arabia cochairs the Counter-ISIS Finance Group of the Global Coalition to Counter ISIS alongside Italy and the United States.

Overall, according to the State Department's 2017 *Country Reports on Terrorism* entry on Saudi Arabia,

> While the Kingdom has maintained strict supervision of the banking sector, tightened the regulation of the charitable sector, and stiffened penalties for financing terrorism, some funds are allegedly collected in secret and illicitly transferred out of the country in cash, sometimes under the cover of religious pilgrimages. To address this issue, the Saudi government continued efforts to counter bulk cash smuggling. Regional turmoil and the sophisticated use of social media have enabled charities outside of Saudi Arabia with ties to terrorists to solicit contributions from

---

[55] U.S. State Department Bureau of Counterterrorism, Country Reports on Terrorism 2017, September 2018. The report included nearly identical language from the 2013, 2014, 2015, and 2016 reports. According to a July 2016 State Department report, "Bulk cash smuggling and money transfers from individual donors and Saudi-based charities have reportedly been a significant source of financing for extremist and terrorist groups over the past 25 years. Despite serious and effective efforts to counter the funding of terrorism originating within the Kingdom, Saudi Arabia is still home to individuals and entities that continue to serve as sources of financial support for Sunni-based extremist groups. Saudi Arabia has publicly imposed targeted sanctions on more than 20 Hizballah-affiliated individuals and companies since May 2015. Funds are allegedly collected in secret and illicitly transferred out of the country in cash, often via pilgrims performing Hajj and Umrah. The government has responded in recent years and increased policing to counter this smuggling. Recent regional turmoil and sophisticated usage of social media have facilitated charities outside of Saudi Arabia with ties to extremists to solicit donations from Saudi donors. Some Saudi officials acknowledge difficulties in following the money trail with regard to illicit finance, in large part due to a preference for cash transactions and regulatory challenges posed by hawala networks, which are illegal and dismantled upon discovery." U.S. State Department, 2016 International Narcotics Control Strategy Report (INCSR)—Volume II: Money Laundering and Financial Crimes Country Database, July 2016.

Saudi donors, but the government has worked to pursue and disrupt such funding streams.[56]

Saudi authorities have forbidden Saudi citizens from travelling to Syria to fight and have taken steps to limit the flow of privately raised funds from Saudis to armed Sunni groups and charitable organizations in Syria. In January 2014, the kingdom issued a decree setting prison sentences for Saudis found to have travelled abroad to fight with extremist groups, including tougher sentences for any members of the military found to have done so. The decree was followed by the release in March 2014 of new counterterrorism regulations under the auspices of the Ministry of Interior outlawing support for terrorist organizations including Al Qaeda and the Islamic State as well as organizations such as the Muslim Brotherhood.[57] The regulations drew scrutiny and criticism from human rights advocates concerned about further restrictions of civil liberties.

In August 2014, Saudi Grand Mufti Shaykh Abd al Aziz bin Abdullah bin Mohammed al Al Shaykh declared "the ideas of extremism ... and terrorism" to be the "first enemies of Muslims," and stated that all efforts to combat Al Qaeda and the Islamic State were required and allowed because those groups "consider Muslims to be infidels."[58] The statement, coupled with state crackdowns on clerics deviating from the government's antiterrorism messaging, appears to signal the kingdom's desire to undercut claims by the Islamic State, Al Qaeda, and their followers that support for the groups and their violent attacks is religiously legitimate. In conjunction with the government's expanded efforts to dissuade Saudi citizens from supporting the Islamic State and other extremist groups, Saudi security entities continue to arrest cells suspected of plotting attacks, recruiting, or fundraising for some terrorist groups.

---

[56] U.S. State Department Bureau of Counterterrorism, Country Reports on Terrorism 2017, September 2018. The 2016 reports had stated that "Despite serious and effective efforts to counter the funding of terrorism within the Kingdom, some individuals and entities in Saudi Arabia probably continued to serve as sources of financial support for terrorist groups."

[57] Saudi Ministry of Interior, List of the Security and Intellectual Prohibitions for the Citizens and Residents, Saudi Press Agency, March 7, 2014.

[58] Saudi Grand Mufti: DA'ISH and Al-Qa'ida Are Not Affiliated to Islam and Muslims" *Al Sharq* (Dammam), August 19, 2014.

U.S. Foreign Assistance to Saudi Arabia

U.S. training and security support to Saudi Arabia remains overwhelmingly Saudi funded via Foreign Military Sales and other contracts, reflecting Saudi ability to pay for costly programs (and limiting opportunities for Congress to affect cooperation through appropriations legislation). Saudi Arabia receives roughly $10,000 per year in International Military Education and Training (IMET) assistance authorized by the Foreign Assistance Act of 1961. This nominal amount makes Saudi Arabia eligible for a discount on training that it purchases through the Foreign Military Sales program.[59]

The Bush Administration requested limited IMET funding for Saudi Arabia from FY2003 through FY2009, and the Obama Administration similarly requested annually that Congress appropriate a small amount of IMET assistance. Successive Administrations have argued that the discount supports continued Saudi participation in U.S. training programs, which in turn supports the maintenance of important military-to-military relationships and improves Saudi capabilities. President Trump's FY2018 budget request sought $10,000 in IMET for Saudi Arabia, but for FY2019 did not specifically request the funds (without explanation). The Senate Appropriations Committee report on the FY2019 State Department and Foreign Operations appropriations bill (S. 3108, S.Rept. 115-282) recommends that $10,000 in IMET assistance be provided for Saudi Arabia.

---

[59] Section 21(c) of P.L.90-629, the Arms Export Control Act (AECA), states that IMET recipient countries are eligible to purchase non-IMET training at reduced cost. Section 108(a) of P.L. 99-83 amended the AECA to provide this reduced cost benefit to IMET recipients. The U.S. Defense Security Cooperation Agency (DSCA) implements the authority provided in P.L. 99-83 to apply a lower cost to U.S. military training purchased by Saudi Arabia and other IMET recipient countries through the Foreign Military Sales (FMS) program. "Incremental rates" applied to the FMS training purchases of IMET recipient countries are calculated according to the terms outlined in Department of Defense Financial Management Regulation (FMR), Volume 15, Chapter 7 (Sections 0711 and 0712). The net benefit in cost savings to the kingdom is not regularly reported, although in the past, Congress has directed the executive branch to report to it on the matter. The conference report for H.R. 3288 (H.Rept. 111-366) required the Obama Administration to report to Congress within 180 days (by June 14, 2010) on the net savings this eligibility provides to Saudi Arabia and other IMET recipients.

In some past years, Congress enacted prohibitions on IMET and other foreign assistance to the kingdom in annual appropriations legislation, subject to waiver provisions. The George W. Bush and Obama Administrations subsequently issued national security waivers enabling the assistance to continue.[60] Saudi officials were privately critical of the congressional prohibitions and appear to prefer to avoid contentious public debate over U.S. foreign assistance, arms sales, and security cooperation. In 2016, the Senate Appropriations Committee narrowly rejected a proposed committee amendment to the Senate version of the FY2017 Foreign Operations Appropriations Act (S. 3117) that sought to condition the provision of FY2017 IMET assistance to Saudi Arabia on certification of Yemen- and terrorism-related criteria.[61]

ARMS SALES, SECURITY ASSISTANCE, AND TRAINING

Arms Sales

Saudi Arabia's armed forces have relied on U.S. arms sales, training, and service support for decades. Congress has broadly supported U.S. arms sales to the kingdom, while seeking to maintain Israel's qualitative military edge (QME) over potential Arab adversaries and expressing concern about the merits or terms of individual sales cases in some instances. Some Members of Congress have at times expressed concern about the potential

---

[60] From 2004 to 2009, Congress adopted several legislative proposals to prohibit the extension of U.S. foreign assistance to Saudi Arabia. As the total amount of U.S. assistance to Saudi Arabia has been relatively minuscule in recent years, the practical effect of the prohibitions was to rescind Saudi Arabia's eligibility to purchase U.S. military training at a reduced cost, absent the issuance of presidential waivers or the assertion of existing executive authority. Some supporters of the prohibitions raised questions regarding Saudi Arabia's reliability as a counterterrorism partner, while opponents of the assistance bans argued that the provisions would unnecessarily jeopardize continuance of cooperative diplomatic and security efforts with a longstanding regional ally. Each legislative proposal differed in its cited reasons for prohibiting aid as well as whether or not it provided national security waiver authority for the President.

[61] Consideration of Amendment offered by Senator Chris Murphy to S. 3117, Senate Appropriations Committee, June 29, 2016. Committee vote—14 in favor, 16 opposed.

for U.S. arms sales to contribute to or help drive arms races in the Gulf region and broader Middle East and about Saudi use of U.S. origin weaponry in Yemen. At present, congressional majorities appear to back continued sales to U.S. partners in the Gulf region, including Saudi Arabia, as a means of improving interoperability, reducing the need for U.S. deployments, deterring Iran, and supporting U.S. industry.

The United States Military Training Mission (USMTM) in Saudi Arabia and the Saudi Arabian National Guard Modernization Program (PM-SANG) oversee U.S. defense cooperation with the kingdom and have been active under special bilateral agreements and funded by Saudi purchases since the 1950s and 1970s, respectively. Saudi military and national-guard forces have, until recently, been under the leadership of two different members of the royal family, and it is unclear what if any effect recent leadership changes may have on patterns of U.S. weapons acquisition and training among these forces.[62] Since 2009, a series of high-value U.S. proposed arms sales to Saudi Arabia have been announced, including the 2010 announcement that the Royal Saudi Air Force (RSAF) would reconstitute and expand its main fighter forces with advanced U.S. F-15 aircraft (see Table B-1.)

In May 2017, President Trump signaled a continuation and deepening of bilateral defense cooperation, announcing completed and proposed defense sales during his visit to Riyadh with a potential value of more than $110 billion (textbox). The sales include cases that the Obama Administration had proposed and notified to Congress, cases developed under the Obama Administration on which Congress had been preliminarily consulted, and new sales that remain under development. Ongoing and proposed sale cases are set to considerably improve Saudi military capabilities, and leaders in both countries appear to view them as symbolic commitments to cooperation during a period of regional turmoil and leadership change.

---

[62] Katie Paul, "Saudi prince, relieved from National Guard, once seen as throne contender," Reuters, November 4, 2017; and, Glen Carey and Zaid Sabah, "Saudi King Replaces Military Commanders as Yemen War Lingers On, *Bloomberg*, February 26, 2018.

President Trump Announces Defense Sales During
May 2017 Visit to Saudi Arabia

In early May 2017, U.S. and Saudi officials accelerated consultations on a package of proposed and new defense sales to deepen U.S.-Saudi defense cooperation. As part of these consultations and in conjunction with President Trump's May 2017 visit, Saudi authorities signed a series of Letters of Offer and Acceptance for sales proposed and notified to Congress by the Obama Administration and U.S. officials presented Memoranda of Intent regarding sales that have been informally discussed with congressional committees of jurisdiction or that the Administration intends to develop further in consultation with Saudi officials and then propose to Congress.[63] In aggregate, the sales concerned may have an approximate value of more than $110 billion dollars. They include the following:

- A Letter of Offer and Acceptance for four Littoral Combat Ships
- A Letter of Offer and Acceptance for 115 M1A2S tanks made by General Dynamics Corp., as well as munitions and heavy equipment recovery systems
- A Letter of Offer and Acceptance for PAC-3 Patriot missiles
- A Letter of Offer and Acceptance for UH-60 Helicopters
- A Letter of Offer and Acceptance for CH-47 Chinook Helicopters
- A memorandum of intent for an $18 billion program to upgrade Saudi Arabia's military command-and-control and defense communications infrastructure
- A memorandum of intent for a potential sale of the THAAD Anti-Missile System
- A proposed FMS sale to further improve the training and capacity of the Royal Saudi Air Force to include enhanced training on precision targeting capabilities, processes, and Law of Armed Conflict
- The formal notification of Congress of three proposed direct commercial sales of precision guided munitions technology (see below)

Several of the LOA agreements signed include provisions calling for the production and/or final assembly of military equipment inside Saudi Arabia as part of the kingdom's initiative to strengthen its local defense production base, as its neighbors in the United Arab Emirates have done in recent years. Saudi Arabia intends to spend 50% of its defense dollars locally as part of its Vision 2030 initiative and has established a state-owned enterprise—Saudi Arabian Military Industries (SAMI)—to oversee local defense production and service development. In conjunction with President Trump's May 2017 visit, Lockheed Martin announced plans to produce 150 Blackhawk helicopters in Saudi Arabia through a joint venture, and Raytheon announced plans to establish a Saudi Arabia-based subsidiary.

---

[63] The executive branch declined to make an accounting of the proposed sales publicly available. Aaron Mehta, "Revealed: Trump's $110 billion weapons list for the Saudis," *Defense News*, June 8, 2017.

Support to Saudi Military Operations in Yemen

Saudi Arabia established a coalition in March 2015 to engage in military operations in Yemen against the Ansar Allah/Houthi movement and loyalists of the previous president of Yemen, the late Ali Abdullah Saleh (see "Conflict in Yemen").[64] The war in Yemen has continued unabated since then, leading, according to the United Nations, to one of the world's largest humanitarian crises. President Trump and Administration officials have signaled support for the Saudi-led coalition's operations in Yemen as a bulwark against Iranian regional interference, while imploring the Saudis and their partners to improve humanitarian access, pursue a settlement to the conflict, and take measures to prevent civilian casualties.

The United States' role in supporting the Saudi-led coalition's military operations in Yemen has evolved over time.[65] At present, it consists of some intelligence sharing, aerial refueling, and the deployment of advisers to Saudi Arabia for border security and anti-ballistic missile purposes.[66] In his latest biannual War Powers letters to Congress on the deployment of U.S. forces abroad in combat operations (P.L. 93-148), President Trump informed Congress about ongoing U.S. counterterrorism operations in Yemen and stated that U.S. forces in noncombat roles were providing "military advice and limited information, logistics, and other support to

---

[64] In early December 2017, the Houthi-Saleh alliance unraveled, culminating in the killing of former President Saleh on December 4, 2017.

[65] For background on the evolution of U.S. military support to Saudi Arabia and the Saudi-led coalition in Yemen, see CRS Report R45046, *The War in Yemen: A Compilation of Legislation in the 115th Congress.*

[66] In February 2018, the Acting Department of Defense General Counsel wrote to Senate leaders describing the extent of then-current U.S. support, and reported that "the United States provides the KSA-led coalition defense articles and services, including air-to-air refueling; certain intelligence support; and military advice, including advice regarding compliance with the law of armed conflict and best practices for reducing the risk of civilian casualties." According to the Department of Defense, "roughly 50" U.S. personnel are in Saudi Arabia for related activities including efforts focused on Houthi ballistic missile threats to the kingdom. Press reports also have included unconfirmed details about U.S. border security and counter-missile operations. See Letter from Department of Defense Acting General Counsel William Castle to Senators Mitch McConnell and Chuck Schumer, February 27, 2018; Assistant Defense Secretary for International Security Affairs Robert S. Karem, Testimony before the Senate Foreign Relations Committee, April 17, 2018; and, Helene Cooper, Thomas Gibbons-Neff and Eric Schmitt, "Army Special Forces Secretly Help Saudis Combat Threat From Yemen Rebels," *New York Times*, May 18, 2018.

regional forces combatting the Houthi insurgency."[67] The Department of Defense argues that "the limited military and intelligence support that the United States is providing to the KSA-led coalition does not involve any introduction of U.S. forces into hostilities for purposes of the War Powers Resolution."[68]

U.S. in-flight refueling to the militaries of Saudi Arabia and the United Arab Emirates (UAE) has been conducted pursuant to the terms of bilateral Acquisition and Cross-Servicing Agreements (ACSAs) between the Department of Defense and the respective ministries of each country.[69] Sales and deliveries of defense articles and services continue pursuant to the Foreign Military Sales and Direct Commercial Sales procedures established in the Arms Export Control Act.

U.S. personnel advised the Saudi-led coalition on the establishment of its Joint Incident Assessment Team (JIAT) for investigation of civilian casualties but are not deployed to Saudi Arabia to assist in ongoing JIAT investigations or to independently verify JIAT conclusions.[70] In the wake of an August 2018 Saudi airstrike that killed dozens of children in northern Yemen, Secretary of Defense Mattis directed Lieutenant General Michael Garrett to travel to Saudi Arabia to urge Saudi authorities to thoroughly

---

[67] See, Text of a Letter from the President to the Speaker of the House of Representatives and the President Pro Tempore of the Senate, The White House, Office of the Press Secretary, June 8, 2018.

[68] Letter from Department of Defense Acting General Counsel William Castle to Senators Mitch McConnell and Chuck Schumer, February 27, 2018.

[69] ACSA agreements are governed by 10 U.S.C. 2341-2350. The agreements provide for reciprocal logistical support under a variety of circumstances, and their underlying statutory authority does not prohibit U.S. support to partner forces engaged in armed conflict. U.S. ACSA agreements with Saudi Arabia and the UAE provide for the transfer of support to third parties with the prior written consent of both the original provider and original recipient. The U.S. agreement with Saudi Arabia was signed in May 2016. The executive branch has not publicly specified what legal authority or agreement provided for refueling support to Saudi aircraft from March 2015 through May 2016. Section 1271 of the FY2019 NDAA (H.R. 5515) amends the underlying authority for ACSA agreements to prohibit the transfer of logistic support, supplies, and services to parties with whom no ACSA agreement has been signed and creates an annual reporting requirement on standing ACSA agreements and their use.

[70] Samuel Oakford "One American's Failed Quest to Protect Civilians in Yemen," The Atlantic, August 17, 2018.

investigate the incident.[71] U.S. officials welcomed the JIAT's findings that the strike had violated coalition rules and best practices and the JIAT's recommendation that those responsible for evident errors be punished.[72]

Coalition officials acknowledge that some of their operations have inadvertently caused civilian casualties, while contesting some reports of civilian casualties by explaining coalition target selection and other factors. The JIAT continues to evaluate allegations of coalition involvement in strikes resulting in civilian deaths and periodically releases accounts assessing the nature and results of individual coalition operations.[73] Saudi leaders frequently state that the coalition military campaign is an act of legitimate self-defense because of their Yemeni adversaries' repeated, deadly cross-border attacks, including ballistic missile attacks.

On September 12, Secretary of State Mike Pompeo certified to Congress that the governments of Saudi Arabia and the United Arab Emirates "are undertaking demonstrable actions to reduce the risk of harm to civilians and civilian infrastructure resulting from military operations" pursuant to Section 1290 of the FY2019 John S. McCain National Defense Authorization Act (P.L. 115-91). Some Members of Congress criticized the certification. Congress continues to debate proposals that would place conditions on or direct an end to U.S. military support to coalition operations in Yemen (see Appendix D below).

Assistance to the Saudi Ministry of Interior

U.S.-Saudi counterterrorism and internal security cooperation has expanded since 2008, when a bilateral technical cooperation agreement established a U.S.-interagency critical infrastructure protection advisory mission to the kingdom. The agreement was extended in 2013 through

---

[71] Eric Schmitt, "U.S. Commander Urges More Transparency in Yemen Strike on School Bus," *New York Times*, August 27, 2018.

[72] *Arab News* (Jeddah), "Coalition 'regrets' Yemen bus strike, JIAT says those responsible should be accountable," September 2, 2018.

[73] Lojien Ben Gassem, "Fact-finding team presents results of 7 incidents in Yemeni conflict," *Arab News* (Jeddah), September 12, 2018.

2023.[74] It is unclear what changes to ongoing cooperation programs, if any, may have resulted from 2017 changes of leadership in the Ministry of Interior (MOI).

The Office of the Program Manager-Ministry of Interior (OPM-MOI) is a Saudi-funded, U.S. staffed senior advisory mission that embeds U.S. advisors into key security, industrial, energy, maritime, and cybersecurity offices within the Saudi government "focused on the protection of critical infrastructure and the Saudi public."[75] According to the State Department, "Through the OPM-MOI program, U.S. agencies are helping Saudi Arabia improve its ability to thwart terrorists before they act and to defend against terrorist attacks if they occur."[76]

In parallel to these advisory efforts, the U.S. Army Material Command-Security Assistance Command oversees a Saudi-funded Ministry of Interior Military Assistance Group (MOI-MAG) and Facilities Security Force-Training Advisor Group (FSF-TAG). The FSF protects key infrastructure locations, such as Abqaiq, the globally critical petroleum operations facility in eastern Saudi Arabia targeted by Al Qaeda in February 2006. According to the Defense Security Cooperation Agency, as of September 2016, the U.S. government had reached sales agreements worth $262 million in support of Saudi Ministry of Interior programs since FY2009.[77]

U.S.-SAUDI TRADE

Saudi Arabia was the largest U.S. trading partner in the Middle East by overall value in 2017.[78] According to the U.S. International Trade

---

[74] Adriane Elliot, "Security assistance growth prompts restructuring," U.S. Army, September 2, 2015.

[75] "Counterterrorism Coordination with Saudi Arabia" in U.S. State Department Bureau of Counterterrorism, Country Reports on Terrorism 2015, April 2016. The program is modeled loosely on embedded advisory and technology transfer programs of the U.S.-Saudi Joint Commission for Economic Cooperation, established in the 1970s.

[76] Ibid.

[77] Defense Security Cooperation Agency Fiscal Year Series Data, September 30, 2017.

[78] Based on U.S. Department of Commerce International Trade Administration Global Patterns of U.S. Merchandise Trade, September 2018. Comparable 2017 figures for Israel, the second

Administration, Saudi exports to the United States in 2017 were worth more than $18.8 billion (down from the 2008 value of $54.8 billion). In 2017, U.S. exports to Saudi Arabia were valued at more than $16.3 billion (up more than $6 billion since 2009). To a considerable extent, the high value of U.S.-Saudi trade is dictated by U.S. imports of hydrocarbons from Saudi Arabia and U.S. exports of weapons, machinery, and vehicles to Saudi Arabia.

Fluctuations in the volume and value of U.S.-Saudi oil trade account for declines in the value of Saudi exports to the United States in some recent years. Declines in global oil prices from 2014 through 2017 and increases in U.S. domestic oil production had pronounced effects on the value of Saudi exports to the United States. According to the U.S. Energy Information Administration (EIA), as of September 2018, Saudi Arabia was the second-largest source of U.S crude oil imports, providing an average of 948 thousand barrels per day of the 7.6 million barrels per day (mbd) in gross U.S. crude imports, behind Canada.[79]

ENERGY ISSUES

Global Energy Trends and Saudi Policy

Saudi Arabia holds the second largest proven oil reserves in the world (16% of global total) and was the largest exporter of crude oil and petroleum products in the world in 2016. The kingdom produces an average of more than 10 mbd of its estimated 12 mbd capacity and has indicated that it may not expand that capacity in light of current trends in international oil markets. In 2016, 69% of Saudi crude oil exports went to Asia, with Japan, China, South Korea, and India as the top consumers.[80]

---

largest U.S. trading partner in the Middle East, were more than $21.9 billion in exports to the United States and more than $12.5 billion in U.S. exports to Israel. U.S. exports to the United Arab Emirates in 2017 were worth more than $20 billion.

[79] Based on EIA data, "Weekly Imports & Exports: Crude" and "Weekly Preliminary Crude Imports by Country of Origin," Four Week Averages, September 7, 2018.

[80] ETA Country Analysis Brief—Saudi Arabia, October 2017.

The reimposition of U.S. sanctions on Iran has raised questions about the kingdom's ability and willingness to durably increase its output and exports to maintain overall market supply. Saudi leaders stated their intent to affect such an increase, and production levels have fluctuated since June 2018. Industry analysts differ on the sustainability and potential effects of longer-term output increases by the kingdom.[81]

Since Saudi Arabia remains dependent on oil export revenues for much of its national budget, a trend of lower oil prices from 2014 through mid-2017 was viewed with some public and official concern in the kingdom. To meet related challenges, Saudi authorities devised a three-track strategy:

1. Negotiation of agreements with other oil producers to reduce and control output,
2. Increases in domestic energy prices to reduce consumption, and
3. A now-delayed plan to offer public shares in the state owned oil company Saudi Aramco and reinvest proceeds in the kingdom's Public Investment Fund (PIF).

Negotiations with Producers

Mutual reliance on oil export revenues creates parallel interests and competition for market share between Saudi Arabia, Russia, Iran, and Iraq. With oil markets adequately supplied after 2014, Saudi officials have attempted to preserve and expand the kingdom's market share, with mixed results.[82] In 2016, Saudi authorities reversed their commitment to maintaining high production levels in the face of sustained competition from U.S. producers and surplus conditions in global oil markets. Instead, Saudi Arabia convinced fellow OPEC members to embrace shared productions cuts and reached an agreement with Russia to support a production cut arrangement that market observers credit with stabilizing

---

[81] Reuters, "Can Saudi Arabia pump much more oil?," July 1, 2018; and, Tom DiChristopher, "OPEC's oil output jumps in June as Saudi Arabia opens the taps to tame crude prices," July 11, 2018.

[82] Anjli Raval, "Saudi Arabia loses oil market share to rivals in key nations," *Financial Times* (UK), March 28, 2016.

prices. In November 2017, officials from Saudi Arabia, other OPEC countries, and Russia agreed to extend agreed joint cuts through 2018, but agreed in general terms to increase production in June 2018 as a response to unrest in Venezuela and U.S. sanctions on Iran. In June 2018, Crown Prince Mohammad bin Salman and Russian President Vladimir Putin announced a bilateral energy cooperation agreement that Saudi and Russian Energy Ministers said would seek "a balanced market that is supported by a reliable and sufficient supply."[83]

Domestic Energy Policy

Saudi energy use has declined since 2016, partly as a result of government-imposed domestic price increases. Prior to increases on prices of subsidized domestic oil products, some reports warned that the volume of oil consumed in Saudi Arabia could exceed oil exports by 2030 if domestic energy consumption patterns did not change.[84] Price increases also may help make stakes in the kingdom's energy producers more attractive to investors drawn by the higher revenue potential of exports over domestic consumption.[85]

Saudi Aramco IPO

Saudi officials apparently have now delayed plans for a partial public offering of shares in Saudi Aramco.[86] Proceeds from the offering were to benefit the kingdom's Public Investment Fund (PIF) and enable it to better support Saudi economic transformation initiatives and help manage the kingdom's fiscal needs.[87] Market analysts vigorously debated the potential value of the share offering, with Saudi officials reportedly having hoped for a valuation of $2 trillion and other sources having suggested a valuation

---

[83] Stanley Reed, "As Their Clout Wanes, Saudi Arabia and Russia Extend Oil Production Cuts," *New York Times*, May 15, 2017.

[84] Glada Lahn and Paul Stevens, *Burning Oil to Keep Cool: The Hidden Energy Crisis in Saudi Arabia*, Chatham House (UK), December 2011; and, John Sfakianakis, "Saudi Arabia's Essential Oil," *Foreign Affairs*, January 8, 2014.

[85] Rania El Gamal, "Burning less oil at home will help Saudi exports and Aramco IPO," Reuters, March 7, 2017.

[86] Matthew Campbell and Glen Carey, "Aramco's Stalled IPO Tarnishes Saudi Prince's Grand Vision," Bloomberg, August 23, 2018.

[87] Anthony Dipaola & Wael Mahdi, "QuickTake: Saudi Aramco," *Bloomberg*, May 5, 2017.

of $1 trillion to $1.5 trillion. Corresponding proceeds of a ~5% offering could have netted the PIF $50 billion to $100 billion.[88] In discussing the potential sale, Crown Prince Mohammed bin Salman said in a May 2017 interview that the Saudi government would retain sovereign control over oil and gas reserves and production decisions under any circumstances.[89] An alternate plan is now under consideration to sell bonds to enable Saudi Aramco to purchase the PIF's stake in the petrochemical company SABIC.[90]

Potential U.S.-Saudi Nuclear Cooperation

Saudi Energy Consumption and Nuclear Plans

In July 2017, the Saudi cabinet approved a National Project for Atomic Energy, including plans to build large and small nuclear reactors for electricity production and sea water desalination. The decision comes amid a larger effort to diversify the economy and expand renewable energy use. Specifically, Saudi officials at the King Abdullah City for Atomic and Renewable Energy (KA CARE) have stated their intent to develop as many as 16 nuclear power reactors by 2040 in order to reduce the domestic consumption of oil and natural gas for electricity production.[91] The Saudi Ministry of Energy, Industry, and Mineral Resources and KA CARE envision these reactors generating up to 17.6 GW of nuclear energy, which could provide 15-20% of Saudi Arabia's projected electricity needs.

---

[88] Summer Said, "Potential Saudi Aramco IPO Wouldn't Include Oil Reserves," *Wall Street Journal*, January 24, 2016; Sam Wilkin, "Saudi Aramco's Valuation Could Top $1 Trillion After Tax Cut," *Bloomberg*, March 28, 2017; Alan Livsey, "Lex in depth: The $2tn Saudi Aramco question," *Financial Times* (UK), April 3, 2017; and, Simeon Kerr and Ahmed Al Omran, "Saudi Aramco IPO sparks fears of loss of cash cow," *Financial Times* (UK), May 10, 2017.

[89] Wael Mahdi, "Saudis to Control Crude Reserves, Output After Aramco IPO," *Bloomberg*, May 3, 2017.

[90] Katie Paul and Tom Arnold, "Saudi sovereign fund picks Goldman, BAML, Klein for SABIC sale: sources," Reuters, September 10, 2018.

[91] KA CARE 2011 statement cited in World Nuclear Association, "Nuclear Power in Saudi Arabia," October 2017.

Saudi Arabia is the largest oil consumer in the Middle East, and oil consumption for electricity generation was estimated in 2017 at 700,000 barrels per day on average and 850,000 barrels per day during peak use. As of 2017, oil and natural gas generated 40% and nearly 60% of the kingdom's electricity, respectively. The use of domestically produced oil and oil products for power generation imposes a fiscal tradeoff, with opportunities lost for export revenue in an environment where market trends have strained Saudi state finances in some recent years.

Saudi leaders have stated that they intend to solicit bids for the construction of two nuclear power reactors in 2018, of a total capacity between 2 GW and 3.2 GW, with contracts to be signed for reactor construction by year's end for delivery by 2027.[92] According to KA CARE consultant Abdul Malik Al Sabery, the kingdom planned to evaluate request-for-information submissions from firms in Russia, the United States, France, China, and South Korea during January and February 2018, with the goal of prequalifying firms from two or three countries for bidding on these reactors by April or May, although that deadline has passed without an announcement.[93]

In January, Al Sabery stated that he expected that the winning firm, to be chosen in late 2018, would enter into a joint venture with the Saudi government in 2019. A separate process with South Korean partners to study the use of relatively small SMART reactors to generate electricity in remote areas also is underway. In recent years, Saudi Arabia has entered into a range of agreements concerning possible civil nuclear cooperation with several countries (Table 2).

Saudi nuclear facilities would be subject to International Atomic Energy Agency (IAEA) safeguards under the terms of the country's comprehensive safeguards agreement, which has been in force since 2009. Such safeguards present a significant hurdle to the development of nuclear weapons.

---

[92] Reuters, "Saudi Arabia aims to prequalify firms by April or May for first nuclear plant," January 15, 2018.

[93] Ibid.

Table 2. Recent Nuclear Cooperation Developments Involving Saudi Arabia

March 2015	Argentine-Saudi joint nuclear R&D venture agreed. Saudi-South Korean mutual nuclear cooperation agreements signed, including an MOU on building two small reactors for Saudi water desalination.
June 2015	KA CARE officials sign a nuclear energy cooperation agreement with Russia's Rosatom. Agreements signed with France on cooperation, including EPR reactor feasibility studies.
January 2016	Saudi Arabia and China memorandum of understanding signed regarding cooperation in the possible future construction of a high-temperature gas-cooled reactor (HTGR) in the kingdom.
October 2016	Saudi Arabia and Kazakhstan sign a nuclear cooperation agreement focused on nuclear fuel.
March 2017	Agreement signed for Chinese-Saudi feasibility study of HTGR construction in Saudi Arabia.
March August 2017	KA CARE officials visit China to begin HTGR study implementation planning. China National Nuclear Corporation (CNNC) and the Saudi Geological Survey sign agreements on uranium exploration cooperation.
December 2017	Russia's Rosatom and KA CARE sign implementing agreement related to small and medium reactors, personnel and fuel management.

Source: Official statements and media reports.

The IAEA completed an Integrated Nuclear Infrastructure Review (INIR) in Saudi Arabia at the kingdom's invitation in July 2018.[94] To date, Saudi Arabia has not agreed to an Additional Protocol to its safeguards agreement. The country also has a Small Quantities Protocol (SQP) to its safeguards agreement, which in some cases the IAEA has noted when suspending certain verification requirements for NPT state-parties with small quantities of fissionable materials. The agency's Board of Governors in 2005 approved changes that were designed to bolster verification obligations under the protocol, and Saudi Arabia has not accepted the modified text. Saudi Arabia would need to rescind its SQP to build nuclear reactors.

---

[94] IAEA, "IAEA Reviews Saudi Arabia's Nuclear Power Infrastructure Development," 35/2018, July 31, 2018.

U.S. Civil Nuclear Cooperation with Saudi Arabia

In 2008, the United States and Saudi Arabia signed a Memorandum of Understanding (MOU), which stated the countries' intentions to cooperate on a variety of nuclear activities in the fields of medicine, industry, and electricity production. Previous U.S. Administrations had explored a civil nuclear energy agreement with Saudi Arabia but had not finalized an agreement.

Assistant Secretary of State for International Security and Nonproliferation Christopher Ford told the Senate Foreign Relations Committee on November 28, 2017, that renewed discussions with Saudi Arabia about a nuclear cooperation agreement are "underway." In 2017, the Trump Administration expedited consideration of required regulatory approvals for U.S. firms to provide marketing information to Saudi officials, and U.S. companies have provided proposals to Saudi authorities in relation to the planned 2018 tender for nuclear reactor construction. In September 2018, Secretary of Energy Rick Perry and Minister of Energy, Industry, and Mineral Resources Khalid al Falih met in Washington, DC, and discussed, inter alia, "the potential for U.S.-Saudi civil nuclear engagement and new technologies such as Small Modular Reactors."[95]

Congressional Views, Legislation, and Administration Perspectives

It remains to be seen whether or when the Trump Administration might propose a bilateral nuclear cooperation agreement for Congress to consider. Nuclear cooperation agreements under Section 123 of the Atomic Energy Act of 1954, as amended (AEA, 22 U.S.C. 2011 et seq), are required for significant nuclear cooperation such as the transfer of certain U.S.-origin nuclear material subject to licensing for commercial, medical, and industrial purposes; the export of reactors and critical reactor components; and other commodities under Nuclear Regulatory Commission export licensing authority. A "123 agreement" is required for any covered nuclear exports but appears to be unnecessary for U.S companies to conclude contracts for nuclear reactors. Whether Saudi

---

[95] U.S. Department of Energy, "Secretary Perry Meets with Khalid Al-Falih, Minister of Energy, Industry and Mineral Resources of the Kingdom of Saudi Arabia," September 10, 2018.

Arabia would be willing to conclude such a contract without a 123 agreement in place that would be required for related exports is unclear. Whether a U.S.-Saudi 123 agreement can enter into force by the end of 2018 depends on a number of variables, such as the length of the governments' negotiations and the adjournment of the 115th Congress. Congress also could enact legislation to approve an agreement notwithstanding the AEA congressional review requirements.[96]

Some Members of Congress have criticized the potential for U.S.-Saudi nuclear cooperation in the absence of a firm Saudi commitment to forego uranium enrichment and fuel reprocessing technologies. In the 115th Congress, H.R. 5357 would amend the procedures for consideration of 123 agreements to require congressional approval of any agreement not containing, inter alia, commitments by cooperating countries to forego enrichment and reprocessing. In July 2018, the Senate Foreign Relations Committee reported S.Res. 541 to the Senate, which would state the sense of the Senate that any United States-Saudi Arabia civilian nuclear cooperation agreement under section 123 of the Atomic Energy Act of 1954 (42 U.S.C. 2153), commonly known as a "123 Agreement", concluded in the future should prohibit the Kingdom of Saudi Arabia from enriching uranium or separating plutonium on Saudi Arabian territory in keeping with the strongest possible nonproliferation "gold standard" as well as require the Kingdom of Saudi Arabia to bring into force the Additional Protocol with the International Atomic Energy Agency.

Some Administration officials and nuclear industry advocates have warned of the potential for Saudi Arabia to pursue nuclear cooperation with other countries, including Russia or China, if the United States insists on including enrichment and reprocessing commitments in a bilateral agreement. Nevertheless, the Trump Administration has indicated it is seeking such commitments in discussions with Saudi authorities. In May 2018, Secretary of State Mike Pompeo said in Senate testimony, "we want a gold-standard Section 123 Agreement from them, which would not

---

[96] Such legislation has precedent; bills introduced in the House and Senate in 2010 would have approved the 123 agreement between the United States and Australia. See CRS Report R41312, *U.S.-Australia Civilian Nuclear Cooperation: Issues for Congress*, by Mary Beth D. Nikitin and Bruce Vaughn.

permit them to enrich."[97] Secretary of Energy Rick Perry also told a House committee that if Saudi Arabia does not reach an agreement with the United States, "the message will be clear to the rest of the world that the kingdom is not as concerned about being leaders when it comes to nonproliferation in the Middle East."[98]

Saudi Views on Fuel Cycle Technologies

Analysts have examined Saudi nuclear plans and proposals for decades in light of the kingdom's economic profile, energy resources, and security dilemmas. Saudi state policy underscores that the kingdom's nuclear energy pursuits are limited to peaceful purposes, but senior officials, including Crown Prince Mohammed bin Salman, also have stated that if Iran pursues or obtains a nuclear weapon, then the kingdom also would work to do so. In March 2018, Crown Prince Mohammed bin Salman said, "Saudi Arabia does not want to acquire any nuclear bomb, but without a doubt if Iran developed a nuclear bomb, we will follow suit as soon as possible."[99]

The 2008 U.S.-Saudi MOU on nuclear cooperation, which is a statement of intent and is not legally binding, described the Saudi government's intent "to rely on existing international markets for nuclear fuel services as an alternative to the pursuit of enrichment and reprocessing." Saudi Arabian officials have not publicly stated that they will reject prohibitions on uranium enrichment and fuel reprocessing if such prohibitions are required to enter into a bilateral nuclear cooperation agreement with the United States. However, Saudi officials also have not forsworn enrichment or reprocessing and have stated their intent to use and develop domestic resources and capabilities to support their nuclear program.

---

[97] Secretary of State Mike Pompeo, Testimony before the Senate Foreign Relations Committee, May 24, 2018.

[98] Sec. of Energy Rick Perry, Testimony before the House Committee on Science, Space, and Technology, May 9, 2018.

[99] Reuters, "Saudi crown prince says will develop nuclear bomb if Iran does: CBS TV," March 15, 2018

Saudi official statements since late 2017 have implied that the country seeks, at a minimum, to preserve the option to pursue uranium enrichment. KA CARE officials have said that the Saudi program may use indigenous uranium resources for fuel,[100] and, in December 2017, Saudi Energy Minister Khalid al Falih said, "we intend to localize the entire value chain with nuclear energy.... Whatever we do is going to be under strict compliance with international agreements. But we will not deprive ourselves of accessing our natural resources and localizing an industry that we intend to be with us for the long term."[101] In February 2018, Saudi Foreign Minister Adel Al Jubeir said "we want to have the same rights as other countries."[102]

Saudi Foreign Policy

Close U.S.-Saudi security cooperation continues in parallel with work to overcome U.S.-Saudi differences of opinion on some regional security threats. The latter years of President Obama's Administration were characterized by reports of tension between U.S. and Saudi leaders on key issues, most notably the conflict in Syria, Iran's nuclear program, and U.S. policy toward Egypt. Many of those issues—in addition to political-military developments in Yemen and campaigns against the Islamic State and other violent extremists—remain prominent on the U.S.-Saudi policy agenda and were identified as issues of interest during President Trump's May 2017 visit to the kingdom and Crown Prince Mohammed bin Salman's March 2018 visit to the United States.

President Trump and King Salman bin Abd al Aziz agreed to a "Strategic Partnership for the 21st Century" during the President's May 2017 trip to Riyadh. King Salman and President Obama had previously formed such a partnership in September 2015. President Trump and King

---

[100] Ibid.

[101] Rania El Gamal and Katie Paul, "Saudi Arabia hopes to start nuclear pact talks with U.S. in weeks – minister," Reuters, December 20, 2017.

[102] CNBC, Interview with Saudi Foreign Minister Adel Al Jubeir, Munich, Germany, February 19, 2018.

Salman further agreed to a "Joint Strategic Vision for the Kingdom of Saudi Arabia and the United States of America" and announced plans for a "Strategic Joint Consultative Group" that is intended to meet "at least once a year, alternating between the two countries" to review bilateral cooperation.[103]

King Salman and Crown Prince Mohammad bin Salman have actively pursued Saudi interests across the Middle East since 2015, challenging Iran, reopening dialogue with Iraq, seeking to isolate Qatar, and fighting an ongoing war in Yemen. This Saudi activism in regional affairs has created new questions for the Trump Administration and Congress to consider, including with regard to defense cooperation.

Iran, Iraq, and Syria

Saudi policies toward Iraq, Syria, and Lebanon continue to reflect the kingdom's overarching concerns about Iran and its ties to state and nonstate actors in these countries. Statements by Saudi leaders suggest that they see Iran's policies as part of an expansionist, sectarian agenda aimed at empowering Shia Muslims in the Middle East at the expense of Sunnis.[104] Iranian leaders attribute similarly sectarian motives to their Saudi counterparts and remain critical of Saudi cooperation with the United States.[105]

Saudi concern about Iranian nuclear activities also persists. The kingdom scrutinized and then accepted the Iran-P5+1 Joint Comprehensive Plan of Action (JCPOA), later calling for its rigorous enforcement and reconsideration. In May 2018, the kingdom welcomed President Trump's decision to withdraw the United States from the JCPOA and announced its support for the reimposition of economic sanctions on Iran and efforts to

---

[103] Joint Statement by President Trump and King Salman bin Abd al-Aziz Al Saud of Saudi Arabia, May 23, 2017.

[104] "Saudi FM to Asharq Al-Awsat: We Reject Iran's Sectarian Strife, Support for Terrorism," July 11, 2018.

[105] Reuters, "Iran's leader accuses Saudis of 'treason' against Muslims," January 16, 2018.

curtail Iranian support to the Syrian government and various nonstate actors in the region.[106]

At present, limits on arms sales to Iran imposed under U.N. Security Council Resolution 2231 are set to remain in place until 2020. In the interim, ongoing initiatives to improve U.S.-Saudi defense cooperation and sales of new defense systems (see "Arms Sales, Security Assistance, and Training") may further improve Saudi Arabia's conventional military advantage over Iran and strengthen its ability to meet unconventional threats from Iran or Iranian proxies.

Short of outright war between the two regional contenders, their apparent proxy competitions may intensify. Such intensification could complicate the Administration's desired outcomes in places like Lebanon, Iraq, Syria, and Yemen, and could affect stated U.S. national security objectives across the Middle East.

Iraq

In December 2015, Saudi officials reopened the kingdom's diplomatic offices in Iraq after a 25 year absence, marking a milestone in a relative normalization of Saudi-Iraqi relations that occurred after the 2014 change in Iraqi leadership from Nouri al Maliki to Prime Minister Hayder al Abadi. U.S. officials have praised a series of official visits by senior Saudis to Iraq intended to strengthen ties with Iraq's government. Border crossings between the two countries have been reopened, although to date Saudi Arabia and the other GCC states have not offered major new economic or security assistance or new debt relief initiatives to help stabilize Iraq.[107] Saudi officials view the empowerment of Iran-linked Shia militia groups in Iraq with suspicion. It remains to be seen whether or how Saudi-Iraqi relations may be affected by the selection of a new government in Iraq following May 2018 elections.[108]

---

[106] Embassy of the Kingdom of Saudi Arabia, Washington, DC, Statement on the United States Withdrawal from the JCPOA, May 8, 2018.

[107] Saudi Arabia claims nearly $16 billion in Iraqi official debt dating to the era of Saddam Hussein's war with Iran.

[108] See CRS Report R45096, *Iraq: In Brief*, by Christopher M. Blanchard.

Syria

With regard to Syria, Saudi authorities back the U.N. Security Council's call for a negotiated settlement to the conflict and would prefer that such a settlement result in a transition away from the Iran-aligned government of Syrian President Bashar al Asad.[109] Saudi efforts to consolidate and align the views of various Syrian opposition actors and armed groups bore some fruit in 2017, but divisions among Syrian factions persist. In conjunction with the Trump Administration's plans to reduce some U.S. spending on stabilization efforts in areas of Syria liberated from the Islamic State, Saudi authorities have agreed to make contributions and, in August 2018, announced plans to spend $100 million on related programs.

Conflict in Yemen

Saudi Arabia has long exercised a strong role in Yemen, seeking to mitigate various threats to the kingdom through liaison relationships and security interventions. Saudi officials expressed increasing concern about developments in Yemen over the course of 2014, as the Saudi- and GCC-backed transition process there stalled. An alliance between the northern-Yemen based Zaydi Shia movement known as the Houthis/*Ansar Allah* (see text box below) and forces loyal to the now deceased former president Ali Abdullah Saleh grew more aggressive in their attempts to coerce transitional authorities.

In mid-2014, pro-Saleh and Houthi forces took control of the Yemeni capital, Sana'a, and, in September 2014, they continued military operations in contravention of an agreed power-sharing arrangement with the Hadi government. Houthi forces' unwillingness to withdraw from the capital and unilateral moves by Houthi leaders and Saleh supporters to circumvent Hadi's authority precipitated a crisis that culminated in the outbreak of renewed conflict and Hadi's resignation and de facto house arrest in January 2015. Houthi leaders announced a new governance plan in

---

[109] U.N. Security Council Resolution (UNSCR) 2254, adopted in 2015, endorsed a "road map" for a political settlement in Syria, including the drafting of a new constitution and the administration of U.N.-supervised elections.

February 2015 and in March launched an offensive against pro-Hadi forces in central and southern Yemen.

In response, the Saudi Foreign Minister decried what the kingdom considered a "serious escalation... carried out by an Al Houthi militia coup against constitutional legitimacy."[110] Days later, as Houthi forces advanced on the southern city of Aden, Saudi Arabia and members of a coalition launched air strikes in response to a specific request from President Hadi.[111] Saudi Arabia has led a military coalition of mostly Arab states since March 2015 in efforts to reinstate the Hadi government.[112]

Yemen's Houthi Movement and Saudi Arabia

The *Ansar Allah* movement is a predominantly Zaydi Shia revivalist political and insurgent movement that formed in the northern province of Sa'da in 2004 under the leadership of members of the Al Houthi family. It originally sought an end to what it viewed as efforts to marginalize Zaydi Shia communities and beliefs, but its goals grew in scope and ambition as it embraced a populist, antiestablishment message following the 2011 uprising in Yemen. Members of its Zaydi Shia base of support are closer in their beliefs to Sunni Muslims than most other Shia, and some Yemeni observers argue that the motives of the Houthi movement are evolving to include new political and social goals that cannot be explained strictly in sectarian terms. Skeptics highlight the movement's ideological roots, its alleged cooperation with Iran, and the slogans prominently displayed on its banners: "God is Great! Death to America! Death to Israel! Curse the Jews! Victory to Islam!"

Saudi air, ground, and border forces fought Houthi militia members in 2009 in a campaign that ejected Houthi fighters who had crossed the Saudi border, but Saudi Arabia failed to defeat the movement or end the potential threat it posed to southern Saudi Arabia and Saudi interests in Yemen. The development and increased sophistication of Houthi military capabilities since 2014 is a source of significant concern to Saudi Arabia, especially the group's demonstrated ability to conduct cross-border missile attacks against targets inside the kingdom.[113] U.S. officials express concern not only about Houthi threats to Saudi Arabia, but the potential for ties between the Houthi movement, Iran, and Iranian-supported groups such as Hezbollah to develop to an extent that Houthi forces could pose a durable, Iranian-linked threat in the southern Arabian Peninsula and Red Sea region.

---

[110] Saudi Ministry of Foreign Affairs, Minister of Foreign Affairs Stresses Depth of Historical and Strong Relations Between Saudi Arabia and Britain, March 24, 2015.

[111] Text of Hadi request letter in "GCC statement: Gulf countries respond to Yemen developments," *The National* (UAE), March 26, 2015.

[112] See CRS Report R43960, *Yemen: Civil War and Regional Intervention*, by Jeremy M. Sharp.

[113] For a detailed discussion, see Michael Knights, "The Houthi War Machine: From Guerrilla War to State Capture," U.S. Military Academy Combatting Terrorism Center, *Sentinel*, Volume 11, Issue 8, September 2018.

Since April 2015, U.N. Security Council Resolution 2216 has demanded that the Houthis take a number of steps immediately and unconditionally that remain unfulfilled, including

- ending their use of violence;
- withdrawing their forces from all areas they have seized, including the capital Sana'a;
- relinquishing all additional arms seized from military and security institutions, including missile systems;
- ceasing all actions that are exclusively within the authority of the legitimate Government of Yemen; and
- refraining from any provocation or threats to Yemen's neighbors, including through acquiring surface-surface missiles and stockpiling weapons in territory adjacent to Yemen's borders.

Since 2015, Houthi fighters have launched attacks on Saudi border areas that have killed Saudi civilians and security personnel, and Saudi military operations have continued to strike Houthi positions across Yemen.

Yemen and U.S.-Saudi Relations

Saudi Arabia's military intervention in neighboring Yemen has placed the United States in a difficult position. On the one hand, U.S. officials share Saudi concerns about the ouster of the Hadi government, Iranian ties to the Houthi movement, and armed extremist threats from Al Qaeda and Islamic State supporters in Yemen. On the other hand, Saudi intervention has embroiled a key U.S. partner in a seemingly intractable armed conflict in which Saudi use of U.S.-origin weaponry appears to have contributed to mass displacement and resulted in civilian casualties and infrastructure damage. As the conflict continues, extremist groups have remained active, and Houthi forces conduct cross-border attacks and threaten maritime security in the Red Sea, with some Iranian support.

The Saudi intervention in Yemen also may have broader implications for the kingdom's future leadership and stability. Insofar as Crown Prince Mohammed bin Sultan has portrayed himself as the architect and leader of the intervention, its relative success or failure may shape perceptions of his competence and judgment. Saudi casualties in the campaign also have cost the kingdom's military some key personnel and added to the domestic political sensitivity of the overall effort. Despite possible concerns over the ramifications of Saudi-led operations, both the Trump and Obama Administrations have voiced diplomatic support for Saudi efforts to reinstall Hadi's government and have provided logistical and intelligence support to Saudi-led military operations. U.S. officials have repeatedly spoken about what they view as the importance of avoiding civilian casualties and reaching a negotiated solution to the crisis.

- Congressional concerns expressed in the 114th and 115th Congress have been driven in part by civilian casualties and deteriorating humanitarian conditions resulting from Saudi and coalition military operations in Yemen.
- Congress reviews proposed foreign military and commercial arms sales pursuant to the provisions of the Arms Export Control Act, and some Members have sought to condition or disapprove of proposed sales to Saudi Arabia.[114] Critics of proposed sales argue that Saudi airstrikes in Yemen using U.S. munitions and weapons platforms violate international humanitarian law and that further U.S. sales of identical or related items risk facilitating further such airstrikes or otherwise indelibly associating the United States with Saudi conduct. Proponents of the sales argue that in order to improve Saudi military operations and targeting, the United States should provide more advanced U.S. technology and expand training and intelligence support to the Saudi air force.
- Congress also authorizes and appropriates funds for Department of Defense activities in support of the Saudi-led coalition, and some Members have proposed conditions on U.S. support and sought certifications on Saudi and coalition activities and additional information about U.S. programs.
- Congress also reviews U.S. military operations pursuant to its war powers under the Constitution and pursuant to the War Powers Resolution (P.L. 93-148). Some Members have proposed legislation directing the President to withdraw U.S. military forces from missions in Yemen not expressly authorized by Congress.

U.S. officials have acknowledged[115] that pressure from Congress has altered how the Administration deals with the coalition over the Yemen conflict, and Congress continues to debate legislative proposals seeking variously to

- Require additional oversight reporting on U.S. activities;
- Restrict or prohibit the deployment of U.S. military personnel or the use of U.S. funds for certain purposes in Yemen; and/or

Condition or prohibit the provision of certain support or the sale of certain weaponry to Saudi Arabia.

---

[114] See CRS Report RL31675, *Arms Sales: Congressional Review Process*, by Paul K. Kerr.

[115] Acting Assistant Secretary of State for Near Eastern Affairs David Satterfield, Testimony before the Senate Foreign Relations Committee, April 17, 2018.

Saudi Arabia 57

Iranian material and advisory support to the Houthi war effort—including the provision of missiles that have been fired into Saudi Arabia—has amplified Saudi leaders' anxieties and concerns. Saudi forces have intercepted missile attacks from Yemen on several occasions, including a missile attack on Riyadh in November 2017.

As the military campaign has continued, reports of civilian casualties and displacement; food, medicine, and water shortages; advances by AQAP forces; Islamic State attacks; and persistence by the Houthis and their allies have fueled international criticism of Saudi policy. In August 2018, U.N. officials estimated that 6,660 civilians have been killed in the conflict since March 2015 and another 10,563 injured.[116] A report issued by the U.N. Human Rights Council-organized Group of International and Regional Eminent Experts on Yemen attributed most direct civilian casualties to coalition airstrikes based on data from the U.N. Office of the High Commissioner for Human Rights and also described potential violations of international law by Houthi forces and their allies.[117] Humanitarian conditions worsened significantly in Yemen in 2017 amid Saudi coalition-enforced limits on air and sea access that have remained in place, with some changes. Periodic coalition strikes that cause civilian casualties continue.

Saudi officials have acknowledged some shortcomings in their operations, while placing most of the blame for reported civilian deaths and for difficult humanitarian conditions on the activities of and threats posed by their adversaries. Saudi officials accuse Houthi forces of conspiring to restrict flows of humanitarian goods to areas under their control and of profiting from the illicit diversion and sale of such goods. Saudi officials also underscore their view of the Houthis as a hostile minority movement that is opposed by many other Yemenis and continues

---

[116] U.N. Document A/HRC/39/43, Report of the United Nations High Commissioner for Human Rights containing the findings of the Group of Independent Eminent International and Regional Experts, August 17, 2018.

[117] According to the OHCHR data, OHCHR, coalition airstrikes have killed at least 4,300 civilians. See Annex 4, U.N. Document A/HRC/39/43, Report of the United Nations High Commissioner for Human Rights containing the findings of the Group of Independent Eminent International and Regional Experts, August 17, 2018.

to benefit from Iranian security support to the detriment of the kingdom's security.

Saudi and coalition officials have taken some steps to improve humanitarian access and implement more effective military targeting, but criticism has grown among some Members of Congress and several legislative proposals have been made to condition, reduce, or eliminate related U.S. assistance (see Appendix D).[118]

Successive U.S. Administrations have expressed varying degrees of criticism of some coalition actions while emphasizing a consistent view that strictly military solutions to the Yemen conflict are not possible. At present, the U.S. government continues to provide limited military support to the Saudi-led coalition in Yemen, while stating that, for the United States, "ending the conflict in Yemen is a national security priority."[119]

In September 2018, the Administration certified to Congress pursuant to the FY2019 NDAA (P.L. 115-232) that the Saudi and Emirati governments are taking steps to reduce the risk of harm to civilians and civilian infrastructure, engaging in good-faith efforts to diplomatically resolve the conflict, and acting to alleviate the humanitarian crisis and reduce unnecessary delays to shipments entering Yemen. The Administration's certifications described steps taken by U.S. government officials to engage Saudi and Emirati officials on related issues and to encourage them to take specific actions. Updated certifications are required under the provisions of the FY2019 NDAA not later than 180 and 360 days from August 13, 2018. Some Members of Congress have criticized the Administration's decision to certify the coalition's actions and may propose new legislation related to U.S. operations in Yemen and arms sales to coalition countries.[120]

---

[118] Also see CRS Report R45046, *The War in Yemen: A Compilation of Legislation in the 115th Congress*, by Jeremy M. Sharp and Christopher M. Blanchard.

[119] Statement by Secretary of State Mike Pompeo, September 12, 2018.

[120] Joe Gould, "Yemen skeptics in Congress see politics shifting their way — and against Trump," *Defense News*, September 13, 2018.

Qatar and Intra-Gulf Cooperation Council (GCC) Tensions

Saudi-Qatari disputes have flared periodically over the last 20-plus years and soured significantly in 2017.[121] Saudi Arabia has taken issue with the pro-Islamist and independent foreign policy pursued by Qatar's leaders and opposed Qatar's maintenance of ties to Iran, with which Qatar shares lucrative natural gas reserves.

Saudi Arabia and Qatar have both sought to shape the outcome of regional uprisings since 2011, in some cases using their own military forces, such as in Libya and Yemen, and, in other cases, such as Syria, supporting different nonstate armed groups. In March 2014, these and related differences—including over the 2013 military overthrow of an elected Muslim Brotherhood-linked President of Egypt—widened to the point where Saudi Arabia, UAE, and Bahrain withdrew their ambassadors from Doha. The ambassadors returned in November 2014 in exchange for mutual pledges not to interfere in each other's affairs. Nevertheless, underlying policy differences remained.

Emir Tamim bin Hamad participated in the May 2017 U.S.-Gulf summit and met with President Donald Trump, but there were indications of Qatari-Saudi discord prior to and during the summit. On June 5, 2017, Saudi Arabia abruptly severed diplomatic relations with Qatar, closed the land border between the two countries, closed its air space and waters to Qatari vessels, prohibited Saudi nationals from visiting or transiting Qatar, and gave Qatari nationals 14 days to leave the kingdom. The moves followed a period of escalation in official Saudi-Qatari confrontation marked by mutual recriminations and accusations.

Saudi Arabia accuses Qatar's government of supporting terrorism, interfering in the internal affairs of fellow Arab states, and facilitating Iranian efforts to destabilize Saudi Arabia and its neighbors.[122] Qatar rejects the charges and views Saudi Arabia as seeking to violate Qatari

---

[121] For background, see Kristian Coates Ulrichsen, "Qatar: The Gulf's Problem Child," *Atlantic Monthly*, June 5, 2017, and, CRS Report R44533, *Qatar: Governance, Security, and U.S. Policy*, by Kenneth Katzman.

[122] Saudi Ministry of Foreign Affairs, Statement, June 5, 2017.

sovereignty and impose its will on the country's leaders and population.[123] Qatar has rejected some demands presented by Saudi Arabia, the United Arab Emirates, Egypt, and Bahrain, but has sought to resolve the confrontation through negotiation. Saudi authorities have kept their isolation measures in place. Both sides of the dispute have sought to influence the United States to support their position.

The United States maintains close defense cooperation, including arms sales, with both Saudi Arabia and Qatar and continues to operate from military bases in Qatar. U.S. officials have called for reconciliation and have offered to facilitate dialogue among the parties. Limitations imposed on travel and transit to Qatar by Saudi Arabia could impact U.S. nationals and businesses, and U.S. nationals and businesses operating in the kingdom may face pressure to limit or curtail their contacts with Qatar as the dispute continues.

Israeli-Palestinian Affairs

For decades, official Saudi statements have been routinely critical of Israeli policies, and many Saudi clerics, including leading official clerics, appear to remain implacably hostile to Israel. Apart from any potential alignment of views or interests with Israel on some regional threats, Saudi leaders and government officials have historically been vocal advocates for the Palestinians in the context of Israeli-Arab disputes. Saudi Arabia supports the international recognition of a Palestinian state and full Palestinian membership at the United Nations.

Shared antipathy to the Iranian government's policies, parallel cooperation with the United States, and shared terrorism concerns do not appear to have contributed to tangibly closer Saudi-Israeli ties in recent years. However, some new, overt contacts have occurred between Saudis and Israeli government officials, and this has driven speculation about the potential for a breakthrough in bilateral engagement.[124]

---

[123] Qatar Ministry of Foreign Affairs, Statement, June 5, 2017.
[124] Israeli Prime Minister Benjamin Netanyahu speculated in January 2016 that "Saudi Arabia recognizes that Israel is an ally rather than an enemy because of the two [principal] threats that threaten them, Iran and Daesh [the Arabic acronym for the Islamic State]." i24 News, "Netanyahu urges EU to adopt policy of moderate Arab states on Israel," January 22, 2016.

In May 2017, President Trump flew directly to Israel from Saudi Arabia and upon his arrival said,

"I was deeply encouraged by my conversations with Muslim world leaders in Saudi Arabia, including King Salman, who I spoke to at great length. King Salman feels very strongly, and I can tell you would love to see peace between Israel and the Palestinians."[125] The U.S.-Saudi joint statement released following President Trump's May 2017 visit to the kingdom says that the President and King Salman "stressed the importance of reaching a comprehensive peace between Israelis and Palestinians" and "agreed to do everything they can to promote an environment that is conducive to advancing peace."[126]

King Salman has remained committed to the terms of the peace initiative his predecessor (the late King Abdullah) put forward under the auspices of the Arab League in 2002. The initiative calls for normalization of Arab relations with Israel if Israel were to

1. withdraw fully from the territories it occupied in 1967,
2. agree to the establishment of a Palestinian state with a capital in East Jerusalem, and
3. provide for the "[a]chievement of a just solution to the Palestinian Refugee problem in accordance with U.N. General Assembly Resolution 194."[127]

---

[125] President Donald Trump, Remarks with Israeli President Reuven Rivlin, May 22, 2017.

[126] The White House, Joint Statement Between the Kingdom of Saudi Arabia and the United States of America, May 23, 2017.

[127] Adopted in December 1948, General Assembly Resolution 194 states that "the refugees wishing to return to their homes and live at peace with their neighbours should be permitted to do so at the earliest practicable date, and that compensation should be paid for the property of those choosing not to return and for loss of or damage to property which, under principles of international law or in equity, should be made good by the Governments or authorities responsible." This resolution is often cited by advocates for the right of Palestinian refugees to return to their former homes in what is now Israel. In April 2013, representatives of the Arab League agreed that land swaps could be an element of a conflict-ending agreement between Israel and the Palestinians. In September 2015, King Salman and President Obama "underscored the enduring importance of the 2002 Arab Peace Initiative, and underlined the necessity of reaching a comprehensive, just and lasting settlement to the conflict based on two states living side-by-side in peace and security." Joint Statement on the Meeting between President Barack Obama and King Salman bin Abd al Aziz Al Saud, September 4, 2015.

In January 2018, King Salman reiterated the kingdom's "firm position on the Palestinian cause and the legitimate rights of the Palestinian people to establish their independent state with Jerusalem as its capital and on continuing efforts to find a just and lasting solution to the Palestinian cause in accordance with relevant international resolutions."[128] Saudi officials reportedly have consulted with other Arab states on joint responses to the Trump Administration's recognition of Jerusalem as the capital of Israel and U.S. decisions to reduce contributions to U.N. relief efforts for Palestinian refugees.

At an Arab League meeting in September 2018, Saudi Foreign Minister Adel al Jubeir said, "the Palestinian cause is the top priority and concern of the Kingdom of Saudi Arabia, which seeks to achieve the legitimate rights of the Palestinian people based on the Arab Peace Initiative and the resolutions of international legitimacy for the establishment of an independent state on the 1967 borders with East Jerusalem as its capital."[129]

Saudi relations with Hamas have evolved over time and have grown strained since 2017, amid the deteriorating relationship between Iran and Saudi Arabia and Saudi confrontation with Qatar. Whereas Saudi authorities vociferously criticized Israeli conduct during the summer 2014 Gaza war with Hamas, condemning what they described as "Israeli inhuman aggression" and pledging Saudi support "to the Palestinian brothers in the West Bank and Gaza Strip to alleviate the difficult conditions in which they live because of the Israeli aggression and terrorism,"[130] in June 2017, Foreign Minister Al Jubeir called on Qatar "to stop supporting groups like Hamas."

---

[128] Ministry of Foreign Affairs, Statement on Phone Conversation between King Salman and Palestinian Authority President Mahmoud Abbas, January 9, 2018.

[129] Foreign Minister Adel al Jubeir, Statement to 150th session of the Arab League Council in Cairo, Sept. 11, 2018.

[130] Saudi Press Agency (Riyadh), Deputy Crown Prince Chairs Cabinet's Session, August 18, 2014.

OUTLOOK

As described above, Saudi Arabia has close defense and security ties with the United States anchored for decades by long-standing military training programs and supplemented by high-value weapons sales, critical infrastructure security cooperation, and counterterrorism initiatives. Joint security ties would be difficult and costly for either side to fully break or replace. While Saudi and U.S. officials have taken steps to maintain and deepen these ties, differences in preferred tactics and methods may continue to complicate bilateral coordination on regional security issues, including on Iran and action against the Islamic State and other terrorist groups. U.S. willingness to arm and train Saudi security forces may reduce potential burdens on U.S. forces, but may also more deeply entangle the United States in dilemmas or disputes in cases where U.S.-equipped or -trained Saudi forces are deployed.

In recent years, U.S. policymakers have engaged with an emerging class of Saudi leaders during a particularly challenging and tumultuous period for the kingdom and its neighbors. Islamic State attacks, leadership transition and consolidation in the kingdom, the collapse of the Saudi-backed transitional government in neighboring Yemen, oil market trends, Russian military intervention in Syria, and Iranian nuclear policy and regional activism have all created pressure on Saudi leaders and tested U.S.-Saudi relations. Saudi Arabia's pursuit of an independent and assertive course on regional security issues and its leaders' ambitious plans to transform the kingdom's economy and fiscal base reflect these concerns and offer both new opportunities for U.S.-Saudi partnership and shared risks.

Over time, Saudi and U.S. officials have periodically attempted to articulate a shared "strategic vision" that includes, but extends beyond, defense and counterterrorism partnership. As the kingdom repositions itself as a hub for global investment, commercial ties and investment opportunities may forge new bonds between Saudis and Americans, even if U.S. firms may not enjoy the privileged role they once held in the increasingly open Saudi market. In June 2017, former U.S. Ambassador to

Saudi Arabia Joseph Westphal identified education and judicial reform as potential areas for expanded U.S.-Saudi cooperation.

Changes to succession arrangements have elevated Crown Prince Mohammed bin Salman and raised the prospect that, while still in his 30s, he could succeed his father and potentially remain as monarch for decades. The Crown Prince's economic and social reform proposals would overturn decades of precedent, and he has taken dramatic steps against high-profile individuals accused of corruption and/or abuse of power, including fellow royal family members. The changes unfolding may eliminate uncertainty about the consolidation of power among the next generation of Saudi leaders, but also may signal an end to the system of ostensibly consensus-based rule among the Al Saud family that has prevailed since the 1960s. Successive U.S. Administrations have cultivated ties to different royal actors and security entities in Saudi Arabia in an effort to build a broad-based partnership with different power centers. Consolidated control could alter the dynamics of U.S.-Saudi cooperation, particularly with regard to Saudi purchases of military equipment. Alternatively, if the Crown Prince's initiatives stall or fail, recent events could mark the beginning of a more volatile period in the kingdom and in U.S.- Saudi relations, with varying and potentially serious economic and security consequences.

If past patterns in the bilateral relationship prevail, leaders on both sides may seek to maintain U.S.-Saudi solidarity, while managing points of friction and resisting calls from some parties on both sides for a more fundamental reevaluation of a productive, if imperfect, partnership. Congress may continue to shape bilateral relations through its oversight of U.S.-Saudi security cooperation and its engagement on regional economic and diplomatic policy issues.

APPENDIX A. HISTORICAL BACKGROUND

The modern kingdom of Saudi Arabia is the third state established in the Arabian Peninsula since the end of the 18th century based on the hereditary rule of members of the Al Saud family. In the mid-18th century, a local alliance developed between the Al Saud and the members of a puritanical Sunni Islamic religious movement led by a cleric named Mohammed ibn Abd Al Wahhab. Alliances between the Al Saud family and supporters of Abd Al Wahhab (referred to by some as Wahhabis) built two states in the Arabian Peninsula during the next century. Each eventually collapsed under pressure from outside powers and inter- and intrafamily rivalries.

During the first quarter of the 20th century, an Al Saud chieftain named Abd al Aziz ibn Abd al Rahman Al Saud (commonly referred to as Ibn Saud) used force to unify much of the Arabian Peninsula under a restored Al Saud state. Ibn Saud's forces overcame numerous tribal rivals with the support of an armed Wahhabi contingent known as the Ikhwan (or brotherhood), and, at times, with the financial and military backing of the British government. By 1932, King Abd al Aziz and his armies had crushed an Ikhwan revolt, consolidated control over most of the Arabian

Peninsula, and declared the establishment of the Kingdom of Saudi Arabia. Six of Ibn Saud's sons—Kings Saud, Faisal, Khaled, Fahd, Abdullah, and Salman—have succeeded him as rulers of the Saudi kingdom during the subsequent eight decades. This era has been dominated by the development and export of the kingdom's massive oil resources, the resulting socioeconomic transformation of the country, and accompanying religious and cultural debates spurred by rapid change. During this period, Al Saud rulers have managed a complex consensus-based system of governance, balancing the various interests of tribal, religious, regional, political, and economic constituencies. A series of agreements, statements by successive U.S. Administrations, arms sales, military training arrangements, and military deployments have demonstrated a strong U.S. security commitment to the Saudi monarchy since the 1940s. That security commitment was built on shared economic interests and antipathy to Communism and was tested by regional conflict during the Cold War. It has survived the terrorism-induced strains of the post-Cold War era relatively intact, and has continued as new arms sales to Saudi Arabia—the largest in U.S. history—are implemented. Transition to a new generation of leadership in the Al Saud family, evolution in the Saudi economy, and

Appendix B. Proposed Major U.S. Defense Sales to Saudi Arabia

Table B-1. Proposed Major U.S. Foreign Military Sales to Saudi Arabia January 2009 to September 2018; Possible values in billions of dollars

Formal Notification Date	System	Recipient Force	Pos. Value
August 2009	CNS-ATM	RSAF	$1.500
August 2009	TASS	RSAF	$0.530
December 2009	SANG Modernization	SANG	$0.177
September 2010	Blanket Order Training Program	RSAF	$0.350
October 2010	F-15 Sales, Upgrades, Weaponry and Training	RSAF	$29.400
October 2010	APACHE, BLACKHAWK, AH-6i, and MD-530F Helicopters	SANG	$25.600
October 2010	APACHE Longbow Helicopters	RSLF	$3.300
October 2010	APACHE Longbow Helicopters	Royal Guard	$2.200
November 2010	JAVELIN Missiles and Launch Units	—	$0.071
May 2011	Night Vision and Thermal Weapons Sights	RSLF	$0.330
June 2011	CBU-105D/B Sensor Fuzed Weapons	RSAF	$0.355
June 2011	Light Armored Vehicles	—	$0.263
June 2011	Light Armored Vehicles	SANG	$0.350
September 2011	Howitzers, Fire Finder Radar, Ammunition, HMMWVs	—	$0.886
October 2011	Up-Armored HMMWVs	RSLF	$0.033
December 2011	PATRIOT Systems Engineering Services	—	$0.120
August 2012	RSAF Follow-on Support	RSAF	$0.850
August 2012	Link-16 Systems and ISR Equipment and Training	RSAF	$0.257
November 2012	C-130J-30 Aircraft and KC-130J Air Refueling Aircraft	RSAF	$6.700
November 2012	RSLF Parts, Equipment, and Support	RSLF	$0.300

Saudi Arabia

Formal Notification Date	System	Recipient Force	Pos. Value
November 2012	PATRIOT (PAC-2) Missiles Recertification	RSADF	$0.130
June 2013	SANG Modernization Program Extension	SANG	$4.000
July 2013	Mark V Patrol Boats	RSNF	$1.200
August 2013	RSAF Follow-on Support	RSAF	$1.200
October 2013	U.S. Military Training Mission (USMTM) Program Support Services	MOD	$0.090
October 2013	SLAM-ER, JSOW, Harpoon Block II, GBU-39/B Munitions	RSAF	$6.800
November 2013	C4I System Upgrades and Maintenance	RSNF	$1.100
December 2013	TOW 2A and 2B Missiles	RSLF	$0.170
December 2013	TOW 2A and 2B RF Missiles	SANG	$0.900
April 2014	Facilities Security Forces- Training and Advisory Group (FSF-TAG) Support	MOI	$0.080
August 2014	AWACS Modernization	RSAF	$2.000
October 2014	Patriot Air Defense System with PAC-3 enhancement	—	$1.750
May 2015	MH-60R Multi-Mission Helicopters	—	$1.900
July 2015	Ammunition	RSLF	$0.500
July 2015	Patriot Advanced Capability-3 (PAC-3) Missiles	—	$5.400
October 2015	UH-60M Black Hawk Utility Helicopters	RSLF Aviation Command	$0.495
October 2015	Multi-Mission Surface Combatant Ships	RSNF	$11.250
November 2015	Air-to-Ground Munitions	RSAF	$1.290
February 2016	MK 15 Phalanx Close-In Weapons System (CIWS) Block 1B Baseline 2 Kits	RSNF	$0.154
February 2016	USMTM Technical Assistance Field Teams and other Support	—	$0.200
August 2016	M1A2S Tanks and Related Equipment	RSLF	$1.150
December 2016	CH-47F Chinook Cargo Helicopters	RSLF Aviation Command	$3.510
January 2017	Persistent Threat Detection System (PTDS) Aerostats	RSLF	$0.525
May 2017	Naval Training Blanket Order	RSNF	$0.250
June 2017	Air Force Training Blanket Order	RSAF	$0.750
June 2017	AN/TPQ 53-V Radar and Support (Counter Indirect Fire)	RSLF	$0.662

Table B-1. (Continued)

Formal Notification Date	System	Recipient Force	Pos. Value
October 2017	Terminal High Altitude Area Defense (THAAD)	RSADF	$15.000
January 2018	Missile Support Services	—	$0.500
Formal Notification Date	System	Recipient Force	Pos. Value
March 2018	TOW 2B (BGM-71F-Series) Missiles	—	$0.670
March 2018	RSLF Ordnance Corps FMS Order II	RSLF	$0.300
March 2018	Maintenance Support Services	RSLF Aviation Command	$0.106
April 2018	155mm M109A6 Paladin Howitzer System	RSLF	$1.310
Total			$138.914

Source: U.S. Defense Security Cooperation Agency (DSCA).

Notes: Possible values noted in sale proposals may not match actual values of concluded contract sales. Direct Commercial Sales not included. Table includes proposed sales to Royal Saudi Air Force (RSAF), Saudi Arabian National Guard (SANG), Royal Saudi Land Forces (RSLF), Royal Guard, Royal Saudi Air Defense Force (RSADF), Royal Saudi Naval Forces (RSNF), Ministry of Interior (MOI), and Ministry of Defense (MOD). Dashes indicate unspecified recipient force.

APPENDIX C. SAUDI ARABIA AND INQUIRIES INTO THE TERRORIST ATTACKS OF SEPTEMBER 11, 2001

The report of the congressional Joint Inquiry into Intelligence Community Activities Before and After the Terrorist Attacks of September 11, 2001, released in December 2002, brought attention to the alleged role of Saudi Arabia in supporting terrorism.[131] In the 900-page report, a chapter on alleged foreign support for the September 11 hijackers was redacted virtually in its entirety—Part Four of the report, often referred to as "the 28 pages" (actually 29)—because executive branch officials determined at the time that its public release was contrary to U.S. national security interests.

---

[131] Joint Inquiry into Intelligence Community Activities Before and After the Terrorist Attacks of September 11, 2001, S.Rept. 107-351/H.Rept. 107-792.

The congressional Joint Inquiry's report stated that the committee had "made no final determinations as to the reliability or sufficiency of the information regarding these issues [alleged foreign support for the hijackers] that was found contained in FBI and CIA documents. It was not the task of this Joint Inquiry to conduct the kind of extensive investigation that would be required to determine the true significance of such alleged support to the hijackers." U.S. law enforcement and intelligence agencies subsequently investigated information in the redacted portion of the report further. Some information reportedly remains under investigation.

In the years since, speculation and periodic media reporting focused on the degree to which the redacted pages may have addressed the question of whether or not there was some degree of official Saudi complicity in the September 11 attacks. For years, some people who claimed to have read the formerly classified sections of the report said it addressed some Saudi nationals' links with individuals involved in the attacks.[132] In 2003, the Saudi government appealed to U.S. authorities to publish the redacted pages so as to enable Saudi Arabia to rebut related allegations.[133] On April 19, 2016, President Barack Obama stated that he had asked Director of National Intelligence James Clapper to review the redacted pages of the congressional Joint Inquiry's report for potential release.[134]

On July 15, 2016, the Senate Select Committee on Intelligence released a declassified version of Part Four of the congressional Joint Inquiry as well as two declassified pages from the executive summary of the September 2005 Joint FBI-CIA Intelligence Report Assessing the Nature and Extent of Saudi Government Support of Terrorism.[135] The latter report focused in part on investigating information discussed in the 2002 Joint Inquiry and was originally submitted as required by the classified annex of the Intelligence Authorization Act for FY2004.

---

[132] CBS News 60 Minutes, "Top secret '28 pages' may hold clues about Saudi support for 9/11 hijackers," April 8, 2016.

[133] Josh Meyer, "Saudis to Seek Release of Classified Parts of 9/11 Report," *Los Angeles Times*, July 29, 2003.

[134] President Barack Obama interviewed by Charlie Rose, PBS, April 19, 2016.

[135] Both documents are available on the website of the Senate Select Committee on Intelligence.

The "28 pages" of the congressional Joint Inquiry released in 2016 address a number of reports that individual Saudi nationals had contact with and may have provided assistance to some of the September 11, 2001, hijackers. Specifically, the pages discuss information that suggested that (*emphasis* added).

> "...while in the United States, some of the September 11 hijackers were in contact with, and received support or assistance from, individuals who *may be* connected to the Saudi Government. There is information, primarily from FBI sources, that at least two of those individuals were *alleged by some* to be Saudi intelligence officers. The Joint Inquiry's review confirmed that the Intelligence Community also has information, much of it which has *yet be independently verified*, indicating that individuals associated with the Saudi Government in the United States *may have* other ties to al-Qa'ida and other terrorist groups."

As noted above, the pages of the 2002 report discuss allegations that were then under consideration and not investigatory conclusions of law enforcement or intelligence officials.

The declassified pages from the September 2005 FBI-CIA report state that, "There is no evidence that either the Saudi government or members of the Saudi royal family knowingly provided support for the attacks of 11 September 2001 or that they had foreknowledge of terrorist operations in the Kingdom or elsewhere." The executive summary of the joint FBI-CIA report further states that "there is evidence that official Saudi entities, [redacted portion], and associated nongovernmental organizations provide financial and logistical support to individuals in the United States and around the world, some of whom are associated with terrorism-related activity. The Saudi Government and many of its agencies have been infiltrated and exploited by individuals associated with or sympathetic to al-Qa'ida."

The 2004 final report of the bipartisan National Commission on Terrorist Attacks Upon the United States (aka "The 9/11 Commission") states that the commission "found no evidence that the Saudi government as an institution or senior Saudi officials individually funded [Al

Qaeda]."[136] The report also states that Saudi Arabia "was a place where Al Qaeda raised money directly from individuals and through charities," and indicates that "charities with significant Saudi government sponsorship" may have diverted funding to Al Qaeda.

In July 2016, Saudi Foreign Minister Adel al Jubeir argued that the pages' release exonerated the Saudi government with regard to allegations that it supported or had foreknowledge of the September 11 attacks, saying that "when the appropriate agencies, the 9/11 Commission and the FBI and CIA investigated those leads and came out with their conclusions they said that 'there's no there there.'"[137] The Saudi Embassy in Washington, DC, has consistently responded to news reports about the so-called 28 pages' contents by citing some of the findings of later investigations and noting the dismissal of some lawsuits against the kingdom.[138]

APPENDIX D. LEGISLATIVE DEVELOPMENTS

Developments in the 114th Congress

When the Obama Administration informally notified Congress of a proposed sale of precision guided munitions (PGMs) to Saudi Arabia, some Senators sought to delay its formal notification. After the formal notification in November 2015,[139] Senate Foreign Relations Committee leaders jointly requested that the Administration notify Congress 30 days prior to associated shipments.[140]

---

[136] Final Report of the National Commission on Terrorist Attacks Upon the United States, July 22, 2004.

[137] Royal Embassy of Saudi Arabia Information Office, "Saudi Foreign Minister: '28 Pages' Were Misleading," July 16, 2016.

[138] Royal Embassy of Saudi Arabia Information Office, "Saudi Arabia Responds to 60 Minutes Report," April 10, 2016.

[139] Defense Security Cooperation Agency Transmittal No. 15-57, November 16, 2015.

[140] The request marked the first time that Congress has invoked an authority it added to the Arms Export Control Act in December 2014 through an amendment included in the Naval Vessel Transfer Act of 2013 (P.L. 113-276). Section 201 of the Naval Vessel Transfer Act of 2013 (P.L. 113-276) added Section 36(i) to the AECA. Potentially applicable to any foreign military sale requiring notification pursuant to Section 36(b) of the AECA, the 36(i)

No related joint resolutions of disapproval of this proposed sale were introduced during the 30 calendar-day consideration period outlined in the AECA (22 U.S.C. 2776), but the delay and additional notification request demonstrated congressional concern. Then, in April 2016, legislation was introduced that sought to place conditions on future proposed sale notifications, previously approved sales, or transfers of PGMs to Saudi Arabia (S.J.Res. 32 and H.J.Res. 90). Proposed amendments to FY2017 defense legislation would have added some similar conditions on the use of funds to implement sales of PGMs (FY2017 National Defense Authorization Act, S. 2943) or prohibited the transfer of cluster munitions to Saudi Arabia (Defense Appropriations Act, H.R. 5293).

The Senate did not consider the PGM amendment submitted in conjunction with its consideration of the FY2017 NDAA, but the House narrowly defeated the Saudi cluster munitions prohibition amendment in a June 2016 House floor vote.[141] Saudi use of U.S. cluster munitions in Yemen has been reported, and unnamed U.S. officials have indicated that the Obama Administration placed a hold on further cluster munitions transfers.[142]

In August 2016, the Obama Administration notified Congress of a proposed sale of M1A2S tanks to Saudi Arabia, and some lawmakers wrote to request that President Obama withdraw the proposal, citing concerns about Yemen.[143] In September 2016, joint resolutions of disapproval of the proposed tank sale were introduced in the Senate (S.J.Res. 39) and House (H.J.Res. 98). U.S. tanks form the core of the Royal Saudi Land Forces fleet, and a series of contracts concluded since

---

mechanism requires both the chair and ranking member of either of the two committees of jurisdiction (SFRC/HFAC) to jointly request that the President provide such a "pre-shipment notification" 30 days prior to a shipment. The preshipment notification would inform Congress that a shipment was about to occur, but would not require or preclude Congress from taking further action to modify or block the shipment.

[141] Hon. Conyers Amendment No. 40, Roll Call Vote 327, Consideration of H.R. 5293, June 16, 2016.

[142] John Hudson, "White House Blocks Transfer of Cluster Bombs to Saudi Arabia," Foreign Policy (online), May 27, 2016. U.S. officials had previously said that they "have discussed reports of the alleged use of cluster munitions" in Yemen with Saudi officials and consider their use "permissible" if "used appropriately" and according to "end-use rules." State Department Daily Press Briefing, August 20, 2015.

[143] See Hon. Lieu et al., Letter to President Barack Obama, August 29, 2016.

2006 has seen Saudi M1 series tanks first sold to the kingdom in the 1990s upgraded to the M1A2S standard.[144] On September 21, 2016, the Senate voted to table a motion to discharge the Senate Foreign Relations Committee from further consideration of S.J.Res. 39 (71-27, Record Vote 145).[145]

In the wake of an October 2016 Saudi airstrike on a funeral hall in Sana'a that killed 140 people, the Obama Administration announced that it was initiating a review of U.S. security assistance to Saudi Arabia. In December 2016, press reports cited Obama Administration officials as stating that a planned commercial sale of precision guided munitions technology, including more than 16,000 air-to-ground munitions kits, would not proceed and that U.S. intelligence sharing would be further limited in favor of enhanced training for the Saudi Air Force.[146]

Developments in the 115th Congress

The Trump Administration has attempted to balance its condemnation of the Houthis and their Iranian backers with more direct calls for the coalition to ease its restrictions on access to Yemen, limit civilian casualties, and pursue negotiations. Some lawmakers have suggested that U.S. arms sales and military support to the coalition have enabled alleged violations of international humanitarian law, while others have argued that U.S. support to the coalition improves its effectiveness and helps minimize civilian casualties. Some Senators have focused on Yemen-related questions in considering nominations, some Members of both chambers have conducted enhanced oversight, and Congress has considered but has

---

[144] A series of contracts have been signed to implement the sale proposed in Defense Security Cooperation Agency Transmittal No. 06-31, July 28, 2006.

[145] Congressional Record, September 21, 2016, pp. S5921-S5935.

[146] Helene Cooper, "U.S. Blocks Arms Sale to Saudi Arabia Amid Concerns Over Yemen War," New York Times, December 13, 2016.

74   *Christopher M. Blanchard*

not enacted proposals to curtail or condition U.S. defense sales to Saudi Arabia or to prohibit the use of funds for coalition support operations.[147]

Legislation seeking to place conditions on future transfers or sales of precision guided munitions technology was modified and reintroduced in the 115th Congress (S.J.Res. 40 and H.J.Res. 104) and sought to condition the sale or transfer of munitions on a presidential certification that the Saudi government and coalition were taking "all feasible precautions" to protect civilians, "demonstrable efforts" to facilitate flows of aid and goods, and "effective measures" to target Islamic State and AQAP terrorists. Neither resolution has been considered, but their formulations have influenced other legislation, including Section 1290 of the FY2019 NDAA, which requires a similar set of certifications as a condition for the use of FY2019 defense funding for refueling support to Saudi and coalition aircraft engaged in certain missions in Yemen.

On March 19, 2017, just prior to his visit to the kingdom, President Trump notified Congress that he is proceeding with three proposed direct commercial sales of precision guided munitions technology deferred by the Obama Administration, subject to congressional review.[148] The proposed sales would include equipment and services related to joint direct attack munitions (JDAMs), Paveway laser-guided munitions kits, and

---

[147] In late 2017, Senators Todd Young and Christopher Murphy placed a hold on the confirmation of the State Department's nominee for legal advisor, Jennifer Newstead, until the Administration took certain steps to address the coalition's blockade of Yemen. Dan De Luce and Robbie Gramer, "GOP Senator Presses Trump Administration Over Deadly Saudi Blockade in Yemen," *Foreign Policy*, December 4, 2017; and, Dan De Luce, "Trump Nominee Concedes Saudi Siege of Yemen Could Be Violating U.S. Law," *Foreign Policy*, December 19, 2017. On December 14, Senator Young sent a letter to President Trump thanking the President for his December 6 statement, while asserting that the coalition's blockade triggers, per the Foreign Assistance Act of 1961 as amended (22 U.S. Code §2378–1(a)), a prohibition on U.S. foreign assistance to Saudi Arabia. Newstead was confirmed by the Senate on December 19 after promising the Senate Foreign Relations Committee to consider evidence of any possible foreign government restriction of the delivery of U.S. humanitarian assistance to Yemen in determining whether to apply statutory prohibitions found in 22 U.S. Code §2378-1(a). See, Senator Todd Young, Young: Law Triggered by Saudi Arabia's Actions in Yemen, December 14, 2017, and Newstead response online at https://www.documentcloud.org/documents/4333104-20171114- Young-Newstead-QFRs-Round-3-1.html.

[148] DDTC Transmittals No. DDTC 15-132 (JDAM), No. DDTC 16-011 (FMU-152A/B bomb fuzes), No. DDTC 16 043 (Paveway II & III, Enhanced Paveway II & III, Paveway IV), May 19, 2017.

programmable bomb fuzes. Pursuant to Section 36(c) of the Arms Export Control Act, the executive branch may proceed with a proposed direct commercial sale case 30 days after formally notifying Congress. Legislation in the House (H.J.Res. 102) and Senate (S.J.Res. 42) was proposed to disapprove of the three proposed sales. On June 13, the Senate voted to reject a motion to discharge the Senate Foreign Relations Committee from further consideration of S.J.Res. 42 (47-53, Record Vote 143).

On March 20, 2018, the Senate voted to table a motion to discharge the Senate Foreign Relations Committee from further consideration of S.J.Res. 54, a joint resolution that would direct the President to remove U.S. forces from "hostilities in or affecting" Yemen (except for those U.S. forces engaged in counterterrorism operations directed at al Qaeda or associated forces).

In May, the Senate Foreign Relations Committee reported S.J.Res. 58 to the Senate; it would prohibit the obligation or expenditure of U.S. funds for in-flight refueling operations of Saudi and Saudi-led coalition aircraft that are not conducting select types of operations if certain certifications cannot be made and maintained at 30-, 180-, and 360-day intervals. The joint resolution identified several certification criteria, although, reported as amended by the committee, it would enable the Secretary of State to waive the certification requirement for national security purposes if the Secretary provides an unclassified explanatory justification to the appropriate committees. The joint resolution also would require a report on, among other things, United States objectives in Yemen and a detailed strategy to accomplish those objectives.

The Senate Armed Services Committee incorporated the provisions of the Senate Foreign Relations Committee-reported text of S.J.Res. 58 as Section 1266 of the version of the FY2019 John S. McCain National Defense Authorization Act (NDAA) that it reported to the Senate on June 5, 2018 (S. 2987). The provision was modified further and passed by both the House and Senate as Section 1290 of the conference version of the FY2019 NDAA (P.L. 115-91). The potential restrictions on the use of U.S. funds for in-flight refueling of coalition aircraft do not apply to certain types of operations, including missions related to Al Qaeda and the Islamic State or "related to countering the transport, assembly, or employment of ballistic missiles or components in Yemen." Under the modified version, the Administration must certify that the Saudi and Emirati governments are undertaking

- an urgent and good faith effort to support diplomatic efforts to end the civil war in Yemen;
- appropriate measures to alleviate the humanitarian crisis in Yemen by increasing access for Yemenis to food, fuel, medicine, and medical evacuation, including through the appropriate use of Yemen's Red Sea ports, including the port of Hudaydah, the airport in Sana'a, and external border crossings with Saudi Arabia; and
- demonstrable actions to reduce the risk of harm to civilians and civilian infrastructure resulting from military operations of the Government of Saudi Arabia and the Government of the United Arab Emirates in Yemen, including by (1) complying with applicable agreements and laws regulating defense articles purchased or transferred from the United States, and (2) taking appropriate steps to avoid disproportionate harm to civilians and civilian infrastructure

With specific regard to Saudi Arabia, the Administration also must certify that "the Government of Saudi Arabia is undertaking appropriate actions to reduce any unnecessary delays to shipments associated with secondary inspection and clearance processes other than UNVIM." The Administration may waive the certification requirement if certain explanatory submissions are made. Reporting and strategy submission requirements also were included in the final version.

On September 12, 2018, Secretary of State Mike Pompeo announced that the Saudi and Emirati governments are "undertaking demonstrable actions to reduce the risk of harm to civilians" in Yemen.

Senator Robert Menendez, the Ranking Member on the Senate Foreign Relations Committee, has refused to consent to formal congressional notification of a potential U.S. sale of precision guided munitions to Saudi Arabia and the United Arab Emirates. In a June 28 letter to Secretary of State Pompeo and Secretary of Defense Mattis, Senator Menendez said,

> I am not confident that these weapons sales will be utilized strategically as effective leverage to push back on Iran's actions in Yemen, assist our partners in their own self- defense, or drive the parties toward a political settlement that saves lives and mitigates humanitarian suffering.... Even worse, I am concerned that our policies are enabling perpetuation of a conflict that has resulted in the world's worst humanitarian crisis.[149]

Several Senators also submitted an amendment to the FY2019 Defense Department appropriations act (H.R. 6157) that would have prohibited the use of funds made available by the act to support the Saudi-led coalition operations in Yemen until the Secretary of Defense certified in writing to Congress that the coalition air campaign "does not violate the principles of distinction and proportionality within the rules for the protection of civilians." The provision would not have applied to support for ongoing counterterrorism operations against Al Qaeda and the Islamic State in Yemen. The amendment was not considered after an objection on the Senate floor.[150]

---

[149] Senate Foreign Relations Committee, Ranking Member's Press, Menendez Demands more Answers from Trump Admin before letting Arms Sales to United Arab Emirates and Saudi Arabia move forward," June 28, 2018.

[150] Congressional Record, Volume 164, Number 140, August 22, 2018, p. S5797.

In: The Middle East
Editor: Doyle Keller

ISBN: 978-1-53616-191-5
© 2019 Nova Science Publishers, Inc.

Chapter 2

SAUDI ARABIA*

Christopher M. Blanchard

CHANGE, CONTINUITY AND CONTROVERSY

The kingdom of Saudi Arabia, ruled by the Al Saud family since its founding in 1932, wields significant global influence through its administration of the birthplace of the Islamic faith and by virtue of its large oil reserves. Saudi leaders' domestic and foreign policy decisions are fueling calls from some U.S. leaders for a reassessment of longstanding bilateral ties. The Al Saud have sought protection, advice, technology, and armaments from the United States, along with support in developing their country's natural and human resources and in facing national security threats. U.S. leaders have valued Saudi cooperation in security and counterterrorism matters and have sought to preserve the secure, apolitical flow of the kingdom's energy resources and capital to global markets. The Trump Administration seeks to strengthen U.S.-Saudi ties as the kingdom

---

* This is an edited, reformatted and augmented version of Congressional Research Service Publication No. IF10822, dated April 9, 2019.

Leadership and Public Confidence

King Salman bin Abd al Aziz Al Saud (age 83) assumed the throne in 2015 after the death of his half-brother, the late King Abdullah bin Abd al Aziz. King Salman since has altered the responsibilities and relative power of leading members of the next generation of the Al Saud family, the grandsons of the kingdom's founder. King Salman's son, Crown Prince Mohammed bin Salman (age 33), is now the central figure in Saudi policymaking, having asserted control over key national security forces, sidelined potential rivals, and begun implementing ambitious policy changes.

In parallel, channels for expressing dissent within the kingdom appear to have narrowed considerably. Since 2017, security forces have detained dozens of activists, Islamist figures, and journalists. Prosecutors have detained and/or pursued various charges against some well-known figures, including prominent clerics, human rights advocates, and women's rights campaigners. In late 2017, authorities also imprisoned dozens of wealthy individuals (and potential family rivals of the crown prince) for months in the Ritz Carlton hotel in Riyadh as part of a nominal anticorruption campaign. Most of this latter group of detainees were released after reaching undisclosed financial settlement arrangements, amid accounts of abuse.

Many Saudis and outside observers have expressed surprise about the scope and rapidity of post-2015 developments and continue to speculate about their potential implications. Saudi decision-making had long appeared to be relatively risk-averse and rooted in rulers' concerns for maintaining consensus among different constituencies, including factions of the royal family, business elites, and conservative religious figures. Crown Prince Mohammed bin Salman's bolder and more centralized leadership has challenged each of these interest groups, and is leading Saudis and outsiders alike to reexamine their assumptions.

Vision 2030 and Social Change

The centerpiece of Saudi leaders' domestic agenda is the Vision 2030 initiative, which seeks to transform the kingdom's economy by diversifying the government's sources of revenue and reducing long-standing oil export dependence by promoting investment and private sector growth. Plans for an initial public offering of shares in state oil company Saudi Aramco have been delayed to 2021. Authorities have reduced some consumer and industrial subsidies and introduced a value-added tax. Amid some domestic criticism, authorities also have offered citizens relief payments, salary increases, and tax exemptions.

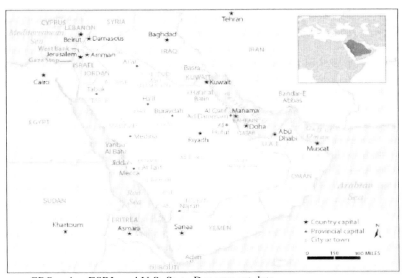

Source: CRS, using ESRI, and U.S. State Department data.

Figure 1. Saudi Arabia.

Economic transformation has driven social change in the kingdom since the early 20th century, and the Vision 2030 initiative is being accompanied by significant changes in the state's approach to some sensitive social matters. Authorities reversed the kingdom's long-standing ban on women driving in June 2018, in part to expand women's participation in the workforce. Parallel changes have created more public space for women in some social and cultural events, but most male guardianship rules restricting women's activities remain in place. Some Saudis welcome changes made to date and call for more, while others express opposition or concern about the changes' potential effects on religious and social values.

Human Rights

The October 2018 killing of Saudi journalist Jamal Khashoggi by Saudi government officials in the Saudi consulate in Istanbul, Turkey has led to increased congressional scrutiny of the kingdom's human rights practices. The Trump Administration has described the killing as a "horrific act," stated its intent to pursue accountability for those responsible, and imposed travel and financial sanctions on some Saudi officials suspected of involvement. The kingdom is prosecuting some officials on charges of involvement. Other suspects, such as Crown Prince Mohammed bin Salman's former adviser Saud al Qahtani, reportedly have not been charged. Some in Congress continue to advocate for a more forceful U.S. response to the Khashoggi killing and speak on behalf of Saudi human rights activists detained and on trial.

> "We want to make sure that everyone understands that the United States doesn't believe that the killing of Jamal Khashoggi was anything other than a horrific act. And we hope that we can work together, both with Congress and our allies, to hold those responsible accountable."
> Secretary of State Michael Pompeo, October 2018

Saudi Nuclear Plans

Saudi leaders seek to recast the role of energy resources in the kingdom's economy and plan to develop domestic civilian nuclear power infrastructure. They have solicited bids for the construction of two nuclear power reactors. The Trump Administration expedited consideration of required regulatory approvals for U.S. firms to provide marketing information to Saudi officials, and may propose a bilateral nuclear cooperation agreement to the 116th Congress. Saudi officials have not forsworn uranium enrichment and have stated their intent to use and develop domestic capabilities. Saudi nuclear facilities are subject to International Atomic Energy Agency (IAEA) safeguards, The IAEA has reviewed Saudi nuclear infrastructure and recommends adoption and implementation of an additional protocol.

Combatting Terrorism and Extremism

The U.S. government describes U.S.-Saudi cooperation on counterterrorism as robust and credits Saudi officials with reducing the financing of terrorism by Saudi nationals and with contributing to global efforts to undermine terrorist propaganda. The Islamic State group has been highly critical of Saudi authorities and religious officials, and U.S. threat assessments judge that the Islamic State and Al Qaeda pose continuing risks to the kingdom's security. The Saudi government's relationship with conservative religious figures is evolving, with the state promoting potentially controversial social policy changes while enlisting religious leaders to counteract extremist messages. In December 2017, King Salman said "there is no place among us for an extremist who sees moderation as degeneration."

SAUDI FOREIGN POLICY

The King and Crown Prince have actively pursued several initiatives across the Middle East since 2015, challenging Iran, reopening dialogue with Iraq, seeking to isolate Qatar, and fighting an ongoing war in Yemen. New Saudi activism in regional affairs has created new questions for Congress to consider, including with regard to defense cooperation.

Iran, Iraq, and the Levant

Saudi policies toward Iraq, Syria, and Lebanon continue to reflect the kingdom's overarching concerns about Iran and the Iranian government's ties to state and nonstate actors in these countries. Saudi authorities back the U.N. Security Council's call for a negotiated settlement to the conflict in Syria and seek more progress in settlement talks before reengagement with the Iran-aligned Syrian government of Bashar al Asad. U.S. officials have praised Saudi efforts to strengthen ties with Iraq's government, including the reopening of border crossings between the two countries.

Conflict in Yemen

Saudi Arabia has led a military coalition of mostly Arab states since March 2015 in efforts to reinstate the government of Yemeni President Abdu Rabbu Mansour Hadi, who was ousted in a 2014-2015 offensive by the Zaydi Shia Houthi movement of northern Yemen. Iranian material and advisory support to the Houthi war effort— including the provision of ballistic missiles and drones used to attack Saudi Arabia—has amplified Saudi leaders' anxieties and concerns. The Trump Administration lifted some limits on U.S. arms sales to Saudi Arabia that the Obama Administration had imposed to protest airstrikes that resulted in civilian casualties, but announced plans to end U.S. refueling of Saudi coalition aircraft in November 2018. The United Nations considers Yemen to be the world's worst humanitarian crisis and cites Houthi malfeasance and Saudi coalition-enforced limits on air and sea access as contributing to shortages of food and goods. The 116th Congress continues to debate proposals to restrict or condition U.S. military aid to Saudi operations, and the House and Senate passed S.J.Res. 7 directing President Trump to end some U.S. military involvement in Yemen.

Intra-Gulf Cooperation Council (GCC) Tensions

Saudi Arabia has led an effort to isolate the government of Qatar internationally since mid-2017, citing concerns about reported Qatari support for terrorism and aspects of Qatar's independent foreign policy approach. Various GCC-based figures describe close Qatari ties with regional Islamist actors, including the Muslim Brotherhood, as problematic. The Trump Administration favors negotiation and compromise by parties to the ongoing intra-GCC dispute.

Israeli-Palestinian Affairs

Saudi Arabia is a leader among Arab states in supporting key Palestinian demands, but Saudi leaders also have engaged quietly with Israel in light of the two countries' shared interest in countering Iran. In January 2018, King Salman reiterated the kingdom's "firm position on the Palestinian cause and the legitimate rights of the Palestinian people to establish their independent state with Jerusalem as its capital and on continuing efforts to find a just and lasting solution to the Palestinian cause in accordance with relevant international resolutions."

Relations with China and Russia

Greater Saudi energy exports to China have underwritten new Sino-Saudi economic and diplomatic ties, and bilateral meetings of senior officials are often followed by announcements of new cooperation initiatives. Saudi leaders also have opened substantive dialogue and cooperation with Russia, encompassing coordination on oil production decisions to bolster global oil prices, discussion of arms sales, and talks on Syria and other regional issues.

In: The Middle East
Editor: Doyle Keller

ISBN: 978-1-53616-191-5
© 2019 Nova Science Publishers, Inc.

Chapter 3

IRAQ: ISSUES IN THE 115TH CONGRESS*

Christopher M. Blanchard

ABSTRACT

Iraq's government declared military victory against the Islamic State organization (IS, aka ISIS/ISIL) in December 2017, but insurgent attacks by remaining IS fighters threaten Iraqis as they shift their attention toward recovery and the country's political future. Security conditions have improved since the Islamic State's control of territory was disrupted, but IS fighters are active in some areas and security conditions are fluid.

Meanwhile, daunting resettlement, reconstruction, and reform needs occupy citizens and leaders. Internally displaced Iraqis are returning home in greater numbers, but stabilization and reconstruction needs in liberated areas are extensive. An estimated 1.9 million Iraqis remain as internally displaced persons (IDPs), and Iraqi authorities have identified $88 billion in reconstruction needs over the next decade. Large protests in southern Iraq during August and September 2018 highlighted some citizens' outrage with poor service delivery and corruption.

National legislative elections were held in May 2018, but results were not certified until August, delaying the formal start of required steps

---

* This is an edited, reformatted and augmented version of Congressional Research Service, Publication No. R45096, dated October 4, 2018.

to form the next government. Iraqi Prime Minister Haider al Abadi sought reelection, but his electoral list's third-place showing and lack of internal cohesion undermined his chances for a second term. On October 2, Iraq's Council of Representatives (COR) chose former Kurdistan Regional Government Prime Minister and former Iraqi Deputy Prime Minister Barham Salih as Iraq's President. Salih, in turn, named former Oil Minister Adel Abd al Mahdi as Prime Minister-designate and directed him to assemble a slate of cabinet officials for COR approval within 30 days.

Paramilitary forces have grown stronger and more numerous since 2014, and have yet to be fully integrated into national security institutions. Some figures associated with the Popular Mobilization Forces (PMF) that were organized to fight the Islamic State participated in the 2018 election campaign and won seats in the Council of Representatives, including individuals with ties to Iran. Iraqi politicians have increasingly employed cross-sectarian political and economic narratives in an attempt to appeal to disaffected citizens, but identity-driven politics continue to influence developments. Iraq's neighbors and other outsiders, including the United States, are pursuing their respective interests in Iraq, at times in competition.

The Kurdistan Region of northern Iraq (KRI) enjoys considerable administrative autonomy under the terms of Iraq's 2005 constitution, and the Kurdistan Regional Government (KRG) held legislative elections on September 30, 2018. The KRG had held a controversial advisory referendum on independence in September 2017, amplifying political tensions with the national government, which moved to reassert security control of disputed areas that had been secured by Kurdish forces after the Islamic State's mid-2014 advance. Iraqi and Kurdish security forces remain deployed across from each other along contested lines of control, while their respective leaders are engaged in negotiations over a host of sensitive issues.

In general, U.S. engagement with Iraqis since 2011 has sought to reinforce Iraq's unifying tendencies and avoid divisive outcomes. At the same time, successive U.S. Administrations have sought to keep U.S. involvement and investment minimal relative to the 2003-2011 era, pursuing U.S. interests through partnership with various entities in Iraq and the development of those partners' capabilities—rather than through extensive deployment of U.S. military forces. The Trump Administration has sustained a cooperative relationship with the Iraqi government and plans to continue security training for Iraqi security forces. To date, the 115th Congress has appropriated funds for U.S. military operations against the Islamic State and for security assistance, humanitarian relief, and foreign aid for Iraq.

OVERVIEW

Iraq's government declared military victory against the Islamic State organization (IS, aka ISIS/ISIL) in December 2017, but insurgent attacks by remaining IS fighters threaten Iraqis as they shift their attention toward recovery and the country's political future. Security conditions have improved since the Islamic State's control of territory was disrupted (Figure 1 and Figure 2), but IS fighters are active in some areas of the country and security conditions are fluid. Meanwhile, daunting resettlement, reconstruction, and reform needs occupy citizens and leaders. Ethnic, religious, regional, and tribal identities remain politically relevant in Iraq, as do partisanship, personal rivalries, economic disparities, and natural resource imbalances.

National legislative elections were held in May 2018, but results were not certified until August, delaying the formal start of required steps to form the next government. Turnout was low relative to past national elections, and campaigning reflected issues stemming from the 2014-2017 conflict with the Islamic State as well as preexisting internal disputes and governance challenges.

Iraqi Prime Minister Haider al Abadi sought reelection, but his electoral list's third-place showing and lack of internal cohesion undermined his chances for a second term. He is serving in a caretaker capacity as government-formation negotiations continue. In September 2018, a statement from the office of leading Shia religious leader Grand Ayatollah Ali al Sistani called for political forces to choose a prime minister from beyond the ranks of current or former officials. Nevertheless, on October 2, Iraq's Council of Representatives chose former Kurdistan Regional Government Prime Minister and former Iraqi Deputy Prime Minister Barham Salih as Iraq's President. Salih, in turn, named former Oil Minister Adel Abd al Mahdi as Prime Minister-designate and directed him to assemble a slate of cabinet officials for approval by the Council of Representatives (COR).

Paramilitary forces have grown stronger and more numerous since 2014, and have yet to be fully integrated into national security institutions.

Some figures associated with the Popular Mobilization Forces (PMF) militias that were organized to fight the Islamic State participated in the 2018 election campaign and won seats in the COR, including individuals with ties to Iran.

Since the ouster of Saddam Hussein in 2003, Iraq's Shia Arab majority has exercised new power in concert with the Sunni Arab and Kurdish minorities. Despite ethnic and religious diversity and political differences, many Iraqis advance similar demands for improved security, government effectiveness, and economic opportunity. Large, volatile protests in southern Iraq during August and September 2018 highlighted some citizens' outrage with poor service delivery and corruption. Iraqi politicians have increasingly employed cross-sectarian political and economic narratives in an attempt to appeal to disaffected citizens, but identity-driven politics continue to influence developments across the country. Iraq's neighbors and other outsiders, including the United States, are pursuing their respective interests in the country, at times in competition.

The Kurdistan Region of northern Iraq (KRI) enjoys considerable administrative autonomy under the terms of Iraq's 2005 constitution, and the Kurdistan Regional Government (KRG) held legislative elections on September 30, 2018. The KRG had held a controversial advisory referendum on independence in September 2017, amplifying political tensions with the national government and prompting criticism from the Trump Administration and the United Nations Security Council. In October 2017, the national government imposed a ban on international flights to and from the KRI, and Iraqi security forces moved to reassert security control of disputed areas that had been secured by Kurdish forces after the Islamic State's mid-2014 advance. Much of the oil-rich governorate of Kirkuk—long claimed by Iraqi Kurds—returned to national government control, and resulting controversies have riven Kurdish politics. Iraqi and Kurdish security forces remain deployed across from each other along contested lines of control while their respective leaders are engaged in negotiations over a host of sensitive issues.

Internally displaced Iraqis are returning home in greater numbers, but stabilization and reconstruction needs in areas liberated from the Islamic State are extensive. An estimated 1.9 million Iraqis remain as internally displaced persons (IDPs), and Iraqi authorities have identified $88 billion in reconstruction needs over the next decade.

In general, U.S. engagement with Iraqis since 2011 has sought to reinforce Iraq's unifying tendencies and avoid divisive outcomes. At the same time, successive U.S. Administrations have sought to keep U.S. involvement and investment minimal relative to the 2003-2011 era, pursuing U.S. interests through partnership with various entities in Iraq and the development of those partners' capabilities—rather than through extensive deployment of U.S. military forces. U.S. economic assistance bolsters Iraq's ability to attract lending support and is aimed at improving the government's effectiveness and public financial management. The United States is the leading provider of humanitarian assistance to Iraq and also supports post-IS stabilization activities across the country through grants to United Nations agencies and other entities.

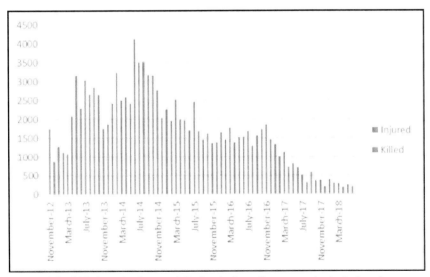

Source: United Nations Assistance Mission in Iraq. Some months lack data from some governorates.

Figure 1. Estimated Iraqi Civilian Casualties from Conflict and Terrorism.

Table 1. Iraq: Map and Country Data

Area: 438,317 sq. km (slightly more than three times the size of New York State)

Population: 39.192 million (July 2017 estimate), —59% are 24 years of age or under

Internally Displaced Persons: 1.9 million (September 15, 2018)

Religions: Muslim 99% (55-60% Shia, 40% Sunni), Christian <0.1%, Yazidi <0.1%

Ethnic Groups: Arab 75-80%; Kurdish 15-20%; Turkmen, Assyrian, Shabak, Yazidi, other —5%.

Gross Domestic Product [GDP; growth rate]: $197.7 billion (2017 est); -0.8% (2017 est.)

Budget (revenues; expenditure; balance): $77.42 billion, $88 billion, -$10.58 billion (2018 est.)

Percentage of Revenue from Oil Exports: 87% (June 2017 est.)

Current Account Balance: $1.42 billion (2017 est.)

Oil and natural gas reserves: 142.5 billion barrels (2017 est., fifth largest); 3.158 trillion cubic meters (2017 est.)

External Debt: $73.43 billion (2017 est.)

Foreign Reserves: —$47.02 billion (December 2017 est.)

Sources: Graphic created by CRS using data from U.S. State Department and Esri. Country data from CIA, *The World Factbook*, September 2018, Iraq Ministry of Finance, and International Organization for Migration.

The Trump Administration has sustained a cooperative relationship with the Iraqi government and has requested funding to support Iraq's stabilization and continue security training for Iraqi security forces. The size and missions of the U.S. military presence in Iraq has evolved as conditions on the ground have changed since 2017 and could change further if newly elected Iraqi officials revise their requests for U.S. and other international assistance.

To date, the 115th Congress has appropriated funds to continue U.S. military operations against the Islamic State and to provide security assistance, humanitarian relief, and foreign aid for Iraq. Appropriations and authorization legislation enacted or under consideration for FY2019 would largely continue U.S. policies and programs on current terms.

DEVELOPMENTS IN 2017 AND 2018

Iraq Declares Victory against the Islamic State, Pursues Fighters

In July 2017, Prime Minister Haider al Abadi visited Mosul to mark the completion of major combat operations there against the Islamic State forces that had taken the city in June 2014. Iraqi forces subsequently retook the cities of Tal Afar and Hawijah, and launched operations in Anbar Governorate in October amid tensions elsewhere in territories disputed between the Kurdistan Regional Government (KRG) and national authorities. On December 9, 2017, Iraqi officials announced victory against the Islamic State and declared a national holiday. Although the Islamic State's exclusive control over distinct territories in Iraq has now ended, the U.S. intelligence community told Congress in February 2018 that the Islamic State "has started—and probably will maintain—a robust insurgency in Iraq and Syria as part of a long-term strategy to ultimately enable the reemergence of its so-called caliphate."[1]

---

[1] Worldwide Threat Assessment of the U.S. Intelligence Community, February 13, 2018.

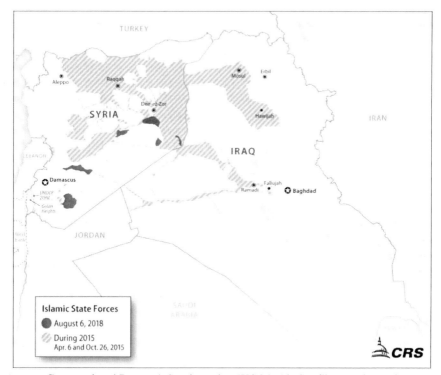

Source: Congressional Research Service using IHS Markit Conflict Monitor, ESRI, and U.S. State Department data.

Figure 2. Islamic State Territorial Control in Syria and Iraq, 2015-2018.

As of October 2018, Iraqi security operations are ongoing in Anbar, Ninewa, Diyala, and Salah al Din against IS fighters. These operations are intended to disrupt IS fighters' efforts to reestablish themselves and keep them separated from population centers. Iraqi officials warn of IS efforts to use remaining safe havens in Syria to support infiltration of Iraq. Press reports and U.S. government reports describe continuing IS attacks, particularly in rural areas of governorates the group formerly controlled. Independent analysts describe dynamics in these areas in which IS fighters threaten, intimidate, and kill citizens in areas at night or where Iraq's national security forces are absent.[2] In some areas, new displacement is occurring as civilians flee IS attacks.

May 2018 Election, Unrest, and Government Formation

On May 12, 2018, Iraqi voters went to the polls to choose national legislators for four-year terms in the 329-seat Council of Representatives, Iraq's unicameral legislature. Turnout was lower in the 2018 COR election than in past national elections, and reported irregularities led to a months-long recount effort that delayed certification of the results until August. Nevertheless, since May, the results have informed Iraqi negotiations aimed at forming the largest bloc within the COR— the parliamentary majority charged with proposing a prime minister and new Iraqi cabinet. Senior officials from Iran and the United States are monitoring the talks closely and consulting with leading Iraqi figures.

The *Sa'irun* (On the March) coalition led by populist Shia cleric and longtime U.S. antagonist Muqtada al Sadr's *Istiqama* (Integrity) list placed first in the election (54 seats), followed by the predominantly Shia *Fatah* (Conquest) coalition led by Hadi al Ameri of the Badr Organization (48 seats). *Fatah* includes several individuals formerly associated with the mostly Shia Popular Mobilization Force (PMF) militias that helped fight the Islamic State, including figures and movements with ties to Iran (see Figure 3 and "Popular Mobilization Forces and Iraqi Security Forces" below). Prime Minister Haider al Abadi's *Nasr* (Victory) coalition underperformed to place third (42 seats), and Abadi, who has been prime minister since 2014, is now serving in a caretaker role.

---

[2] Derek Henry Flood, "From Caliphate to Caves: The Islamic State's Asymmetric War in Northern Iraq," U.S. Military Academy (USMA) Combatting Terrorism Center (CTC) *Sentinel*, September 2018, Vol. 11, Issue 8; Hassan Hassan, "Insurgents Again: The Islamic State's Calculated Reversion to Attrition in the Syria-Iraq Border Region and Beyond," USMA CTC *Sentinel*, Vol. 10, Issue 11, December 2017; Liz Sly and Mustafa Salim, "ISIS is making a comeback in Iraq just months after Baghdad declared victory," *Washington Post*, July 17, 2018.

Coalition/Party	Seats Won	Iraq's 2018 National Legislative Election Seats won by Coalition/Party
Sa'irun	54	
Fatah	48	
Nasr	42	
Kurdistan Democratic Party	25	
State of Law	25	
Wataniya	21	
Hikma	19	
Patriotic Union of Kurdistan	18	
Qarar	14	
Others	63	

Source: Iraq Independent High Electoral Commission.

Former prime minister Nouri al Maliki's State of Law coalition, Ammar al Hakim's *Hikma* (Wisdom) list, and Iyad Allawi's *Wataniya* (National) list also won significant blocs of seats. Among Kurdish parties, the Kurdistan Democratic Party (KDP) and the Patriotic Union of Kurdistan (PUK) won the most seats, and smaller opposition lists protested alleged irregularities.

Escalating frustration in southern Iraq with unemployment, corruption, and electricity and water shortages has driven widespread popular unrest since the May election, amplified in some instances by citizens' anger about heavy-handed responses by security forces and militia groups. Dissatisfaction exploded in the southern province of Basra during August and September, culminating in several days and nights of mass demonstrations and the burning by protestors of the Iranian consulate in Basra and the offices of many leading political groups and militia movements. Reports from Basra in the weeks since the unrest suggest that some protestors have been intimidated or killed by unknown assailants.

Several pro-Iran groups and figures have accused the United States and other outside actors of instigating the unrest, in line with Iran-linked figures' broader accusations about alleged U.S. meddling in government formation talks.[3] U.S. officials have attributed several rocket attacks near

---

[3] The statement said that, "the resistance factions are standing ready to frustrate the foreign meddling and will intervene at the right moment to strip the conspirators of their tools." Kata'ib Hzbollah, Badr, Al Jihad wal Bina' Movement, Asa'ib Ahl al Haq, Kata'ib Sayyid al Shuhada, Kata'ib Jund al Imam, Ansar Allah al Awfiya, Saraya Ashura, Saraya Ansar al

U.S. facilities in Iraq to Iran, stating that the United States would respond directly to attacks on U.S. facilities or personnel by Iranian-backed entities.[4] On September 28, the Trump Administration announced it would temporarily remove U.S. personnel from the U.S. Consulate in Basra in response to threats from Iran and Iranian-backed groups.[5]

The government-formation process in Iraq is ongoing, and leaders have taken formal steps to fill key positions since election results were finalized on August 19. In successive governments, Iraq's Prime Minister has been a Shia Arab, the President has been a Kurd, and the Council of Representatives Speaker has been a Sunni Arab, reflecting an informal agreement among leaders of these communities. On September 3, the first session of the newly elected COR was held, and, on September 15, members elected Mohammed al Halbousi, the governor of Anbar, as Speaker. Hassan al Kaabi of the Sa'iroun list and Bashir Hajji Haddad of the KDP were elected as First and Second Deputy Speaker, respectively.

On October 2, the COR met to elect Iraq's President, with rival Kurdish parties nominating competing candidates.[6] COR members chose the PUK candidate - former KRG Prime Minister and former Iraqi Deputy Prime Minister Barham Salih - in the second round of voting. President Salih immediately named former Minister of Oil Adel Abd al Mahdi as the Prime Minister-designate of the largest bloc of COR members and directed

---

Aqidah, Saraya al Khurasani, and Kata'ib al Imam Ali, [kataibhizbollah.com], September 5, 2017.

[4] U.S. officials blamed Iran-backed groups for "life-threatening attacks" on U.S. diplomatic facilities in Baghdad and Basra after rockets were fired on the airport compound in Basra where the U.S. Consulate is located and the Green Zone in Baghdad where the U.S. Embassy is located. A White House statements said "The United States will hold the regime in Tehran accountable for any attack that results in injury to our personnel or damage to United States government facilities." Statement by the White House Press Secretary, September 11, 2018.

[5] In an interview, an unnamed senior U.S. official described attacks and threats saying that, "The totality of the information available to us leads us to the conclusion that we must attribute ultimate responsibility to the Iranian government, the Qods Force and the proxy militias under the direct command and control of the Qods Force. ...Bottom line, if we are attacked we'll respond. We'll respond swiftly and effectively, and it will not be at proxies." Ben Kesling and Michael Gordon, "U.S. to Close Consulate in Iraq, Citing Threats From Iran," *Wall Street Journal*, September 28, 2018.

[6] The KDP nominated Masoud Barzani's long-time chief of staff Dr. Fouad Hussein, while the PUK nominated former KRG Prime Minister and former Iraqi Deputy Prime Minister Barham Salih. Several other candidates also ran.

him to form a government for COR consideration. Within thirty days (by November 1), the Prime Minister-designate is to present a slate of cabinet members and a government platform for COR approval.

Iraq: Select Shia Political Groups, Leaders, and Militias

Badr Organization
The Badr Organization of Reconstruction and Development was founded in Iran in the early 1980s as the militia force of the Supreme Council for Islamic Revolution in Iraq. Then known as the Badr Brigades or Badr Corps, it received training and support from the Islamic Revolutionary Guard Corps-Qods Force (IRGC-QF) of Iran in its failed efforts to overthrow Saddam Hussein during the 1980s and 1990s. The Badr Organization largely disarmed after Saddam's fall and integrated into the political process, supporting the United States insofar as it facilitated a transition to Shia-majority rule and exercising control over Iraq's interior ministry. Under the administration of Prime Minister Nouri al Maliki, Badr leader Hadi al Ameri served as transportation minister and commanded security forces in Diyala province.
In 2014, Badr mobilized approximately 10,000 fighters under the auspices of the Popular Mobilization Forces (PMF) and Ameri assumed a leadership role in the PMF movement. Ameri leveraged this role as the head of the *Fatah* (Conquest) coalition in the May 2018 national election. *Fatah* won the second-highest number of seats (48) in the Council of Representatives (COR), of which 22 were won by Badr candidates. Ameri withdrew his name from consideration for prime minister in September 2018, but *Fatah*-backed Sunni candidate Mohammed al Halbousi was elected COR speaker.

Kata'ib Hezbollah (Battalions of the Party of God)
Also known as the Hezbollah Brigades, Kata'ib Hezbollah (KH) is an Iranian-backed Shia armed group and U.S.-designated Foreign Terrorist Organization (FTO) founded by Abu Mahdi al Muhandis in 2006. Muhandis was a Shia opposition operative during Saddam's rule, and was convicted in absentia by Kuwaiti courts for a number of attacks there. After these attacks, he served as leader of the Badr Corps, but broke with the group because of its support for the U.S. invasion of Iraq. Muhandis aligned with the Mahdi Army (see below) from 2004-2006, but then broke with it to form KH. The Treasury Department designated KH and Muhandis as threats to Iraqi stability under Executive Order 13438 in 2009. KH has sent troops to fight with Bashar al Asad's regime in Syria, and, since 2013, KH has been fighting IS forces in Iraq. The group claims to have 30,000 fighters, though other estimates are significantly lower. In September 2018, the State Department described KH as "heavily dependent" on Iranian support.

Asa'ib Ahl al Haq (AAH, "League of the Righteous")
Led by Qa'is al Khazali, who previously commanded Mahdi Army "Special Groups" personnel during 2006-2007, until his capture and incarceration by U.S. forces for his role in a 2005 raid that killed five U.S. soldiers. During his imprisonment, his followers formed AAH. After his release in 2010, Khazali took refuge in Iran, returning in 2011 to take resume command of AAH while also converting it into a political movement and social service network. AAH resumed military activities under the auspices of the PMF after the 2014 Islamic State offensive. Khazali and other AAH leaders nominally disassociated themselves from AAH-affiliated PMF units in order to participate in the 2018 election and secured 13 COR seats as part of the *Fatah* coalition.

Saraya al Salaam (Peace Brigades)
Established in 2014, Saraya al Salaam, also known as "The Peace Brigades," are one of several successor militias to the "Mahdi Army" movement that the junior Shia cleric Muqtada Al Sadr formed in 2004 to combat the U.S. military presence in Iraq. Sadr's relationship with Iran has evolved over time, and former Mahdi Army elements with close ties to Iranian security services have broken away to form their own groups. As U.S. forces completed their withdrawal from Iraq in 2011, Sadr's movement evolved into a social services network. In response to the Islamic State threat in 2014, Sadr mobilized fighters under the Saraya al Salaam framework. Though part of the PMF network, Sadrist militia have clashed with Badr and other PMF groups. The Sadr-led *Sa'irun* list won the highest number of seats (54) in the 2018 election.

Harakat Hezbollah al Nujaba (Movement of the Noble Ones of the Party of God)
Harakat Hezbollah al Nujaba (HHN) formed in 2013 and deployed Iraqi volunteers to Syria to assist the Asad regime. HHN forces have participated in a number of Iran-supported operations in Syria, including efforts to recapture city of Aleppo in 2016 and secure areas near the Iraq-Syria border. HHN's leader, Akram al Ka'bi, was designated by the U.S. government as a threat to Iraq's stability under E.O. 13438 in 2008, when he was a leader of an Iran-backed Mahdi Army faction referred to by U.S. forces as the "Special Groups." HHN claims a strength of 9,000 fighters, of which around two-thirds are in Iraq, with the remainder in Syria.

Sources: Graphic created by CRS, September 2018. Information compiled from Iraqi groups' statements and public platforms, U.S. government reports, non-government analyses, and international media accounts.

Figure 3. Select Iraqi Shia Political Groups, Leaders, and Militias.

Iraq: Issues in the 115th Congress

The contest to form the largest bloc and designate a prime minister candidate was shaped by the protests and attacks described above, with candidates drawn from the ranks of former officialdom disadvantaged by the public's apparent anti-incumbent mood. On September 7, the representative of Iraqi Shia supreme religious authority Grand Ayatollah Ali al Sistani decried Iraq's transformation into "an arena for regional and international conflicts" and said, "there should be pressure toward forming a new government that is different from the previous ones and to ensure that it takes into consideration the standards of efficiency, integrity, courage, firmness, and loyalty to the country and people as a basis for the selection of senior officials."[7]

A subsequent statement issued by Sistani's office denied rumors that Sistani had intervened to select or reject specific prime ministerial candidates and emphasized the prerogatives and duties of Iraq's elected leaders to do so.[8] Notably, this second statement further attributed to Sistani the view that current and former Iraqi officials should not lead Iraq's next government. In the wake of these messages from Grand Ayatollah Al Sistani's office, Prime Minister Abadi announced that he would not "cling to power," which many observers regarded as the end of his public campaign for a second term.[9] Badr Organization and *Fatah* coalition leader Hadi al Ameri also announced that would not pursue the position of prime minister.

Many observers of Iraqi politics regard Adel Abd al Mahdi as a compromise candidate acceptable to coalitions that have formed around the *Fatah* list on the one hand and the *Sa'irun* list on the other. While some in Congress have expressed concern about reported Iranian involvement in negotiations that led to Abd al Mahdi's nomination, Administration

---

[7] Shaykh 'Abd-al-Mahdi al-Karbala'i, Representative of Iraqi Supreme Religious Authority Ayatollah 'Ali al-Sistani, 2nd Sermon in the Grand Husayni Mosque in Karbala, Iraq, September 7, 2018.

[8] Statement posted on [https://www.sistani.org], September 10, 2018.

[9] Qassim Abdul-Zahra, "Uncertainties mount as Iraq's PM says he won't seek 2nd term," AP, September 14, 2018.

responses have highlighted past U.S. work with him and suggest they view the nomination as acceptable.[10]

Abd al Mahdi has been a key interlocutor for U.S. officials since shortly after the 2003 U.S.-led invasion that overthrew Saddam Hussein's regime. At the same time, he has been a prominent figure in the Islamic Supreme Council of Iraq (ISCI), which has historically received substantial backing from Iran. He served as Minister of Finance in Iraq's appointed interim government and led the country's debt relief initiatives. He has publicly supported an inclusive approach to sensitive political, religious, and inter-communal issues, but his relationships with other powerful Iraqi Shia forces and Iran raise some questions about his ability to lead independently.[11] Looking ahead, the new government's viability and the Prime Minister's freedom of action on controversial issues will be shaped by the durability of agreements among Iraqi coalitions and progress on citizens' priorities.

Popular Mobilization Forces and Iraqi Security Forces

Since its founding in 2014, Iraq's Popular Mobilization Committee (PMC) and its associated militias—the Popular Mobilization Forces (PMF)—have contributed to Iraq's fight against the Islamic State. Despite appreciating those contributions, some Iraqis and outsiders have raised concerns about the future of the PMC/PMF and some of its members' ties to Iran.[12] At issue has been the apparent unwillingness of some PMC/PMF

---

[10] Senator Marco Rubio, @marcorubio, Twitter, October. 3, 2018, 9:52 AM; and U.S. Embassy Baghdad, October 3, 2018.

[11] See Dexter Filkins, "Shiite Offers Secular Vision of Iraq Future," *New York Times*, February 10, 2005; and, Mustafa Salim and Tamer El-Ghobashy, "After months of deadlock, Iraqis name new president and prime minister," *Washington Post*, October 2, 2018.

[12] The PMC was established by then-Prime Minister Nouri al Maliki in June 2014 to give volunteer forces "a sense of legal justification and a degree of institutionalization." While the PMC falls under the authority of the Prime Minister's office and was led (until August 2018) by the Abadi-appointed Falih al Fayyadh, some allege that KH leader Muhandis, the PMC's deputy leader, has exerted the most influence over its direction. Renad Mansour, "More Than Militias: Iraq's Popular Mobilization Forces Are Here to Stay," *War on the*

entities to subordinate themselves to the command of Iraq's elected government and the ongoing participation in PMC/PMF operations of groups reported to receive direct Iranian support. In February 2018, the U.S. intelligence community told Congress that Iranian support to the PMC and "Shia militants remains the primary threat to U.S. personnel in Iraq." The community assessed that "this threat will increase as the threat from ISIS recedes, especially given calls from some Iranian-backed groups for the United States to withdraw and growing tension between Iran and the United States."[13]

Many PMF-associated groups and figures participated in the May 2018 national elections under the auspices of the *Fatah* coalition headed by Ameri.[14] Ameri and other prominent PMF-linked figures such as *Asa'ib Ahl al Haq* (League of the Righteous) leader Qa'is al Khazali nominally disassociated themselves from the PMF in late 2017, in line with legal prohibitions on the participation of PMF officials in politics.[15] Nevertheless, their movements' supporters and associated units remain integral to some ongoing PMF operations, and the *Fatah* coalition's campaign was arguably boosted by its members' past PMF activities.

During the election and in its aftermath, the key unresolved issue with regard to the PMC/PMF has remained the incomplete implementation of a 2016 law calling for the PMF to be incorporated as a permanent part of Iraq's national security establishment. In addition to outlining salary and benefit arrangements important to individual PMF volunteers, the law calls for all PMF units to be placed fully under the authority of the commander-in-chief [Prime Minister] and to be subject to military discipline and organization.

Through mid-2018, some PMF units were being administered in accordance with the law, but others have remained outside the law's directive structure. This includes some units associated with Shia groups

---

Rocks, April 3, 2018; Renad Mansour and Faleh Jabar, "The Popular Mobilization Forces and Iraq's Future," Carnegie Middle East Center, April 28, 2017.

[13] Worldwide Threat Assessment of the U.S. Intelligence Community, February 13, 2018.

[14] Phillip Smyth, "Iranian Militias in Iraq's Parliament: Political Outcomes and U.S. Response," Washington Institute for Near East Policy, PolicyWatch 2979, June 11, 2018.

[15] Khazali and Ameri made public statements in December 2017 instructing their organizations' political cadres to cut ties to operational PMF units.

identified by U.S. government reports as receiving or as having received Iranian support.[16] According to August 2018 oversight reporting on Operation Inherent Resolve, Defense Department sources report that electioneering and government formation talks had "prevented any meaningful efforts to integrate the PMF into the ISF or the Ministries of Defense or Interior" through mid-year.

In general, the popularity of the PMF and broadly expressed popular respect for the sacrifices made by individual volunteers in the fight against the Islamic State create complicated political questions. From an institutional perspective, one might assume Iraqi political leaders would share incentives to assert full state control over all PMF units and other armed groups and to ensure the full implementation of the 2016 PMF law. However, in practice, different figures appear to favor different approaches, with some Iran-aligned figures appearing to prefer a model that preserves the relative independence of units loyal and responsive to them. Iraqi leaders arguably benefit politically from continuing to embrace the PMF and its personnel and from supporting volunteers during their demobilization or transition into security sector roles. Nevertheless, there also may be political costs to appearing too supportive of the PMF relative to other national security forces or to embracing Iran-linked units in particular.

Proposals for fully dismantling the PMC/PMF structure appear to be politically untenable at present, and, given the ongoing role PMF units are playing in security operations against remnants of the Islamic State in some areas, might create opportunities for IS fighters to exploit. Forceful confrontation between Iraqi security forces and Iran-backed groups within the PMF structure or outside of it could precipitate civil conflict and a crisis in Iraq-Iran relations. Attempts by Iraqi Security Forces to

---

[16] The State Department's 2016 Country Reports on Terrorism mentioned Asa'ib Ahl al Haq and the Badr forces in this regard and warned specifically that the permanent inclusion of the U.S.-designated foreign terrorist organization (FTO) Kata'ib Hezbollah militia in Iraq's legalized PMF "could represent an obstacle that could undermine shared counterterrorism objectives." The 2017 report states that "Iran supported various Iraqi Shia terrorist groups, including Kata'ib Hizballah" and states that "Kata'ib Hizballah continued to combat ISIS alongside the Iraqi military, police, and other Popular Mobilization Force units during the year."

investigate allegations of illicit activity by some PMF units and Shia armed groups have resulted in violence in 2018. The *Fatah* coalition reacted angrily to Abadi's August 2018 decision to dismiss *Fatah*-aligned National Security Advisor and PMC head Falih al Fayyadh, calling the decision "illegal."[17]

Grand Ayatollah Al Sistani's office and his personal representatives have spoken directly about the importance of establishing and maintaining institutional control of all security forces in Iraq. This suggests that Sistani could make further public statements on the issue in the event that a figure with a different view takes office as prime minister or if some armed factions resist future government efforts at security force integration.

Though in a caretaker role, Prime Minister Abadi has made some recent attempts to assert the authority of the prime minister's office over the PMC/PMF and has expressed his desire to see U.S. military support for Iraq's security forces continue. *Sa'irun* leader Muqtada al Sadr remains critical of U.S. policy toward Iraq and the broader Middle East, but has not publicly called for the immediate withdrawal of foreign forces since the election. According to Defense Department sources cited in recent oversight reporting, Ameri and some Iran-aligned groups "appeared to have set aside hostility to the United States" through mid-2018 and "signaled a willingness to accept a continued United States military presence to train Iraqi forces."[18] To date, there are no clear public indications that Iraq's emerging government will seek to substantially change current patterns of U.S.-Iraq cooperation or abandon plans for the integration of the PMF within the Iraqi Security Forces.

The Kurdistan Region and Relations with Baghdad

Following the Kurdistan region of Iraq's September 2017 referendum on independence from Iraq (see textbox below), already tense relations

---

[17] Kosar Nawzad, "Iran-backed militias slam Iraqi PM's sacking of security advisor, call the decision 'illegal,'" Kurdistan 24, August 21, 2018.

[18] Lead Inspector General for Overseas Contingency Operations Quarterly Report, June 11, 2018.

between the semi-autonomous federal region and the national government in Baghdad grew more strained.[19] Kurdish parties had been divided among themselves over the wisdom of the referendum and relations with Baghdad, and post-referendum changes in territorial control in the disputed territories upended the Kurds' oil-based financial prospects and created new political differences among Iraqi Kurds.

The Kurdistan Region's September 2017 Referendum on Independence

The Kurdistan Regional Government (KRG) held an official advisory referendum on independence from Iraq on September 25, 2017, despiterequests from the national government of Iraq, the United States, and other external actors to delay or cancel it. Kurdish leaders held the referendum on time and as planned, with more than 72% of eligible voters participating and roughly 92% voting "Yes." The referendum was held across the KRI and in other areas that were then under the control of Kurdish forces, including some areas subject to territorial disputes between the KRG and the national government, such as the multiethnic city of Kirkuk, adjacent oil-rich areas, and parts of Ninewa governorate populated by religious and ethnic minorities. Kurdish forces had secured many of these areas following the retreat of national government forces in the face of the Islamic State's rapid advance across northern Iraq in 2014.

In the wake of the referendum, Iraqi national government leaders imposed a ban on international flights to and from the Kurdistan region, and, in October 2017, Prime Minister Abadi ordered Iraqi forces to return to the disputed territories that had been under the control of national forces prior to the Islamic State's 2014 advance, including Kirkuk. Iraqi authorities rescinded the international flight ban in 2018 after agreeing on border control, customs, and security at Kurdistan's international airports. Iraqi security forces and KRG *peshmerga* forces remain deployed across from each other at various fronts throughout the disputed territories, including deployments near the strategically sensitive tri-border area of Iraq, Syria, and Turkey (Figure 4).

---

[19] For background on the Kurdistan region, see CRS Report R45025, *Iraq: Background and U.S. Policy.*

Sources: Congressional Research Service using ArcGIS, IHS Markit Conflict Monitor, U.S. government, and United Nations data.

Figure 4. Disputed Territories in Iraq; Areas of Influence as of September 17, 2018.

Elections for the Kurdistan National Assembly were delayed in November 2017 and held on September 30, 2018. Preliminary results suggest that the KDP won a plurality of the 111 seats, with the Patriotic Union of Kurdistan (PUK) and smaller opposition and Islamist parties winning the balance.

U.S. officials have encouraged Kurds and other Iraqis to engage on issues of dispute and to avoid unilateral military actions that could further destabilize the situation. Iraqi national government and KRG officials continue to engage U.S. counterparts on related issues.

Economic and Fiscal Challenges Continue

The public finances of the national government and the KRG remain strained, amplifying the pressure on leaders working to address the country's security and service-provision challenges. On a national basis, the combined effects of lower global oil prices from 2014 through mid-2017, expansive public-sector liabilities, and the costs of the military campaign against the Islamic State have exacerbated budget deficits.[20] The IMF estimated Iraq's 2017-2018 financing needs at 19% of GDP. Oil exports provide nearly 90% of public-sector revenue in Iraq, while non-oil sector growth has been hindered over time by insecurity, weak service delivery, and corruption.

Iraq's oil production and exports have increased since 2016, but fluctuations in oil prices undermined revenue gains until the latter half of 2017. Revenues have since improved, but Iraq has agreed to manage its overall oil production in line with mutually agreed Organization of the Petroleum Exporting Countries (OPEC) output limits. In August 2018, Iraq exported an average of 4 million barrels per day (mbd, including KRG-administered oil exports), above the March 2018 budget's 3.8 mbd export assumption and at prices well above the budget's $46 per barrel benchmark.[21] The IMF projects modest GDP growth over the next five years and expects growth to be stronger in the non-oil sector if Iraq's implementation of agreed measures continues as oil output and exports plateau.

---

[20] IMF Country Report No. 17/251, Iraq: Second Review of the Three-Year Stand-By Arrangement, August 2017.

[21] Ahmed Aboulenein, Ahmed Rasheed, "Iraqi parliament approves budget, Kurdish lawmakers boycott vote," Reuters, March 3, 2018; and, Ben Lando, "Iraqi oil exports and revenues skyrocket in August," Iraq Oil Report, September 2, 2018.

Fiscal pressures are more acute in the Kurdistan region, where the fallout from the national government's response to the September 2017 referendum has further sapped the ability of the KRG to pay salaries to its public-sector employees and security forces. The KRG's loss of control over significant oil resources in Kirkuk governorate coupled with changes implemented by national government authorities over shipments of oil from those fields via the KRG-controlled export pipeline to Turkey have contributed to a sharp decline in revenue for the KRG.

Related issues shaped consideration of the 2018 budget in the COR, with Kurdish representatives criticizing the government's budget proposal to allocate the KRG a smaller percentage of funds in 2018 than the 17% benchmark reflected in previous budgets. National government officials argue that KRG resources should be based on a revised population estimate, and the 2018 budget adopted in March 2018 does not specify a fixed percentage or amount for the KRG and requires the KRG to place all oil exports under federal control in exchange for financial allocations for verified expenses.

HUMANITARIAN ISSUES AND STABILIZATION

Humanitarian Conditions

U.N. officials report several issues of ongoing humanitarian concern including harassment by armed actors and threats of forced return.[22] Humanitarian conditions remain difficult in many conflict-affected areas of Iraq, but December 2017 marked the first month since December 2013 that Iraqis who returned to their home areas outnumbered those who remained as internally displaced persons (IDPs) or became newly displaced. As of

---

[22] "The continued presence of armed actors in some camps across Iraq and reports of some attacks by them on humanitarian personnel, as well as reports of sexual harassment of women and girls with perceived ties to ISIL, detention and disappearance, recruitment activities inside the camps, restrictions on freedom of movement and threats of forced return, remain a grave concern." U.N. Document S/2018/677, Report of the Secretary-General pursuant to Resolution 2367 (2017), July 9, 2018.

September 15, more than 4 million Iraqis had returned to their districts since 2014, while more than 1.9 million individuals remained displaced.[23] These figures include those who were displaced and returned home in disputed areas in the wake of the September 2017 KRG referendum on independence.[24] Ninewa governorate is home to the largest number of IDPs, reflecting the lingering effects of the intense military operations against the Islamic State in Mosul and other areas during 2017 (Table 2). Estimates suggest thousands of civilians were killed or wounded during the Mosul battle, which displaced more than 1 million people. The Kurdistan Region of Iraq (KRI) hosts nearly 38% of the remaining IDP population in Iraq.

Table 2. IOM Estimates of IDPs by Location in Iraq
As of September 15, 2018, Select Governorates

IOM Estimates of IDPs by Location of Displacement				% Change since 2017
Governorate	January 2017	January 2018	September 2018	
Suleimaniyah	153,816	188,142	151,164	-2%
Erbil	346,080	253,116	217,548	-37%
Dohuk	397,014	362,670	349,656	-12%
KRI Total	*896,910*	*806,976*	*718,368*	*-20%*
Ninewa	409,020	795,360	595,632	+46%
Salah al Din	315,876	241,404	158,346	-50%
Baghdad	393,066	176,700	82,494	-79%
Kirkuk	367,188	172,854	117,444	-68%
Anbar	268,428	108,894	71,190	-73%
Diyala	75,624	81,972	61,644	-18%

Source: International Organization for Migration, Iraq Displacement Tracking Monitor Data.

IDP numbers in the KRI have declined since 2017, though not as rapidly as in some other governorates. Conditions for IDPs in Dohuk governorate remain the most challenging in the KRI, with more than 57%

---

[23] International Organization for Migration (IOM), Iraq Displacement Tracking Monitor, September 15, 2018.

[24] As of September 15, more than 72,000 people remained displaced because of the crisis in the disputed territories. According to IOM, approximately 266,000 such individuals had then returned to their home areas. CRS correspondence with IOM Iraq personnel, October 2018.

of Dohuk-based IDPs living in camps or critical shelters as of September 2018 according to International Organization for Migration surveys.

The U.N.'s 2018 Iraq humanitarian appeal expected that as many as 8.7 million Iraqis would require some form of humanitarian assistance in 2018 and sought $569 million to reach 3.4 million of them.[25] As of October 2018, the appeal was 60% met with $342 million in funds provided and more than $250 million in additional funds provided outside the plan.[26]

Stabilization and Reconstruction

At a February 2018 reconstruction conference in Kuwait, Iraqi authorities described more than $88 billion in short- and medium-term reconstruction needs, spanning various sectors and different areas of the country.[27] Countries participating in the conference offered approximately $30 billion worth of loans, investment pledges, export credit arrangements, and grants in response. The Trump Administration actively supported the participation of U.S. companies in the conference and announced its intent to pursue $3 billion in Export-Import Bank support for Iraq.

U.S. stabilization assistance to areas of Iraq that have been liberated from the Islamic State is directed through the United Nations Development Program (UNDP)-administered Funding Facility for Stabilization (FFS).[28] According to UNDP data, the FFS has received more than $690 million in resources since its inception in mid-2015, with 1,100 projects reported completed and a further 1,250 projects underway or planned with the support of UNDP-managed funding.[29] In August 2018, UNDP identified a "funding gap" of $505 million for stabilization projects in what it describes

---

[25] Iraq Humanitarian Response Plan 2018 - Advanced Executive Summary, February 2018.

[26] United Nations Financial Tracking Service, Iraq 2018 (Humanitarian Response Plan), October 1, 2018.

[27] Iraq Ministry of Planning, Reconstruction and Development Framework, February 2018.

[28] FFS includes a Funding Facility for Immediate Stabilization (FFIS), a Funding Facility for Expanded Stabilization (FFES), and Economic Reform Facilities for the national government and the KRI. U.S. contributions to FFIS support stabilization activities under each of its "Four Windows": (1) light infrastructure rehabilitation, (2) livelihoods support, (3) local official capacity building, and (4) community reconciliation programs.

[29] UNDP-Iraq, Funding Facility for Stabilization Quarter II Report - 2018, August 19, 2018.

as "strategic red box zones" (i.e., "the areas that are most vulnerable to the re-emergence of violent extremism and were last to be liberated") in Ninewa, Anbar, and Salah al Din governorates.[30] UNDP highlights unexploded ordnance, customs clearance delays, and the growth in volume and scope of FFS projects as challenges to its ongoing work.[31]

Iraqi leaders hope to attract considerable private sector investment to help finance its reconstruction needs and underwrite a new economic chapter for the country. The size of Iraq's internal market and its advantages as a low-cost energy producer with identified infrastructure investment needs help make it attractive to investors, but overcoming persistent concerns about security, service reliability, and corruption may prove challenging. The formation of the new Iraqi government and its reform plans may provide key signals to parties exploring investment opportunities.

ISSUES IN THE 115TH CONGRESS

As Congress has considered the Trump Administration's requests for FY2019 foreign assistance and defense funding, Iraqis have been engaged in competitive electioneering and government formation negotiations, while working to rebuild war-torn areas of their country. The final FY2018 appropriations acts approved in March 2018 (P.L. 115-141) made additional U.S. funding available for U.S. defense programs and contributions to immediate post-IS stabilization efforts, while also renewing authorities for U.S. economic loan guarantees to Iraq.

Defense authorization (P.L. 115-232) and appropriation (Division A of P.L. 115-245) legislation enacted for FY2019 extends congressional authorization for U.S. training, equipping, and advisory programs for Iraqi

---

[30] Ibid. Specifically, the report identifies western Anbar, Mosul, western Ninewa, "the Baiji-Hatra Corridor," and Hawijah district in Salah al Din as priority areas where UNDP considers funding constraints to pose risks.

[31] Past UNDP FFS self-assessment reports have highlighted growth in the number of projects undertaken nationwide since 2016 and resulting strains created on program systems including procurement, management, and monitoring.

security forces until December 2020 and makes $850 million in additional defense funding available for security assistance programs through FY2020. Congress has limited the availability of these funds, authorizing the obligation or expenditure of no more than $450 million for Iraq train and equip efforts until the Administration submits required strategy and oversight reporting.[32]

The FY2018 NDAA [Section 1224(c) of P.L. 115-91] modified the authority of the Office of Security Cooperation at the U.S. Embassy in Iraq (OSC-I) to widen the range of forces that the office may engage with professionalization and management assistance from Ministry of Defense and Counter Terrorism Service personnel to include all "military and other security forces with a national security mission."[33] The Administration's FY2019 defense funding request outlines plans for U.S. training of Iraqi border security forces, energy security forces, emergency response police units, Counterterrorism Service forces, and ranger units.

The FY2019 Continuing Appropriations Act (Division C of P.L. 115-245) makes funds available for foreign operations programs in Iraq on the terms and at the levels provided for in FY2018 appropriations through December 7, 2018. Foreign operations appropriations bills considered by the House and Senate would appropriate FY2019 funds for Iraq programs differently.

- The House version of the FY2019 Foreign Operations Appropriations bill (H.R. 6385) would make funds available "to promote governance and security, and for stabilization programs,

---

[32] Section 1233 of P.L. 115-232 conditions the availability of funding on the submission of the report on U.S. strategy in Iraq required by the joint explanatory statement of the committee of the conference accompanying H.Rept. 115-404, and a new report on the purpose, size, roles, missions, responsibilities, beneficiaries, and projected costs of U.S. training efforts in Iraq through FY2024. President Trump objected to this provision in his signing statement accompanying P.L. 115-232 as purporting "to mandate or regulate the submission to the Congress or the publication of information protected by executive privilege." The statement said, "My Administration will treat these provisions consistent with the President's constitutional authority to withhold information, the disclosure of which could impair national security, foreign relations, law enforcement, or the performance of the President's constitutional duties."

[33] The underlying authority for OSC-I activities remains Section 1215 of P.L. 112-81, as amended.

including in the Kurdistan Region of Iraq ...in accordance with the Constitution of Iraq." The accompanying report (H.Rept. 115-829) would direct $50 million in funds made available by the act for stabilization and recovery be used "for assistance to support the safe return of displaced religious and ethnic minorities to their communities in Iraq."

- The Senate version (S. 3108) and accompanying report (S.Rept. 115-282) would make $429.4 million available in FY2019 funding across various accounts, including $250 million in Foreign Military Financing assistance not requested by the Trump Administration. The Senate version also would direct that additional assistance monies in various accounts be made available for a $250 million Relief and Recovery Fund (RRF) for areas liberated or at risk from the Islamic State and other terrorist organizations, and the accompanying report contains a further direction that $100 million in funds appropriated for RRF purposes in prior acts be made available for programs in Iraq.

The Trump Administration signaled that decisions about future U.S. assistance efforts will be shaped by the outcome of Iraqi government formation talks. In September 2018, U.S. officials suggested they would like to see prevailing patterns of U.S. assistance continue, but an unnamed senior U.S. official also said that the Administration is prepared to reconsider U.S. support to Iraq if individuals perceived to be close to or controlled by Iran assume positions of authority in Iraq's new government.[34] Legislation enacted and under consideration in the second session of the 115th Congress would require annual reporting on Iraqi entities and individuals receiving Iranian support and would codify authorities currently available to the President under executive order to place sanctions on individuals threatening the security or stability of Iraq (see "The United States and Iran in Iraq" below).

---

[34] Katie Bo Williams, "U.S. Official: We May Cut Support for Iraq If New Government Seats Pro-Iran Politicians," *Defense One*, September 26, 2018.

U.S. Military Operations

Iraqi military and counterterrorism operations against scattered supporters of the Islamic State group are ongoing, and the United States military and its coalition partners continue to provide support to those efforts at the request of the Iraqi government. U.S. military operations against the Islamic State in Iraq and Syria are organized under the command of Combined Joint Task Force – Operation Inherent Resolve (CJTF-OIR).

The Trump Administration, like the Obama Administration, has cited the 2001 Authorization for Use of Military Force (AUMF, P.L. 107-40) as the domestic legal authorization for U.S. military operations against the Islamic State in Iraq and refers to both collective and individual self-defense provisions of the U.N. Charter as the relevant international legal justifications for ongoing U.S. operations in Iraq and Syria. The U.S. military presence in Iraq is governed by an exchange of diplomatic notes that reference the security provisions of the 2008 bilateral Strategic Framework Agreement.[35] This arrangement has not required approval of a separate security agreement by Iraq's Council of Representatives. In July 2018, NATO inaugurated a "non-combat training and capacity-building mission" at the request of the Iraqi government.

The overall volume and pace of U.S. strikes against IS targets in Iraq has diminished since the end of 2017, with U.S. training efforts for various Iraqi security forces ongoing at various locations, including in the Kurdistan region, pursuant to the authorities granted by Congress for the Iraq Train and Equip Program and for the activities of the OSC-I.[36] As of August 2018, U.S. and coalition training had benefitted more than 150,000

---

[35] Section III of the agreement states: "In order to strengthen security and stability in Iraq, and thereby contribute to international peace and stability, and to enhance the ability of the Republic of Iraq to deter all threats against its sovereignty, security, and territorial integrity, the Parties shall continue to foster close cooperation concerning defense and security arrangements without prejudice to Iraqi sovereignty over its land, sea, and air territory."

[36] Specific authority for the Iraq train and equip program is provided in Section 1236 of the FY2015 National Defense Authorization Act (P.L. 113-291), as amended. OSC-I activities are authorized by Section 1215 of the FY2012 National Defense Authorization Act (P.L. 112-81), as amended.

Iraqi security personnel since 2014. From FY2015 through FY2019, Congress authorized and appropriated more than $5.8 billion for train and equip assistance in Iraq (Table 3).

Assistance to the Kurdistan Regional Government and in the Kurdistan Region

Congress has authorized the President to provide U.S. assistance to the Kurdish *peshmerga* and certain Sunni and other local security forces with a national security mission in coordination with the Iraqi government, and to do so directly under certain circumstances. Pursuant to a 2016 U.S.-KRG memorandum of understanding (MOU), the United States has offered more than $400 million in defense funding and in-kind support to the Kurdistan Regional Government of Iraq, delivered in smaller monthly installments. The December 2016 continuing resolution (P.L. 114-254) included $289.5 million in FY2017 Iraq training program funds to continue support for *peshmerga* forces. In 2017, the Trump Administration requested an additional $365 million in defense funding to support programs with the KRG and KRG-Baghdad cooperation as part of the FY2018 train and equip request. The Administration also proposed a sale of infantry and artillery equipment for *peshmerga* forces that Iraq agreed to finance using a portion of its U.S.-subsidized Foreign Military Financing loan proceeds.

The Administration's FY2019 Iraq Train and Equip program funding request refers to the *peshmerga* as a component of the ISF and discusses the *peshmerga* in the context of a $290 million request for potential ISF-wide sustainment aid. The conference report (H.Rept. 115-952) accompanying the FY2019 Defense Appropriations Act (Division A of P.L. 115-245) says the United States "should" provide this amount for "operational sustainment" for Ministry of Peshmerga forces.

Kurdish officials report that U.S. training support and consultation on plans to reform the KRG Ministry of Peshmerga and its forces continue. The Department of Defense reports that it has resumed paying the salaries of *peshmerga* personnel in units aligned by the Ministry of Peshmerga, after a pause following the September 2017 independence referendum.

Congress has directed in recent years that U.S. foreign assistance, humanitarian aid, and loan guarantees be implemented in Iraq in ways that benefit Iraqis in all areas of the country, including in the Kurdistan region.

The Trump Administration has not reported the number of U.S. personnel in Iraq since September 2017.[37] In February 2018, General Joseph Votel, Commander of U.S. Central Command, stated that there has been a reduction in the number of U.S. military personnel and changes in U.S. capabilities in Iraq from 2017 levels.[38] U.S. military sources have stated that the "continued coalition presence in Iraq will be conditions-based, proportional to the need, and in coordination with the government of Iraq."[39] As of October 2018, 67 U.S. military personnel and DOD civilians have been killed or have died as part of OIR, and 72 U.S. persons have been wounded. Through March 2018, OIR operations since August 2014 had cost $23.5 billion.[40]

Table 3. Iraq Train and Equip Program: Appropriations and Requests in thousands of dollars

	FY2015	FY2016	FY2017 Requests	FY2018 Iraq-Specific Request	FY2019 Iraq-Specific Request
Iraq Train and Equip Fund	1,618,000	715,000	630,000 289,500 (FY17 CR)	-	-
Additional Counter-ISIL Train and Equip Fund	-	-	446,400	1,269,000	850,000
Total	1,618,000	715,000	1,365,900	1,269,000	850,000

Source: Executive branch appropriations requests and appropriations legislation.

---

[37] As of September 2017, the Department of Defense (DOD) Defense Manpower Data Center (DMDC) reported that there were then nearly 8,900 U.S. uniformed military personnel in Iraq, although precise numbers have been fluid based on operational needs and deployment schedules.

[38] Gen. Joseph Votel, Testimony before House Armed Services Committee, February 27, 2018.

[39] Saad al Hadithi and U.S. Army Col. Ryan Dillon quoted in Susannah George and Qassim Abdul-Zahra, "US begins reducing troops in Iraq after victory over IS," Associated Press, February 5, 2018.

[40] Lead Inspector General for Operation Inherent Resolve and Operation Pacific Eagle-Philippines, Quarterly Report to the United States Congress, April 1, 2018 - June 30, 2018, released August 6, 2018.

U.S. Foreign Assistance

In recent years, the U.S. government has provided State Department- and USAID-administered assistance to Iraq to support a range of security and economic objectives. U.S. Foreign Military Financing (FMF) funds have supported the costs of continued loan-funded purchases of U.S. defense equipment and helped fund Iraqi defense institution building efforts. Congressionally authorized U.S. loan guarantees also have supported successful Iraqi bond issues to help Baghdad cover its fiscal deficits. Since 2014, the United States has contributed more than $1.7 billion to humanitarian relief efforts in Iraq,[41] including more than $607 million in humanitarian support in FY2017 and FY2018.[42]

The Administration's FY2019 request seeks more than $199 million for stabilization and other non-military assistance programs in Iraq (Table 4). The Senate version of the FY2019 foreign operations appropriations act (S. 3108, S.Rept. 115-282) would appropriate $150 million in ESF, along with $250 million in Foreign Military Financing and other security assistance funds. The Senate version also would direct that $50 million in FY2019 ESF funds be provided for stabilization in Iraq, in addition to $100 million in previously appropriated Relief and Recovery Fund-designated monies.[43] The report accompanying the House version of the bill (H.Rept. 115-829, H.R. 6385) would direct $50 million in FY2019 funds available for stabilization programs "for assistance to support the

---

[41] Iraq-Complex Emergency Fact Sheet #1, Fiscal Year (FY) 2018, November 27, 2017.

[42] Iraq-Complex Emergency Fact Sheet #9, Fiscal Year (FY) 2018, July 20, 2018.

[43] Section 8004 of the FY2017 Foreign Operations Appropriations Act (Division J of P.L. 115-31) and its accompanying explanatory statement designated amounts to be made available from various accounts for a $169 million Relief and Recovery Fund (RRF). The act states that RRF funding is "for assistance for areas liberated from, or under the influence of, the Islamic State of Iraq and Syria, other terrorist organizations, or violent extremist organizations in and around the Near East and Africa." According to the act, the funds were to be in addition to funds otherwise available for countries for such purposes and may not be made available "for the costs of significant infrastructure projects." The act stated that funds were to be made available "the maximum extent practicable on a cost-matching basis from sources other than the United States." Section 7041(j) of the FY2018 Foreign Operations Appropriations Act (Division K of P.L. 115-141) designated an additional $500 million in FY2018 funding from various accounts as RRF funding for similar purposes and on similar terms.

Iraq: Issues in the 115th Congress

safe return of displaced religious and ethnic minorities to their communities in Iraq."

Table 4. U.S. Assistance to Iraq: Select Obligations, Allocations, and Requests in millions of dollars

Account	FY 2012	FY 2013	FY 2014	FY 2015	FY 2016	FY 2017	FY 2018	FY 2019
	Obligated	Obligated	Obligated	Obligated	Obligated	Actual	Req.	Req.
FMF	79.555	37.290	300.000	150.000	250.000	250.00	-	-
ESF/ ESDF	275.903	128.041	61.238	50.282	116.452	553.50	300.000	150.000
INCLE	309.353	-	11.199	3.529	-	0.20	-	2.000
NADR	16.547	9.460	18.318	4.039	38.308	56.92	46.860	46.860
DF	0.540	26.359	18.107	-	.028	-	-	
IMET	1.997	1.115	1.471	0.902	0.993	0.70	1.000	1.000
Total	683.895	202.265	410.333	208.752	405.781	1061.12	347.860	199.860

Sources: Obligations data derived from U.S. Overseas Loans and Grants (Greenbook), January 2017. FY2016- FY2019 data from State Department Congressional Budget Justification and other executive branch documents.

Notes: FMF = Foreign Military Financing; ESF/ESDF = Economic Support Fund/Economic Support and Development Fund; INCLE = International Narcotics Control and Law Enforcement; NADR = Nonproliferation, Antiterrorism, Demining, and Related Programs; DF = Democracy Fund; IMET = International Military Education and Training.

Stabilization and Issues Affecting Religious and Ethnic Minorities

State Department reports on human rights conditions and religious freedom in Iraq have documented the difficulties faced by religious and ethnic minorities in the country for years. In some cases, these difficulties and security risks have driven members of minority groups to flee the country or to take shelter in different areas of the country, whether with fellow group members or in new communities. Minority groups that live in areas subject to long-running territorial disputes between Iraq's national government and the KRG face additional interference and exploitation by larger groups for political, economic, or security reasons. Members of diverse minority communities express a variety of territorial claims and administrative preferences, both among and within their own groups. While much attention is focused on potential intimidation or coercion of minorities by majority groups, disputes within and among minority communities also have the potential to generate tension and violence. In October 2017, Vice President Mike Pence said in a speech that the U.S. government would direct more support to persecuted religious minority groups in the Middle East, including in Iraq. As part of this initiative, the Trump Administration has negotiated with UNDP to direct U.S. contributions to the UNDP Funding Facility for Stabilization (FFS) to the Ninewa Plains and other minority populated areas of northern Iraq. In October 2017, USAID solicited proposals in a Broad Agency Announcement for cooperative programs "to facilitate the safe and voluntary return of Internally Displaced Persons (IDPs) to their homes in the Ninewa plains and western Ninewa of Iraq and to encourage those who already are in their communities to remain there."[44] In parallel, USAID notified Congress of its intent to obligate $14 million in FY2017 ESF-OCO for stabilization programs.

In January 2018, USAID officials released to UNDP a $75 million first tranche of stabilization assistance from an overall pledge of $150 million that had been announced in July 2017 and notified for planned obligation to Congress in April 2017. According to the January 2018 announcement, USAID "renegotiated" the contribution agreement with UNDP so that $55 million of the $75 million payment "will address the needs of vulnerable religious and ethnic minority communities in Ninewa Province, especially those who have been victims of atrocities by ISIS" with a focus on "restoring services such as water, electricity, sewage, health, and education."[45] USAID Administrator Mark Green visited Iraq in June 2018 and engaged with ethnic and religious minority groups in Ninewa. He also announced $10 million in awards under USAID's October 2017 proposal solicitation.

Inclusive of the January announcement, the United States has provided $198.65 million to support the FFS—which remains the main international conduit for post-IS stabilization assistance in liberated areas of Iraq. According to UNDP, overall stabilization priorities for the FFS program are set by a steering committee chaired by the government of Iraq, with governorate-level Iraqi authorities directly responsible for implementation. UNDP officials report that earmarking of funding by donors "can result in funding being directed away from areas highlighted by the Iraqi authorities as being in great need."[46] At the end of the second quarter of 2018, UNDP reported that 214 projects in minority communities of were complete out of 416 overall projects completed, planned, or under way in the Ninewa Plains.[47]

---

[44] USAID Solicitation Number: BAA-267-Ninewa-2017, October 30, 2017.

[45] USAID, "Continued U.S. Assistance to Better Meet the Needs of Minorities in Iraq," January 8, 2018.

[46] UNDP response to CRS inquiry, May 2018.

[47] UNDP-Iraq, Funding Facility for Stabilization Quarter II Report - 2018, August 19, 2018.

The FY2018 foreign operations appropriations act (Division K, P.L. 115-141) stated that funds shall be available for stabilization in Iraq, and U.S. support to stabilization programs is ongoing using funds appropriated in FY2017. Since mid-2016, the executive branch has notified Congress of its intent to obligate $265.3 million in assistance funding to support UNDP FFS programs, including post-IS stabilization funding made available in the December 2016 continuing resolution (Division B of P.L. 114-254, see textbox below).[48] Trump Administration requests for FY2018 and FY2019 monies for Iraq programs included requests to fund continued U.S. contributions to post-IS stabilization programs. No new contributions to U.N.-managed stabilization programs have been announced in 2018.

The United States also contributes to Iraqi programs to stabilize the Mosul Dam on the Tigris River, which remains at risk of collapse due to structural flaws, overlooked maintenance, and its compromised location. The State Department notes that Iraq is working to stabilize the dam, but "it is impossible to accurately predict the likelihood of the dam's failing...."[49]

The United States and Iran in Iraq

The Trump Administration seeks to more proactively challenge, contain, and roll back Iran's regional influence, while attempting to solidify a long-term partnership with the government of Iraq and ensure Iraq's economic stability.[50] These dual, and sometimes competing, goals raise several policy questions for U.S. officials and Members of Congress to consider. These include questions about

---

[48] In P.L. 114-254, Congress appropriated $1.03 billion in Economic Support Fund (ESF) monies available through FY2018 for programs to counter the Islamic State, including in minority populated areas of Iraq.

[49] State Department Bureau of Consular Affairs, Iraq Country Information Page: Iraq, September 2018.

[50] Secretary of State Michael Pompeo, "Remarks at the United Against Nuclear Iran Summit," New York City, September 25, 2018; and, State Department and Defense Department appropriations requests, FY2018-2019.

- the makeup and viability of the emergent Iraqi government,
- Iraqi leaders' approaches to Iran-backed groups and the future of militia forces mobilized to fight the Islamic State,
- Iraq's compliance with U.S. sanctions on Iran,
- the future extent and roles of the U.S. military presence in Iraq,
- the terms and conditions associated with U.S. security assistance to Iraqi forces,
- U.S. relations with Iraqi constituent groups such as the Kurds, and
- potential responses to U.S. efforts to contain or confront Iran-aligned entities in Iraq or elsewhere in the region.

The 115th Congress has considered proposals to direct the Administration to impose U.S. sanctions on some Iran-aligned Iraqi groups, and has enacted legislation containing reporting requirements focused on Iranian support to non-state actors in Iraq and other countries.

- The FY2018 NDAA augmented annual reporting requirements on Iran to include reporting on the use of the Iranian commercial aviation sector to support U.S.- designated terrorist organization Kata'ib Hezbollah and other groups (Section 1225 of P.L. 115-91).
- An amendment adopted to the House version of the FY2019 National Defense Authorization Act would have required the President to impose specified sanctions on Asa'ib Ahl al Haq, Harakat Hezbollah al Nujaba, and certain associated persons (Section 1230F of H.R.5515EH). The provision was not included in the conference version of the bill (P.L. 115-232). The conference report encourages the Secretary of State "to continuously review whether groups that are affiliated with Iran meet the criteria for designation as a foreign terrorist organization or the application of sanctions pursuant to Executive Order 13224." S. 3431, introduced in September 2018, would also require the imposition of sanctions on those groups. A similar bill, H.R. 4238, was introduced in the House in November 2017.

- The House version of the FY2019 National Intelligence Authorization Act would require the Director of National Intelligence to report within 90 days of enactment on Iranian government spending on terrorist and military activities outside Iran's borders including support to "proxy forces" in Iraq (Section 2515 of H.R. 6237EH). The annually required report on Iran's military power includes criteria focused on Iranian support to non-state groups around the world.

- In September 2018, the House Foreign Affairs Committee approved and reported to the House an amended version of H.R. 4591, which, subject to national security waiver, would direct the President to impose sanctions on "any foreign person that the President determines knowingly commits a significant act of violence that has the direct purpose or effect of—(1) threatening the peace or stability of Iraq or the Government of Iraq; (2) undermining the democratic process in Iraq; or (3) undermining significantly efforts to promote economic reconstruction and political reform in Iraq or to provide humanitarian assistance to the Iraqi people."

- H.R. 4591 would further require the Secretary of State to submit a determination as to whether Asa'ib Ahl al Haq, Harakat Hizballah al Nujaba, or affiliated persons and entities meet terrorist designation criteria or the sanctions criteria of the bill. The bill also would direct the Secretary of State to prepare, maintain, and publish a "a list of armed groups, militias, or proxy forces in Iraq receiving logistical, military, or financial assistance from Iran's Revolutionary Guard Corps or over which Iran's Revolutionary Guard Corps exerts any form of control or influence."

Iran-linked actors in Iraq have directly targeted U.S. forces in the past, and some maintain the ability and state their willingness to do so again under certain circumstances. U.S. officials blamed these groups for apparent indirect weaponry attacks on U.S. diplomatic facilities in Basra and Baghdad in late September. These attacks followed reports that Iran had transferred short range ballistic missiles to Iran-backed militias in Iraq, reportedly including Kata'ib Hezbollah. Efforts to punish or sideline these groups, via sanctions or other means, could reduce Iran's influence in Iraq in ways that could serve U.S. national security interests. However, U.S. efforts to counter Iranian activities in Iraq, and elsewhere in the region, have the potential to complicate other U.S. interests in Iraq. Aggressively confronting Iran and its allies in Iraq could disrupt relations among parties to the emerging government in Baghdad, or even precipitate further civil conflict, undermining the U.S. goal of ensuring the stability and authority of the Iraqi government.

Additionally, while a wide range of Iraqi actors have ties to Iran, the nature of those ties differs, and treating these diverse groups uniformly risks ostracizing potential U.S. partners or neglecting opportunities to create divisions between these groups and Iran. With regard to the imposition of U.S. sanctions, some analysts have argued, "the timing and sequencing of any such move is critical to maximizing desired effects and minimizing Tehran's ability to exploit Iraqi blowback."[51]

While much attention focuses on the future of Iran-backed armed groups, the new Iraqi government's decisions about compliance with U.S. sanctions on Iran also may prove sensitive in coming months. Newly elected COR Speaker Halbousi has said that "Iraq will always be alongside the Iranian people" and that he and others in the COR "opposed the exercise of any economic pressure and embargo on Iran."[52]

Iraq's relations with the Arab Gulf states also shape the balance of Iranian and U.S. interests. U.S. officials have praised Saudi efforts since 2015 to reengage with the Iraqi government and support normalization of ties between the countries. In December 2015, Saudi officials reopened the kingdom's diplomatic offices in Iraq after a 25-year absence, and border crossings between the two countries have been reopened. Saudi Arabia and the other GCC states have not offered major new economic or security assistance or new debt relief initiatives to help stabilize Iraq, but actively

---

[51] Michael Knights, et al., "The Smart Way to Sanction Iranian-Backed Militias in Iraq," Washington Institute for Near East Policy, September 17, 2018.

[52] Shaafaq News (Iraq), "Al Halbousi in his First Statement: We Oppose the Embargo on Iraq," September 16, 2018.

engaged in and supported the February 2018 reconstruction conference held by Iraq in Kuwait. Saudi and other GCC state officials generally view the empowerment of Iran-linked Shia militia groups in Iraq with suspicion and, like the United States, seek to limit Iran's ability to influence political and security developments in Iraq.

OUTLOOK

Negotiations among Iraqi factions following the May 2018 election have not fully resolved outstanding questions about the future of U.S.-Iraqi relations. Prime Minister Abadi, with whom the U.S. government worked closely, could not translate his list's third-place finish into a mandate for a second term. His designated successor, Prime Minister-designate Adel Abd al Mahdi served in Abadi's government and is an individual with whom U.S. officials have worked positively in the past. Yet, the nature and durability of the political coalition arrangements supporting his leadership are unclear, and he lacks a strong personal electoral mandate. Similarly, Iraqi President Barham Salih is familiar to U.S. officials as a leading and friendly figure among Iraqi Kurds, but his election comes at time of significant political differences among Kurds and amid strained relations between Kurds and the national government.

There is little public indication at present that Iraqi authorities intend to request that the United States dramatically alter its assistance approach to or end its military presence in Iraq, including with regard to the Kurdistan region. However, the United States could face countervailing requests from its various Iraqi partners in the event that anti-U.S. political forces emerge more empowered from remaining government formation steps or through the new government's policies. It remains possible that the national government could more strictly assert its sovereign prerogatives with regard to the presence of foreign military forces and foreign assistance to sub-state entities, and/or that KRG representatives could seek expanded or more direct foreign support.

Some Iraqi groups, such as the Shia militant organization Kata'ib Hezbollah, remain vocally critical of the remaining U.S. and coalition military presence in the country and argue that the defeat of the Islamic State's main forces means that U.S. and other foreign forces should depart. These and similar groups also accuse the United States of seeking to undermine the Popular Mobilization Forces or otherwise subordinate Iraq to U.S. preferences. Most mainstream Iraqi political movements or leaders did not use the U.S. military presence as a major wedge issue in the run-up to or aftermath of the May 2018 election and have not directly called for an end to security partnership with the United States.

Members of Congress and U.S. officials face difficulties in developing policy options that can secure U.S. interests on specific issues without provoking levels of opposition from Iraqi constituencies that may jeopardize wider U.S. goals. Debates over U.S. military support to Iraqi national forces and sub-state actors in the fight against the Islamic State illustrated this dynamic, with some U.S. proposals for the provision of aid to all capable Iraqi forces facing criticism from Iraqi groups suspicious of U.S. intentions or fearful that U.S. assistance could empower their domestic rivals. U.S. aid to the Kurds to date has been provided with the approval of the Baghdad government, though some Members have advocated for assistance to be provided directly to the KRG.

U.S. assistance to Baghdad is provided on the understanding that U.S. equipment will be responsibly used by its intended recipients, and some Members have expressed concerns about the use of U.S.-origin defense equipment by actors or in ways that Congress has not intended, including a now-resolved case involving the possession and use of U.S.-origin tanks by elements of the Popular Mobilization Forces. The strained relationship between national government and Kurdish forces along the disputed territories and the future of the Popular Mobilization Forces implicate these issues directly and may remain relevant to debates over the continuation of prevailing patterns of U.S. assistance.

Once negotiations over cabinet positions are completed and a new government is seated, debate over the 2019 budget, reform of the water and electricity sectors, employment initiatives, and national security issues are expected to define the political agenda in Iraq. It seems reasonable to expect that Iraqis will continue to assess and respond to U.S. initiatives (and those of other outsiders) primarily through the lenses of their own domestic political rivalries, anxieties, and agendas. Reconciling U.S. preferences and interests with Iraq's evolving politics and security conditions may thus require continued creativity, flexibility, and patience.

In: The Middle East
Editor: Doyle Keller

ISBN: 978-1-53616-191-5
© 2019 Nova Science Publishers, Inc.

Chapter 4

JORDAN: BACKGROUND AND U.S. RELATIONS (UPDATED)*

Jeremy M. Sharp

ABSTRACT

This chapter provides an overview of Jordanian politics and current issues in U.S.-Jordanian relations. It provides a brief discussion of Jordan's government and economy and of its cooperation with U.S. policies in the Middle East.

Several issues are likely to figure in decisions by Congress and the Administration on future aid to and cooperation with Jordan. These include Jordan's continued involvement in attempting to promote Israeli-Palestinian peace and the stability of the Jordanian regime, particularly in light of ongoing conflicts in neighboring Syria and Iraq. U.S. officials may also consider potential threats to Jordan from the Islamic State organization (IS, also known as ISIL, ISIS, or the Arabic acronym *Da'esh*).

Although the United States and Jordan have never been linked by a formal treaty, they have cooperated on a number of regional and international issues over the years. Jordan's small size and lack of major

---

* This is an edited, reformatted and augmented version of Congressional Research Service, Publication No. RL33546, dated October 17, 2018.

economic resources have made it dependent on aid from Western and various Arab sources. U.S. support, in particular, has helped Jordan address serious vulnerabilities, both internal and external. Jordan's geographic position, wedged between Israel, Syria, Iraq, and Saudi Arabia, has made it vulnerable to the strategic designs of more powerful neighbors, but has also given Jordan an important role as a buffer between these countries in their largely adversarial relations with one another.

Public dissatisfaction with the economy is probably the most pressing concern for the Jordanian monarchy. Over the summer of 2018, widespread protests erupted throughout the kingdom in opposition to a draft tax bill and price hikes on fuel and electricity. Though peaceful, the protests drew immediate international attention because of their scale. Since then, the government has continued to work with the International Monetary Fund (IMF) on fiscal reforms to address a public debt that has ballooned to 96.4% of Gross Domestic Product (GDP).

The United States has provided economic and military aid to Jordan since 1951 and 1957, respectively. Total bilateral U.S. aid (overseen by the Departments of State and Defense) to Jordan through FY2016 amounted to approximately $19.2 billion.

On February 14, 2018, then-U.S. Secretary of State Rex W. Tillerson and Jordanian Minister of Foreign Affairs Ayman Safadi signed a new Memorandum of Understanding (or MOU) on U.S. foreign assistance to Jordan. The MOU, the third such agreement between the United and Jordan, commits the United States to provide $1.275 billion per year in bilateral foreign assistance over a five-year period for a total of $6.375 billion (FY2018-FY2022). This latest MOU represents a 27% increase in the U.S. commitment to Jordan above the previous iteration and is the first five-year MOU with the kingdom. The previous two MOU agreements had been in effect for three years. In line with the new MOU, for FY2019 President Trump is requesting $1.271 billion for Jordan, including $910.8 million in ESF, $350 million in FMF, and $3.8 million in International Military Education and Training (IMET).

OVERVIEW

Since assuming the throne from his late father on February 7, 1999, Jordan's 56-year-old monarch King Abdullah II bin Al Hussein (hereinafter King Abdullah II) has maintained Jordan's stability and strong ties to the United States. Although many commentators frequently caution that Jordan's stability is fragile, the monarchy has remained resilient owing to a number of factors. These include a relatively strong sense of social cohesion, strong support for the government from both Western powers and the Gulf Arab monarchies, and an internal security apparatus that is highly capable and, according to human rights groups, uses vague and broad criminal provisions in the legal system to dissuade dissent.[1]

U.S. officials frequently express their support for Jordan. President Trump has acknowledged Jordan's role as a key U.S. partner in countering the Islamic State, as U.S. policymakers advocate for continued robust U.S. assistance to the kingdom. Annual aid to Jordan has nearly quadrupled in historical terms over the last 15 years. Jordan also hosts thousands of U.S. troops. According to President Trump's June 2018 War Powers Resolution Report to Congress, "At the request of the Government of Jordan, approximately 2,600 United States military personnel are deployed to Jordan to support Defeat-ISIS operations, to enhance Jordan's security, and to promote regional stability."[2]

COUNTRY BACKGROUND

Although the United States and Jordan have never been linked by a formal treaty, they have cooperated on a number of regional and international issues for decades. Jordan's small size and lack of major economic resources have made it dependent on aid from Western and various Arab sources. U.S. support, in particular, has helped Jordan deal with serious vulnerabilities, both internal and external. Jordan's geographic position, wedged between Israel, Syria, Iraq, and Saudi Arabia, has made it vulnerable to the strategic designs of its powerful neighbors, but has also given Jordan an important role as a buffer between these countries in their largely adversarial relations with one another.

---

[1] Human Rights Watch, Jordan. See https://www.hrw.org/middle-east/n-africa/jordan.
[2] The White House, Office of the Press Secretary, Text of a Letter from the President to the Speaker of the House of Representatives and the President Pro Tempore of the Senate, June 8, 2018.

Jordan, created by colonial powers after World War I, initially consisted of desert or semidesert territory east of the Jordan River, inhabited largely by people of Bedouin tribal background. The establishment of the state of Israel in 1948 brought large numbers of Palestinian refugees to Jordan, which subsequently unilaterally annexed a Palestinian enclave west of the Jordan River known as the West Bank.[3] The original "East Bank" Jordanians, though probably no longer a majority in Jordan, remain predominant in the country's political and military establishments and form the bedrock of support for the Jordanian monarchy. Jordanians of Palestinian origin comprise an estimated 55% to 70% of the population and generally tend to gravitate toward the private sector due to their general exclusion from certain public-sector and military positions.[4]

The Hashemite Royal Family

Jordan is a hereditary constitutional monarchy under the prestigious Hashemite family, which claims descent from the Prophet Muhammad. King Abdullah II (age 56) has ruled the country since 1999, when he succeeded to the throne upon the death of his father, the late King Hussein, after a 47-year reign. Educated largely in Britain and the United States, King Abdullah II had earlier pursued a military career, ultimately serving as commander of Jordan's Special Operations Forces with the rank of

---

[3] Though there was little international recognition of Jordan's annexation of the West Bank, Jordan maintained control of it (including East Jerusalem) until Israel took military control of it during the June 1967 Arab-Israeli War, and maintained its claim to it until relinquishing the claim to the Palestine Liberation Organization in 1988.

[4] Speculation over the ratio of East Bankers to Palestinians (those who arrived as refugees and immigrants since 1948) in Jordanian society tends to be a sensitive domestic issue. Jordan last conducted a national census in 2004, and it is unclear whether or not the government maintains such statistics. Over time, intermarriage has made it more difficult to discern distinct differences between the two communities, though divisions do persist.

major general. The king's son, Prince Hussein bin Abdullah (born in 1994), is the designated crown prince.[5]

The king appoints a prime minister to head the government and the Council of Ministers (cabinet). On average, Jordanian governments last no more than 15 months before they are dissolved by royal decree. This seems to be done in order to bolster the king's reform credentials and to distribute patronage among a wide range of elites. The king also appoints all judges and is commander of the armed forces.

Political System and Key Institutions

The Jordanian constitution, most recently amended in 2016, empowers the king with broad executive powers. The king appoints the prime minister and may dismiss him or accept his resignation. He also has the sole power to appoint the crown prince, senior military leaders, justices of the constitutional court, and all 75 members of the senate. The king appoints cabinet ministers. The constitution enables the king to dissolve both houses of parliament and postpone lower house elections for two years.[6] The king can circumvent parliament through a constitutional mechanism that allows provisional legislation to be issued by the cabinet when parliament is not sitting or has been dissolved.[7] The king also must approve laws before they can take effect, although a two-thirds majority of both houses of parliament can modify legislation. The king also can issue royal decrees, which are not subject to parliamentary scrutiny. The king commands the armed forces, declares war, and ratifies treaties. Finally, Article 195 of the Jordanian Penal Code prohibits insulting the dignity of

---

[5] In July 2009, King Abdullah II named Prince Hussein (then 15 years old), as crown prince. The position had been vacant since 2004, when King Abdullah II removed the title from his half-brother, Prince Hamzah.

[6] The king also may declare martial law. According to Article 125, "In the event of an emergency of such a serious nature that action under the preceding Article of the present Constitution will be considered insufficient for the defense of the Kingdom, the King may by a Royal Decree, based on a decision of the Council of Ministers, declare martial law in the whole or any part of the Kingdom."

[7] New amendments to Article 94 in 2011 have put some restrictions on when the executive is allowed to issue temporary laws.

the king (lèse-majesté), with criminal penalties of one to three years in prison.

Jordan's constitution provides for an independent judiciary. According to Article 97, "Judges are independent, and in the exercise of their judicial functions they are subject to no authority other than that of the law." Jordan has three main types of courts: civil courts, special courts (some of which are military/state security courts), and religious courts. In Jordan, state security courts administered by military (and civilian) judges handle criminal cases involving espionage, bribery of public officials, trafficking in narcotics or weapons, black marketeering, and "security offenses." Overall, the king may appoint and dismiss judges by decree, though in practice a palace-appointed Higher Judicial Council manages court appointments, promotions, transfers, and retirements.

Although King Abdullah II has envisioned Jordan's gradual transition from a constitutional monarchy into a full-fledged parliamentary democracy,[8] in reality, successive Jordanian parliaments have mostly complied with the policies laid out by the Royal Court. The legislative branch's independence has been curtailed not only by a legal system that rests authority largely in the hands of the monarch, but also by carefully crafted electoral laws designed to produce propalace majorities with each new election.[9] Due to frequent gerrymandering in which electoral districts are drawn to favor more rural progovernment constituencies over densely populated urban areas, parliamentary elections have produced large progovernment majorities dominated by representatives of prominent tribal families. In addition, voter turnout tends to be much higher in progovernment areas since many East Bank Jordanians depend on family/tribal connections as a means to access patronage jobs.

---

[8] See "Making Our Democratic System Work for All Jordanians," Abdullah II ibn Al Hussein, January 16, 2013, available online at http://kingabdullah.jo/index.php/en_US/pages/view/id/248.html.

[9] "How Jordan's Election Revealed Enduring Weaknesses in Its Political System," *Washington Post*, October 3, 2016.

SHORT-TERM OUTLOOK

In late 2018, the outlook for the Hashemite Kingdom of Jordan, a vital U.S. partner in the Middle East, is mixed. On the one hand, as conflicts in Syria and Iraq have abated somewhat, the kingdom faces improved prospects for stable borders, a resumption of trade with its neighbors, and the possible repatriation of hundreds of thousands of refugees. On the other hand, continuing economic discontent and sensitivity among the public regarding recent U.S. policy changes on Israel and the Palestinians have placed Jordan in a difficult political position.

Public dissatisfaction with the economy is probably the most pressing concern for the monarchy. Over the summer of 2018, widespread protests erupted throughout the kingdom in opposition to a draft tax bill and price hikes on fuel and electricity. Though peaceful, the protests drew immediate international attention because of their scale. Since summer, the government has continued to work with the International Monetary Fund (IMF) on fiscal reforms to address a public debt that has ballooned to 96.4% of Gross Domestic Product (GDP).

As the Trump Administration has enacted changes to long-standing U.S. policies on Israel and the Palestinians, which have been perceived by the Palestinians to be unfairly punitive and biased toward Israel, Jordan has been placed in a difficult political position. While King Abdullah II seeks to maintain strong relations with the United States, he rules over a country where the issue of Palestinian rights resonates with much of the Jordanian population; it is estimated that more than half of all Jordanian citizens originate from either the West Bank or the area now comprising the state of Israel. In trying to balance U.S.-Jordanian relations with concern for Palestinian rights, King Abdullah II has refrained from directly criticizing the Trump Administration on its recent moves, while urging the international community to return to the goal of a two-state solution that would ultimately lead to an independent Palestinian state with East Jerusalem as its capital.[10]

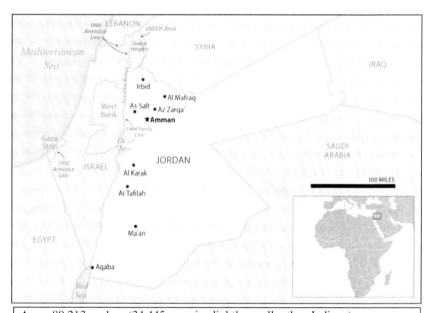

Area: 89,213 sq. km. (34,445 sq. mi., slightly smaller than Indiana)
Population: 8,185,384 (2016); *Amman (capital): 1.155 million (2015)*
Ethnic Groups: Arabs 98%; Circassians 1%; Armenians 1%
Religion: Sunni Muslim 97.2%; Christian 2%
Percent of Population under Age 25: 55% (2016)
Literacy: 95.4% (2015)
Youth Unemployment: 29.3% (2012)
Source: Graphic created by CRS; facts from CIA World Factbook.

Figure 1. Jordan at a Glance.

THE ECONOMY

With few natural resources and a small industrial base, Jordan has an economy that depends heavily on external aid, tourism, expatriate worker

---

[10] For example, see Remarks by His Majesty King Abdullah II at the Plenary Session of the 73rd General Assembly of the United Nations, New York, New York, September 25, 2018.

remittances, and the service sector. Among the long-standing problems Jordan faces are poverty, corruption, slow economic growth, and high levels of unemployment. The government is by far the largest employer, with between one-third and two-thirds of all workers on the state's payroll. These public sector jobs, along with government-subsidized food and fuel, have long been part of the Jordanian government's "social contract" with its citizens.

In the past decade, this arrangement between state and citizen has become more strained. When oil prices skyrocketed between 2007 and 2008, the government had to increase its borrowing in order to continue fuel subsidies. The 2008 global financial crisis was another shock to Jordan's economic system, as it depressed worker remittances from expatriates. The unrest that spread across the region in 2011 further exacerbated Jordan's economic woes, as the influx of hundreds of thousands Syrian refugees increased demand for state services and resources. Moreover, tourist activity, trade, and foreign investment decreased in Jordan after 2011 due to regional instability.

Finally, Jordan, like many other countries, has experienced uneven economic growth, with higher growth in the urban core of the capital Amman and stagnation in the historically poorer and more rural areas of southern Jordan. According to the *Economist Intelligence Unit*, Amman is the most expensive Arab city to live in.[11]

Popular economic grievances have spurred the most vociferous protests in Jordan. Youth unemployment is high, as it is elsewhere in the Middle East, and providing better economic opportunities for younger Jordanians outside of Amman is a major challenge. Large-scale agriculture is not sustainable because of water shortages, so government officials are generally left providing young workers with low-wage, relatively unproductive civil service jobs. How the Jordanian education system and economy can respond to the needs of its youth has been and will continue to be one of the defining domestic challenges for the kingdom in the years ahead.

---

[11] "Asian and European Cities Compete for the Title of most Expensive City," *Economist*, March 18, 2018.

In 2016, the IMF and Jordan reached a three-year, $723 million extended fund facility (EFF) agreement that commits Jordan to improving the business environment for the private sector, reducing budget expenditures, and reforming the tax code. As a result, in 2017 Jordan enacted a Value Added Tax (VAT) on common goods to raise revenue. The government also is in the process of eliminating popular subsidies on critical commodities such as flour.

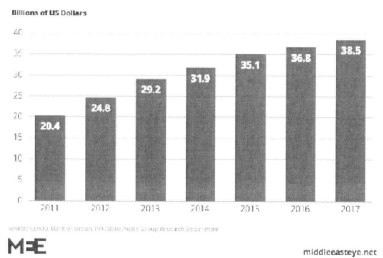

Source: Middle East Eye.

Figure 2. Rising Debt in Jordan.

To comply with IMF-mandated reforms, the Jordanian government drafted a new tax bill to increase personal income taxes and thus raise government revenue and ease the public debt burden (see Figure 2). The draft tax bill would have lowered the minimum taxable income in order to expand the tax base from 4.5% of workers to 10%.[12] It also would have raised corporate taxes on banks and reclassified tax evasion as a felony rather than a misdemeanor.

---

[12] "Austerity and Fury in Jordan," *Economist*, June 7, 2018.

In late May 2018, as the bill drew closer to passage and after an IMF team visited Jordan to review its economic reform plan, demonstrations began across the country. On May 30, Jordanian unions and professional associations held a massive general strike against the tax bill and were joined by many younger protesters who denounced recent price hikes on fuel and electricity. Days later, King Abdullah II ordered the government to freeze a 5.5% increase in the price of fuel and a 19% increase in electricity prices. For days, protests continued throughout the country, with some protesters calling for parliament to be dissolved and the political system to be reformed.

On June 4, Prime Minister Hani Mulki resigned, and King Abdullah II appointed Education Minister and former World Bank economist Omar Razzaz as prime minister. A change in prime minister is considered fairly routine in Jordanian politics, and protesters decried it as an insufficient response to their demands. Large-scale demonstrations continued for two more days, and on June 7 the government announced that it was withdrawing the bill from immediate consideration and sending it back to parliament for revision.

On June 11, Kuwait, the United Arab Emirates, and Saudi Arabia held a summit in Mecca, Saudi Arabia, where they collectively pledged $2.5 billion for Jordan. The aid includes a deposit at the Central Bank of Jordan. The IMF also is supporting the Jordanian government's decision to revise the tax bill, noting that fiscal reforms should not come at the expense of political stability.[13]

This was not the first time that the Jordanian monarchy backtracked on reforms in the face of public pressure. In 1989, 1996, and 2012, Jordanian monarchs responded to mass demonstrations with limited political reforms (new elections and electoral laws, constitutional amendments, anticorruption measures) that did not fundamentally alter the political system.

---

[13] "IMF Reassures Jordan of Continuing Support," *Economist Intelligence Unit*, June 13, 2018.

In times of crisis, the government often appeals for Jordanian unity, while calling the opposition divisive or even disloyal.[14] King Abdullah II's turn toward the Gulf for a financial bailout also has precedents. In 2012, at the height of unrest in the Middle East, the Gulf Cooperation Council countries pledged $5 billion to Jordan.

While the government has used familiar tools in its response to protests, the protesters themselves do not necessarily fit the profile of previous demonstrations. This year's demonstrations were not organized by Islamists or pro-Palestinian activists focusing primarily on political grievances, but were decentralized and focused mainly on economic themes.[15] Many protesters hailed from traditional strongholds of the monarchy, calling into question how King Abdullah II will be able to manage in the future if he is pressured to enact fiscal austerity measures.

In fall 2018, the Jordanian government proposed a new draft tax bill which raises personal and family exemptions for the poorest citizens. The Gulf monarchies also followed through with their $2.5 billion pledge to Jordan, providing $1 billion in central bank deposits, $600 million in loan guarantees, $750 million in direct budgetary support (spread over five years), and $150 million for school construction.[16]

THE WAR IN SYRIA AND ITS IMPACT ON JORDAN

Throughout Syria's civil war, Jordan has prioritized stability on its northern border and has worked with select Syrian rebel groups, the Asad regime, Israel, the United States, and—since its intervention in 2015— the Russian government, in ways intended to shield the kingdom from the war's fallout. In 2017, the United States, Russia, and Jordan agreed to a de-escalation zone along the Jordanian-Syrian border in order to reduce

---

[14] "Jordan's Solid National Unity is what makes it Special — King," *Jordan Times*, September 16, 2015.

[15] "Jordan's Young Protesters say they Learned from Arab Spring Mistakes," *Christian Science Monitor*, June 5, 2018.

[16] "Gulf Allies Pledge Billions in Aid Deals for Bahrain and Jordan," *Bloomberg*, October 4, 2018.

fighting and ensure that no Iranian-backed militias would be based near Jordan or Israel.

In summer 2018, Syrian military forces recaptured southwest Syria. Since then, the Syrian and Jordanian governments have engaged in talks about opening border crossings to allow for a resumption in bilateral trade and the possible return of Syrian refugees residing in Jordan.[17] The kingdom had wanted to ensure that before Syria and Jordan fully normalize relations and reopen borders, the two sides work out a process for legally dealing with Jordanian fighters who traveled to Syria and Iraq.[18] On October 15, 2018, Syria and Jordan reopened the Nassib border crossing to people and goods with the Jordanian government noting that Syrians entering Jordan must first obtain the necessary clearance.[19]

Islamic State (IS) Sympathizers Kill Four Security Personnel in Jordan

In August 2018, IS sympathizers placed an improvised explosive device (IED) under a police vehicle which was stationed at a music festival in a predominately Christian area in the town of Fuheis. The IED remotely detonated, killing one officer. In the process of searching for the perpetrators of the attack, security forces laid siege to their hideout in a residential area of the town of Salt. In an exchange of fire that killed three militants, three more Jordanian personnel were killed. Several other suspects were arrested. This incident was the first terrorist attack inside Jordan since December 2016. According to one analysis, "Returning Jordanian jihadists with operational experience in Syria and Iraq are bringing with them IED and tactical expertise, and the attack shows increased bomb-making capabilities."[20]

---

[17] "Taking It Slow at Jordan's Nasib Border Crossing with Syria," *Policywatch* #3010, The Washington Institute, August 30, 2018.

[18] "Russia key to Reset of Jordanian-Syrian Ties," *Al Monitor*, July 23, 2018.

[19] "Jordan and Syria Reopen Nassib Border Crossing," *Reuters*, October 15, 2018.

[20] "Successful Attack Demonstrates Militant intent to target Jordan's Security Forces and Christians, likely improved IED Capabilities," *Jane's Country Risk Daily Report*, August 13, 2018.

Syrian Refugees in Jordan

Since 2011, the influx of Syrian refugees has placed tremendous strain on Jordan's government and local economies, especially in the northern governorates of Mafraq, Irbid, Ar Ramtha, and Zarqa.

As of October 2018, the United Nations High Commissioner for Refugees (UNHCR) estimates that there are 671,919 registered Syrian refugees in Jordan; 83% of all Syrian refugees live in urban areas, while the remaining 17% live in three camps—Azraq, Zaatari, and the Emirati Jordanian Camp (Mrajeeb al Fhood). Due to Jordan's small population size, it has one of the highest per capita refugee rates in the world.

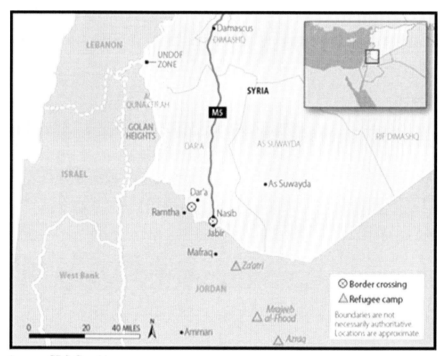

Source: CRS Graphics.
Note: M5 (purple line) is the main north-south highway in Syria.

Figure 3. Syria-Jordan Border.

Another 45,000 refugees are stranded in the desert along the northeastern Jordanian area bordering Syria and Iraq, known as Rukban. Though most of the refugees stranded at Rukban are women and children, a June 2016 IS terrorist attack near the border led Jordanian authorities to close the area, and access to Rukban is sporadic. In fall 2018, Syrian regime forces prevented food from entering the area from the Syrian side, eventually permitting a United Nations aid food delivery on October 17, 2018. According to one report, Rukban is located within a 35-mile, U.S. established "de-confliction zone" surrounding U.S. forces based at the Tanf garrison near the Syrian-Iraqi-Jordanian triborder area.[21]

Source: U.N. Office for the Coordination of Humanitarian Affairs.

Figure 4. Rukban Encampment (June 2018).

---

[21] "Syria approves U.N. Aid Delivery to Remote Camp on Jordan-Syria Border," *Reuters*, October 17, 2018.

Israel, the Palestinians, and U.S. Policy

> **Holy Sites in Jerusale[22]**
>
> Per arrangements with Israel dating back to 1967 and then subsequently confirmed in their 1994 bilateral peace treaty, Israel acknowledges a continuing role for Jordan vis-à-vis Jerusalem's historic Muslim shrines.[23] A Jordanian *waqf* (or Islamic custodial trust) has long administered the Temple Mount (known by Muslims as the Haram al Sharif or Noble Sanctuary) and its holy sites, and this role is key to bolstering the religious legitimacy of the Jordanian royal family's rule. Successive Jordanian monarchs trace their lineage to the Prophet Muhammad. Disputes over Jerusalem that appear to circumscribe King Abdullah II's role as guardian of the Islamic holy sites create a domestic political problem for the King. Jewish worship on the Mount/Haram is prohibited under a long-standing "status quo" arrangement.

The Jordanian government has long described efforts to secure a lasting end to the Israeli-Palestinian conflict as one of its highest priorities. In 1994, Jordan and Israel signed a peace treaty,[24] and King Abdullah II has used his country's relationship with Israel to improve Jordan's standing with Western governments and international financial institutions, on which it relies heavily for external support and aid. Nevertheless, the

---

[22] For more information on Jerusalem and its holy sites, see CRS Report RL33476, *Israel: Background and U.S. Relations*, by Jim Zanotti.

[23] Article 9, Clause 2 of the peace treaty says that "Israel respects the present special role of the Hashemite Kingdom of Jordan in Muslim Holy shrines in Jerusalem. When negotiations on the permanent status will take place, Israel will give high priority to the Jordanian historic role in these shrines." In 2013, the Palestine Liberation Organization (PLO) reaffirmed in a bilateral agreement with Jordan that the King of the Hashemite Kingdom of Jordan will continue to serve as the "Custodian of the Holy Sites in Jerusalem," a title that successive Jordanian monarchs have used since 1924.

[24] Jordan and Israel signed the peace treaty on October 26, 1994. Later, the two countries exchanged ambassadors, Israel returned approximately 131 square miles of territory near the Rift Valley to Jordan, the parliament repealed laws banning contacts with Israel, and the two countries signed a number of bilateral agreements between 1994 and 1996 to normalize economic and cultural links. Water sharing, a recurring problem, was partially resolved in May 1997 when the two countries reached an interim arrangement under which Israel began pumping 72,000 cubic meters of water from Lake Tiberias (the Sea of Galilee) to Jordan per day (equivalent to 26.3 million cubic meters per year—a little over half the target amount envisioned in an annex to the peace treaty).

persistence of Israeli-Palestinian conflict continues to be a major challenge for Jordan. The issue of Palestinian rights resonates with much of the population; it is estimated that more than half of all Jordanian citizens originate from either the West Bank or the area now comprising the state of Israel.[25]

Since December 2017, when the Palestinians broke off high-level political contacts with the United States after President Trump's decision to recognize Jerusalem as Israel's capital and relocate the U.S. embassy there, Jordan has been caught in the middle of ongoing acrimony between the Trump Administration and the Palestinian Authority. Jordan has expressed solidarity with the Palestinians while also trying to encourage the Trump Administration to commit to the two-state solution. In a recent interview with Fox News, King Abdullah II said the following:

> The President [Trump] from day one was committed to a fair and balanced deal for the Israelis and Palestinians to move the process forward. We're not too sure what the plan is, that's part of the problem, so it's more difficult for us to be able to step in and help. What I'm worried about is that we will go from the two state sol ution to a one state sol ution, which is a disaster for all of us in the region, including Israel. If most of the final status issues are being taken off the table then you can understand Palestinian frustration. So how do we build the bridges of confidence between Palestinians and the United States? Whatever people say, you cannot achieve a two state solution or a peace deal without the role of the Americans. So at the moment the Americans are speaking to one side and not speaking to the others and so that's the impasse we are at.[26]

During his January 2018 visit to Jordan, Vice President Mike Pence tried to reassure King Abdullah II that the United States is committed to "continue to respect Jordan's role as the custodian of holy sites; that we take no position on boundaries and final status. Those are subject to

---

[25] For additional background on Jordanian citizens of Palestinian origin, see https://fanack.com/jordan/population/.

[26] "King Abdullah of Jordan on Syria, ISIS and Mideast Peace," *Fox News*, September 26, 2018.

negotiation.... the United States of America remains committed, if the parties agree, to a two-state solution."[27]

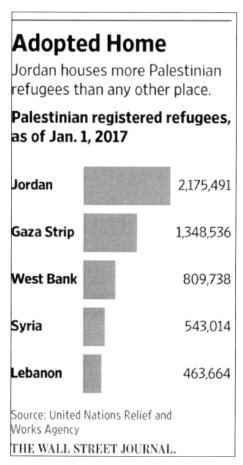

Source: Wall Street Journal and UNRWA.

Figure 5. Jordan and Palestinian Refugees.

In September 2018, the Administration announced that it would end all U.S. contributions to UNRWA. In Jordan, there are 2.1 million registered Palestinian refugees (or descendants of refugees) who have Jordanian citizenship. UNRWA serves the neediest of this population, administering

---

[27] Remarks by Vice President Mike Pence and His Majesty King Abdullah II of Jordan, Al Husseiniya Palace, Amman, Jordan, January 22, 2018.

facilities such as schools and health clinics within refugee "camps" (mostly urban neighborhoods) throughout Jordan.[28] In 2017, UNRWA spent $175.8 million on operations in Jordan.[29] To raise funds to cover UNRWA's budgetary shortfall, Jordan, the European Union, Sweden, Turkey, Germany, and Japan cochaired a September 2018 donor meeting in New York to garner financial and political support for UNRWA on the sidelines of the U.N. General Assembly.

Water Scarcity and Israeli-Jordanian-Palestinian Water Deal

Jordan is among the most water-poor nations in the world and ranks among the top 10 countries with the lowest rate of renewable freshwater per capita.[30] According to the Jordan Water Project at Stanford University, Jordan's increase in water scarcity over the last 60 years is attributable to an approximate 5.5-fold population increase since 1962, a decrease in the flow of the Yarmouk River due to the building of dams upstream in Syria, gradual declines in rainfall by an average of 0.4 mm/year since 1995, and depleting groundwater resources due to overuse.[31]

To secure new sources of freshwater, Jordan has pursued water cooperative projects with its neighbors. On December 9, 2013, Israel, Jordan, and the Palestinian Authority signed a regional water agreement (officially known as the Memorandum of Understanding on the Red-Dead Sea Conveyance Project, see Figure 6) to pave the way for the Red-Dead Canal, a multibillion-dollar project to address declining water levels in the Dead Sea. The agreement was essentially a commitment to a water swap, whereby half of the water pumped from the Red Sea is to be desalinated in a plant to be constructed in Aqaba, Jordan. Some of this water is to then be used in southern Jordan. The rest is to be sold to Israel for use in the Negev

---

[28] There are ten Palestinian refugee camps in Jordan. Throughout the kingdom, UNRWA administers 171 schools and 25 healthy centers.

[29] "Jordan Seeks to Replace Lost Aid," *Wall Street Journal*, September 20, 2018.

[30] See https://data.worldbank.org/indicator/ER.H2O.INTR.PC.

[31] Dr. Steven Gorelick, Cyrus F. Tolman Professor and Senior Fellow, Woods Institute for the Environment - Stanford University, Jordan Water Project, https://pangea.stanford.edu/researchgroups/jordan/.

Desert. In return, Israel is to sell fresh water from the Sea of Galilee to northern Jordan and sell the Palestinian Authority discounted fresh water produced by existing Israeli desalination plants on the Mediterranean. The other half of the water pumped from the Red Sea (or possibly the leftover brine from desalination) is to be channeled to the Dead Sea. The exact allocations of swapped water were not part of the 2013 MOU and were left to future negotiations.

In 2017, with Trump Administration officials seemingly committed to reviving the moribund Israeli-Palestinian peace process, U.S. officials focused on finalizing the terms of the 2013 MOU. In July 2017, the White House announced that U.S. Special Representative for International Negotiations Jason Greenblatt had "successfully supported the Israeli and Palestinian efforts to bridge the gaps and reach an agreement," with the Israeli government agreeing to sell the Palestinian Authority (PA) 32 million cubic meters (MCM) of fresh water.[32]

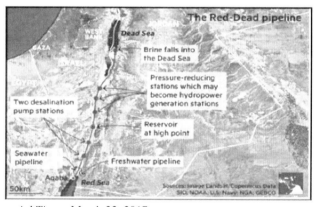

Source: *Financial Times*, March 22, 2017.

Figure 6. Red-Dead Sea Conveyance Project.

However, one recent report indicates that some Israeli officials may have misgivings about the project and are seeking to pull out of the deal.[33] According to one unnamed U.S. official cited by the report, "The United

---

[32] The White House, Office of the Press Secretary, Donald J. Trump Administration Welcomes Israeli-Palestinian Deal to Implement the Red-Dead Water Agreement, July 13, 2017.
[33] "Scoop: U.S. Pressing Israel to implement Pipeline Project with Jordan," *Axios*, July 26, 2018.

States told Israel that the U.S. supports the project and expects Israel to live up to its obligations under the Red-Dead agreement or find a suitable alternative that is acceptable to Israel and Jordan."[34]

Congress has supported the Red-Dead Sea Conveyance Project. P.L. 114-113, the FY2016 Omnibus Appropriations Act, specifies that $100 million in Economic Support Funds be set aside for water sector support for Jordan, to support the Red Sea-Dead Sea water project. In September 2016, USAID notified Congress that it intended to spend the $100 million in FY2016 ESF-OCO on Phase One of the project.[35]

U.S. FOREIGN ASSISTANCE TO JORDAN

Table 1. U.S. Foreign Assistance to Jordan, SFOPS Appropriations: FY2014-FY2019 Request current dollars in millions

Account	FY2014	FY2015	FY2016	FY2017	FY2018 est.	FY2019 Request
ESF	$700.000	$615.000	$812.350	$832.350	$1,082.400	$910.800
FMF	$300.000	$385.000	$450.000	$470.000	$425.000	$350.000
NADR	$7.000	$7.700	$8.850	$13.600	$13.600	—
IMET	$3.500	$3.800	$3.733	$3.879	$4.000	$3.800
Total	$1,010.500	$1,011.500	$1,274.933	$1,319.830	$1,525.000	$1,264.600

Source: U.S. State Department.

Notes: Funding levels in this table include both enduring (base) and Overseas Contingency Operation (OCO) funds. The Department of Defense also has provided Jordan with military assistance. According to the Department of State, "Jordan is the third largest recipient of FMF funds globally and the single largest recipient of DoD Section 333 funding."

---

[34] Ibid.

[35] According to USAID, "Phase 1 includes construction of a seawater desalination plant located in Aqaba, Jordan on the Red Sea, that will produce 65 MCM of water to be shared between Israel and Jordan, and a pipeline to convey approximately 100 MCM of brine mixed with 135 MCM of seawater, to the Dead Sea. Plans include 35 MCM of desalinated water from Aqaba to the Israeli Water Authority to serve populations in southern Israel, and the purchase up to 50 MCM of fresh water from the Sea of Galilee for use in northern Jordan. As part of the regional project, Israel will sell up to 30 MCM of fresh water to the Palestinian Authority for use in the West Bank and Gaza." See, USAID Congressional Notification # 146, Jordan Country Narrative, September 30, 2016.

The United States has provided economic and military aid to Jordan since 1951 and 1957, respectively. Total bilateral U.S. aid (overseen by State and the Department of Defense) to Jordan through FY2016 amounted to approximately $19.2 billion. Jordan also has received hundreds of millions in additional military aid since FY2014 channeled through the Defense Department's various security assistance accounts.

New U.S.-Jordanian Agreement on Foreign Assistance

On February 14, 2018, then-U.S. Secretary of State Rex W. Tillerson and Jordanian Minister of Foreign Affairs Ayman Safadi signed a new Memorandum of Understanding (or MOU) on U.S. foreign assistance to Jordan (Figure 7). The MOU, the third such agreement between the United and Jordan, commits the United States to provide $1.275 billion per year in bilateral foreign assistance over a five-year period for a total of $6.375 billion (FY2018-FY2022).

Source: U.S. State Department.

Figure 7. New U.S.-Jordanian MOU; Amman, Jordan.

This latest MOU represents a 27% increase in the U.S. commitment to Jordan above the previous iteration and is the first five-year MOU with the kingdom. The previous two MOU agreements had been in effect for three

Jordan: Background and U.S. Relations 149

years. According to the U.S. State Department, the United States is the single largest donor of assistance to Jordan, and the new MOU commits the United States to provide a minimum of $750 million of Economic Support Funds (ESF) and $350 million of Foreign Military Financing (FMF) to Jordan between FY2018 and FY2022.[36] In line with the new MOU, for FY2019 President Trump is requesting $1.271 billion for Jordan, including $910.8 million in ESF, $350 million in FMF, and $3.8 million in International Military Education and Training (IMET).

Economic Assistance

The United States provides economic aid to Jordan both as a cash transfer and for USAID programs in Jordan. The Jordanian government uses cash transfers to service its foreign debt. Approximately 40% to 60% of Jordan's ESF allotment may go toward the cash transfer.[37] USAID programs in Jordan focus on a variety of sectors including democracy assistance, water preservation, and education (particularly building and renovating public schools). In the democracy sector, U.S. assistance has supported capacity-building programs for the parliament's support offices, the Jordanian Judicial Council, the Judicial Institute, and the Ministry of Justice.

The International Republican Institute and the National Democratic Institute also have received U.S. grants to train, among other groups, the Jordanian Independent Election Commission (IEC), Jordanian political parties, and members of parliament. In the water sector, the bulk of U.S. economic assistance is devoted to optimizing the management of scarce water resources, as Jordan is one of the most water-deprived countries in the world. USAID is currently subsidizing several waste treatment and water distribution projects in the Jordanian cities of Amman, Mafraq,

---

[36] U.S. State Department, New U.S.-Jordan Memorandum of Understanding on Bilateral Foreign Assistance to Jordan, Fact Sheet, February 14, 2018.

[37] In 2016, the United States provided $470 million in ESF to Jordan as a cash transfer (59% of the total ESF allocation for Jordan).

Aqaba, and Irbid. USAID also is helping Jordanian water utilities on advanced leak detection capability.[38]

Humanitarian Assistance for Syrian Refugees in Jordan

The U.S. State Department estimates that, since large-scale U.S. aid to Syrian refugees began in FY2012, it has allocated more than $1.1 billion in humanitarian assistance from global accounts for programs in Jordan to meet the needs of Syrian refugees and, indirectly, to ease the burden on Jordan.[39] U.S. aid supports refugees living in camps (~141,000) and those living in towns and cities (~500,000). According to the State Department, U.S. humanitarian assistance is provided both as cash assistance and through programs to meet basic needs, such as child health care, water, and sanitation.

The U.S. government provides cross-border humanitarian and stabilization assistance to Syrians via programs monitored and implemented through the Embassy Amman-based Southern Syria Assistance Platform. This includes humanitarian assistance to areas of southern and eastern Syria that are otherwise inaccessible, as well as congressionally authorized stabilization and nonlethal assistance to opposition-held areas in southern Syria. According to USAID, U.S. humanitarian assistance funds are enabling UNICEF to provide health assistance for Syrian populations sheltering at the informal Rukban and Hadalat settlements along the Syria-Jordan border berm, including daily water trucking, the rehabilitation of a water borehole, and installation of a water treatment unit in Hadalat.[40]

---

[38] Congressional Notification #53, Country Narrative, Jordan, USAID, February 16, 2018.
[39] U.S. State Department, Fact Sheet: New U.S.-Jordan Memorandum of Understanding on Bilateral Foreign Assistance to Jordan, February 14, 2018.
[40] USAID, "Syria Complex Emergency - Fact Sheet #4," April 27, 2017.

Loan Guarantees

The Obama Administration provided three loan guarantees to Jordan, totaling $3.75 billion.[41] These include the following:

- In September 2013, the United States announced that it was providing its first-ever loan guarantee to the Kingdom of Jordan. USAID notified Congress of its intent to obligate up to $120 million in FY2013 ESF-OCO to support a $1.25 billion, seven-year sovereign loan guarantee for Jordan.
- In February 2014, during a visit to the United States by King Abdullah II, the Obama Administration announced that it would offer Jordan an additional five-year, $1 billion loan guarantee. USAID notified Congress of its intent to obligate $72 million out of the $340 million of FY2014 ESF-OCO for Jordan to support the subsidy costs for the second loan guarantee.
- In June 2015, the Obama Administration provided its third loan guarantee to Jordan of $1.5 billion. USAID notified Congress of its intent to obligate $221 million in FY2015 ESF to support the subsidy costs of the third loan guarantee to Jordan.[42]

Military Assistance

Foreign Military Financing

U.S.-Jordanian military cooperation is a key component in bilateral relations. U.S. military assistance is primarily directed toward enabling the

---

[41] Congress initially authorized additional economic assistance to Jordan in Section 7041 of P.L. 112-74, the Consolidated Appropriations Act, 2012. P.L. 113-6, the Consolidated and Further Continuing Appropriations Act, 2013 specified that such assistance should take the form of a loan guarantee. Section 1706 (j) of the same act also appropriated $30 million (from FY2011) for the initial cost of sovereign loan guarantees. Congress reauthorized loan guarantees for Jordan in Section 7034(r)(1) of P.L. 113-235 (Consolidated and Further Continuing Appropriations Act, 2015). P.L. 114-113, the FY2016 Omnibus Appropriations Act, once again reauthorized loan guarantees to Jordan.
[42] Op. cit., Congressional Notification #74.

Jordanian military to procure and maintain conventional weapons systems.[43] The United States and Jordan have jointly developed a five-year procurement plan for the Jordanian Armed Forces in order to prioritize Jordan's needs and procurement budget using congressionally appropriated Foreign Military Financing (FMF). FMF grants have enabled the Royal Jordanian Air Force to procure munitions for its F-16 fighter aircraft and a fleet of 28 UH-60 Blackhawk helicopters.[44] On February 18, 2016, President Obama signed the United States-Jordan Defense Cooperation Act of 2015 (P.L. 114-123), which authorizes expedited review and an increased value threshold for proposed arms sales to Jordan for a period of three years.

Defense Department Assistance

As a result of the Syrian civil war and Operation Inherent Resolve against IS, the United States has increased military aid to Jordan and channeled these increases through Defense Department-managed accounts. Although Jordan still receives the bulk of U.S. military aid from the FMF account, Congress has authorized defense appropriations to strengthen Jordan's border security. Jordan may receive funding from various DOD accounts, such as the following:

- 10 U.S.C. 333—Commonly referred to as DOD's "Global Train and Equip authority." The Secretary of Defense may use this to build the capacity of a foreign country's national security forces for a range of purposes, including counterterrorism, countering weapons of mass destruction, counternarcotics, maritime security, military intelligence, and participation in coalition operations.[45]

---

[43] According to *Jane's Defence Procurement Budgets*, Jordan's 2017 defense budget was $2.01billion. See *Jane's Defence Budgets*, Jordan, February 6, 2018.

[44] U.S. Department of State, U.S. Security Cooperation with Jordan, Fact Sheet, Bureau of Political-Military Affairs, March 23, 2018.

[45] DOD's global train and equip activities were originally authorized by Section 1206 (FY2006 NDAA, P.L. 109-163), as amended. Section 1206 was the first major DOD authority to be used expressly for the purpose of training and equipping the national military forces of foreign countries worldwide. The authority was later codified as 10 U.S.C. 2282 in the FY2015 NDAA (P.L. 113-291). Activities permitted under 10 U.S.C. 2282 have been

- Counterterrorism Partnerships Fund (CTPF) (FY2015-FY2016)—Under the FY2015 NDAA (P.L. 113-291) and the defense appropriations measure for the same year (P.L. 113-235), Congress established a DOD Counterterrorism Partnerships Fund (CTPF), which provided increased funding resources for counterterrorism training and equipment transfers in Africa and the Middle East.[46] Section 1534 of FY2015 NDAA stipulated that funds could be transferred to other accounts for use under existing DOD authority established by "any other provision of law." The FY2017 NDAA (P.L. 114-328) expanded and consolidated DOD's "global train and equip" authority, along with various others, under Section 333 of a new Chapter 16 of Title 10, U.S.C (see above). Since then, Congress has not appropriated funds for DOD's CTPF, instead directing funds under DOD's Operation and Maintenance, Defense-Wide account for a range of security cooperation activities.

- Coalition Support Fund (CSF)—CSF authorizes the Secretary of Defense to reimburse key cooperating countries for logistical, military, and other support, including access, to or in connection with U.S. military operations in Iraq, Afghanistan, or Syria and to assist such nations with U.S.-funded equipment, supplies, and training. CSF is authorized by Section 1233 (FY2008 NDAA, P.L. 110-181), as amended and extended.

- Counter-ISIS Train and Equip Fund (CTEF)—The National Defense Authorization Act for Fiscal Year 2017 (P.L. 114-328) and The Consolidated Appropriations Act, 2017 (P.L. 115-31) created the Counter-ISIL Train and Equip Fund (CTEF), since

---

incorporated into a new, broader global train and equip authority established by Section 1241(c) of the FY2017 NDAA: 10 U.S.C. 333. This provision also repealed prior authorities, such as: 10 U.S.C. 2282: Building capacity of foreign forces; Section 1204 (FY2014 NDAA , P.L. 113-66): Authority to conduct activities to enhance the capabilities of foreign countries to respond to incidents involving weapons of mass destruction; Section 1207 (FY2014 NDAA, P.L. 113-66): Assistance to the Government of Jordan for border security operations; and Section 1033 (FY1998 NDAA, P.L. 105-85, as amended): Assistance for additional counternarcotics support for specified countries.

[46] See CRS In Focus IF10040, *DOD Train and Equip Authorities to Counter the Islamic State*, by Nina M. Serafino.

renamed the Counter-ISIS Train and Equip Fund. The CTEF is designed to allow the Secretary of Defense, with the concurrence of the Secretary of State, to transfer funds, equipment, and related capabilities to partner countries in order to counter emergent ISIS threats. The CTEF is the primary account for the Syria and Iraq Train and Equip Programs.[47] It replaced the Iraq Train and Equip Fund (ITEF).

- Cooperative Threat Reduction—DOD is authorized, under Chapter 48 of Title 10, U.S.C., to build foreign countries' capacity to prevent nuclear proliferation. Over the past five years, the Defense Threat Reduction Agency has provided training and equipment to border security forces in several Middle Eastern countries under this authority, including Jordan, Iraq, Turkey, and Tunisia.[48]

Excess Defense Articles

In 1996, the United States granted Jordan Major Non-NATO Ally (MNNA) status, a designation that, among other things, makes Jordan eligible to receive excess U.S. defense articles, training, and loans of equipment for cooperative research and development.[49] In the last five years, Jordan has received excess U.S. defense articles, including two C-130 aircraft, HAWK MEI-23E missiles, and cargo trucks.

RECENT LEGISLATION

P.L. 115-14, the Consolidated Appropriations Act, 2018, provided the following for Jordan:

---

[47] The underlying authorities for the Department of Defense Syria and Iraq train and equip programs are Sections 1209 and 1236 of P.L. 113-291, as amended.

[48] CRS Report R43143, *The Evolution of Cooperative Threat Reduction: Issues for Congress*, by Mary Beth D. Nikitin and Amy F. Woolf.

[49] See Designation of Jordan As Major Non-NATO Ally, Determination of President of the United States, No. 97-4, November 12, 1996, 61 F.R. 59809.

Jordan: Background and U.S. Relations

- Appropriates "not less than" $1.525 billion in total U.S. assistance for Jordan, of which "not less than" $1.082 billion is ESF and "not less than" $425 million is FMF;
- Reauthorizes funds from the Operation and Maintenance, Defense-Wide account to "enhance the ability of the armed forces of Jordan to increase or sustain security along its borders";
- Appropriates "up to" $500 million for the Defense Security Cooperation Agency in the Operation and Maintenance, Defense-Wide account to be used to support the armed forces of Jordan and to enhance security along its borders;
- Reauthorizes funds from the Counter-ISIS Train And Equip Fund (CTEF) to enhance the border security of nations adjacent to conflict areas including Jordan, Lebanon, Egypt, and Tunisia resulting from actions of the Islamic State of Iraq and Syria;
- Reauthorizes ESF to be used to support possible new loan guarantees for Jordan;
- Authorizes ESF to be used to support the creation of an Enterprise Fund in Jordan.

P.L. 115-245, the Department of Defense and Labor, Health and Human Services, and Education Appropriations Act, 2019 and Continuing Appropriations Act, 2019, provides the following for Jordan:

- Reauthorizes funds from the Operation and Maintenance, Defense-Wide account to "enhance the ability of the armed forces of Jordan to increase or sustain security along its borders";
- Appropriates "up to" $500 million for the Defense Security Cooperation Agency in the Operation and Maintenance, Defense-Wide account to be used to support the armed forces of Jordan and to enhance security along its borders;
- Reauthorizes funds from the Counter-ISIS Train and Equip Fund (CTEF) to enhance the border security of nations adjacent to conflict areas including Jordan, Lebanon, Egypt, and Tunisia resulting from actions of the Islamic State of Iraq and Syria.

H.R. 2646, United States-Jordan Defense Cooperation Extension Act, would amend the United States-Jordan Defense Cooperation Act of 2015 to extend Jordan's inclusion among the countries eligible for certain streamlined defense sales until December 31, 2022. The bill also would authorize an enterprise fund to provide assistance to Jordan. It was passed in the House on February 5, 2018.

Table 2. U.S. Foreign Aid Obligations to Jordan: 1946-2016 current U.S. dollars in millions

Account	1946-2011	FY2012	FY2013	FY2014	FY2015	FY2016	1946-2016
FMF	3,380.800	300.000	284.800	300.000	385.000	450.000	5,100.600
ESF	6,043.800	485.500	542.900	329.600	594.700	812.350	8,808.850
INCLE	3.800	1.200	—	0.800	0.200	—	6.000
NADR	110.600	18.400	12.200	6.100	5.400	8.850	166.300
IMET	70.700	3.700	3.600	3.600	3.800	3.733	89.400
MRA	82.100	35.200	167.100	157.600	162.500	tbd	604.500
Other	2,963.500	330.100	199.400	345.700	365.400	322.930	4,527.030
Total	12,655.300	1,174.100	1,210.000	1,143.400	1,517.000	1,597.863	19,297.663

Source: USAID Overseas Loans and Grants, July 1, 1945-September 30, 2015.

Notes: "Other" accounts include economic and military assistance programs administered by USAID, State, and other federal agencies which are funded at less than $2 million annually. It also includes larger, more recent funding through the International Disaster Assistance account (IDA), Millennium Challenge Account, and several defense department funding accounts. It also encapsulates much larger legacy programs (food aid), some of which have been phased out over time.

In: The Middle East
Editor: Doyle Keller

ISBN: 978-1-53616-191-5
© 2019 Nova Science Publishers, Inc.

Chapter 5

LEBANON*

Carla E. Humud

ABSTRACT

Since having its boundaries drawn by France after the First World War, Lebanon has struggled to define its national identity. Its population included Christian, Sunni Muslim, and Shia Muslim communities of roughly comparable size, and with competing visions for the country. Seeking to avoid sectarian conflict, Lebanese leaders created a confessional system that allocated power among the country's religious sects according to their percentage of the population. The system continues to be based on Lebanon's last official census, which was conducted in 1932.

As Lebanon's demographics have shifted over the years, Muslim communities have pushed for the political status quo, favoring Maronite Christians, to be revisited, while the latter have worked to maintain their privileges. This tension has at times manifested itself in violence, such as during the country's 15-year civil war, but also in political disputes such as disagreements over revisions to Lebanon's electoral law. To date,

---

* This is an edited, reformatted and augmented version of Congressional Research Service, Publication No. R44759, dated October 5, 2018.

domestic political conflicts continue to be shaped in part by the influence of external actors, including Syria and Iran.

The United States has sought to bolster forces that could serve as a counterweight to Syrian and Iranian influence in Lebanon, providing more than $1.7 billion in military assistance to Lebanon with the aim of creating a national force strong enough to counter nonstate actors and secure the country's borders. Hezbollah's armed militia is sometimes described as more effective than the Lebanese Armed Forces (LAF), and has also undertaken operations along the border to counter the infiltration of armed groups from the war in neighboring Syria. U.S. policy in Lebanon has been undermined by Iran and Syria, both of which exercise significant influence in the country, including through support for Hezbollah. The question of how best to marginalize Hezbollah and other anti-U.S. Lebanese actors without provoking civil conflict among Lebanese sectarian political forces has remained a key challenge for U.S. policymakers.

U.S. assistance to Lebanon also has addressed the large-scale refugee crisis driven by the ongoing war in neighboring Syria. There are over 1 million Syrian refugees registered with the U.N. High Commissioner for Refugees (UNHCR) in Lebanon, in addition to a significant existing community of Palestinian refugees. This has given Lebanon (a country of roughly 4.3 million citizens in 2010) the highest per capita refugee population in the world. Lebanon's infrastructure has been unable to absorb the refugee population, which some government officials describe as a threat to the country's security. Since 2015, the government has taken steps to close the border to those fleeing Syria, and has implemented measures that have made it more difficult for existing refugees to remain in Lebanon legally.

At the same time, Hezbollah has played an active role in the ongoing fighting in Syria. The experience gained by Hezbollah in the Syria conflict has raised questions about how the eventual return of these fighters to Lebanon could impact the country's domestic stability or affect the prospects for renewed conflict with Israel.

This chapter provides an overview of Lebanon and current issues of U.S. interest. It provides background information, analyzes recent developments and key policy debates, and tracks legislation, U.S. assistance, and recent congressional action.

HISTORICAL BACKGROUND

Prior to World War I, the territories comprising modern-day Lebanon were governed as separate administrative regions of the Ottoman Empire.

After the war ended and the Ottoman Empire collapsed, the 1916 Sykes-Picot agreement divided the empire's Arab provinces into British and French zones of influence.

Population: 6,229,794 (2017 est., includes Syrian refugees)
Religion: Muslim 54% (27% Sunni, 27% Shia), Christian 40.5% (includes 21% Maronite Catholic, 8% Greek Orthodox, 5% Greek Catholic, 6.5% other Christian), Druze 5.6%, very small numbers of Jews, Baha'is, Buddhists, Hindus, and Mormons.
Note: 18 religious sects recognized
Land: (Area) 10,400 sq km, 0.7 the size of Connecticut; (Borders) Israel, 81 km; Syria, 403 km GDP: (PPP, growth rate, per capita 2017 est.) $87.8 billion, 1.5%, $19,500
Budget: (spending, deficit, 2017 est.) $15.99 billion, -9.7% of GDP
Public Debt: (2017 est.) 142.2% of GDP
Source: Created by CRS using ESRI, Google Maps, and Good Shepherd Engineering and Computing. CIA, The World Factbook data, June 7, 2018.

Figure 1. Lebanon at a Glance.

The area constituting modern day Lebanon was granted to France, and in 1920, French authorities announced the creation of Greater Lebanon. To

160 *Carla E. Humud*

form this new entity, French authorities combined the Maronite Christian enclave of Mount Lebanon— semiautonomous under Ottoman rule—with the coastal cities of Beirut, Tripoli, Sidon, and Tyre and their surrounding districts. These latter districts were (with the exception of Beirut) primarily Muslim and had been administered by the Ottomans as part of the *vilayet* (province) of Syria. These administrative divisions created the boundaries of the modern Lebanese state; historians note that "Lebanon, in the frontiers defined on 1 September 1920, had never existed before in history."[1] The new Muslim residents of Greater Lebanon—many with long-established economic links to the Syrian interior—opposed the move, and some called for integration with Syria as part of a broader postwar Arab nationalist movement. Meanwhile, many Maronite Christians—some of whom also self-identified as ethnically distinct from their Arab neighbors—sought a Christian state under French protection. The resulting debate over Lebanese identity would shape the new country's politics for decades to come.

Independence

In 1943, Lebanon gained independence from France. Lebanese leaders agreed to an informal National Pact, in which each of the country's officially recognized religious groups were to be represented in government in direct relation to their share of the population, based on the 1932 census. The presidency was to be reserved for a Maronite Christian (the largest single denomination at that time), the prime minister post for a Sunni Muslim, and the speaker of parliament for a Shia. Lebanon has not held a census since 1932, amid fears (largely among Christians) that any demographic changes revealed by a new census—such as a Christian population that was no longer the majority—would upset the status quo.[2]

---

[1] Fawwaz Traboulsi, *A History of Modern Lebanon*, Pluto Press, London, 2007, p. 75.
[2] A demographic study conducted in 2011 by Statistics Lebanon, a Beirut-based research firm, reported that Lebanon's population was 27% Sunni, 27% Shia, and 21% Maronite Christian, with the remainder composed of smaller Christian denominations, and Druze. See, "Lebanon," State Department International Religious Freedom Report for 2011. See

Civil War

In the decades that followed, Lebanon's sectarian balance remained a point of friction between communities. Christian dominance in Lebanon was challenged by a number of events, including the influx of (primarily Sunni Muslim) Palestinian refugees as a result of the Arab-Israeli conflict, and the mobilization of Lebanon's Shia Muslim community in the south—which had been politically and economically marginalized. These and other factors would lead the country into a civil war that lasted from 1975 to 1990 and killed an estimated 150,000 people. While the war pitted sectarian communities against one another, there was also significant fighting within communities.

Foreign Intervention

The civil war drew in a number of external actors, including Syria, Israel, Iran, and the United States. Syrian military forces intervened in the conflict in 1976, and remained in Lebanon for another 29 years. Israel sent military forces into Lebanon in 1978 and 1982, and conducted several subsequent airstrikes in the country. In 1978, the U.N. Security Council established the United Nations Interim Force in Lebanon (UNIFIL) to supervise the withdrawal of Israeli forces from southern Lebanon, which was not complete until 2000.[3] In the early 1980s, Israel's military presence in the heavily Shia area of southern Lebanon began to be contested by an emerging militant group that would become Hezbollah, backed by Iran. The United States deployed forces to Lebanon in 1982 as part of a multinational peacekeeping force, but withdrew its forces after the 1983 marine barracks bombing in Beirut, which killed 241 U.S. personnel.

---

also, "Lebanon," CIA World Factbook, November 2016. Other studies estimate that Lebanese Shia slightly outnumber Sunnis See: "Lebanon: Census and sensibility," *The Economist*, November 5, 2016.

[3] UNIFIL forces remain deployed in southern Lebanon, comprising more than 10,500 peacekeepers from 41 countries.

Taif Accords

In 1989, the parties signed the Taif Accords, beginning a process that would bring the war to a close the following year. The agreement adjusted and formalized Lebanon's confessional system, further entrenching what some described as an unstable power dynamic between different sectarian groups at the national level. The political rifts created by this system allowed Syria to present itself as the arbiter between rivals, and pursue its own interests inside Lebanon in the wake of the war. The participation of Syrian troops in Operation Desert Storm to expel Iraqi forces from Kuwait reportedly facilitated what some viewed as the tacit acceptance by the United States of Syria's continuing role in Lebanon. The Taif Accords also called for all Lebanese militias to be dismantled, and most were reincorporated into the Lebanese Armed Forces. However, Hezbollah refused to disarm—claiming that its militia forces were legitimately engaged in resistance to the Israeli military presence in southern Lebanon.

Hariri Assassination

In February 2005, former Lebanese Prime Minister Rafik Hariri—a prominent anti-Syria Sunni politician—was assassinated in a car bombing in downtown Beirut. The attack galvanized Lebanese society against the Syrian military presence in the country and triggered a series of street protests known as the "Cedar Revolution." Under pressure, Syria withdrew its forces from Lebanon in the subsequent months, although Damascus continued to influence domestic Lebanese politics. While the full details of the attack are unknown, the Special Tribunal for Lebanon (STL) has indicted five members of Hezbollah and is conducting trials in absentia.[4]

---

[4] The United Nations Security Council created the STL as an independent judicial organization in Resolution 1757 of May 2007. The STL has worked from its headquarters in Leidschendam, the Netherlands, since March 2009, and consists of three chambers, prosecutors and defense offices, and an administrative Registrar. For additional details, see Special Tribunal for Lebanon Seventh Annual Report (2015-2016). See also, "The Hezbollah Connection," *New York Times Magazine*, February 15, 2015.

Closing arguments in the case were concluded in September 2018; a verdict is expected in 2019.[5] The Hariri assassination reshaped Lebanese politics into the two major blocks known today: March 8 and March 14, which represented pro-Syria and anti-Syria segments of the political spectrum, respectively (see Figure 2).

2006 Hezbollah-Israel War

In July 2006, Hezbollah captured two Israeli soldiers along the border, sparking a 34-day war. The Israeli air campaign and ground operation aimed at degrading Hezbollah resulted in widespread damage to Lebanon's civilian infrastructure, killing roughly 1,190 Lebanese, and displacing a quarter of Lebanon's population.[6] In turn, Hezbollah launched thousands of rockets into Israel, killing 163 Israelis.[7] U.N. Security Council Resolution 1701 brokered a cease-fire between the two sides.

2008 Doha Agreement

In late 2006, a move by the Lebanese government to endorse the STL led Hezbollah and its Shia political ally Amal to withdraw from the government, triggering an 18 month political crisis. In May 2008, a cabinet decision to shut down Hezbollah's private telecommunications network—which the group reportedly viewed as critical to its ability to fight Israel—led Hezbollah fighters to seize control of parts of Beirut. The resulting sectarian violence raised questions regarding Lebanon's risk for renewed civil war, as well as concerns about the willingness of Hezbollah to deploy its militia force in response to a decision by Lebanon's civilian government. Qatar helped broker a political settlement between rival

---

[5] "Hariri verdict likely in 2019 as STL enters final stretch," *Daily Star*, August 18, 2018.
[6] Human Rights Watch, *Why They Died: Civilian Casualties in Lebanon during the 2006 War*, September 5, 2007.
[7] Human Rights Watch, *Civilians under Assault: Hezbollah's Rocket Attacks on Israel in the 2006 War*, August 2007.

War in Syria

In 2011, unrest broke out in neighboring Syria. Hezbollah moved to support the Asad regime, eventually mobilizing to fight inside Syria. Meanwhile, prominent Lebanese Sunni leaders sided with the Sunni rebels. As rebel forces fighting along the Lebanese border were defeated by the Syrian military—with Hezbollah assistance—rebels fell back, some into Lebanon. Syrian refugees also began to flood into the country. Beginning in 2013, a wave of retaliatory attacks targeting Shia communities and Hezbollah strongholds inside Lebanon threatened to destabilize the domestic political balance as each side accused the other of backing terrorism. The Lebanese Armed Forces (LAF) and Hezbollah have both worked to contain border attacks by Syria-based groups such as the Islamic State and the Nusra Front.

ISSUES FOR CONGRESS

U.S. policy in Lebanon has sought to limit threats posed by Hezbollah both domestically and to Israel, bolster Lebanon's ability to protect its borders, and build state capacity to deal with the refugee influx. Iranian influence in Lebanon via its ties to Hezbollah, the potential for renewed armed conflict between Hezbollah and Israel, and Lebanon's internal political dynamics complicate the provision of U.S. assistance. Lebanon continues to be an arena for conflict between regional states, as local actors aligned with Syria and Iran vie for power against those that seek support from Saudi Arabia, which backs Sunni elements in Lebanon, and the United States.

As Congress reviews aid to Lebanon, Members continue to debate the best ways to meet U.S. policy objectives:

- Weakening Hezbollah and building state capacity. The United States has sought to weaken Hezbollah without provoking a direct confrontation that could undermine Lebanon's stability. Both Obama and Trump Administration officials have argued that Hezbollah's influence in Lebanon can be addressed by strengthening Lebanon's legitimate security institutions, including the LAF.[8] However, some Members have argued that Hezbollah has increased cooperation with the LAF, and questioned requests for continuing Foreign Military Financing (FMF) assistance to Lebanon.[9] Adjacent Hezbollah and LAF operations along the Syrian border in mid-2017 against Islamic State and Al Qaeda-affiliated militants raised additional questions about de-confliction and coordination between the military and Hezbollah fighters.

- Defending Lebanon's borders. Beginning in late 2012, Lebanon faced a wave of attacks from Syria-based groups, some of which sought to gain a foothold in Lebanon. U.S. policymakers have sought to ensure that the Lebanese Armed Forces have the tools they need to defend Lebanon's borders against encroachment by the Islamic State and other armed nonstate groups.

- Assisting Syrian refugees. While seeking to protect Lebanon's borders from infiltration by the Islamic State and other terrorist groups, the United States also has called for Lebanon to keep its border open to Syrian refugees fleeing violence. The United States had, as of February 2018, provided nearly $1.6 billion in humanitarian aid to Lebanon since FY2012,[10] much of it designed to lessen the impact of the refugee surge on host communities.

---

[8] State Department Daily Press Briefing by Spokesperson John Kirby, March 8, 2016; "Background Briefing: Updating on Secretary Tillerson's Trip to Amman, Jordan; Ankara, Turkey; Beirut, Lebanon; Cairo, Egypt; and Kuwait City, Kuwait," State Department Press Release, February 14, 2018.

[9] Transcript, House Foreign Affairs Subcommittee on Middle East and North Africa hearing on U.S. policy towards Lebanon, April 28, 2016; Transcript, Senate Foreign Relations Subcommittee on Near East, South Asia, Central Asia, and Counterterrorism hearing on Lebanon, March 21, 2018.

[10] Remarks of former Secretary of State Rex Tillerson at press availability with Lebanese Prime Minister Saad Hariri, February 15, 2018.

- Strengthening government institutions. U.S. economic aid to Lebanon aims to strengthen Lebanese institutions and their capacity to provide essential public services. Slow economic growth and high levels of public debt have limited government spending on basic public services, and this gap has been filled in part by sectarian patronage networks, including some affiliated with Hezbollah. U.S. programs to improve education, increase service provision, and foster economic growth are intended to make communities less vulnerable to recruitment by extremist groups.

POLITICS

Lebanon is a parliamentary republic. The confessional political system established by the 1943 National Pact and formalized by the 1989 Taif Accords divides power among Lebanon's three largest religious communities (Christian, Sunni, Shia) in a manner designed to prevent any one group from dominating the others. Major decisions can only be reached through consensus, setting the stage for prolonged political deadlock.

2018 Legislative Elections

Lebanon was due for parliamentary elections in 2013. However, disagreements over the details of a new electoral law (passed in June 2017) delayed the elections until May 6, 2018. The results of the May elections gave parties allied with Hezbollah an increase in their share of seats from roughly 44% to 53%. The political coalition known as March 8, which includes Hezbollah, the Shia Amal Movement, the Free Patriotic Movement (FPM) and allied parties, won 68 seats according to Lebanese vote tallies.[11] This is enough to secure a simple majority (65 out of 128 seats) in parliament, but falls short of the two-thirds majority needed to push through major initiatives such as a revision to the constitution. Hezbollah itself did not gain any additional seats.

The rival March 14 coalition (which includes the Sunni Future Movement, the Maronite Lebanese Forces, and allied MPs) lost 10 seats. Prime Minister Hariri's Future Movement absorbed the largest loss (roughly a third of its seats) but remains the largest Sunni bloc in parliament. The Lebanese Forces party was among the largest winners, increasing its share of seats from 8 to 14.

Government Formation Stalls

The conclusion of legislative elections cleared the way for the formation of a new government, in the shape of a new cabinet. Known formally as the Council of Ministers, the cabinet is comprised of 30 ministerial posts, currently distributed among 10 parties. On May 24, President Aoun reappointed Saad Hariri as prime minister and charged him with forming a new government. This will be Hariri's third term as prime minister (he previously served from 2009 to 2011 and 2016 to 2018). Since May, Hariri has held consultations with political blocs to select ministers for a new cabinet, which must be approved by the president. In early September, Hariri presented a draft cabinet proposal to President Aoun, who declined to endorse it—reportedly over concerns regarding Christian and Druze representation.[12] Aoun stated,

> Once the [Cabinet] formula is balanced, the formation of a government will take place [...] it's not permissible for any side or sect to monopolize [Cabinet representation], or marginalize one side in favor of another, or exclude anyone.[13]

---

[11] "Official election results—How Lebanon's next parliament will look," *Daily Star*, May 8, 2018.

[12] "Aoun calls for 'balanced' govt, rejects accusations," *Daily Star*, September 11, 2018.

[13] Ibid.

The process has sparked debate regarding the respective roles and prerogatives of the president and prime minister in government formation.[14] As of October 2018, cabinet formation remained stalled as a result of disagreements among political blocks over their share of cabinet posts. Stumbling blocks include the following:

- Christian Representation. The two largest Christian parties in parliament—the Free Patriotic Movement (FPM) and the Lebanese Forces (LF)—have struggled to agree on the allocation of Christian seats in the cabinet. The two are political rivals, allied with March 8 and March 14, respectively (see Figure 2). The FPM holds a larger share of seats in parliament. The LF, which nearly doubled its share of parliamentary seats in the May elections, has sought either the deputy premiership or a "sovereign ministry" (Foreign Affairs, Defense, Interior, or Finance).[15] Traditionally, Lebanon's largest sectarian communities (Maronite, Shia, Sunni, Greek Orthodox) each receive one sovereign ministry, although these are not formally assigned to a particular sect.[16] In the outgoing cabinet, the FPM holds both the Maronite and the Greek Orthodox seats (the Foreign Affairs and Defense portfolios), and appears unwilling to cede either to the LF.
- Druze Representation. MP Walid Jumblatt, head of the Druze Progressive Socialist Party (PSP), has sought to name the three Druze ministers expected to sit in the new cabinet. According to some reports, Jumblatt seeks to prevent a key Druze rival—an ally of President Aoun—from obtaining a cabinet seat.[17]
- Sunni Representation. Prime Minister Hariri's Future Movement is the largest Sunni party in Lebanon and reportedly has sought to claim all ministerial seats allotted to Sunnis in the cabinet. However, a group of Sunni MPs not affiliated with the Future

---

[14] "Aoun naming ministers tips delicate balance," *Daily Star*, September 3, 2018.
[15] "Slim chance new talks will break Cabinet deadlock," *Daily Star*, August 28, 2018.
[16] "Lebanon's leaders and the marathon task of cabinet formation," *The National*, June 4, 2018.
[17] "Slim chance new talks will break Cabinet deadlock," *Daily Star*, August 28, 2018.

Movement has challenged this approach and called for non-Future Sunni MPs to be represented in the new cabinet.[18]

The cabinet is Lebanon's primary executive body. As the term of the previous cabinet has expired and no agreement on a new cabinet has been reached, the Lebanese government is technically in caretaker status. In late September, parliament convened in a two-day session to consider what was described as "legislation of necessity."[19] Bills passed by parliament in this session will not become effective until they are endorsed by a new cabinet. Government formation in Lebanon over the past decade has ranged from 44 days (2008) to over 10 months (2014).[20]

Hezbollah in the Lebanese Cabinet

Hariri's Temporary Resignation

In November 2017, Prime Minister Hariri unexpectedly announced his resignation during a visit to Saudi Arabia, issuing a statement condemning the role of Iran and Hezbollah in Lebanon. The move was widely viewed as orchestrated by Riyadh, which has sought to isolate Iran and Hezbollah in the region.[21] Lebanese President Michel Aoun stated that he would not accept Hariri's resignation or begin the process of forming a new government until the prime minister returned to Lebanon. Lebanese from across the political spectrum also called for the return of the prime minister, and criticized Saudi Arabia for what many viewed as undue influence in Lebanese internal affairs. Hariri withdrew his resignation a month later, upon his return to Lebanon. The Lebanese cabinet unanimously endorsed a policy statement calling on all Lebanese groups, including Hezbollah, to recommit to the policy of dissociation from regional conflicts (as established by the 2012 Baabda Declaration.) Since then, Hariri has sought to repair his relationship with Saudi Arabia, and visited the kingdom in March 2018.

---

[18] "Berri positive Cabinet formation nearing: Sunni MPs," *Daily Star*, August 28, 2018.

[19] "Parliament waves through key bills in first legislative session," *Daily Star*, September 25, 2018.

[20] Joe Macaron, "Cabinet stalemate in Lebanon may be delaying a political confrontation," Arab Center Washington DC, September 24, 2018.

[21] "Why Saad Hariri had that strange sojourn in Saudi Arabia," *New York Times*, December 24, 2017.

Hezbollah has held either one or two seats in each of the six Lebanese governments formed since July 2005, complicating U.S. engagement with successive Lebanese administrations. In mid-May 2018, the United States imposed additional sanctions on Hezbollah officials, and Assistant Secretary of the Treasury for Terrorist Financing Marshall Billingslea told the Lebanese newspaper *Daily Star* that, "We are gravely concerned by the role that Hezbollah is trying to play in the government and I would urge extreme caution for any future government for the inclusion of this terrorist group in the political system."[22] It is unclear whether U.S. preferences will affect government formation. In response to a question about whether Hezbollah would be excluded from the new government, Hariri stated, "When we are talking about a government that [ensures] agreement in the country [then] it [will include] everyone."[23] Some reports suggest that Hariri's September cabinet proposal would have included three ministerial seats for Hezbollah.[24]

2016 Presidential Election

On October 31, 2016, Lebanon's parliament elected Christian leader and former LAF commander Michel Aoun [pronounced AWN] as president, filling a post that had stood vacant since the term of former President Michel Sleiman expired in May 2014. More than 40 attempts by the parliament to convene an electoral session had previously failed, largely due to boycotts by various parties that prevented the body from attaining the necessary quorum for the vote.[25] Those most frequently boycotting sessions were MPs allied with the FPM and Hezbollah.[26]

---

[22] "U.S. official warns against Hezbollah Cabinet role," *Daily Star*, May 18, 2018.

[23] "Lebanon enters new political phase," *Daily Star*, May 21, 2018.

[24] Joe Macaron, "Cabinet stalemate in Lebanon may be delaying a political confrontation," Arab Center Washington DC, September 24, 2018.

[25] "Lebanon records 44th failed attempt to elect president," *Daily Star*, September 7, 2016.

[26] Alex Rowell, "Revealed: The MPs who aren't voting for a president," *NOW*, September 28, 2016.

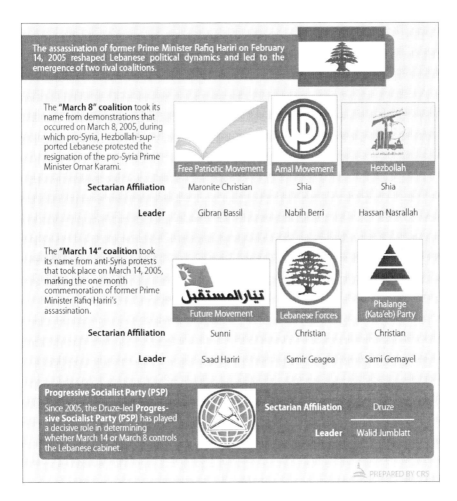

Figure 2. Lebanon's Political Coalitions; Reflects those parties with the largest number of seats in Parliament.

In addition to creating an electoral stalemate, boycotts had also prevented parliament from attaining the necessary quorum to convene regular legislative sessions, effectively paralyzing many functions of the central government. In 2015, the country saw mass protests over the government's failure to collect garbage. Over the past two years, some parties have used legislative boycotts as a way to block the consideration of controversial issues, such as the proposal for a new electoral law.

The election of a president in 2016 was made possible in part by a decision by Future Movement leader Saad Hariri—head of the largest single component of the March 14 coalition—to shift his support from presidential candidate Suleiman Franjieh to Michel Aoun, giving Aoun the votes necessary to secure his election. In return, Aoun was expected to appoint Hariri as prime minister. In December 2016, a new 30-member cabinet was announced, headed by Hariri.

Aoun is a former military officer and founder of the Maronite Christian Free Patriotic Movement. He has been allied with Hezbollah since 2005. At the same time, he represents a Christian community which views Hezbollah's interference in Syria as endangering Lebanese stability.

Evolution of March 8 and March 14 Political Coalitions

Many observers and Lebanese political leaders contend that the alliances that previously defined March 8 and March 14 have evolved since the formation of the two coalitions in 2005, with some arguing that the coalitions—particularly March 14—are weakened or defunct. However, the broad contours of March 8 and March 14 may still impact government formation.

SECURITY CHALLENGES

Lebanon faces numerous security challenges from a combination of internal and external sources. Some of these stem from the conflict in neighboring Syria, while others are rooted in longstanding social divisions and the marginalization of some sectors of Lebanese society. The Syria conflict appears to have exacerbated some of the societal cleavages.

According to the State Department's 2017 Country Reports on Terrorism (released in September 2018), Lebanon remains a safe haven for certain terrorist groups:

> Lebanon remained a safe haven for certain terrorist groups in both undergoverned and Hizballah-controlled areas. Hizballah used areas

Lebanon 173

under its control for terrorist training, fundraising, financing, and recruitment. The Government of Lebanon did not take significant action to disarm Hizballah, even though Hizballah maintained its weapons in defiance of UNSCR 1701. The government was unable to limit Hizballah's travel to and from Iraq or Syria to fight in support of the Assad regime. The Lebanese government did not have complete control of all regions of the country, or fully control its borders with Syria and Israel. Hizballah controlled access to parts of the country and had influence over some elements within Lebanon's security services.[27]

The report also noted that in 2017, ungoverned areas along Lebanon's border with Syria served as safe havens for extremists groups such as the Islamic State and the Al Qaeda-linked Syrian militants (such as the Nusra Front, part of which evolved into *Ha'ia Tahrir al Sham*, or HTS). In mid-2017 both the LAF and Hezbollah carried out operations aimed at clearing the border area of Islamic State and HTS forces (see "2017 Border Operations," below).

Spillover from Syria Conflict

Despite the Lebanese government's official policy of disassociation from the war in neighboring Syria, segments of Lebanese society have participated to varying degrees in the conflict, resulting in a range of security repercussions for the Lebanese state.

In May 2013, Hezbollah leader Hasan Nasrallah publicly announced Hezbollah's military involvement in the Syria conflict in support of the Asad government. In July 2013, Nusra Front leader Abu Muhammad al Jawlani warned that Hezbollah's actions in Syria "will not go unpunished."[28] In December 2013, a group calling itself the Nusra Front in Lebanon released its first statement. The group claimed responsibility for a

---

[27] State Department, *Country Reports on Terrorism 2017*, Chapter 4: Terrorist Safe Havens.
[28] Audio statement attributed to Abu Muhammad al Jawlani released by *Al Manarah al Bayda* [Nusra Front media arm], July 22, 2013.

number of suicide attacks in Lebanon, which it described as retaliation for Hezbollah's involvement in Syria.[29]

The Islamic State has also conducted operations inside Lebanon targeting Shia Muslims and Hezbollah. In November 2015, the Islamic State claimed responsibility for twin suicide bombings in the Beirut suburb of Burj al Barajneh—a majority Shia area. The attack killed at least 43 and wounded more than 200.[30] As a result of the targeting of Shia areas, Hezbollah has worked in parallel to the Lebanese Armed Forces to counter the Nusra Front and the Islamic State in Lebanon. In 2016, U.S. defense officials described the relationship between Hezbollah and the LAF as one of "de-confliction."[31]

While Hezbollah backed the Asad government, sympathy for the largely Sunni Syrian opposition was widespread among Lebanon's Sunni community. Some areas of Lebanon's border region became an enclave for armed groups. In 2013, fighting in the Qalamoun mountain region located between Syria and Lebanon transformed the Lebanese border town of Arsal into a rear base for Syrian armed groups.[32]

In August 2014, clashes broke out between the LAF and Islamic State/Nusra Front militants in Arsal. Nineteen LAF personnel and 40 to 45 Lebanese and Syrians were killed, and 29 LAF and Internal Security Forces were taken hostage.[33] It was generally believed that nine of the hostages were still being held by the Islamic State, until the location of their remains was disclosed as part of an August 2017 cease-fire arrangement with the group. U.S. officials described the August 2014 clashes between the Islamic State and the LAF in Arsal as a watershed moment for U.S. policy toward Lebanon, accelerating the provision of

---

[29] "Jabhat al-Nusra claims deadly Lebanon bombing," *Al Jazeera*, February 1, 2014.
[30] "ISIS claims responsibility for blasts that killed dozens in Beirut," *New York Times*, November 12, 2015.
[31] Andrew Exum, Deputy Assistant Defense Secretary for Middle East Policy, at a hearing entitled "U.S. Policy Towards Lebanon," before the House Foreign Affairs Subcommittee on Middle East and North Africa, April 28, 2016.
[32] "Arsal in the Crosshairs: The Predicament of a Small Lebanese Border Town," International Crisis Group, February 23, 2016.
[33] "Lebanon," State Department Annual Report on Human Rights, 2015.

equipment and training to the LAF.[34] The situation in Arsal was compounded by the refugee crisis—by 2016, the border town hosted more than 40,000 refugees, exceeding the Lebanese host population by more than 15%.[35]

Security Issues and Antirefugee Sentiment

Some Lebanese have described the country's growing Syrian refugee population as a risk to Lebanon's security. In June 2016, eight suicide bombers attacked the Christian town of Al Qaa near the Syrian border, killing five and wounding dozens. The attack heightened antirefugee sentiment, as the attackers were initially suspected to be Syrians living in informal refugee settlements inside the town. Lebanese authorities arrested hundreds of Syrians following the attack, although Lebanon's interior minister later stated that seven out of the eight bombers had traveled to Lebanon from the Islamic State's self-declared capital in Raqqah, Syria, and were not residing in Lebanon.[36]

In June 2017, five suicide bombers struck two refugee settlements in Arsal, killing a child and wounding three LAF soldiers. The attacks came during an LAF raid against IS militants thought to be hiding in the area. In the wake of the attacks, the LAF detained some 350 people, including several alleged IS officials.[37] Four Syrian detainees died in LAF custody, drawing criticism from Syrian opposition groups and human rights organizations. A Lebanese military prosecutor ordered an investigation into the deaths. Following the attack, Hezbollah released a statement supporting LAF operations around Arsal and calling for "coordinated efforts" to prevent terrorist infiltration across Lebanon's eastern border.[38] In a cabinet meeting on July 5, President Aoun praised LAF efforts to

---

[34] CRS conversation with State Department official, October 2016.

[35] "Humanitarian Bulletin, Lebanon," Issue 25, 1-30 November 2016, United Nations Office for the Coordination of Humanitarian Affairs (OCHA).

[36] "Lebanon's tough options as backlash against Syrian refugees grows," *Christian Science Monitor*, July 1, 2016.

[37] "Lebanon refugee camps hit by five suicide bombers," *BBC*, June 30, 2017.

[38] "Hezbollah Hails the Lebanese Army Raids in Arsal, Calls for Unifying Efforts," *Al-Manar TV Online*, June 30, 2017.

176 Carla E. Humud

combat terrorism and warned that Syrian refugee camps in Lebanon were turning into "enabling environments for terrorism."[39]

Some Lebanese officials continue to describe the country's Syrian refugee population as destabilizing, and argue that Syrian refugees should return home. In May 2018, President Aoun reiterated his call for the repatriation of Syrian refugees, stating that their return would "end the repercussions of this displacement on Lebanon socially, economically, educationally, and in terms of security."[40] President Aoun has said that the return of refugees should not be contingent on a political solution to the Syrian conflict.[41] Prime Minister Hariri has stated that Lebanon will not force Syrian refugees to return to Syria, but has agreed that the final solution to the refugee issue will require refugees to return home.[42] Hariri has opposed coordinating refugee returns with the Syrian government, an option supported by President Aoun's Free Patriotic Movement (FPM) as well as by Hezbollah.[43]

For additional details on the refugee situation in Lebanon, see "Syrian and Palestinian Refugees and Lebanese Policy."

2017 Border Operations

In an effort to counter the infiltration of militants from Syria, both the LAF and Hezbollah have deployed forces at various points along Lebanon's eastern border. In May 2017, Hezbollah withdrew from a 67 km area stretching from the Masnaa border crossing with Syria (the primary official land crossing between the two countries) to Arsal, and was

---

[39] "Aoun: Refugees Encampments Could Turn into Safe Haven for Terrorism," *Naharnet*," July 5, 2017; "Cabinet pledges more progress on key public issues, postpones refugee return discussion," *The Daily Star*, July 5, 2017.

[40] "Aoun pleads for Arab intervention in refugee return," *Daily Star*, May 3, 2018.

[41] "Aoun Calls for Gradual Return of Syrian Refugees," *Asharq Al Awsat*, March 8, 2018.

[42] "Lebanon says will not force Syrian refugees to return," *Reuters*, February 1, 2018; "Hariri: Solution to Syrian refugee crisis in Lebanon is returning to Syria," *Al Arabiya*, June 13, 2018.

[43] "Lebanese divided over efforts to repatriate Syrian refugees," Al Monitor, July 25, 2018.

replaced by LAF forces.[44] In July 2017, Hezbollah launched an operation to clear HTS militants from Arsal. In August, the LAF conducted a separate operation to clear Islamic State militants from border areas north of Arsal. Hezbollah's role in operations along Lebanon's eastern border has been controversial, with some Lebanese politicians arguing that the job of clearing militants from the area should rest with the Lebanese government alone.[45]

Hezbollah Offensive Near Arsal

In late July 2017, Hezbollah began operations around Arsal. Within days, Nasrallah announced that Hezbollah had retaken most of the territory held by HTS. On July 27, a cease-fire was announced between Hezbollah and HTS fighters, brokered by Lebanon's Chief of General Security.[46] As part of the agreement, HTS fighters agreed to relocate with their families to Syria's Idlib province. Nasrallah stated that "we will be ready to hand all the recaptured Lebanese lands and positions over to the Lebanese Army if the army command requests this and is ready to take responsibility for them."[47] Prime Minister Hariri said that the LAF did not participate in Hezbollah's operations around Arsal.[48] However, in a public address, Nasrallah stated that the LAF secured the area to the west of Arsal to ensure that HTS militants along the border did not escape into Lebanon.[49] Praising the role of the LAF in the July Arsal operation, Nasrallah stated, "What the Lebanese Army did around Aarsal, on the outskirts of Aarsal, and along the contact line within the Lebanese territories was essential for scoring this victory."[50]

---

[44] "Lebanese army takes over Hizbullah positions on Syrian border," *Jane's Defense Weekly*, May 30, 2017.

[45] "MP Houri blasts Hezbollah role in Arsal," *Daily Star*, July 13, 2017.

[46] "Ceasefire Deal Agreed in Arsal Outskirts," *National News Agency*, July 27, 2017.

[47] Transcript, televised remarks by Lebanese Hezbollah Secretary General Hasan Nasrallah, July 26, 2017.

[48] "Saad Hariri: The Full Transcript," *Politico*, July 31, 2017.

[49] Transcript, televised remarks by Lebanese Hezbollah Secretary General Hasan Nasrallah, July 26, 2017.

[50] Ibid.

LAF Border Operation against the Islamic State

In August 2017, the Lebanese government launched a 10-day offensive to clear Islamic State militants from the outskirts of the towns of Ras Baalbeck and Al Qaa, north of Arsal along Lebanon's northeast border. According to media reports, the LAF operation occurred in conjunction with a separate but simultaneous attack on the militants by Syrian government and Hezbollah forces from the Syrian side of the border, trapping the militants in a small enclave.[51] On August 30, 2017, LAF Commander General Joseph Aoun declared the operation, which resulted in the deaths of seven LAF soldiers and dozens of IS fighters, complete.[52] In a phone call with CENTCOM Commander General Votel, General Aoun "confirmed that the U.S. aid provided to the LAF had an efficient and main role in the success of this operation."[53]

The conclusion of the operation also involved an agreement to allow the roughly 300 IS fighters to withdraw from their besieged enclave along with their families, and head to IS-controlled Abu Kamal on the Syrian border with Iraq. In return, the Islamic State revealed the location of the remains of nine LAF soldiers captured in 2014, as well as the bodies of five Hezbollah fighters.[54]

Domestic Sunni Extremism

Since the start of the Syria conflict, some existing extremist groups in Lebanon who previously targeted Israel refocused on Hezbollah and Shia communities. The Al Qaeda-linked Abdallah Azzam Brigades (AAB), formed in 2009, initially targeted Israel with rocket attacks. However, the group began targeting Hezbollah in 2013 and is believed to be responsible for a series of bombings in Hezbollah-controlled areas of Beirut, including

---

[51] "Ceasefire halts Syria-Lebanon border fight against Islamic State," *Reuters*, August 27, 2017.

[52] "President, Army chief declare victory over Daesh," *Daily Star*, August 31, 2017.

[53] "Command General Joseph Votel to the Armed Forces Commander General Joseph Aoun," August 30, 2017, http://www.lebarmy.gov.lb.

[54] "DNA Results Match Identities of Soldiers," *Naharnet*, September 6, 2017; "In a deal, remains of Lebanon soldiers held by IS located," *Washington Post*, August 27, 2017.

a November 2013 attack against the Iranian Embassy that killed 23 and wounded more than 140.[55]

In addition to the AAB, there are numerous Sunni extremist groups based in Lebanon that predate the Syria conflict. These include Hamas, the Popular Front for the Liberation of Palestine (PFLP), Palestinian Islamic Jihad, Fatah al Islam, and Jund al Sham. These groups operate primarily out of Lebanon's 12 Palestinian refugee camps. Due to an agreement between the Lebanese government and the late Palestine Liberation Organization (PLO) chairman Yasser Arafat, Lebanese forces generally do not enter Palestinian camps in Lebanon, instead maintaining checkpoints outside them. These camps operate as self-governed entities, and maintain their own security and militia forces outside of government control.[56]

HEZBOLLAH

Lebanese Hezbollah, a Shia Islamist movement, is Iran's most significant nonstate ally. Iran's support for Hezbollah, including providing thousands of rockets and short-range missiles, helps Iran acquire leverage against key regional adversaries such as Israel and Saudi Arabia. It also facilitates Iran's intervention on behalf of a key ally, the Asad regime in Syria. The Asad regime has been pivotal to Iran and Hezbollah by providing Iran a secure route to deliver weapons to Hezbollah. Iran has supported Hezbollah by providing "hundreds of millions of dollars" to the group and training "thousands" of Hezbollah fighters inside Iran.[57] In June 2018, Treasury Under Secretary for Terrorism and Financial Intelligence Sigal Mandelker estimated that Iran provides Hezbollah with more than

---

[55] "Abdallah Azzam Brigades," State Department Country Reports on Terrorism 2017, Chapter 5, "Foreign Terrorist Organizations."

[56] "Lebanon," State Department Annual Country Reports on Human Rights, 2015.

[57] Department of State Country Reports on Terrorism 2015, p. 300.

180 Carla E. Humud

$700 million per year,[58] significantly more than previously released U.S. government estimates.[59]

Clashes with Israel

Hezbollah emerged in the early 1980s during the Israeli occupation of southern Lebanon. Israel invaded Lebanon in 1978 and again in 1982, with the goal of pushing back (in 1978) or expelling (in 1982) the leadership and fighters of the Palestine Liberation Organization (PLO)—which used Lebanon as a base to wage a guerrilla war against Israel until the PLO relocated to Tunisia in 1982.[60] In 1985 Israel withdrew from Beirut and its environs to southern Lebanon—a predominantly Shia area. Shia leaders disagreed about how to respond to the Israeli occupation, and many of those favoring a military response gradually coalesced into what would become Hezbollah.[61] The group launched attacks against Israeli Defense Forces (IDF) and U.S. military and diplomatic targets, portraying itself as the leaders of resistance to foreign military occupation.

In May 2000, Israel withdrew its forces from southern Lebanon, but Hezbollah has used the remaining Israeli presence in the Sheb'a Farms (see below) and other disputed areas in the Lebanon-Syria-Israel triborder region to justify its ongoing conflict with Israel—and its continued existence as an armed militia alongside the Lebanese Armed Forces.

---

[58] Transcript of remarks by Treasury Under Secretary for Terrorism and Financial Intelligence Sigal Mandelker at the Foundation for Defense of Democracies, June 5, 2018.

[59] The Obama Administration's 2010 report on Iran's military power stated that Iran provides "roughly $100-200 million per year in funding to support Hizballah." (U.S. Department of Defense, Annual Unclassified Report on Military Power of Iran, Required by Section 1245 of the FY2010 National Defense Authorization Act [P.L. 111-84], April 2010).

[60] According to various accounts, Israel's 1982 invasion included additional goals of countering Syrian influence in Lebanon and helping establish an Israel-friendly Maronite government there.

[61] The Shia group Amal took a more nuanced view of the Israeli occupation, which it saw as breaking the dominance of Palestinian militia groups operating in southern Lebanon.

The Sheb'a Farms Dispute

When Israel withdrew from southern Lebanon in 2000, several small but sensitive territorial issues were left unresolved, notably, a roughly 10-square-mile enclave at the southern edge of the Lebanese-Syrian border known as the Sheb'a Farms. Israel did not evacuate this enclave, arguing that it is not Lebanese territory but rather is part of the Syrian Golan Heights, which Israel occupied in 1967. Lebanon, supported by Syria, asserts that this territory is part of Lebanon and should have been evacuated by Israel when the latter abandoned its self-declared security zone in May 2000.

Ambiguity surrounding the demarcation of the Lebanese-Syria border has complicated the task of determining ownership over the area. France, which held mandates for both Lebanon and Syria, did not define a formal boundary between the two, although it did separate them by administrative divisions. Nor did Lebanon and Syria establish a formal boundary after gaining independence from France in the aftermath of World War II—in part due to the influence of some factions in both Syria and Lebanon who regarded the two as properly constituting a single country.

Advocates of a "Greater Syria" in particular were reluctant to establish diplomatic relations and boundaries, fearing that such steps would imply formal recognition of the separate status of the two states. The U.N. Secretary-General noted in May 2000 that "there seems to be no official record of a formal international boundary agreement between Lebanon and the Syrian Arab Republic."[62] Syria and Lebanon did not establish full diplomatic relations until 2008.[63]

2006 Hezbollah-Israel War

Hezbollah's last major clash with Israel occurred in 2006—a 34-day war that resulted in the deaths of approximately 1,190 Lebanese and 163 Israelis,[64] and the destruction of large parts of Lebanon's civilian infrastructure. The war began in July 2006, when Hezbollah captured two members of the IDF along the Lebanese-Israeli border. Israel responded by carrying out air strikes against suspected Hezbollah targets in Lebanon,

---

[62] United Nations Security Council, Report of the Secretary-General on the implementation of Security Council resolutions 425 (1978) and 426 (1978), S/2000/460, May 22, 2000.

[63] Syrian Government, Presidential Decree No. 358, October 14, 2008.

[64] See "Lebanon"—Amnesty International Report 2007, and "Israel-Hizbullah conflict: Victims of rocket attacks and IDF casualties," Israel Ministry of Foreign Affairs.

and Hezbollah countered with rocket attacks against cities and towns in northern Israel. Israel subsequently launched a full-scale ground operation in Lebanon with the stated goal of establishing a security zone free of Hezbollah militants. Hostilities ended following the issuance of U.N. Security Council Resolution (UNSCR) 1701, which imposed a cease-fire.

In the years since the 2006 war, Israeli officials have sought to draw attention to Hezbollah's weapons buildup—including reported upgrades to the range and precision of its projectiles—and its alleged use of Lebanese civilian areas as strongholds.[65] In addition, Israel has reportedly struck targets in Syria or Lebanon in attempts to prevent arms transfers to Hezbollah in Lebanon.[66] In February 2016, Israeli Prime Minister Netanyahu said the following:

> We will not agree to the supply of advanced weaponry to Hezbollah from Syria and Lebanon. We will not agree to the creation of a second terror front on the Golan Heights. These are the red lines that we have set and they remain the red lines of the State of Israel.[67]

Some media reporting in 2017 has focused on claims that Iran has helped Hezbollah set up underground factories in Lebanon to manufacture weapons previously only available from outside the country.[68] In August 2017, the former commander of the Israel Air Force (IAF) claimed that Israel had hit convoys of weapons headed to Hezbollah almost 100 times since civil war broke out in Syria in 2012.[69] In September 2017, the IAF allegedly struck an area in northwestern Syria—reportedly targeting a Syrian chemical weapons facility[70] and/or a factory producing precision

---

[65] "Ten years after last Lebanon war, Israel warns next one will be far worse," *Washington Post*, July 23, 2016.

[66] See, e.g., "Israel has hit 'dozens' of Hezbollah arms transfers, Netanyahu says," *Times of Israel*, April 11, 2016; "Lebanon: New Skirmish Between Israel and Hezbollah in Disputed Territory," *New York Times*, January 5, 2016.

[67] "Netanyahu Welcomes Cease-Fire in Syria, but Adds a Warning," *New York Times*, February 29, 2016.

[68] See, e.g., Gili Cohen, "Iran Reportedly Built Weapons Factories in Lebanon for Hezbollah," Ha'aretz, March 14, 2017.

[69] "Israel said to have hit Hezbollah convoys dozens of times," Times of Israel, August 17, 2017.

[70] "Israel airstrike hits suspected Syrian chemical weapons plant," Deutsche Welle, September 7, 2017.

weapons transportable to Hezbollah.[71] In October, the IAF acknowledged striking a Syrian antiaircraft battery that apparently targeted Israeli aircraft flying over Lebanon.[72] Russia's actions could affect future Israeli operations, given that it maintains advanced air defense systems and other interests in Syria.

United Nations Force in Lebanon

Since 1978, the United Nations Force in Lebanon (UNIFIL) has been deployed in the Lebanon Israel-Syria triborder area.[73] UNIFIL's initial mandate was to confirm the withdrawal of Israeli forces from southern Lebanon, restore peace and security, and assist the Lebanese government in restoring its authority in southern Lebanon (a traditional Hezbollah stronghold). In May 2000, Israel withdrew its forces from southern Lebanon. The following month, the United Nations identified a 120 km line between Lebanon and Israel to use as a reference for the purpose of confirming the withdrawal of Israeli forces. The Line of Withdrawal, commonly known as the Blue Line, is not an international border demarcation between the two states. In 2007, Israel and Lebanon agreed to visibly mark the Blue Line on the ground. As of July 2017, UNIFIL has measured 282 points along the Blue Line and constructed 268 Blue Line Barrels as markers.[74]

Following the 2006 Israel-Hezbollah war, UNIFIL's mandate was expanded via UNSCR 1701 (2006) to including monitoring the cessation of hostilities between the two sides, accompanying and supporting the Lebanese Armed Forces as they deployed throughout southern Lebanon, and helping to ensure humanitarian access to civilian populations. UNSCR 1701 states that UNIFIL shall assist the Lebanese government in "taking steps toward" the establishment of "an area free of any armed personnel, assets and weapons other than those of the Government of Lebanon and of

---

[71] Ben Caspit, "Will Russia Tolerate Israeli Actions in Syria?" Al-Monitor Israel Pulse, September 11, 2017.

[72] "Israel Carries Out Air Strike on Syrian Anti-Aircraft Battery," Reuters, October 17, 2017.

[73] The formal boundaries dividing the three countries remain disputed.

[74] "Working with UNIFIL, LAF confirms 8 new Blue Line points," unifil.unmissions.org, July 13, 2017.

UNIFIL" between the Blue Line and the Litani River (which UNIFIL defines as its area of operations).[75] Separately, UNSCR 1701 also calls upon the government of Lebanon to secure its borders and requests UNIFIL "to assist the Government of Lebanon at its request."

UNIFIL is headquartered in the Lebanese town of Naqoura and maintains more than 10,500 peacekeepers drawn from 41 countries.[76] This includes more than 9,400 ground troops and over 850 naval personnel of the Maritime Task Force. In July 2018, Major General Stefano Del Col (Italy) was appointed as head of UNIFIL, succeeding Major General Michael Beary (Ireland). U.S. personnel do not participate in UNIFIL, although U.S. contributions to U.N. peacekeeping programs support the mission. The United States provides security assistance to the Lebanese Armed Forces aimed at supporting Lebanese government efforts to implement UNSCR 1701.

Since the discovery in 2009 of large offshore gas fields in the Mediterranean, unresolved issues over the demarcation of Lebanon's land border with Israel have translated into disputes over maritime boundaries, and in 2011 Lebanese authorities called on the U.N. to establish a maritime equivalent of the Blue Line. UNIFIL has maintained a Maritime Task Force since 2006, which assists the Lebanese Navy in preventing the entry of unauthorized arms or other materials to Lebanon. However, U.N. officials have stated that UNIFIL does not have the authority to establish a maritime boundary.[77] (For more information, see "Eastern Mediterranean Energy Resources and Disputed Boundaries," below.)

UNIFIL continues to monitor violations of UNSCR 1701 by all sides, and the U.N. Secretary-General reports regularly to the U.N. Security Council on the implementation of UNSCR 1701. These reports have listed violations by Hezbollah—including an April 2017 media tour along the

---

[75] United Nations Interim Force in Lebanon, http://unifil.unmissions.org/faqs.
[76] Ibid.
[77] United Nations Security Council, Fifteenth report of the Secretary-General on the implementation of Security Council Resolution 1701 (2006) S/2011/91, February 28, 2011.

Israeli border—as well as violations by Israel—including "almost daily" violations of Lebanese airspace.[78]

In January 2017, UNIFIL underwent a strategic review. The scope of the review did not include the mandate of the mission or its authorized maximum strength of 15,000 troops. In March, the results of the strategic review were presented to the Security Council. The review found that "overall, the Force was well configured to implement its mandated tasks," and also outlined a number of recommendations.[79]

2017 UNIFIL Mandate Debate

On August 30, 2017, the U.N. Security Council voted to renew UNIFIL's mandate for another year. The vote followed what U.S. Ambassador to the U.N. Nikki Haley described as "tense negotiations" over the mission's mandate,[80] with the United States and Israel reportedly pushing for changes that would allow UNIFIL to access and search private property for illicit Hezbollah weapons stockpiles or other violations of UNSCR 1701.[81] Ambassador Haley has been critical of UNIFIL, which she argues has failed to prevent Hezbollah violations of UNSCR 1701 and whose patrols in southern Lebanon are sometimes restricted by roadblocks.[82]

Changes to UNIFIL's mandate were opposed by countries contributing troops to the mission, including France and Italy.[83] Lebanon's Foreign Minister also called on the Security Council to renew the mission's mandate without change. Other critics of the proposed changes questioned whether troop-contributing countries would be willing to deploy forces for

---

[78] For details, see United Nations Security Council, *Report of the Secretary General on the implementation of Security Council resolution 1701 (2006)* issued every four months.

[79] "Letter dated 8 March 2017 from the Secretary-General addressed to the President of the Security Council," March 9, 2017, S/2017/202.

[80] Nikki Haley, "Confronting Hezbollah in Lebanon," *Jerusalem Post*, September 5, 2017.

[81] "Report Says UNIFIL Mission Extended for One Year, Adjustments 'Not Up To Washington's Ambitions,'" *Al Sharq al Awsat*, September 1, 2017.

[82] Nikki Haley, "Confronting Hezbollah in Lebanon," *Jerusalem Post*, September 5, 2017.

[83] "Vote on a Resolution Renewing UNIFIL," *What's in Blue*, August 30, 2017.

a mission that could require direct confrontation with Hezbollah in heavily Shia areas of southern Lebanon.[84]

The renewal of UNIFIL's mandate in UNSCR 2373 included limited wording changes, which were praised by all sides.[85] The new language requests that the existing U.N. Secretary-General's reports on the implementation of UNSCR 1701 include, among other things, "prompt and detailed reports on the restrictions to UNIFIL's freedom of movement, reports on specific areas where UNIFIL does not access and on the reasons behind these restrictions."[86]

Source: U.N. Geospatial Information Section.

Figure 3. UNIFIL Area of Operations.

In his July 2018 report to the Security Council on the implementation of UNSCR 1701, the U.N. Secretary-General stated that, "The freedom of

---

[84] "New UNIFIL mandate? Business as usual," *Daily Star*, September 1, 2017.
[85] Ibid; "UNIFIL changes provide transparency: Haley," *Daily Star*, September 6, 2017.
[86] UN Security Council Resolution 2373 (2017).

movement of UNIFIL was generally respected, except for those occasions detailed in annex I."[87] Annex I of the July report, which covers the period between March 1 and June 20, lists 10 incidents. On August 31, 2018, the U.N. Security Council voted to renew UNIFIL's mandate for another year.

Domestic Politics

Hezbollah was widely credited for forcing the withdrawal of Israeli troops from southern Lebanon in 2000, and this elevated the group into the primary political party among Lebanese Shia.[88] In addition, Hezbollah—like other Lebanese confessional groups—vies for the loyalties of its constituents by operating a vast network of schools, clinics, youth programs, private business, and local security. These services contribute significantly to the group's popular support base, although some Lebanese criticize Hezbollah's vast apparatus as "a state within the state." The legitimacy that this popular support provides compounds the challenges of limiting Hezbollah's influence.

Hezbollah has participated in elections since 1992, and it has achieved a modest but steady degree of electoral success. Hezbollah entered the cabinet for the first time in 2005, and has held one or two seats in each of the six Lebanese governments formed since then. Hezbollah candidates have also fared well in municipal elections, winning seats in conjunction with allied Amal party representatives in many areas of southern and eastern Lebanon.

On May 6, 2018, Lebanon held its first legislative elections in nine years. The results showed that parties allied with Hezbollah increased their share of seats from roughly 44% to 53%. The political coalition known as March 8 (see Figure 2), which includes Hezbollah, Amal, the FPM, and

---

[87] "Implementation of Security Council resolution 1701 (2006)," Report of the Secretary-General to the U.N. Security Council, July 13, 2018, S/2018/703.

[88] Lina Khatib and Maxwell Gardiner, "Lebanon: Situation Report," Carnegie Middle East Center, April 17, 2015.

188   Carla E. Humud

allied parties, won 68 seats according to Lebanese vote tallies.[89] This is enough to secure a simple majority (65 out of 128 seats) in parliament, but falls short of the two-thirds majority needed to push through major initiatives such as a revision to the constitution. Hezbollah itself did not gain any additional seats.

Hezbollah has at times served as a destabilizing political force, despite its willingness to engage in electoral politics. In 2008, Hezbollah-led fighters took over areas of Beirut after the March 14 government attempted to shut down the group's private telecommunications network—which Hezbollah leaders described as key to the group's operations against Israel.[90] Hezbollah has also withdrawn its ministers from the cabinet to protest steps taken by the government (in 2008 when the government sought to debate the issue of Hezbollah's weapons, and in 2011 to protest the expected indictments of Hezbollah members for the Hariri assassination). On both occasions, the withdrawal of Hezbollah and its political allies from the cabinet caused the government to collapse. At other times, Hezbollah leaders have avoided conflict with other domestic actors, possibly in order to focus its resources elsewhere—such as on activities in Syria.

Top Lebanese leaders have acknowledged that despite their differences with Hezbollah, they do confer with the group on issues deemed to be critical to Lebanon's security. In July 2017, Prime Minister Saad Hariri stated that although he disagreed with Hezbollah on politics,

> when it comes for the sake of the country, for the economy, how to handle those 1.5 million refugees, how to handle the stability, how to handle the governing our country, we have to have some kind of understanding, otherwise we would be like Syria. So, for the sake of the stability of Lebanon, we agree on certain things, and we disagree on political issues that we—until today, we disagree. So, ... there is an

---

[89] "Official election results—How Lebanon's next parliament will look," *Daily Star*, May 8, 2018.
[90] "Row over Hezbollah phone network," *Al Jazeera*, May 9, 2008.

understanding or a consensus in the country, with all political parties including the president, [and it] is how to safeguard Lebanon.[91]

Intervention in Syria

Syria is important to Hezbollah because it serves as a key transshipment point for Iranian weapons. Following Hezbollah's 2006 war with Israel, the group worked to rebuild its weapons cache with Iranian assistance, a process facilitated or at minimum tolerated by the Syrian regime. While Hezbollah's relationship with Syria is more pragmatic than ideological, it is likely that Hezbollah views the prospect of regime change in Damascus as a fundamental threat to its interests—particularly if the change empowers Sunni groups allied with Saudi Arabia.

Hezbollah has played a key role in helping to suppress the Syrian uprising, in part by "advising the Syrian Government and training its personnel in how to prosecute a counter insurgency."[92] Hezbollah fighters in Syria have worked with the Syrian military to protect regime supply lines, and to monitor and target rebel positions. They also have facilitated the training of Syrian forces by the IRGC-QF.[93] The involvement of Hezbollah in the Syrian conflict has evolved since 2011 from an advisory to an operational role, with forces fighting alongside Syrian troops—most recently around Aleppo.[94] The International Institute for Strategic Studies estimated in 2016 that Hezbollah maintains between 4,000 and 8,000 fighters in Syria.[95] In mid-September 2017, Nasrallah declared that "we have won the war (in Syria)" and described the remaining fighting as "scattered battles."[96]

---

[91] "Saad Hariri: The Full Transcript," *Politico*, July 31, 2017.
[92] "Briefing on the designation of Hezbollah for supporting the Syrian regime," Department of State Press Release, August 10, 2012.
[93] Ibid.
[94] "In Syria's Aleppo, Shiite militias point to Iran's unparalleled influence," *Washington Post*, November 20, 2016.
[95] The Military Balance 2016, International Institute for Strategic Studies.
[96] "Hezbollah declares Syria victory, Russia says much of country won back," Reuters, September 12, 2017.

SYRIAN AND PALESTINIAN REFUGEES AND LEBANESE POLICY

Refugees began to stream into Lebanon in 2011, following the outbreak of conflict in neighboring Syria. Initially, Lebanon maintained an open-border policy, permitting refugees to enter without a visa and to renew their residency for a nominal fee. By 2014, Lebanon had the highest per capita refugee population in the world, with refugees equaling one-quarter of the resident population.[97] (See Figure 4.) In May 2015, UNHCR suspended new registration of refugees in response to the government's request. Thus, while roughly 1 million Syrian refugees were registered with UNHCR in late 2016, officials estimate that the actual refugee presence is closer to 1.2 million to 1.5 million (Lebanon's prewar population was about 4.3 million).

In addition, there are 450,000 Palestinian refugees registered with the U.N. Relief and Works Agency for Palestine Refugees in the Near East (UNRWA) in Lebanon, although not all of those registered reside in Lebanon. A 2017 census of Palestinian refugees in Lebanon found that roughly 174,422 Palestinians live in 12 formal camps and 156 informal "gatherings."[98] About 20,725 other refugees and asylum seekers are registered in Lebanon; 84% of these are Iraqi refugees.[99]

As the number of refugees continued to increase, it severely strained Lebanon's infrastructure, which was still being rebuilt following the 2006 war between Hezbollah and Israel. It also created growing resentment among Lebanese residents, as housing prices increased and some felt as though an influx of cheap Syrian labor was displacing Lebanese from their jobs. The influx has also affected the Lebanese education system, as roughly 500,000 of the Syrian refugees in Lebanon are estimated to be school-age children.[100]

---

[97] United Nations High Commissioner for Refugees (UNHCR), "Syrian refugees in Lebanon surpass 1 million," April 3, 2014.

[98] Ibid.

[99] "Refugees and Asylum-Seekers," *Lebanon: Global Focus*, UNHCR.

[100] Human Rights Watch, *Growing Up Without an Education: Barriers to Education for Syrian Refugee Children in Lebanon*, July 2016.

The Lebanese government has been unwilling to take steps that it sees as enabling Syrians to become a permanent refugee population akin to the Palestinians—whose militarization in the 1970s was one of the drivers of Lebanon's 15-year civil war. Some Christian leaders also fear that the influx of largely Sunni refugees could upset the country's sectarian balance. The government has blocked the construction of refugee camps like those built to house Syrian refugees in Jordan and Turkey, presumably to prevent Syrian refugees from settling in Lebanon permanently. As a result, most Syrian refugees in Lebanon have settled in urban areas, in what UNCHR describes as "sub-standard shelters" (garages, worksites, unfinished buildings) or apartments. Less than 20% live in informal tented settlements. Syrian refugees have also settled in existing Palestinian refugee camps in Lebanon, and in some cases outnumber the Palestinian residents of those camps.[101]

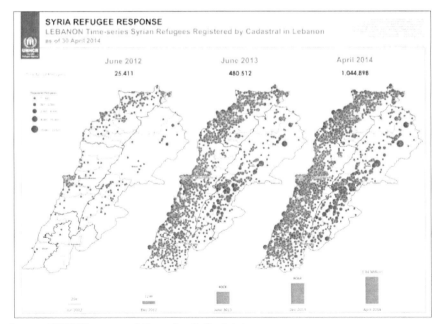

Source: UNHCR, accessed through reliefweb.int.

Figure 4. Registered Syrian Refugees in Lebanon.

---

[101] UNOCHA, Humanitarian Bulletin: Lebanon, Issue 30, 1 November 2017-31 January 2018.

Entry Restrictions

In May 2014, the government enacted entry restrictions effectively closing the border to Palestinian refugees from Syria.[102] In January 2015, the Lebanese government began to implement new visa requirements for all Syrians entering Lebanon, raising concerns among U.S. officials.[103] Under the new requirements, Syrians can only be admitted if they are able to provide documentation proving that they fit into one of the seven approved categories for entry, which do not include fleeing violence.[104] While there is an entry category for displaced persons, the criteria specifically apply to "unaccompanied and/or separated children with a parent already registered in Lebanon; persons living with disabilities with a relative already registered in Lebanon; persons with urgent medical needs for whom treatment in Syria is unavailable; persons who will be resettled to third countries."[105]

Legal Status

Refugees registered with UNHCR are required to provide a notarized pledge not to work, as a condition of renewing their residency. Nevertheless, the January 2015 regulations increased the costs of residency renewal to an annual fee of $200 per person over 15 years of age, beyond the means of the 70% of Syrian refugee households living at or below the poverty line. As a result, most Syrian refugees in Lebanon lost their legal status. To survive, many sought employment in the informal labor market.

---

[102] Amnesty International, *Lebanon: Denied refuge: Palestinians from Syria seeking safety in Lebanon*, July 1, 2014.

[103] See for example, State Department Daily Press Briefing, January 5, 2015.

[104] According to Amnesty International, "Category one is for tourism, shopping, business, landlords, and tenants; category two is for studying, category three is for transiting to a third country, category four is for those displaced; category five for medical treatment; category six for an embassy appointment; and category seven for those entering with a pledge of responsibility (a Lebanese sponsor)." See, *Pushed to the Edge: Syrian Refugees Face Increased Restrictions in Lebanon*, Amnesty International, June 2015.

[105] Ibid.

According to a Human Rights Watch report, the loss of legal status for refugees in Lebanon made them vulnerable to labor and sexual exploitation by employers.[106] In February 2017, Lebanese authorities lifted the $200 residency fee for Syrian refugees registered with UNHCR. The waiver will not apply to the estimated 500,000 Syrian refugees who arrived after the Lebanese government directed UNHCR to stop registering refugees in May 2015, or to refugees who renewed their residency through a Lebanese sponsor.[107]

Palestinian Refugees

Palestinian refugees have been present in Lebanon for at least 70 years, as a result of displacements stemming from various Arab-Israeli wars. Like Syrian refugees, Palestinian refugees and their Lebanese-born children cannot obtain Lebanese citizenship.[108] In addition, the State Department notes that Palestinian refugees in Lebanon are

> prohibited from accessing public health and education services or owning land; they were barred from employment in many fields, making refugees dependent upon UNRWA as the sole provider of education, health care, and social services. A 2010 labor law revision expanded employment rights and removed some restrictions on Palestinian refugees. This law was not fully implemented, however, and Palestinians remained barred from working in most skilled professions, including almost all those that require membership in a professional association.[109]

---

[106] "'I Just Wanted to be Treated Like a Person' How Lebanon's Residency Rules Facilitate Abuse of Syrian Refugees," Human Rights Watch, January 2016.

[107] "General Security waives residency fee for over million registered Syrian refugees," *Daily Star*, February 16, 2017.

[108] Citizenship in Lebanon is derived exclusively from the father. Thus, a child born to a Palestinian refugee mother and a Lebanese father could obtain Lebanese citizenship. However, a Palestinian refugee father would transmit his stateless status to his children, even if the mother was a Lebanese citizen.

[109] "Lebanon," State Department Annual Country Reports on Human Rights, 2017.

In August 2018, the State Department announced that the United States will not make further contributions to UNRWA.[110] The United States contributed approximately one-third of UNRWA's annual budget in 2017. The long-standing presence of Palestinians in Lebanon has shaped the approach of Lebanese authorities to the influx of Syrian refugees. It is unclear whether Lebanese authorities will take a comparable approach to the Syrian population over the long term, particularly as a new generation of Syrian children comes to share Palestinian refugees' status as stateless persons. Some observers worry that government policies limiting nationality, mobility, and employment for refugees and their descendants risk creating a permanent underclass vulnerable to recruitment by terrorist groups.

International Humanitarian Funding

The U.N. Regional Refugee and Resilience Plan (3RP) is a coordinated regional framework designed to address the impact of the Syria crisis on the five most affected neighboring countries: Lebanon, Jordan, Iraq, Turkey, and Egypt. The 2018 3RP appeal seeks $5.6 billion and as of October 2018 was funded at 42%.[111] The Lebanon Crisis Response Plan (LCRP) is nested within the broader 3RP, and targets not only the roughly 1.5 million Syrian refugees in Lebanon but also vulnerable Lebanese communities whose economic security has been adversely affected by the refugee influx. The LCRP also focuses on strengthening the stability of the Lebanese state and civil society. The 2018 LCRP was launched in February 2018 and seeks $2.68 billion. As of July it was funded at 34%.[112]

Return of Syrian Refugees

Since 2017, the LAF and the Directorate for General Security (DGS) have played a role in facilitating the return of several thousand refugees to

---

[110] "On U.S. Assistance to UNRWA," State Department Press Statement, August 31, 2018.
[111] https://fts.unocha.org/appeals/overview/2018.
[112] UNOCHA, Humanitarian Bulletin: Lebanon, Issue 32, 1 May-31 July 2018.

Syria.[113] As part of the arrangement, many refugees have been transferred to rebel-held portions of Syria's Idlib province, as well as to villages in the province of Rural Damascus. It is unclear whether all refugees departed voluntarily.[114]

The government's facilitation of refugee return has generated some tension between Lebanese officials and international humanitarian actors. In June 2018, a UNHCR spokesperson stated, "in our view, conditions in Syria are not yet conducive for an assisted return."[115] Lebanese Foreign Minister Gibran Bassil has accused UNHCR of discouraging refugees from returning to Syria, and on June 8 ordered a freeze on the renewal of residency permits for UNHCR staff in Lebanon.[116] UNHCR released a statement emphasizing, "we do not discourage returns that are based on individual free and informed decisions."[117] The statement also noted that the freeze on residency permit renewals "directly impacts UNHCR's ability to effectively carry out critical protection and solutions work in Lebanon."[118]

Russian Initiative for Refugee Return

Reports suggest that Russian officials have circulated detailed logistical plans for facilitating the return of refugees from neighboring countries to Syria under Syrian government auspices. Efforts would include the preparation of special crossing points and camps for accommodation paired with requests for increased international contributions to reconstruction efforts.

Many Lebanese leaders have embraced Russian efforts to return Syrian refugees in Lebanon to Syria. Caretaker Foreign Minister Gibran Bassil

---

[113] "More than 50 Syrian refugee families return to Syria," *National News Agency*, June 10, 2017; "The return of Syrian refugee families from the camps of Ersal to the village of Essal el-Ward in Syria," July 12, 2017, http://www.lebarmy.gov.lb; "Return of Syrian refugees signals shift in Lebanese policy," *The National*, August 2, 2017.

[114] "Lebanon: Refugees in Border Zone at Risk," Human Rights Watch, September 20, 2017.

[115] "Lebanon blocks UNHCR residency permits over Syria refugee spat," *France24*, June 8, 2018.

[116] "Lebanon freezes UNHCR staff residency applications in row over Syrian refugees," *Reuters*, June 8, 2018.

[117] "Spokesperson's comment on Lebanon," unhcr.org, June 12, 2018.

[118] Ibid.

has stated that Lebanon is fully committed to the success of Russia's proposal and added that, "Lebanon refuses to tie the return of refugees to the political solution [in Syria]."[119] Bassil also stated, "Our basic case is the preservation of [Lebanese] identity. We don't want what happened with the Palestinians to happen with the Syrians."[120]

UNHCR Representative in Lebanon Mireille Girard has stated that, "The position of UNHCR, and of the UN in general, is that at the moment we cannot encourage or promote refugee returns."[121] She noted that UNHCR is working to resolve a number of obstacles facing refugees, including the recovery of national identity documents, potential repercussions for failure to complete military service in Syria, and challenges regarding property restitution. However, she added that refugees have the right to make their own decisions regarding when to return, stating, "We are not here to decide on their behalf and we respect their decisions."

ECONOMY AND FISCAL ISSUES

Lebanon's economy is service oriented (69.5% of GDP), and primary sectors include banking and financial services as well as tourism. The country faces a number of economic challenges, including high unemployment and the third-highest debt-to-GDP ratio in the world (142%, 2017 est).[122] In October 2018, the World Bank estimated that Lebanon's debt-to-GDP ratio is expected to "persist in an unsustainable path towards 155% by end-2018."[123] Moody's Investors Service has warned that the cost of servicing Lebanon's public debt could reach 58.6% of government revenue by 2021.[124]

---

[119] "Lebanon should not be a hostage to Syria crisis: Lavrov," *Daily Star*, August 21, 2018.
[120] Ibid.
[121] Interview with UNHCR Representative Mireille Girard in UNOCHA, Humanitarian Bulletin: Lebanon, Issue 32, 1May-31 July 2018.
[122] "Lebanon," CIA World Factbook, May 15, 2018.
[123] World Bank, "Lebanon's Economic Outlook – October 2018."
[124] "Lebanese economy hammered by political crisis, debt," *Daily Star*, August 25, 2018.

The war in neighboring Syria has significantly affected Lebanon's traditional growth sectors— tourism, real estate, and construction. Economic growth has slowed from an average of 8% between 2007 and 2009 to 1% to 2% since the outbreak of the Syrian conflict in 2011 and the resulting refugee influx.[125] Foreign direct investment fell 68% during the first year of the Syria conflict (from $3.5 billion to $1.1 billion),[126] but reached $2.5 billion in 2016.[127]

The Lebanese government is unable to consistently provide basic services such as electricity, water, and waste treatment, and the World Bank notes that the quality and availability of basic public services is significantly worse in Lebanon than both regional and world averages.[128] As a result, citizens rely on private providers, many of whom are affiliated with political parties. The retreat of the state from these basic functions has enabled a patronage network whereby citizens support political parties— including Hezbollah—in return for basic services.

Unresolved political dynamics have exacerbated Lebanon's economic and fiscal struggles. Between 2014 and 2016, when the office of the presidency remained unfilled, Lebanon lost international donor funding when parliamentary boycotts prevented the body from voting on key matters, including the ratification of loan agreements. In October 2017, Parliament voted to pass the budget—the first time since 2005 that a state budget has been approved.[129]

Lebanon's economy is also affected by fluctuations in the country's relationship to the Gulf states, which are a key source of tourism, foreign investment, and aid. In early 2016, Saudi Arabia suspended $3 billion in pledged aid to Lebanon's military after Lebanon's foreign minister declined to endorse an otherwise unanimous Arab League statement condemning attacks against Saudi diplomatic missions in Iran.[130] Saudi Arabia and other Gulf states instituted a travel warning to Lebanon and

---

[125] "Lebanon," CIA World Factbook, December 20, 2016.
[126] "FDI Declines by 68Pct in 2012 to $1.1 billion," *The Daily Star*, March 19, 2013.
[127] "Only Lebanon sees positive FDI growth in MENA," *Daily Star*, August 23, 2017.
[128] World Bank, *Lebanon Economic Monitor*, Fall 2015, pp. 24-29.
[129] "Lebanon Passes First State Budget in 12 Years as Deadlock Eases," *Bloomberg*, October 20, 2017.
[130] "Saudis Cut Off Funding for Military Aid to Lebanon," *New York Times*, February 19, 2016.

urged their citizens to leave the country—impacting Lebanon's real estate and tourism sectors, which depend on spending by wealthy Gulf visitors. Lebanon's relationship with Saudi Arabia continues to fluctuate (see "Hariri's Temporary Resignation" above).

Despite these numerous challenges, the Central Bank of Lebanon under the leadership of long-serving Governor Riad Salameh has played a stabilizing role. The Central Bank maintains more than $43 billion in foreign reserves,[131] and the Lebanese pound, which is pegged to the dollar, has remained stable. Despite sporadic violence targeting Lebanese banks, Salameh has supported the implementation of the Hizballah International Financing Prevention Act, which seeks to bar from the U.S. financial system any bank that knowingly engages with Hezbollah.

The Capital Investment Plan

At the CEDRE international donor conference, held in Paris in April 2018, Lebanese officials presented the Capital Investment Plan (CIP). The plan, which was endorsed by the Lebanese cabinet, seeks $20 billion in funding (in the form of public-private partnerships, grants, and concessional loans). The project would fund the rehabilitation and expansion of Lebanon's aging and overstretched infrastructure, although funding the project would significantly increase Lebanon's public debt. The Paris CEDRE conference generated $11.8 billion, mainly in soft loans, with significant pledges from the World Bank, European Bank for Reconstruction and Development, the European Investment Bank, the Islamic Development Bank, and others.

Regional and Western states also pledged funding, including Saudi Arabia, France, Qatar, and the United States.[132]

---

[131] "Lebanon Reserves Recovered After Hariri Crisis, Salameh Says," *Bloomberg*, February 22, 2018.

[132] $11.8 billion promised at the Paris CEDRE conference," businessnews.com.lb, April 6, 2018.

Eastern Mediterranean Energy Resources and Disputed Boundaries

In 2010, the U.S. Geological Survey estimated that there are considerable undiscovered oil and gas resources that may be technically recoverable in the Levant Basin, an area that encompasses coastal areas of Syria, Lebanon, Israel, Gaza, and Egypt and adjacent offshore waters.[133] A 2018 report by Lebanon's Bank Audi estimated that Lebanon could generate over $200 billion in revenues from offshore gas exploration, with the potential to significantly reduce the country's debt to GDP ratio.[134]

However, maritime boundary disputes persist between Lebanon and Israel. The two states hold differing views of the correct delineation points for their joint maritime boundary relative to the Israel-Lebanon 1949 Armistice Line that serves as the de facto land border between the two countries.[135] Lebanon objects to an Israeli-Cypriot agreement that draws a specific maritime border delineation point relative to the 1949 Israel-Lebanon Armistice Line and claims roughly 330 square miles of waters that overlap with areas claimed by Israel. Resolution of Israel-Lebanon disputes over the Armistice Line are further complicated by Israel's military presence in the Sheba'a Farms area claimed by Lebanon adjacent to the Israeli-occupied Golan Heights, captured from Syria in 1967.

After a three-year delay, Lebanon's Energy Ministry in January 2017 announced that it would auction energy-development rights to five offshore areas. The announcement followed the approval by the Lebanese cabinet of two decrees defining the exploration blocks and setting out conditions for tenders and contracts. In February 2018, Lebanon signed its first offshore oil and gas exploration agreement for two blocks, including one disputed by Israel. A consortium of Total (France), Eni (Italy), and Novatek (Russia) was awarded two licenses to explore blocks 4 and 9.

---

[133] USGS, Assessment of Undiscovered Oil and Gas Resources of the Levant Basin Province, Eastern Mediterranean, March 2010.

[134] "Audi: Lebanon's share from gas over $200B," *Daily Star*, February 8, 2018.

[135] The Armistice Line is not the final agreed border between Lebanon and Israel, but coastal points on the line appear likely to be incorporated into any future Lebanon-Israel border agreement.

Israel has disputed part of Block 9. Total has said that drilling, which will begin in 2019, will be more than 15 miles from the border claimed by Israel.

Source: *The Economist*.
Notes: Boundaries and locations are approximate and not necessarily authoritative.

Figure 5. Eastern Mediterranean Maritime Territory Disputes and Energy Resources.

U.S. POLICY

The United States has sought to bolster forces that could serve as a counterweight to Syrian and Iranian influence in Lebanon through a variety of military and economic assistance programs. U.S. security assistance priorities reflect increased concern about the potential for Sunni jihadist groups such as the Islamic State to target Lebanon, as well as long-standing U.S. concerns about Hezbollah and preserving Israel's qualitative military edge (QME). U.S. economic aid to Lebanon is designed to promote democracy, stability, and economic growth, particularly in light of the challenges posed by the ongoing conflict in neighboring Syria. Congress places several certification requirements on U.S. assistance funds for Lebanon annually in an effort to prevent their misuse or the transfer of U.S. equipment to Hezbollah or other designated terrorists. Hezbollah's participation in the Syria conflict on behalf of the Asad government is presumed to have strengthened the group's military capabilities and has increased concern among some in Congress over the continuation of U.S. assistance to the LAF.

Current Funding and the FY2019 Request

According to the FY2019 Congressional Budget Justification for Foreign Operations, the executive branch obligated $208 million in assistance for Lebanon during 2017, including $110 million in Economic Support Fund (ESF) aid and $80 million in Foreign Military Financing (FMF) aid. President Trump's FY2018 budget request sought $103 million in total aid to Lebanon, mostly in economic aid ($85 million). The FY2018 appropriations act makes economic and military aid available for Lebanon on conditional terms, and the explanatory statement accompanying the act allocates $115 million in ESF for Lebanon.

FMF has been one of the primary sources of U.S. funding for the LAF, along with the CounterISIL Train and Equip Fund (CTEF). The FY2018 Consolidated Appropriations Act (P.L. 115-141) provides $1.8 billion for CTEF, some of which may be made available to enhance the border security of nations adjacent to conflict areas—including Lebanon. The act and explanatory statement also require the Administration to submit by September 1, 2018, a report on military assistance to Lebanon, including an assessment of the capability and performance of the LAF over time in strengthening border security and combatting terrorism, securing Lebanon's borders, interdicting arms shipments, preventing the use of Lebanon as a safe haven for terrorist groups, and implementing U.N. Security Council Resolution 1701.

The Administration's FY2019 aid request for Lebanon seeks $152 million in total funding, including $85 million in economic aid (ESDF) and $50 million in FMF.

Economic Aid

The influx of over 1 million Syrian refugees into Lebanon has strained the country's already weak infrastructure. Slow economic growth and high levels of public debt have limited government spending on basic public services, and this gap has been filled by various confessional groups affiliated with local politicians. In light of these challenges, U.S. programs are aimed at increasing the capacity of the public sector to provide basic services to both refugees and Lebanese host communities. This includes reliable access to potable water, sanitation, and health services. It also involves increasing the capacity of the public education system to cope with the refugee influx. Other U.S. programs are designed to foster inclusive economic growth, particularly among impoverished and underserved communities. This includes efforts to extend financial lending to small firms, create more jobs, and increase incomes. Taken together, these programs also aim to make communities less vulnerable to recruitment by extremist groups.[136]

Military Aid

The United States has provided more than $1.7 billion to LAF since 2006.[137] Following the legislative elections in early May, the State Department released a statement reiterating,

> U.S. assistance for the LAF is a key component of our policy to reinforce Lebanon's sovereignty and secure its borders, counter internal threats, and build up its legitimate state institutions. Additionally, U.S. security assistance supports implementation of UN Security Council Resolutions 1559, 1680, and 1701, and promotes the LAF's ability to

---

[136] For more information, see *USAID/Lebanon Country Development Cooperation Strategy, December 2014-December 2019.*

[137] "U.S. Security Cooperation with Lebanon," State Department Fact Sheet, Bureau of Political-Military Affairs, May 11, 2018.

extend full governmental control throughout the country in conjunction with the UN Interim Forces in Lebanon (UNIFIL).[138]

In June 2018, the United States delivered four A-29 Super Tucano aircraft to the LAF, completing a delivery of six. U.S. Ambassador to Lebanon Elizabeth Richard noted that six MD-530G light attack helicopters would be forthcoming. The helicopters, valued at $94 million, were announced in December 2017 during the visit of U.S. Central Command Commander General Joseph Votel to Lebanon, together with an additional $27 million package that includes unmanned aerial vehicles and communications and electronic equipment.[139]

Since late 2014, the United States (in some cases using grants from Saudi Arabia) has also delivered Hellfire air-to-ground missiles, precision artillery, TOW-II missiles, M198 howitzers, small arms, and ammunition to Lebanon. Related U.S. training and advisory support is ongoing. The United States conducts annual bilateral military exercises with the LAF. Known as Resolute Response, these exercises include participants from the U.S. Navy, Coast Guard, and Army. In June 2018, Ambassador Richard noted that the United States has trained over 32,000 Lebanese troops.[140]

In August 2017, a Pentagon spokesperson confirmed the presence of U.S. Special Operations Forces in Lebanon, which he described as providing training and support to the LAF.[141] While he would not comment on the size of the contingent, some observers estimate that more than 70 Special Operations Command Central (SOCCENT) trainers and support personnel operate in Lebanon at any given time.[142] According to a U.S.

---

[138] Ibid.

[139] "CENTCOM Commander General Joseph Votel's Visit to Lebanon," U.S. Embassy Beirut Press Release, December 13, 2017.

[140] Remarks by U.S. Ambassador to Lebanon Elizabeth Richard, U.S. Embassy Beirut Press Release, June 13, 2018.

[141] "US Special Forces operating in Lebanon 'close to Hizballah,'" The New Arab, August 6, 2017.

[142] Aram Nerguizian, "The Lebanese Armed Forces, Hezbollah and the Race to Defeat ISIS," Center for Strategic and International Studies, July 31, 2017.

204   *Carla E. Humud*

Army publication, U.S. Special Operations Forces have been deployed to Lebanon since at least 2012.[143]

Table 1. Select U.S. Foreign Assistance Funding for Lebanon-Related Programs. $, millions, Fiscal Year of Appropriation unless noted

Account/Program	FY2016	FY2017 Actual	FY2018 Request	FY2019 Request
FMF	-	-	-	50
FMF-OCO	85.9	80	-	-
ESF-OCO	110	110	-	-
ESDF	-	-	-	85
ESDF-OCO	-	-	85	-
IMET	2.79	2.6	2.75	2.75
INCLE	10	-	-	6.2
INCLE-OCO	10	10	6.25	-
NADR	4.76	-	-	8.8
NADR-OCO	1.8	5.7	9.82	-

Source: U.S. State Department FY2018 and FY2019 Budget Request Materials.

Notes: Table does not reflect all funds or programs related to Lebanon. Does not account for all reprogramming actions of prior year funds or obligation notices provided to congressional committees of jurisdiction. Some programs may be designed and implemented in ways that also meet non-IS related objectives.

FMF = Foreign Military Financing; ESF = Economic Support Fund; ESDF = Economic Support and Development Fund; IMET = International Military Education and Training; INCLE = International Narcotics Control and Law Enforcement; NADR = Nonproliferation, Antiterrorism, Demining and Related Programs.

U.S. assistance for border security improvements in Lebanon has drawn particular attention from Congress because of threats stemming from the conflict in Syria. As noted above, both Hezbollah and the LAF have deployed forces to the mountainous border area separating Lebanon and Syria in a bid to halt infiltrations. Longer-standing U.S. concerns about improving Lebanon's border control and security capabilities focus on stemming flows of weapons to Hezbollah and other armed groups in Lebanon, as called for by UNSCR 1701.

---

[143] "Operationalizing Strategic Policy in Lebanon," *Special Warfare*, April-June 2012, http://www.soc.mil/swcs/swmag/archive/SW2502/SW2502OperationalizingStrategicPolicyInLebanon.html.

The FY2017 NDAA realigned CTPF funding to Operation and Maintenance, Defense-Wide, and made it available for a wide range of security cooperation activities. In FY2017, Lebanon received $42.9 million via CTPF-funded border security improvement programs authorized by Section 1226 of the FY2016 NDAA (P.L. 114-92). Under Section 1226, as amended, DOD may, with State Department concurrence, provide security assistance to the armed forces of Lebanon, Jordan, Egypt, and Tunisia in support of border security improvement efforts on their respective borders with Syria, Iraq, and Libya.

Table 2. Select DOD Security Assistance Funding for Lebanon-Related Programs
$, millions

Authority or Appropriation Category	FY2015	FY2016	FY2017	FY2018
CTPF	48,339	42,032	118,357	-
10 U.S.C. 333	-	-	-	110,445

Source: U.S. Defense Department Obligation Notifications to Congress, 2017-2018.
Notes: Figures provided by year of obligation/expenditure, as reported in the appendices of DOD obligation notifications to Congress. Figures for FY2017 and FY2018 are for notified amounts to Congress only. Since CTPF was only an authorized DOD appropriations account for FY2015-FY2016, CTPF funds listed in FY2017 are for funds appropriated in prior years. *CTPF = Counterterrorism Partnerships Fund.*
Funds include notifications for military and security force train and equip assistance as well as funds for border security enhancement authorized by Section 1226 of the FY2016 National Defense Authorization Act (NDAA P.L. 114-92), as amended. Section 1204 of the Senate version of the FY2019 NDAA (H.R. 5515 EAS) would extend and aim to clarify this authority with regard to Lebanon and other countries.

Recent Legislation

Annual appropriations bills have established conditions for ESF and security assistance for Lebanon. Most recently, Section 7041(e) of the 2018 Consolidated Appropriations Act (P.L. 115 141) states that funding for the Lebanese Internal Security Forces (ISF) and the LAF may not be appropriated if either body is controlled by a U.S.-designated foreign terrorist organization. ESF funding for Lebanon may be made available notwithstanding Section 1224 of the FY2003 Foreign Relations Authorization Act (P.L. 107-228), which states that ESF funds for Lebanon may not be obligated until the President certifies to the appropriate congressional committees that the LAF has been deployed to the Israeli-Lebanese border and that the government of Lebanon is effectively asserting its authority in the area in which the LAF is deployed. FMF assistance to the LAF may not be obligated until the Secretary of State submits to the appropriations committees a spend plan, including actions to be taken to ensure equipment provided to the LAF is used only for intended purposes.

FY2019 Legislation

The House version of the FY2019 Foreign Operations appropriations bill (H.R. 6385) would not provide the notwithstanding 1224 exception that has enabled unrestricted ESF provision to Lebanon in recent years, in spite of ESF restrictions contained in Section 1224 of the FY2003 Foreign Relations Authorization Act (P.L. 107-228). The Senate bill (S. 3108) would provide the notwithstanding 1224 exception for ESF. The House and Senate bills would both state that

> funds appropriated by this Act under the heading 'Foreign Military Financing Program' for assistance for Lebanon may be made available only to professionalize the LAF and to strengthen border security and combat terrorism, including training and equipping the LAF to secure Lebanon's borders, interdicting arms shipments, preventing the use of Lebanon as a safe haven for terrorist groups, and to implement United Nations Security Council Resolution 1701.

This is consistent with the approach taken by successive Congresses to FMF aid to Lebanon in appropriations bills going back to the Omnibus Appropriations Act, 2009 (P.L. 111-8). The FY2019 Continuing Appropriations Act (Division C of P.L. 115-245) makes funds available for foreign operations programs in Lebanon on the terms and at the levels provided for in FY2018 appropriations through December 7, 2018.

The FY2019 NDAA (P.L. 115-232) does not specify a specific amount for Lebanon. Section 1213 notes that the Secretary of Defense, with the concurrence of the Secretary of State, is authorized to provide support on a reimbursement basis "to the Government of Lebanon for purposes of supporting and enhancing efforts of the armed forces of Lebanon to increase security and sustain increased security along the border of Lebanon with Syria."

The defense appropriations act for FY2019 (Division A of P.L. 115-245) makes $1.3 billion in CTEF funds available until September 2020 to assist in counter-IS activities—including to enhance the border security of nations adjacent to conflict areas including Jordan, Lebanon, Egypt, and Tunisia. Funds are to be made available provided that recipients are assessed for associations with terrorist groups or groups associated with the government of Iran.

Hezbollah Sanctions

Hezbollah, as an entity, is listed as a Specially Designated Terrorist (1995); a Foreign Terrorist Organization (1997); and a Specially Designated Global Terrorist or SDGT (2001). Hezbollah was designated again in 2012 under E.O. 13582, for its support to the Syrian government. Several affiliated individuals and entities have also been designated, including Secretary-General Hasan Nasrallah (1995) and the Hezbollah-run satellite television network Al Manar.

In May, the U.S. Department of the Treasury's Office of Foreign Assets Control (OFAC) announced a set of additional sanctions on Hezbollah members:

- On May 15, OFAC designated Muhammad Qasir as a SDGT. Qasir served as a conduit for financial disbursements from the Iranian Revolutionary Guard CorpsQods Force to Hezbollah.
- On May 16, OFAC together with six Arab Gulf states designated members of Hezbollah's Shura Council, the group's primary decisionmaking body.

- On May 17, OFAC designated two additional Hezbollah members as SDGTs: Hezbollah financier Muhammad Ibrahim Bazzi, and Hezbollah's representative to Iran, Abdullah Safi al Din.

Hizballah International Financing Prevention Act of 2015

In December 2015, the 114th Congress enacted a sanctions bill targeting parties that facilitate financial transactions for Hezbollah's benefit (H.R. 2297, P.L. 114-102). The Hizballah International Financing Prevention Act of 2015 (HIFPA) requires, inter alia, that the President, subject to a waiver authority, prohibit or impose strict conditions on the opening or maintaining in the United States of a correspondent account or a payable-through account by a foreign financial institution that knowingly

- facilitates a transaction or transactions for Hezbollah;
- facilitates a significant transaction or transactions of a person on specified lists of specially designated nationals and blocked persons, property, and property interests for acting on behalf of or at the direction of, or being owned or controlled by, Hezbollah;
- engages in money laundering to carry out such an activity; or
- facilitates a significant transaction or provides significant financial services to carry out such an activity.

Some Lebanese observers have expressed concern that the legislation could inadvertently damage Lebanon's economy or banking sector if regulations written or actions taken to implement the law broadly target Lebanese financial institutions or lead other jurisdictions to forgo business in Lebanon because of difficulties associated with distinguishing between legitimate and illegitimate institutions and activities.[144] Items of particular interest to Lebanese parties, as U.S. Treasury officials craft implementing regulations for the law, include whether or not the United States will consider Lebanese government payments of salaries to Hezbollah members

---

[144] Hassan Al-Qishawi, "Assessing financial sanctions on Hizbullah," Al Ahram Weekly (Egypt), February 18, 2016; and, Jean Aziz, "How Lebanese banks are handling US sanctions on Hezbollah," Al Monitor (Washington), January 12, 2016.

who hold public office to be activities of terrorist financing or money laundering concern.

Hezbollah's leader, Hassan Nasrallah, has sought to downplay the effects of this law, stating the following in a June 2016 speech:

> Hizballah's budget, salaries, expenses, arms and missiles are coming from the Islamic Republic of Iran. Is this clear? This is no one's business. As long as Iran has money, we have money. Can we be any more frank about that? Our allocated money is coming to us, not through the banks. Just as we receive rockets with which we threaten Israel, our money is coming to us. No law can prevent this money from reaching us.[145]

At the same time, Nasrallah also criticized Lebanese banks for what he described as overcompliance with the legislation, saying, "[...] there are banks in Lebanon that went too far. They were American more than the Americans. They did some things that the Americans did not even ask them to do."[146]

Some analysts have questioned the effect of U.S. sanctions on Hezbollah, noting that the group maintains a largely cash-based economy and that Iran is still able to use land and air corridors to conduct cash transfers.[147]

Lebanese leaders have raised concerns about potential unintended consequences of any new sanctions on groups with ties to Hezbollah, given that Hezbollah is deeply embedded in Lebanon's political and social spheres through its membership in Lebanon's governing coalition and management of a vast network of social services. Some have also noted that sanctions imposing new regulations on the Lebanese banking sector could lower the inflow of foreign remittances into Lebanon, estimated at 15% of the country's GDP.[148] According to one analyst, "expatriate

---

[145] Transcript, televised remarks by Hezbollah Secretary General Hasan Nasrallah, June 24, 2016.
[146] Ibid.
[147] "Iran pays Hezbollah $700 million a year, U.S. official says," *The National*, June 5, 2018.
[148] Nicholas Blanford, "US sanctions on Hezbollah cause fallout on Lebanon's economy," *The Arab Weekly*, June 4, 2017; World Bank Open Data Indicators, *Personal remittances, received (% of GDP)*, 2015, http://data.worldbank.org/indicator/BX.TRF.PWKR. DT.GD.ZS.

remittances support the solvency of Lebanon's banks, thus consolidating the banks' potential to finance the economy, in particular their ability to buy Lebanese treasury bonds."[149]

Since the enactment of HIFPA in late 2015, congressional leaders raised the possibility of imposing additional sanctions on Hezbollah and/or groups that maintain political or economic ties to Hezbollah. Some analysts have argued for the use of secondary sanctions under HIFPA to target Hezbollah associates or allies, emphasizing the involvement of Hezbollah in a range of transnational criminal activities.[150] U.S. policymakers have stressed that any new sanctions would seek to target Hezbollah, not the broader Lebanese state.

Hizballah International Financing Prevention Amendments Act of 2017

In July 2017, the Hizballah International Financing Prevention Amendments Act of 2017 was introduced by Representatives Royce and Engel in the House (H.R. 3329) and by Senators Rubio and Shaheen in the Senate (S. 1595).[151] In October 2017, H.R. 3329 was passed by the House as amended and S. 1595 was passed by the Senate as amended. S. 1595 was passed by the House in September 2018, and amended by the Senate in October.

The bill expands upon HIFPA 2015 in a number of ways. It would require the President to impose sanctions on foreign persons that he determines to have knowingly provided "significant support" to a fixed list of Hezbollah-linked entities (including, but not limited to, Al Manar TV), as well as sanctions on foreign persons determined to be engaged in fundraising or recruitment activities for Hezbollah. It would require a report on foreign financial institutions that are owned, located in, or controlled by state sponsors of terrorism. It would require the President to

---

[149] "Remittances key for Lebanon's economy, "*Al Monitor*, November 7, 2014.
[150] Matthew Levitt, "Attacking Hezbollah's Financial Network: Policy Options," testimony submitted to the House Committee on Foreign Affairs, June 8, 2017.
[151] H.R. 3329 was referred to the House Committees on Foreign Affairs, Financial Services, and Judiciary. S. 1595 was referred to the Senate Committee on Banking, Housing, and Urban Affairs.

impose sanctions on any agency of a foreign state that knowingly provides significant financial or material support to Hezbollah (or to an entity owned by it or acting on its behalf), as well as sanctions on Hezbollah for narcotics trafficking and transnational criminal activities.

The bill would also require a report on jurisdictions outside Lebanon that knowingly allow Hezbollah to use their territory to carry out terrorist activities, including training, financing, and recruitment. It would call on the President to prescribe, as necessary, enhanced due diligence policies for U.S. financial institutions (and foreign financial institutions maintaining correspondent accounts with them) that the President determines provide significant financial services for persons and entities operating in those jurisdictions.

The bill includes a national security waiver which would allow the Administration to waive the imposition of sanctions.

Other Pending Hezbollah-Related Legislation

The 115th Congress continues to consider a range of Hezbollah-related legislation, including the following:

- Urging the European Union to designate Hizballah in its entirety as a terrorist organization and increase pressure on it and its members (H.Res. 359). Introduced in May 2017 by Representative Deutch, passed by the House in October 2017.
- Sanctioning Hizballah's Illicit Use of Civilians as Defenseless Shields Act (H.R. 3342). Introduced by Representative Gallagher in July 2017, passed the House in October 2017.
- Hezbollah Kingpin Designation Act (H.R. 5035). Introduced by Representative Budd in February 2018, referred to the House Committee on Foreign Affairs.
- Disarm Hizballah Act (H.R. 5540). Introduced in April 2018 by Representative Suozzi.

OUTLOOK

The momentum that drove the passage of a new electoral law in June 2017 and the holding of long-delayed elections in May 2018 appears to have stalled amid the challenges of government formation. With Lebanon's government in caretaker status pending the selection of a new cabinet, disputes among various political factions threaten to generate renewed paralysis. This in turn limits the government's ability to take up key issues—including economic reforms whose implementation has been described by international donors as a condition of the funds pledged for Lebanon's Capital Investment Plan (CIP).

Regional tensions remain another potentially destabilizing force. As the United States and its allies seek to curb Iranian activities in the region, Lebanon remains vulnerable as an arena for Iran (via Hezbollah) to assert its influence. Despite pressure by the United States and others, Lebanese leaders appear reluctant to risk civil conflict by confronting Hezbollah directly. Prime Minister Hariri has argued that Hezbollah is a regional, rather than purely Lebanese, phenomenon, and that the resolution of this issue should not fall to Lebanon alone. Meanwhile, tensions between Israel and Iran in neighboring Syria continue to escalate, risking spillover into Lebanon.

Lebanon's bilateral relationship with Syria is likely to evolve over the coming year, as the conflict there shifts militarily in the Syrian government's favor. Lebanese leaders face pressure to normalize relations with Syria, in part to access primary overland trade routes via border crossings recently recaptured by the Syrian government. Lebanese leaders also must determine how to balance policies favoring refugee return to Syria with the safety concerns expressed by international humanitarian organizations.

In: The Middle East
Editor: Doyle Keller

ISBN: 978-1-53616-191-5
© 2019 Nova Science Publishers, Inc.

Chapter 6

TURKEY: BACKGROUND AND U.S. RELATIONS (UPDATED)*

Jim Zanotti and Clayton Thomas

ABSTRACT

Turkey, a NATO ally since 1952, significantly affects a number of key U.S. national security issues in the Middle East and Europe. U.S.-Turkey relations have worsened throughout this decade over several matters, including Syria's civil war, Turkey-Israel tensions, Turkey-Russia cooperation, and various Turkish domestic developments. The United States and NATO have military personnel and key equipment deployed to various sites in Turkey, including at Incirlik air base in the southern part of the country.

Bilateral ties have reached historic lows in the summer of 2018. The major flashpoint has been a Turkish criminal case against American pastor Andrew Brunson. U.S. sanctions on Turkey related to the Brunson case and responses by Turkey and international markets appear to have seriously aggravated an already precipitous drop in the value of Turkey's currency.

---

* This is an edited, reformatted and augmented version of Congressional Research Service, Publication No. R41368, dated August 31, 2018.

Amid this backdrop, Congress has actively engaged on several issues involving Turkey, including the following:

- Turkey's possible S-400 air defense system acquisition from Russia.
- Turkey's efforts to acquire U.S.-origin F-35 Joint Strike Fighter aircraft and its companies' role in the international F-35 consortium's supply chain.
- Complex U.S.-Turkey interactions in Syria involving several state and non-state actors, including Russia and Iran. Over strong Turkish objections, the United States continues to partner with Syrian Kurds linked with Kurdish militants in Turkey, and Turkey's military has occupied large portions of northern Syria to minimize Kurdish control and leverage.
- Turkey's domestic situation and its effect on bilateral relations. In addition to Pastor Brunson, Turkey has detained a number of other U.S. citizens (most of them dual U.S.-Turkish citizens) and Turkish employees of the U.S. government. Turkish officials and media have connected these cases to the July 2016 coup attempt in Turkey, and to Fethullah Gulen, the U.S.-based former cleric whom Turkey's government has accused of involvement in the plot.

In the FY2019 National Defense Authorization Act (NDAA, P.L. 115-232) enacted in August 2018, Congress has required a comprehensive report from the Trump Administration on (1) U.S.-Turkey relations, (2) the potential S-400 deal and its implications for U.S./NATO activity in Turkey, (3) possible alternatives to the S-400, and (4) various scenarios for the F-35 program with or without Turkey's participation. Other proposed legislation would condition Turkey's acquisition of the F-35 on a cancellation of the S-400 deal (FY2019 State and Foreign Operations Appropriations Act, S. 3180), place sanctions on Turkish officials for their role in detaining U.S. citizens or employees (also S. 3180), and direct U.S. action at selected international financial institutions to oppose providing assistance to Turkey (Turkey International Financial Institutions Act, S. 3248). The S-400 deal might also trigger sanctions under existing law (CAATSA).

The next steps in the fraught relations between the United States and Turkey will take place in the context of a Turkey in political transition and growing economic turmoil. Turkish President Recep Tayyip Erdogan, who has dominated politics in the country since 2002, won reelection to an empowered presidency in June 2018. Given Erdogan's consolidation of power, observers now question how he will govern a polarized electorate and deal with the foreign actors who can affect Turkey's financial solvency, regional security, and political influence. U.S.

officials and lawmakers can refer to Turkey's complex history, geography, domestic dynamics, and international relationships in evaluating how to encourage Turkey to align its policies with U.S. interests.

INTRODUCTION AND ISSUES FOR CONGRESS

U.S.-Turkey ties, always complicated, appear to have reached crisis levels in the summer of 2018. Although the United States and Turkey, NATO allies since 1952, share some vital interests, harmonizing priorities can be difficult. These priorities sometimes diverge irrespective of who leads the two countries, based on contrasting geography, threat perceptions, and regional roles. Current points of tension in the relationship include the following:

- Sanctions and worsening U.S.-Turkey relations. Policy differences and public acrimony between the two countries have fueled concern about their relationship and about Turkey's status as a U.S. ally. In August 2018, the Trump Administration levied sanctions against Turkey in connection with the continued detention of Andrew Brunson, an American pastor charged with terrorism. The sanctions appear to have quickened the decline in value of Turkey's already depreciating currency, which has lost considerable value against the dollar (see "Currency Decline: U.S.-Turkey Crisis and Sanctions" below). The crisis in bilateral relations has appeared to deepen as Turkey has retaliated with its own sanctions, and as each country has raised tariffs on imports from the other.
- Congressional initiatives.[1] Within the tense bilateral context, Congress has required the Trump Administration—in the FY2019

---

[1] According to the Turkish Coalition of America, a non-governmental organization that promotes positive Turkish-American relations, as of June 2018, there are at least 132 Members of the House of Representatives (127 of whom are voting Members) and four Senators in the

National Defense Authorization Act (NDAA, P.L. 115-232)—to report on the status of U.S.-Turkey relations. Also, some Members of Congress have proposed legislation to limit arms sales and strategic cooperation—particularly regarding the F-35 Joint Strike Fighter—or to place additional sanctions on Turkish officials. While Turkish President Recep Tayyip Erdogan and other Turkish leaders have sharply criticized U.S. policies on many issues, questions in U.S. public debate about Turkey's status as an ally and its relationship with Russia have intensified.

- Possible S-400 acquisition from Russia. Turkey's planned purchase of an S-400 air defense system from Russia could trigger U.S. sanctions under existing law. The possible transaction has sparked broader concern over Turkey's relationship with Russia and implications for NATO. U.S. officials seek to prevent the deal, and reports suggest that they may be offering alternatives to Turkey such as Patriot air defense systems.

- Syria and the Kurds. Turkey's political stances and military operations in Syria have fed U.S.-Turkey tensions, particularly regarding Kurdish-led militias supported by the United States against the Islamic State (IS, also known as ISIS/ISIL) over Turkey's strong objections.

- Turkey's domestic trajectory and financial distress. President Erdogan rules in an increasingly authoritarian manner. Presidential and parliamentary elections held in June 2018 consolidated Erdogan's power pursuant to constitutional changes approved in a controversial 2017 referendum. Meanwhile, even before the U.S. sanctions in August, Turkey's currency had fallen considerably in value amid concerns about rule of law, regional and domestic political uncertainty, significant corporate debt, and a stronger dollar.

Congressional Caucus on Turkey and Turkish Americans. See http://www.tcamerica.org/in-congress/caucus.htm.

Turkey

Geography: *Area:* 783,562 sq km (302,535 sq. mile), slightly larger than Texas.
People: *Population:* 80,845,215 (2017) Most populous cities: Istanbul 14.2 mil, Ankara 4.8 mil, Izmir 3mil, Bursa 1.9 mil, Adana 1.8 mil, Gaziantep 1.5 mil (2015).
% of Population 14 or Younger: 24.7% (2017).
Ethnic Groups: Turks 70%-75%; Kurds 19%; Other minorities 7%-12% (2016).
Religion: Muslim 99.8% (mostly Sunni), Others (mainly Christian and Jewish) 0.2% (2017).
Literacy: 95.6% (male 98.6%, female 92.6%) (2015).
Economy: *GDP Per Capita (at purchasing power parity):* $28,350.
Real GDP Growth: 4.4%.
Inflation: 15.4%.
Unemployment: 10.7%.
Budget Deficit as % of GDP: 2.9%.
Public Debt as % of GDP: 27.8%.
Current Account Deficit as % of GDP: 5.4%.
International reserves: $74 billion.
Source: Graphic created by CRS. Map boundaries and information generated by Hannah Fischer using Department of State Boundaries (2011); Esri (2014); ArcWorld (2014); DeLorme (2014). Fact information (2018 estimates unless otherwise specified) from International Monetary Fund, World Economic Outlook Database; Turkish Statistical Institute; World Bank; Economist Intelligence Unit; and Central Intelligence Agency, *The World Factbook*.

Figure 1. Turkey at a Glance.

COUNTRY OVERVIEW AND THE ERDOGAN ERA

Turkey's large, diversified economy, Muslim majority population, and geographic position straddling Europe and the Middle East make it a significant regional power. Important political developments in Turkey since 2002 have occurred within the context of significant socioeconomic changes that began in the 1980s. The military-guided governments that came to power after Turkey's 1980 coup helped establish Turkey's export-driven economy. This led to the gradual empowerment of a largely Sunni Muslim middle class from Turkey's Anatolian heartland.

These socioeconomic changes helped fuel political transformation led by the Islamist-leaning Justice and Development Party (*Adalet ve Kalkinma Partisi*, or AKP) and President (formerly Prime Minister) Recep Tayyip Erdogan. The AKP won governing majorities four times—2002, 2007, 2011, and 2015—during a period in which Turkey's economy generally enjoyed growth and stability. For decades since its founding in the 1920s, the Turkish republic had relied upon its military, judiciary, and other bastions of its Kemalist (a term inspired by Turkey's republican founder, Mustafa Kemal Ataturk) "secular elite" to protect it from political and ideological extremes—sacrificing at least some of its democratic vitality in the process.

Erdogan has worked to reduce the political power of the "secular elite" and has clashed with other possible rival power centers, including previous allies in the Fethullah Gulen movement.[2] Domestic polarization has intensified since 2013: nationwide antigovernment protests that began in Istanbul's Gezi Park took place that year, and corruption allegations later surfaced against a number of Erdogan's colleagues in and out of government.[3]

After Erdogan became president in August 2014 via Turkey's first-ever popular presidential election, he claimed a mandate for increasing his

---

[2] For more on Gulen and the Gulen movement, see CRS In Focus IF10444, *Fethullah Gulen, Turkey, and the United States: A Reference*, by Jim Zanotti and Clayton Thomas.
[3] Freedom House, *Democracy in Crisis: Corruption, Media, and Power in Turkey*, February 3, 2014.

power and pursuing a "presidential system" of governance. Analyses of Erdogan sometimes characterize him as one or more of the following: a pragmatic populist, a protector of the vulnerable, a budding authoritarian, an indispensable figure, an Islamic ideologue.[4]

July 2016 Failed Coup

On July 15-16, 2016, elements within the Turkish military operating outside the chain of command mobilized air and ground forces in a failed attempt to seize political power from President Erdogan and Prime Minister Binali Yildirim.[5] Resistance by security forces loyal to the government and civilians in key areas of Istanbul and Ankara succeeded in foiling the coup,[6] with around 270 killed on both sides.[7] Turkish officials publicly blame the plot on military officers with alleged links to Fethullah Gulen—formerly a state-employed imam in Turkey and now a permanent U.S. resident. Allies at one point, the AKP and Gulen's movement had a falling out in 2013 that complicated existing struggles in Turkey regarding power and political freedom. Gulen denied taking part in the July 2016 coup plot, but acknowledged that he "could not rule out" involvement by some of his followers.[8] Gulen's U.S. residency and Turkish dissatisfaction with the U.S. response to the coup plot probably intensified anti-American sentiment, which Erdogan has actively used to bolster his domestic appeal. Shortly after the failed coup, Erdogan placed Turkey's military and intelligence institutions more firmly under the civilian government's control.[9] In the two years since, Turkey's government has dismissed around 130,000 Turks from government posts, detained more than 60,000,[10] and taken over or closed various businesses, schools, and media outlets.[11] The government largely justified its actions by claiming that those affected are associated with the Gulen movement, even though the measures may be broader in terms of whom they directly impact.[12] The UN and others have expressed concern over reports alleging that some detainees have been subjected to beatings, torture, and other human rights violations.[13]

---

[4] See, e.g., Soner Cagaptay, *The New Sultan: Erdogan and the Crisis of Modern Turkey*, New York: I.B. Tauris & Co. Ltd, 2017; Burak Kadercan, "Erdogan's Last Off-Ramp: Authoritarianism, Democracy, and the Future of Turkey," War on the Rocks, July 28, 2016.

[5] Metin Gurcan, "Why Turkey's coup didn't stand a chance," *Al-Monitor Turkey Pulse*, July 17, 2016.

[6] Nathan Gardels, "A Former Top Turkish Advisor Explains Why Erdogan Is the Coup's Biggest Winner," *Huffington Post*, July 19, 2016.

[7] Ray Sanchez, "Fethullah Gulen on 'GPS': Failed Turkey coup looked 'like a Hollywood movie,'" CNN, July 31, 2016.

[8] Stephanie Saul, "An Exiled Cleric Denies Playing a Leading Role in Coup Attempt," *New York Times*, July 16, 2016.

[9] Cinar Kiper and Elena Becatoros, "Turkey's Erdogan brings military more under gov't," Associated Press, August 1, 2016; Yesim Dikmen and David Dolan, "Turkey culls nearly 1,400 from army, overhauls top military council," Reuters, July 31, 2016.

[10] Carlotta Gall, "Turkish Leader's Next Target in Crackdown on Dissent: The Internet," *New York Times*, March 4, 2018.

[11] Kareem Fahim, "As Erdogan prepares for new term, Turkey dismisses more than 18,000 civil servants," *Washington Post*, July 8, 2018.

[12] Chris Morris, "Reality Check: The numbers behind the crackdown in Turkey," BBC, June 18, 2018.

Erdogan's consolidation of power has continued. He outlasted the July 2016 coup attempt, and then scored victories in the April 2017 constitutional referendum and the June 2018 presidential and parliamentary elections. U.S. and European Union officials have expressed a number of concerns about rule of law and civil liberties in Turkey,[14] including the government's influence on media[15] and Turkey's reported status as the country with the most journalists in prison.[16]

While there may be some similarities between Turkey under Erdogan and countries like Russia, Iran, or China, some factors distinguish Turkey from them. For example, unlike Russia or Iran, Turkey's economy cannot rely on significant rents from natural resources if foreign sources of revenue or investment dry up. Unlike Russia and China, Turkey does not have nuclear weapons under its command and control. Additionally, unlike all three others, Turkey's economic, political, and national security institutions and traditions have been closely connected with those of the West for decades.

Erdogan and various other key Turkish figures (including political party leaders) are profiled in Appendix A.

Erdogan's Expanded Powers and June 2018 Victory

In an election that President Erdogan moved up to June 2018 from November 2019, he was reelected to a five-year presidential term with about 53% of the vote. The election reinforced his dominant role in Turkish politics because a controversial April 2017 popular referendum had determined that the presidential victor would govern with expanded

---

[13] "Turkey: UN expert says deeply concerned by rise in torture allegations," United Nations Office of the High Commissioner for Human Rights, February 27, 2018.

[14] See, e.g., State Department, Country Reports on Human Rights Practices for 2017, Turkey; European Commission, Turkey 2018 Report, April 17, 2018.

[15] See, e.g., "Turkish Media Group Bought by Pro-Government Conglomerate," *New York Times*, March 22, 2018.

[16] State Department Press Briefing, May 3, 2018; Elana Beiser, "Record number of journalists jailed as Turkey, China, Egypt pay scant price for repression," Committee to Protect Journalists, December 13, 2017.

powers. To obtain a parliamentary majority in the June elections, Erdogan's AKP relied on the Nationalist Action Party (*Milliyet Halk Partisi*, or MHP) (see Figure 2 below).

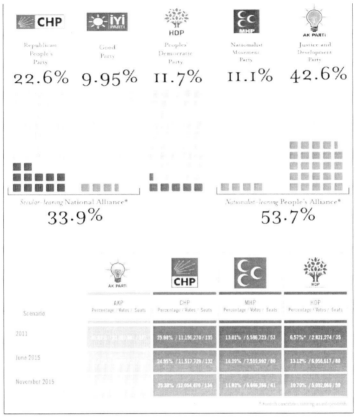

Sources: Institute for the Study of War; Bipartisan Policy Center. Note: Each square represents 12 parliamentary seats.

Figure 2. Turkey: 2018 Parliamentary Election Results in Context.

The MHP is the country's traditional Turkish nationalist party, and is known for opposing political accommodation with the Kurds. The MHP also had provided key support for the constitutional amendments approved in 2017. If the MHP's role in parliament influences policy, the government may be less inclined to make conciliatory overtures to the Kurdish militant group PKK (*Partiya Karkeren Kurdistan*, or Kurdistan Workers Party).[17] However, given his expanded powers, Erdogan might be less sensitive to parliamentary developments.

The New Presidential System

As the presidential system in Turkey gets underway, observers debate how the formalities of government and the surrounding politics will affect checks and balances.[18] As part of the debate, commentators routinely compare Turkey's system with other presidential systems, particularly those in the United States and France.[19] Under Turkey's constitutional changes, a president may serve for up to two five-year terms, and presidential and parliamentary elections occur at the same time. The parliament (expanded from 550 seats to 600) has some ability to counter presidential actions. It retains power to legislate, appoint some judges and bureaucrats, and approve the president's budget proposals. It also may impeach the president with a two-thirds majority. The president can declare a state of emergency, but parliament can reverse this action, and decrees made during a state of emergency lapse if parliament does not approve them within three months. In July 2018, President Erdogan appointed Fuat Oktay as vice president. Oktay had previously served as undersecretary in the prime ministry. In making his other appointments, Erdogan reduced the number of government ministries from 25 to 16, and established eight presidential directorates that overlap with various ministry portfolios.[20]

Most of the constitutional changes, which significantly affect Turkey's democracy and will probably have ripple effects for Turkey's foreign relations, went into effect after the June 2018 elections. Among other things, the changes

- eliminate the position of prime minister, with the president serving as both chief executive and head of state;
- allow the president to appoint ministers and other senior officials without parliamentary approval;
- prohibit ministers from serving as members of parliament;

---

[17] Semih Idiz, "Erdogan still faces uphill battle despite electoral victory," *Al-Monitor Turkey Pulse*, June 25, 2018.

[18] See, e.g., "Turkey's powerful new executive presidency," Reuters, June 22, 2018.

[19] See, e.g., Chris Morris, "Turkey elections: How powerful will the next Turkish president be?" BBC News, June 25, 2018.

[20] Murat Yetkin, "Erdoğan wants to start the new system by September," *Hurriyet Daily News*, July 26, 2018; "Turkey's powerful new executive presidency," op. cit.; "Turkish President Erdogan unveils 16-minister cabinet," Anadolu Agency, July 9, 2018.

- transfer responsibility for preparing the national budget from parliament to the president; and
- increase the proportion of senior judges chosen by the president from about half to over two-thirds.

As with the 2017 constitutional referendum,[21] some allegations of voter fraud and manipulation surfaced in connection with the 2018 elections.[22] Muharrem Ince of the Republican People's Party (*Cumhuriyet Halk Partisi*, or CHP), Erdogan's main challenger in the presidential race, noted these allegations in his concession message. He claimed that the campaign, which was conducted under a state of emergency and featured media coverage disproportionately favoring Erdogan and the AKP, was "unfair." However, Ince also said that the alleged manipulation did not affect the outcome.[23]

Economy

Overview

The AKP's political successes have been aided considerably by robust Turkish economic growth since the early 2000s. Growth rates have been comparable at times to other major emerging markets, such as the BRIC economies of Brazil, Russia, India, and China. Key Turkish businesses include diversified conglomerates (such as Koc and Sabanci) from traditional urban centers as well as "Anatolian tigers" (small- to medium-sized export-oriented companies) scattered throughout the country. According to the World Bank, Turkey's economy ranked 17th worldwide in annual GDP in 2017; when Erdogan came to power in 2003, Turkey was ranked 21st.

---

[21] Organisation for Security and Co-operation in Europe (OSCE), Limited Referendum Observation Mission Final Report, Turkey, April 16, 2017 (published June 22, 2017).

[22] OSCE, International Election Observation Mission, Statement of Preliminary Findings and Conclusions, Turkey, Early Presidential and Parliamentary Elections, June 24, 2018 (published June 25, 2018).

[23] Erin Cunningham and Louisa Loveluck, "Erdogan opponent concedes election defeat, warns against Turkey's 'one-man regime,'" *Washington Post*, June 25, 2018.

However, despite a real GDP growth rate of over 7% in 2017, a number of indicators suggest that the Turkish economy may be entering a period of volatility and perhaps crisis, with potentially significant implications for the global economy.[24] Some observers assert that the "low-hanging fruit"—numerous large infrastructure projects and the scaling up of low-technology manufacturing—that largely drove the previous decade's economic success is unlikely to produce similar results going forward.[25] Turkey's relatively large current account deficit increases its vulnerability to higher borrowing costs.

Prospects are uncertain for how the economy and foreign investors will respond under Erdogan's new government. In July 2018, Erdogan gave himself the power to appoint central bank rate-setters and appointed his son-in-law Berat Albayrak (the former energy minister) to serve as treasury and finance minister, exacerbating concerns about greater politicization of Turkey's monetary policy.[26] Some observers have speculated that if investment dries up, Turkey may need to turn to the International Monetary Fund (IMF) for a financial assistance package.[27] This would be a sensitive challenge for Erdogan because his political success story is closely connected with helping Turkey become independent from its most recent IMF intervention in the early 2000s.[28]

Currency Decline: U.S.-Turkey Crisis and Sanctions[29]

The Turkish lira has depreciated significantly as of August 2018. Even before U.S. sanctions were enacted in August, Turkey's lira had faced a downward trend in value, with that trend becoming more pronounced

---

[24] Peter Goodman, "In an Uncertain Global Economy, Turkey May Be the Most at Risk," *New York Times*, July 10, 2018; David J. Lynch and Kareem Fahim, "Turkey's currency plunge fans fears of new global financial crisis," *Washington Post*, August 13, 2018.

[25] See, e.g., Stephen Starr, "Turkey's economy on the up, but deep-rooted problems remain," *Irish Times*, January 6, 2018.

[26] Marcus Ashworth, "Erdogan's New Dynasty Makes Turkey Uninvestable," Bloomberg, July 10, 2018.

[27] Mustafa Sonmez, "Is Turkey headed for IMF bailout?" *Al-Monitor Turkey Pulse*, May 31, 2018.

[28] Onur Ant, et al., "Erdogan's Road Map out of Market Meltdown Is Full of U-Turns," Bloomberg, August 8, 2018.

[29] For more information, see CRS In Focus IF10957, *Turkey's Currency Crisis*, by Rebecca M. Nelson.

around 2015. The lira's decline and accompanying inflation appear to have been driven in part by a strengthening of the U.S. dollar and in part by concerns about Turkey's central bank independence and rule of law.[30] These factors compounded the problem of the country's corporate debt, which stands at nearly 80% of GDP.[31] The U.S. sanctions related to Pastor Andrew Brunson's case (see "Sanctions, Pastor Brunson, and Other Criminal Cases" below) and the historic crisis they may augur for U.S.-Turkey relations could be speeding the lira's decline. The lira has depreciated against the dollar by around 40% from January through August of 2018. In August, President Erdogan called on Turks to help with a "national struggle" by converting their savings from dollars and gold to lira.[32]

Energy

Turkey's importance as a regional energy transport hub makes it relevant for world energy markets while also providing Turkey with opportunities to satisfy its own domestic energy needs. Turkey's location has made it a key country in the U.S. and European effort to establish a southern corridor for natural gas transit from diverse sources.[33] However, Turkey's dependence on other countries for energy—particularly Russia and Iran—may somewhat constrain Turkey from pursuing foreign policies in opposition to those countries.[34]

---

[30] Onur Ant, "Investors Ask 'Does Turkey Even Have a Central Bank Anymore?'" Bloomberg, May 23, 2018; "Turkey's president hopes to turn huge building projects into votes," *Economist*, April 26, 2018.

[31] Matthew C. Klein, "Turkey's Crisis Was Years in the Making," *Barron's*, August 15, 2018.

[32] David Levy, "Lira collapses as Erdogan tells Turks: They have 'their dollars,' we have 'our god,'" CNBC, August 10, 2018.

[33] The focus of U.S. efforts has been on establishing a southern corridor route for Caspian and Middle Eastern natural gas supplies to be shipped to Europe, generally through pipelines traversing Turkey. State Department press statement, The Importance of Diversity in European Energy Security, June 29, 2018.

[34] According to one report, Turkey received almost 55% percent of its oil used for the first four months of 2018 from Iran. "Turkey says will not cut off trade ties to Iran at behest of others," Reuters, June 29, 2018. Another report indicates that Russia and Iran remain the top two importers of natural gas to Turkey. "Iran reduces gas exports to Turkey," Iran Daily, April 30, 2018. For U.S. government information on the main sources of Turkish energy imports, see http://www.eia.gov/beta/international/analysis.cfm?iso=TUR.

Construction on the Turkish Stream pipeline, which would carry Russian natural gas through Turkey into Europe, has proceeded apace since 2017; the first gas deliveries are projected for the end of 2019.[35]

As part of a broad Turkish strategy to reduce the country's dependence on foreign actors, Turkey appears to be trying to diversify its energy imports. In late 2011, Turkey and Azerbaijan reached deals for the transit of natural gas to and through Turkey via the Trans-Anatolian Pipeline (TANAP);[36] the project was inaugurated in June 2018.[37] The deals have attracted attention as a potentially significant precedent for transporting non-Russian, non-Iranian energy to Europe. In June 2013, the consortium that controls the Azerbaijani gas fields elected to have TANAP connect with a proposed Trans Adriatic Pipeline (TAP) to Italy, though political developments in Italy and elsewhere could complicate these arrangements.[38] Turkey also has shown interest in importing natural gas from new fields in the Eastern Mediterranean, and possibly even developing its own gas fields, but difficult relations with Cyprus, Israel, and Egypt could hamper these efforts.[39]

Another part of Turkey's strategy to become more energy independent is to increase domestic energy production. Turkey has entered into an agreement with a subsidiary of Rosatom (Russia's state-run nuclear company) to have it build and operate what would be Turkey's first nuclear power plant in Akkuyu near the Mediterranean port of Mersin.

---

[35] "Gazprom resumes construction of second line of Turkish Stream pipeline," TASS, June 26, 2018.

[36] The terms of Turkish-Azerbaijani agreement specified that 565 billion-700 billion cubic feet (bcf) of natural gas would transit Turkey, of which 210 bcf would be available for Turkey's domestic use.

[37] "Leaders open TANAP pipeline carrying gas from Azerbaijan to Europe," *Hurriyet Daily News*, June 12, 2018.

[38] Vanand Meliksetian, "A Storm Is Brewing in the Southern Gas Corridor," *Oil Price*, June 23, 2018. For more information, see CRS Report R42405, *Europe's Energy Security: Options and Challenges to Natural Gas Supply Diversification*, coordinated by Michael Ratner.

[39] Yigal Chazon, "Race to exploit Mediterranean gas raises regional hackles," *Financial Times*, March 9, 2018.

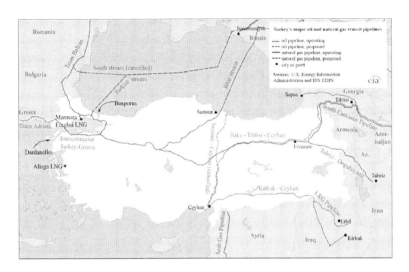

Figure 3. Major Pipelines Traversing Turkey.

Construction, which had been delayed for several years, began in April 2018, with operations expected to begin in 2023.[40] Some observers have expressed both skepticism about the construction timeline and concerns that the plant could provide Russia with additional leverage over Turkey.[41] Japan has agreed to assist with the construction of a second nuclear power plant for Turkey in Sinop on the Black Sea coast, and Turkey is reportedly discussing cooperation with China to build a third plant in Thrace (northwest Turkey).[42]

The Kurdish Issue

Background

Ethnic Kurds reportedly constitute approximately 19% of Turkey's population.[43] Kurds are largely concentrated in the relatively impoverished southeast, though populations are found in urban centers across the

---

[40] See, e.g., Aram Ekin Duran, "Akkuyu nuclear plant: Turkey and Russia's atomic connection," Deutsche Welle, April 3, 2018.
[41] See, e.g., Ibid.
[42] "Turkey's third nuclear power plant likely to be built in Thrace," *Daily Sabah*, June 14, 2018.
[43] CIA World Factbook, Turkey (accessed August 31, 2018).

country. Some Kurds have been reluctant to recognize Turkish state authority in various parts of the southeast—a dynamic that also exists between Kurds and national governments in Iraq, Iran, and Syria. This reluctance and harsh Turkish government measures to quell Kurdish demands for rights have fed tensions that have occasionally escalated since the foundation of the republic in 1923. Since 1984, the Turkish military has periodically countered an on-and-off separatist insurgency and urban terrorism campaign by the PKK.[44] The initially secessionist demands of the PKK have since ostensibly evolved toward the less ambitious goal of greater cultural and political autonomy.[45] According to the U.S. government and European Union, the PKK partially finances its activities through criminal activities, including its operation of a Europe-wide drug trafficking network.[46]

The struggle between Turkish authorities and the PKK was most intense during the 1990s, but has flared periodically since then. The PKK uses safe havens in areas of northern Iraq under the nominal authority of Iraq's Kurdistan Regional Government (KRG). The Turkish military's approach to neutralizing the PKK has been routinely criticized by Western governments and human rights organizations for being overly hard on ethnic Kurds. Thousands have been imprisoned and hundreds of thousands have been displaced or had their livelihoods disrupted for suspected PKK involvement or sympathies.

---

[44] According to the International Crisis Group, around 14,000 Turks have been killed since fighting began in the early 1980s. This figure includes Turkish security personnel of various types and Turkish civilians (including Turkish Kurds who are judged not to have been PKK combatants). Estimates of PKK dead run from 33,000 to 43,000. International Crisis Group, "Turkey's PKK Conflict: The Rising Toll" (interactive blog updated into 2018); *Turkey: Ending the PKK Insurgency*, Europe Report No. 213, September 20, 2011.

[45] Kurdish nationalist leaders demand that any future changes to Turkey's constitution (in its current form following the 2017 amendments) not suppress Kurdish ethnic and linguistic identity. The first clause of Article 3 of the constitution reads, "The Turkish state, with its territory and nation, is an indivisible entity. Its language is Turkish." Because the constitution states that its first three articles are unamendable, even proposing a change could face judicial obstacles.

[46] European Union Terrorism Situation and Trend Report 2018; U.S. Department of the Treasury Press Release, "Five PKK Leaders Designated Narcotics Traffickers," April 20, 2011.

Government Approaches to the Kurds

Until the spring of 2015, Erdogan appeared to prefer negotiating a political compromise with PKK leaders over the prospect of armed conflict.[47] However, against the backdrop of PKK-affiliated Kurdish groups' success in Syria and domestic political considerations, Erdogan then adopted a more confrontational political stance with the PKK. Within that context, a complicated set of circumstances involving terrorist attacks and mutual suspicion led to a resumption of violence between government forces and the PKK in the summer of 2015. As a result of the violence, which has been concentrated in southeastern Turkey and has tapered off somewhat since late 2016, hundreds of fighters and civilians have died.[48] In addition to mass population displacement, infrastructure in the southeast has suffered significant damage. U.S. officials, while supportive of Turkey's prerogative to defend itself from attacks, have advised Turkey to show restraint and proportionality in its actions.[49]

PKK Designations by U.S. Government	
Designation	Year
Foreign Terrorist Organization	1997
Specially Designated Global Terrorist	2001
Significant Foreign Narcotics Trafficker	2008

Under the state of emergency enacted after the failed July 2016 coup attempt, Turkey's government cracked down on Turkey's Kurdish minority. Dozens of elected Kurdish mayors were removed from office and replaced with government-appointed "custodians." In November 2016, the two co-leaders of the pro-Kurdish HDP were arrested along with nine other parliamentarians under various charges of crimes against the state. Turkish officials routinely accuse Kurdish politicians of support for the PKK, but these politicians generally deny close ties.

---

[47] As prime minister, Erdogan had led past efforts to resolve the Kurdish question by using political, cultural, and economic development approaches, in addition to the traditional security-based approach, in line with the AKP's ideological starting point that common Islamic ties among Turks and Kurds could transcend ethnic differences.

[48] International Crisis Group, "Turkey's PKK Conflict: The Rising Toll," op. cit.

[49] Mark Landler and Carlotta Gall, "As Turkey Attacks Kurds in Syria, U.S. Is on the Sideline," *New York Times*, January 22, 2018.

The future trajectory of Turkey-PKK dealings may depend on a number of factors, including

- which Kurdish figures and groups (imprisoned PKK founder Abdullah Ocalan [profiled in Appendix A], various PKK militant leaders, the professedly nonviolent HDP) are most influential in driving events;
- Erdogan's approach to the issue, which has alternated between conciliation and confrontation; and
- possible incentives to Turkey's government and the Kurds from the United States or other actors for mitigating violence and promoting political resolution.

Religious Minorities

Many Members of Congress follow the status of religious minorities in Turkey. Adherents of non-Muslim religions and minority Muslim sects (most prominently, the Alevis) rely to some extent on legal appeals, political advocacy, and support from Western countries to protect their rights in Turkey.

The Turkish government controls or closely oversees religious activities in the country. The Turkish arrangement (often referred to as "laicism") was originally used to enforce secularism, partly to prevent religion from influencing state actors and institutions as it did under Ottoman rule. However, since at least 2015, observers have detected some movement by state religious authorities in the direction of the AKP's Islamic-friendly worldview.[50]

---

[50] See, e.g., Ahmet Erdi Ozturk, "Diyanet as a Turkish Foreign Policy Tool: Evidence from the Netherlands and Bulgaria," *Politics and Religion*, March 2018; Svante Cornell, "The Rise of Diyanet: the Politicization of Turkey's Directorate of Religious Affairs," *Turkey Analyst*, October 9, 2015.

Christians and Jews

U.S. concerns focus largely on the rights of Turkey's Christian and Jewish communities, which have sought greater freedom to choose leaders, train clergy, own property, and otherwise function independently of the Turkish government.[51] According to the State Department's International Religious Freedom Report for 2017, "Members of the Jewish community continued to express concern about anti-Semitism and increased threats of violence throughout the country."[52]

Some Members of Congress routinely express grievances through proposed congressional resolutions and letters on behalf of the Ecumenical (Greek Orthodox) Patriarchate of Constantinople, the spiritual center of Orthodox Christianity based in Istanbul.[53] The Patriarchate, along with various U.S. and European officials, continues to press for the reopening of its Halki Theological School,[54] which was closed after a 1971 Constitutional Court ruling prohibiting the operation of private institutions of higher education. After an April 2018 meeting with President Erdogan, Patriarch Bartholomew said that he was "optimistic" that the seminary would be opened in the fall.[55]

Turkey has converted some historic Christian churches into mosques, and may be considering additional conversions. A popular movement to convert Istanbul's landmark Hagia Sophia (which became a museum in the

---

[51] Since 2009, the U.S. Commission on International Religious Freedom (USCIRF) has given Turkey designations ranging from "country of particular concern" (highest concern) to "monitored." From 2014 through 2017, Turkey has been included in Tier 2, the intermediate level of concern. For additional information on Turkey's religious minorities, see the State Department's International Religious Freedom Report for 2017.

[52] See "Israel" within this chapter for context.

[53] On December 13, 2011, for example, the House passed H.Res. 306—"Urging the Republic of Turkey to safeguard its Christian heritage and to return confiscated church properties"—by voice vote. In June 2014, the House Foreign Affairs Committee favorably reported the Turkey Christian Churches Accountability Act (H.R. 4347). The Turkish government does not acknowledge the "ecumenical" nature of the Patriarchate, but does not object to others' reference to the Patriarchate's ecumenicity.

[54] The Patriarchate also presses for the Turkish government to lift the requirement that the Patriarch be a Turkish citizen, and for it to return previously confiscated properties.

[55] Stelyo Berberakis, "Patriarch hopes to reopen seminary after talks with president," *Daily Sabah*, May 11, 2018. In the past, Erdogan has reportedly conditioned Halki's reopening on measures by Greece to accommodate its Muslim community. "Turkey ready to open Halki Seminary in return for a mosque in Greece: report," *Hurriyet Daily News*, May 8, 2015.

early years of the Turkish republic) into a mosque has gained strength in recent years. Bills to effect that conversion have been introduced in the Turkish parliament, but none have been enacted.[56] In June 2016, the government permitted daily televised Quran readings from Hagia Sophia during Ramadan, prompting criticism from the Greek government,[57] and calls from the State Department for Turkey to respect the site's "traditions and complex history."[58] As part of a cultural event in March 2018, President Erdogan recited a prayer from the Quran at the Hagia Sophia.[59]

Alevis

About 10 to 20 million Turkish Muslims are Alevis (of whom about 20% are ethnic Kurds). The Alevi community has some relation to Shiism[60] and may contain strands from pre-Islamic Anatolian and Christian traditions.[61] Alevism has been traditionally influenced by Sufi mysticism that emphasizes believers' individual spiritual paths, but it defies precise description owing to its lack of centralized leadership and reliance on secret oral traditions. Despite a decision by Turkey's top appeals court in August 2015 that the state financially support cemevis (Alevi houses of worship), the government still does not do so.[62]

Alevis have long been among the strongest supporters of secularism in Turkey, which they reportedly see as a form of protection from the Sunni

---

[56] Nikolia Apostolou, "Turks push to turn iconic Hagia Sophia back into a mosque," *USA Today*, February 25, 2017; Stephen Starr, "Istanbul's Hagia Sophia is at the centre of a battle for Turkey's soul," *Irish Times*, January 2, 2018.

[57] Pinar Tremblay, "The battle for Haghia Sophia in Istanbul escalates," *Al-Monitor Turkey Pulse*, June 15, 2016.

[58] Philip Chrysopoulos, "Turkey Should Respect Hagia Sophia Tradition, Says State Dept. Spokesperson," usa.greekreporter.com, June 10, 2016.

[59] Zeynep Bilginsoy, "Turkish President Recites Muslim Prayer at the Hagia Sophia," Associated Press, March 31, 2018.

[60] For information comparing and contrasting Sunnism and Shiism, see CRS Report RS21745, *Islam: Sunnis and Shiites*, by Christopher M. Blanchard.

[61] For additional historical background, see Elise Massicard, *The Alevis in Turkey and Europe: Identity and managing territorial diversity*, New York: Routledge, 2013, pp. 11-18.

[62] Patrick Kingsley, "Turkey's Alevis, a Muslim Minority, Fear a Policy of Denying Their Existence," *New York Times*, July 22, 2017.

majority.[63] Arab Alawites in Syria and southern Turkey are a distinct Shia-related religious community.

U.S.-TURKEY RELATIONS: QUESTIONS ABOUT ALLY STATUS

Numerous points of bilateral tension have raised questions within the United States and Turkey about the two countries' alliance. In the context of concerns about Turkey's strategic orientation (see "Turkey's Strategic Orientation and Foreign Policy"), many Members of Congress are increasingly active in proposing legislation and exercising oversight on U.S.-Turkey matters that include arms sales and strategic cooperation, various criminal cases, and economic sanctions. For its part, Turkey may bristle because it feels like it is treated as a junior partner, and may seek greater foreign policy diversification through stronger relationships with more countries.[64]

U.S./NATO Cooperation with Turkey

Overview

Turkey's location near several global hotspots makes the continuing availability of its territory for the stationing and transport of arms, cargo,

---

[63] According to a scholar on Turkey, "Alevis suffered centuries of oppression under the Ottomans, who accused them of not being truly Muslim and suspected them of colluding with the Shi'i Persians against the empire. Alevi Kurds were victims of the early republic's Turkification policies and were massacred by the thousands in Dersim [now called Tunceli] in 1937-39. In the 1970s, Alevis became associated with socialist and other leftist movements, while the political right was dominated by Sunni Muslims. An explosive mix of sectarian cleavages, class polarization, and political violence led to communal massacres of Alevis in five major cities in 1977 and 1978, setting the stage for the 1980 coup." Jenny White, *Muslim Nationalism and the New Turks*, Princeton: Princeton University Press, 2013, p. 14.

[64] Recep Tayyip Erdogan, "Erdogan: How Turkey Sees the Crisis With the U.S.," *New York Times*, August 10, 2018; Umut Uzer, "The Revival of Ottomanism in Turkish Foreign Policy: 'The World Is Greater Than Five,'" *Turkish Policy Quarterly*, March 21, 2018.

and personnel valuable for the United States and NATO. From Turkey's perspective, NATO's traditional value has been to mitigate its concerns about encroachment by neighbors. Turkey initially turned to the West largely as a reaction to aggressive post-World War II posturing by the Soviet Union. In addition to Incirlik air base (see textbox below), other key U.S./NATO sites include an early warning missile defense radar in eastern Turkey and a NATO ground forces command in Izmir (see Figure 4 below). Turkey also controls access to and from the Black Sea through its straits pursuant to the Montreux Convention of 1936.

Current tensions have fueled discussion from the U.S. perspective about the advisability of continued U.S./NATO use of Turkish bases. Reports in 2018 suggest that some Trump Administration officials have contemplated permanent reductions in the U.S. presence in Turkey.[65] There are historical precedents for such changes. On a number of occasions, the United States has withdrawn military assets from Turkey or Turkey has restricted U.S. use of its territory or airspace. These include the following:

- 1962 - Cuban Missile Crisis. The United States withdrew its nuclear-tipped Jupiter missiles following this crisis.
- 1975 - Cyprus. Turkey closed most U.S. defense and intelligence installations in Turkey during the U.S. arms embargo that Congress imposed in response to Turkey's military intervention in Cyprus.
- 2003 - Iraq. A Turkish parliamentary vote did not allow the United States to open a second front from Turkey in the Iraq war.

The July 2016 coup plotters apparently used Incirlik air base, causing temporary disruptions of some U.S. military operations. This raised questions about Turkey's stability and the safety and utility of Turkish territory for U.S. and NATO assets. As a result of these questions and U.S.

---

[65] Gordon Lubold, Felicia Schwartz, and Nancy A. Youssef, "U.S. Pares Back Use of Turkish Base Amid Strains with Ankara," *Wall Street Journal*, March 11, 2018.

Turkey tensions, some observers have advocated exploring alternative basing arrangements in the region.[66]

The cost to the United States of finding a temporary or permanent replacement for Incirlik and other sites in Turkey would likely depend on a number of variables including the functionality and location of alternatives, the location of future U.S. military engagements, and the political and economic difficulty involved in moving or expanding U.S. military operations elsewhere. An August 2018 media report claimed that U.S. officials have been "quietly looking for alternatives to Incirlik, including in Romania and Jordan."[67] Another August report cited a Department of Defense spokesperson as saying that the United States is not leaving Incirlik.[68]

Incirlik Air Base

Turkey's Incirlik (pronounced een-jeer-leek) air base in the southern part of the country has long been the symbolic and logistical center of the U.S. military presence in Turkey. Since 1991, the base has been critical in supplying U.S. military missions in Iraq and Afghanistan.
The United States's 39th Air Base Wing is based at Incirlik. Turkey opened its territory for anti-IS coalition surveillance flights in Syria and Iraq in 2014 and permitted airstrikes starting in 2015. U.S. drones (both unarmed and armed) have reportedly flown anti-IS missions. At one point, the number of U.S. forces at the base was reportedly around 2,500 (previously, the normal force deployment had been closer to 1,500), but a March 2018 article, citing U.S. officials, indicated that the U.S. military has sharply reduced combat operations at Incirlik owing to U.S.-Turkey tensions.[69] Turkey's 10th Tanker Base Command (utilizing KC-135 tankers) is also based at Incirlik. Turkey maintains the right to cancel U.S. access to Incirlik with three days' notice.

---

[66] Testimony of Steven Cook of the Council on Foreign Relations, Senate Foreign Relations Committee Hearing, September 6, 2017; John Cappello, et al., "Covering the Bases: Reassessing U.S. Military Deployments in Turkey After the July 2016 Attempted Coup d'Etat," Foundation for Defense of Democracies, August 2016.

[67] Adam Goldman and Gardiner Harris, "U.S. Imposes Sanctions on Turkish Officials Over Detained American Pastor," *New York Times*, August 2, 2018.

[68] Nimet Kirac, "US-Turkey cooperation against Islamic State ongoing, Pentagon says," *Al-Monitor Turkey Pulse*, August 27, 2018.

[69] Gordon Lubold, et al., "U.S. Pares Operations at Base in Turkey," *Wall Street Journal*, March 12, 2018.

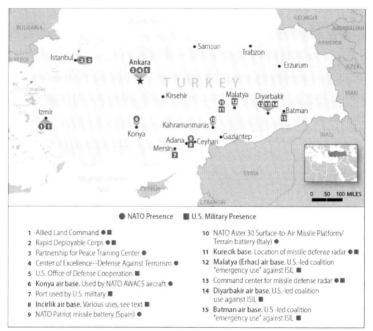

Sources: Department of Defense, NATO, and various media outlets; adapted by CRS.
Notes: All locations are approximate. All bases are under Turkish sovereignty, with portions of them used for limited purposes by the U.S. military and NATO.

Figure 4. Map of U.S. and NATO Military Presence in Turkey.

Calculating the costs and benefits to the United States of a U.S./NATO presence in Turkey, and of potential changes in U.S./NATO posture, revolves to a significant extent around three questions:

- To what extent does strengthening Turkey relative to other regional actors serve U.S. interests?
- To what extent does the United States rely on the use of Turkish territory or airspace to secure and protect U.S. interests?
- To what extent does Turkey rely on U.S./NATO support, both in principle and in functional terms, for its security and regional influence?

U.S. Arms Sales and Aid to Turkey

Turkey has historically been one of the largest recipients of U.S. arms (see more information in Appendix B), owing to its status as a NATO ally, its large military, and its strategic position. Presently, however, Turkey seeks to build up its domestic defense industry (including through technology-sharing and coproduction arrangements with other countries) as much as possible, while minimizing "off-the-shelf" arms purchases from the United States and other countries.

Since 1948, the United States has provided Turkey with approximately $13.8 billion in overall military assistance (nearly $8.2 billion in grants and $5.6 billion in loans). Current annual military and security grant assistance, however, is limited to approximately $3-5 million annually in International Military Education and Training (IMET); and Nonproliferation, Antiterrorism, Demining and Related Programs (NADR) funds.

State Department FY2019 Aid Request for Turkey
IMET: $3.1 million NADR: $600,000 **Total: $3.7 million**

Possible S-400 Acquisition from Russia

In December 2017, Turkey and Russia reportedly signed a finance agreement for Turkey's purchase of the Russian-made S-400 surface-to-air defense system. Media reports indicate that the deal, if finalized, would be worth approximately $2.5 billion.[70] Turkey's procurement agency anticipates initial delivery in July 2019, which is sooner than the first reports of the deal had indicated.[71] (An expedited delivery could increase the purchase price.[72]) Alongside Turkey's pursuit of the S-400 deal to address short-term needs, Turkey also is exploring an arrangement to co-

---

[70] Tuvan Gumrukcu and Ece Toksabay, "Turkey, Russia sign deal on supply of S-400 missiles," Reuters, December 29, 2017. According to this article, the portion of the purchase price not paid for up front (55%) would be financed by a Russian loan.

[71] Charles Forrester, "Turkey, Russia accelerate S-400 sale," *Jane's Defence Weekly*, April 4, 2018.

[72] Ibid.

develop a long-range air defense system with the Franco-Italian Eurosam consortium by the mid-2020s.[73]

Turkey's planned acquisition of the S-400 has raised a number of U.S. and NATO concerns, ranging from technical aspects of military cooperation within NATO to broader political considerations. For some observers, the S-400 issue raises the possibility that Russia could take advantage of U.S.-Turkey friction to undermine the NATO alliance.[74] In a May 3, 2018, press briefing, a State Department spokesperson said, "Under NATO and under the NATO agreement ... you're only supposed to buy ... weapons and other materiel that are interoperable with other NATO partners. We don't see [an S-400 system from Russia] as being interoperable."[75] In March 2018, Czech General Petr Pavel, who chairs the NATO Military Committee, voiced concerns about the possibility that Russian personnel helping operate an S-400 system in Turkey could gain significant intelligence on NATO assets stationed in the country.[76] Additionally, in November 2017, an Air Force official raised specific concerns related to Turkey's operation of the S-400 system alongside F-35 aircraft, citing the potential for Russia to obtain sensitive data related to F-35 capabilities.[77] A Turkish columnist noted in July 2018 that a number of

---

[73] Turkey's procurement agency and two Turkish defense companies signed a contract in January 2018 with Eurosam to do an 18-month definition study to prepare a production and development contract to address Turkish demands. According to one source, a co-developed long-range system with Eurosam would comprise part of an air defense umbrella that would include the S-400 as a high-altitude system and domestic systems as low- and medium-altitude options. Lale Sariibrahimoglu, "Turkey awards Eurosam and Turkish companies contract to define air and missile defence system," *Jane's Defence Weekly*, January 8, 2018.

[74] See, e.g., Yaroslav Trofimov, "Russia, Turkey Forge a Tactical Bond," *Wall Street Journal*, April 6, 2018.

[75] Various NATO assets are deployed to Turkey, as depicted in Figure 4, including a U.S. forward-deployed early warning radar at the Kurecik base near the eastern Turkish city of Malatya as part of NATO's Active Layered Theater Ballistic Missile Defense (ALTBMD) system.

[76] Paul McLeary, "Top NATO General (A Czech) To Europe: 'Grow Up,'" Breaking Defense, March 7, 2018.

[77] Valerie Insinna, "US official: If Turkey buys Russian systems, they can't plug into NATO tech," *Defense News*, November 16, 2017. Air Force Secretary Heather Wilson reiterated these concerns in May 2018. Pat Host, "Turkey purchase of Russian S-400 air defence system draws US Air Force concern," *Jane's Defence Weekly*, May 30, 2018.

Turkey   239

other countries planning to acquire the F-35 share U.S. worries about S-400 information-gathering on F-35s in Turkish airspace.[78]

Turkey has justified its preliminary decision to acquire S-400s instead of U.S. or European alternatives by claiming that it turned to Russia because its attempts to purchase an air defense system from NATO allies were rebuffed.[79] Turkey has also cited various practical reasons, including cost, technology sharing, and territorial defense coverage.[80] However, one analysis from December 2017 asserted that the S-400 deal would not involve technology transfer, would not defend Turkey from ballistic missiles (because the system would not have access to NATO early-warning systems), and could weaken rather than strengthen Turkey's geopolitical position by increasing Turkish dependence on Russia.[81] According to one Turkish press report, Turkey may be taking various steps intended to assuage U.S. concerns, such as insisting on systems and training that allow Turkish technicians to operate the S-400 without Russian involvement, and allowing U.S. officials to examine the S-400.[82] Nevertheless, a Turkish columnist has predicted that "either these S-400s are going to be stored somewhere without being installed, or Turkey will purchase something else from Russia...to appease Moscow."[83]

In March 2018, Turkish Foreign Minister Cavusoglu said that Turkey would also be willing to purchase U.S.-origin Patriot systems if the Administration "guarantees that the US Congress [would] approve the

---

[78] Barcin Yinanc, "With or without S-400, in both cases the loser is the Turkish taxpayer," *Hurriyet Daily News*, July 24, 2018.

[79] Sebastian Sprenger, "Turkey defiant on purchase of Russian S-400 anti-missile system," *Defense News*, July 11, 2018.

[80] Burak Ege Bekdil, "Turkey makes deal to buy Russian-made S-400 air defense system," *Defense News*, December 27, 2017; Umut Uras, "Turkey's S-400 purchase not a message to NATO: official," Al Jazeera, November 12, 2017. Turkish Foreign Minister Mevlut Cavusoglu insisted in February that Turkey needs additional air defense coverage "as soon as possible," and referenced previous withdrawals of Patriot systems by NATO allies. State Department website, Remarks by Cavusoglu, Press Availability with Turkish Foreign Minister Mevlut Cavusoglu, Ankara, Turkey, February 16, 2018.

[81] Gonul Tol and Nilsu Goren, "Turkey's Quest for Air Defense: Is the S-400 Deal a Pivot to Russia?" Middle East Institute, December 2017.

[82] Ragip Soylu, "Turkey extends S-400 offer to Washington," *Daily Sabah*, June 27, 2018.

[83] Yinanc, op. cit.

sale."[84] In April, following a meeting in Brussels in which Secretary of State Pompeo reportedly asked Cavusoglu to "closely consider NATO interoperable systems," Cavusoglu said that the S-400 process was a "done deal," and that further purchases would be in addition to, not in place of, S-400s.[85] At a public event in May, Air Force Secretary Heather Wilson referred to U.S.-Turkey discussions aimed at preventing the F-35 from being close to the S-400. In expressing an opinion about room for improvement with U.S. export controls, she added that the United States sometimes should design defense systems "to be exportable from the very beginning so that we can all operate off the same equipment [with allies]."[86] In July, a State Department official confirmed ongoing talks with Turkey about the Patriot system.[87]

As mentioned above, the planned S-400 acquisition could trigger sanctions under existing U.S. law. In a September 2017 letter to President Trump, Senators John McCain and Ben Cardin cited the deal as a possible violation of section 231 of the Countering America's Adversaries Through Sanctions Act (CAATSA, P.L. 115-44)—relating to transactions with Russian defense and intelligence sectors—that was enacted on August 2, 2017.[88] In April 18, 2018, testimony before the House Foreign Affairs Committee, Assistant Secretary of State for European and Eurasian Affairs

---

[84] Kerry Herschelman, "US discourages Turkey from buying S-400s," *Jane's Defence Weekly*, March 19, 2018.

[85] "Pompeo presses Turkey on S-400 missiles purchase from Russia," Reuters, April 27, 2018.

[86] Ellen Mitchell, "Air Force secretary advocates for export control fixes amid concerns over Turkey," thehill.com, May 29, 2018.

[87] "U.S. in Talks with Turkey to Sell Patriot Missile System to Block Russian Purchase," Reuters, July 16, 2018.

[88] Richard Lardner, "Senators Urge Trump to Robustly Enforce Russia Sanctions Law," Associated Press, September 29, 2017. CAATSA requires the President to impose at least five of the 12 sanctions described in section 235 "with respect to a person the President determines knowingly, on or after such date of enactment, engages in a significant transaction with a person that is part of, or operates for or on behalf of, the defense or intelligence sectors of the Government of the Russian Federation." CAATSA permits the President to waive sanctions only if he submits "(1) a written determination that the waiver—(A) is in the vital national security interests of the United States; or (B) will further the enforcement of this title; and (2) a certification that the Government of the Russian Federation has made significant efforts to reduce the number and intensity of cyber intrusions conducted by that Government." See also State Department, Public Guidance on Sanctions with Respect to Russia's Defense and Intelligence Sectors Under Section 231 of the Countering America's Adversaries Through Sanctions Act of 2017, October 27, 2017.

Wess Mitchell said that a Turkish S-400 purchase from Russia could "potentially lead to sanctions under section 231 of CAATSA and adversely impact Turkey's participation in an F-35 program."[89]

Previously, in 2013, Turkey reached a preliminary agreement to purchase a Chinese air and missile defense system, but later (in 2015) withdrew from the deal, perhaps partly due to concerns voiced within NATO, as well as China's reported reluctance to share technology.[90]

Selected Points of Bilateral Tension

The U.S.-Turkey relationship has always been complicated. Since the 2016 coup attempt, several differences and increased public acrimony have developed between the two countries. Turkey's possible S-400 acquisition from Russia has been discussed above, and U.S.-Turkey disputes over Syria are discussed in a later section of this chapter. This section discusses other points of bilateral tension.

Turkey's Strategic Orientation and Foreign Policy

Turkish actions and statements on a number of foreign policy issues have contributed to problems with the United States and other NATO allies. For example, Turkey's dealings with Russia on Syria, arms sales, and energy;[91] its openness to better relations with China;[92] and its periodic public spats with U.S. and European officials[93] have fueled questions about its commitment to NATO and its Western orientation. Additionally,

---

[89] Transcript of the testimony is available at http://www.cq.com/doc/congressionaltranscripts-5301736?0.

[90] "Turkey confirms cancellation of $3.4 billion missile defence project awarded to China," Reuters, November 18, 2015.

[91] See, e.g., Trofimov, op. cit.; Pepe Escobar, "From Ankara to Moscow, Eurasia integration is on the move," *Asia Times*, April 5, 2018.

[92] See, e.g., Selcuk Colakoglu, "Turkey-China Relations: From 'Strategic Cooperation' to 'Strategic Partnership'?" Middle East Institute, March 20, 2018; Elif Binici, "Close cooperation on Belt and Road to fuel Chinese investments in Turkey," *Daily Sabah*, October 27, 2017.

[93] See, e.g., Semih Idiz, "Erdogan's not doing Turks in Europe any favors," *Al-Monitor Turkey Pulse*, June 12, 2018.

President Erdogan has taken a leading role in rallying regional and international opposition to President Trump's decision to recognize Jerusalem as Israel's capital and move the U.S. embassy to Israel there, and in condemning U.S. support of Israel during rounds of Israeli-Palestinian violence. Erdogan also has vocally opposed the May 2018 U.S. withdrawal from the international agreement on Iran's nuclear program, amid questions about Turkey's willingness to comply with sanctions that the United States is reimposing on Iran's oil exports. Also during 2018, Turkey's interactions have become increasingly contentious with Greece and Cyprus over airspace and maritime access issues that have implications for NATO and the European Union.[94] For more information, see "Turkish Foreign Policy" below.

Sanctions, Pastor Brunson, and Other Criminal Cases[95]

On August 1, 2018, the Treasury Department levied sanctions against Turkey's justice and interior ministers, blocking any property interests they might have within U.S. jurisdiction due to their "leading roles in the organizations responsible for the arrest and detention of Pastor Andrew Brunson."[96] Turkey reacted with reciprocal sanctions against the U.S. Secretary of the Interior and Attorney General. Reciprocal sanctions of this type between the United States and an ally are unusual and suggest a crisis in bilateral relations.[97] With the impasse on Brunson's situation ongoing, on August 10 President Trump announced a doubling of tariffs on Turkish

---

[94] "Rough seas," *Economist*, April 12, 2018; Yiannis Baboulias, "Greece and Turkey Are Inching Toward War," foreignpolicy.com, April 18, 2018.

[95] For more information on U.S.-Turkey trade relations, see CRS In Focus IF10961, *U.S.-Turkey Trade Relations*, by Shayerah Ilias Akhtar.

[96] Treasury Department press release, Treasury Sanctions Turkish Officials with Leading Roles in Unjust Detention of U.S. Pastor Andrew Brunson, August 1, 2018. The sanctions were authorized pursuant to Executive Order 13818, "Blocking the Property of Persons Involved in Serious Human Rights Abuse or Corruption," which builds upon authorities from the Global Magnitsky Human Rights Accountability Act (section 1261, et seq. of P.L. 114-328). For more information, see CRS In Focus IF10576, *The Global Magnitsky Human Rights Accountability Act*, by Dianne E. Rennack.

[97] See, e.g., Therese Raphael, "U.S.-Turkey Relations Will Never Be the Same," Bloomberg, August 10, 2018.

steel and aluminum imports.[98] This prompted retaliatory action from Turkey.[99]

Pastor Brunson's case and a number of other cases that have stoked U.S.-Turkey tensions have some connection with the 2016 coup attempt. Shortly after the attempt, Turkey's government called for the extradition of Fethullah Gulen, and the matter remains pending before U.S. officials.[100] Sharp criticism of U.S. actions related to Gulen's case has significantly increased in Turkish media since the coup attempt. Parallel with nationwide efforts to imprison and marginalize those with connections to Gulen, Turkish authorities have detained Brunson (see textbox below) and a number of other U.S. citizens (most of them dual U.S.-Turkish citizens), along with Turkish employees of the U.S. government.[101]

On August 15, 2018, White House press secretary Sarah Sanders drew a distinction between the Treasury Department sanctions and the new tariff levels on steel. She said that the sanctions were "specific to Pastor Brunson and others that we feel are being held unfairly," but that the tariffs that are in place on steel are specific to national security and "would not be removed with the release of Pastor Brunson."[102]

Separately, two prominent Turkish citizens with government ties were arrested by U.S. authorities in 2016 and 2017 for conspiring to evade sanctions on Iran. One, Reza Zarrab, received immunity for cooperating with prosecutors, while the other, Mehmet Hakan Atilla, was convicted and sentenced in May 2018 to 32 months in prison.

---

[98] https://twitter.com/realDonaldTrump/status/1027899286586109955. The formal presidential proclamation only explicitly referred to action on steel tariffs. White House, Presidential Proclamation Adjusting Imports of Steel into the United States, August 10, 2018. Earlier in the year, President Trump had applied new tariffs on steel and aluminum globally, with exceptions for some countries, but not Turkey. Ceyda Caglayan, "U.S. steel tariffs slash Turkey's exports; future orders recovering—association," Reuters, June 27, 2018.

[99] Jethro Mullen, "Turkey ramps up US spat with huge tariffs on cars and other goods," CNN, August 15, 2018.

[100] CRS In Focus IF10444, *Fethullah Gulen, Turkey, and the United States: A Reference*, by Jim Zanotti and Clayton Thomas. For information on Turkish allegations about Gulen's link to the coup plot, see Carlotta Gall, "104 Turks Get Life Terms for Failed Coup," *New York Times*, May 23, 2018.

[101] Henri J. Barkey and Eric Edelman, "Fight for these State Department workers detained in Turkey," *Washington Post*, July 29, 2018.

[102] White House, Press Briefing by Press Secretary Sarah Sanders, August 15, 2018.

Detention of Pastor Brunson in Turkey

The most high-profile case of an American detained in Turkey after the July 2016 coup attempt is that of Andrew Brunson, a Presbyterian pastor who had been living with his family and working with a small congregation in Izmir since 1993. Brunson and his wife were arrested in October 2016; she was released 13 days later but he remained in custody. In September 2017, President Erdogan appeared to suggest an exchange of Brunson for Fethullah Gulen, but a State Department spokesperson said in response to a question on the issue, "I can't imagine that we would go down that road."[103] In March 2018, after nearly 18 months of detention without indictment, Brunson was charged with espionage and with working on behalf of terrorist groups (the Gulen movement and Kurdish militants). If convicted, he could face up to 35 years in prison. Also in March, Senator Thom Tillis visited Brunson in prison and reported a number of concerns about Brunson's well-being, including that Brunson's physical health had deteriorated and that he had lost 50 pounds.[104] U.S. officials have been openly critical of Turkish authorities in the case. On April 17, 2018, President Trump tweeted, "Pastor Andrew Brunson, a fine gentleman and Christian leader in the United States, is on trial and being persecuted in Turkey for no reason."[105] In testimony the following day (April 18) before the House Foreign Affairs Committee, Assistant Secretary of State for European and Eurasian Affairs Wess Mitchell said that "the Turks claim to have a very high standard of justice. The indictment suggests otherwise, the claims in the indictment were laughable. This [Brunson] is clearly an innocent man."[106] On April 20, 66 Senators sent a letter to President Erdogan on Brunson's behalf,[107] and 154 Representatives followed with a similar letter on May 4. In addition to denouncing the charges against Brunson, both letters said that the indictment's suggestion that Brunson's religious teachings undermined the Turkish state "brings a new and deeply disturbing dimension to the case."[108] Both letters also stated that "other measures will be necessary to ensure that the Government of Turkey respects the right of law-abiding citizens and employees of the United States to travel to, reside in, and work in Turkey without fear of persecution." Brunson is the only U.S. citizen on the "prisoners of conscience" list issued by the U.S. Commission on International Religious Freedom,[109] and his case has influenced some of the legislation on Turkey pending before Congress. In July 2018, Brunson's case was scheduled for further action in October, and he was transferred from prison to house arrest, ostensibly for medical

---

[103] State Department Press Briefing, September 28, 2017.

[104] Senator Tillis press release, Senator Tillis Visits Pastor Andrew Brunson at Turkish Prison, March 28, 2018. In November 15, 2017, testimony before the Commission on Security and Cooperation in Europe (Helsinki Commission), Brunson's daughter Jacqueline Furnari stated that Brunson was battling anxiety and depression. https://www.csce.gov/sites/helsinkicommission.house.gov/files/PrisonersofPurge.pdf.

[105] Brett Samuels, "Trump calls for release of jailed pastor in Turkey," *The Hill*, April 17, 2018. In May, while welcoming the return of a U.S. citizen previously imprisoned in Venezuela, the President spoke about working for Brunson's release. White House, Remarks by President Trump in Meeting with U.S. Citizen Freed From Venezuela, May 26, 2018.

[106] Transcript of the testimony is available at http://www.cq.com/doc/congressionaltranscripts-5301736?0.

[107] The text of the letter is available at https://www.tillis.senate.gov/public/_cache/files/e10f1ffc-be39-4330-8157- c5aa4fcc69be/andrew-brunson-senators-letter.pdf.

[108] The text of the letter is available at https://mchenry.house.gov/news/documentsingle.aspx?DocumentID=398915.

[109] http://www.uscirf.gov/pastor-andrew-brunson.

> reasons. In response, President Trump and Vice President Pence demanded that Turkey release Brunson or face sanctions, amid conflicting reports about whether the United States and Turkey had reached an understanding for Brunson to go free.[110] The U.S. sanctions mentioned above came days later, with Brunson still under house arrest.

The case was repeatedly denounced by Turkish leaders, who were reportedly concerned about the potential implications for Turkey's economy if the case led U.S. officials to impose penalties on Turkish banks.[111] This has not happened to date.

May 2017 Security Detail Incident in Washington, DC

On some occasions during Erdogan's trips outside Turkey, members of his security detail have gotten into physical confrontations with those they perceive as Erdogan's critics or political opponents.[112] Several Members of Congress became particularly concerned about an incident in May 2017 in Washington, DC, outside the Turkish ambassador's residence. The incident featured confrontation between the security guards and largely Kurdish protestors, and 19 people who acted to quell the protest were indicted by a DC grand jury on charges of conspiracy to commit violent crime.[113] The House unanimously passed a resolution (H.Res. 354) in June 2017 that condemned the violence against "peaceful protesters," and Congress included a provision in FY2018 appropriations legislation (section 7046(d) of P.L. 115-141) that prohibited the use of U.S. funds to facilitate arms sales to Erdogan's security detail. Section 7046(d)(2) of the Senate FY2019 State Department, Foreign Operations, and Related Programs Appropriations bill (S. 3108) would maintain that prohibition.

---

[110] Raphael, op. cit.; Goldman and Harris, op. cit.; Michael C. Bender and Dion Nissenbaum, "U.S. Slaps Sanctions on Turkish Officials," *Wall Street Journal*, August 2, 2018; Murat Yetkin, "Here is the Brunson row in Erdogan's words," *Hurriyet Daily News*, July 30, 2018.

[111] Adam Klasfeld, "Turkish Markets Brace for Banker's Sentencing in NY," Courthouse News Service, May 11, 2018.

[112] Haykaram Nahapetyan, "Erdogan's bodyguards have been beating up people around the world. Here's how to stop them," washingtonpost.com, June 8, 2017.

[113] For more detailed information about the status of the charges, see Masood Farivar, "2 Turkish-Americans Sentenced for Brawl During Erdogan's US Visit," Voice of America, April 5, 2018.

Legislation and Congressional Proposals

Bilateral tensions have contributed to various legislative proposals by Members of Congress, alongside a public debate about the potential costs and benefits of sanctions against Turkey.[114] The most significant congressional action against Turkey to date has been an arms embargo that Congress enacted in response to Turkish military intervention in Cyprus. That embargo lasted from 1975 to 1978.

Report: U.S.-Turkey Relations and F-35 Program (FY2019 NDAA)

The FY2019 NDAA (P.L. 115-232) enacted in August 2018 includes a provision (section 1282) that requires a report to congressional armed services and foreign affairs committees within 90 days from the Secretary of Defense (in consultation with the Secretary of State) on the status of U.S.-Turkey relations. The provision prohibits the delivery of F-35 aircraft to Turkey until the report is submitted. The report will include

- an assessment of the U.S. military and diplomatic presence in Turkey, including military activities conducted from Incirlik air base;
- an assessment of Turkey's potential S-400 purchase from Russia and the effects it might have on the U.S.-Turkey relationship, including on other U.S. weapon systems and platforms operated with Turkey (aircraft, helicopters, surface-to-air missiles);
- an assessment of Turkey's participation in the F-35 program, including how changing Turkey's participation could impact the program and what steps might mitigate negative impacts for the United States and other program partners; and

---

[114] See, e.g., Soner Cagaptay, "Sanctions on Turkey: Reconciling Washington's Diverging Views," Washington Institute for Near East Policy, June 1, 2018; Amberin Zaman, "Congress, State Department divided on sanctions against Turkey," *Al-Monitor Turkey Pulse*, February 28, 2018; Nicholas Danforth, "Things to Think about When Thinking about Sanctioning Turkey," Bipartisan Policy Center, February 27, 2018.

- an identification of potential alternative air and missile defense systems for Turkey, including military air defense artillery systems from the United States or other NATO member states.

Turkey is a cooperative partner in developing the F-35,[115] and as part of its involvement, several Turkish companies are assisting with development and manufacture of various F-35 components.[116] Media reports indicate that Turkey plans to purchase 100 F-35s; the first was handed over in Texas at a June 21, 2018 ceremony, and training on the aircraft for Turkish pilots is now underway on U.S. soil.[117] This first aircraft is reportedly scheduled to leave the United States for Turkey sometime in 2020.[118] Secretary of State Mike Pompeo, in May 23, 2018, testimony before the House Foreign Affairs Committee, said that the State Department had not yet decided whether to permit Turkey's purchase of F-35s, and in the same sentence mentioned continuing efforts to persuade Turkey not to acquire the S-400 from Russia.[119]

Some Members of Congress have sought to prevent or place conditions on Turkey's acquisition of F-35s because of the S-400 deal, Pastor Brunson's imprisonment, or other U.S.-Turkey tensions described above.[120] In a June 2018 Senate Armed Services Committee (SASC) report (S.Rept. 115-262) accompanying an early version of the FY2019 NDAA (S. 2987), SASC described Turkey as a NATO ally and critical strategic

---

[115] A 2007 memorandum of understanding among the participants is available at https://www.state.gov/documents/ organization/102378.pdf, and an earlier 2002 U.S.-Turkey agreement is available at https://www.state.gov/documents/ organization/196467.pdf. For information on the consortium and its members, see CRS Report RL30563, *F-35 Joint Strike Fighter (JSF) Program*, by Jeremiah Gertler.

[116] For details on Turkish companies' participation in the F-35 program, see https://www.f35.com/global/participation/ turkey-industrial-participation.

[117] Dylan Malyasov, "Source: Turkey to receive first F-35 Lightning II fighter jet on June 21," Defence Blog, June 5, 2018; Sarp Ozer and Ahmet Sultan Usul, "First F-35 jet delivery to Turkey slated for June 21," Anadolu Agency, May 11, 2018.

[118] Aaron Stein, "The Clock is Ticking: S-400 and the Future of F-35 in Turkey," Atlantic Council, July 24, 2018.

[119] Transcript of testimony available at http://www.cq.com/doc/congressionaltranscripts-5323 484?0.

[120] Some Members of Congress are preparing a letter to urge Secretary of Defense Jim Mattis to prevent the sale of F-35s to Turkey. The text of the letter is available at http://dearcolleague.us/2018/05/deadline-extended-prevent-sale-of-f-35s-to-turkey/.

partner of the United States, but also said that a Turkish purchase of the S-400 from Russia would be incompatible with Turkey's NATO commitments. Additionally, the report expressed concerns about U.S. citizens detained in Turkey (including Pastor Brunson) and called upon Turkey to uphold its obligations under the North Atlantic Treaty to "safeguard the freedom, common heritage and civilization of their peoples, founded on the principles of democracy, individual liberty and the rule of law." In May, Senator Jeanne Shaheen had said, "There is tremendous hesitancy in transferring sensitive F35 planes and technology to a nation who has purchased a Russian air defense system designed to shoot these very planes down."[121]

Because the F-35 program is multinational, unwinding Turkey's involvement could be costly and complicated. One source has said that "the Pentagon last year awarded [Lockheed Martin, a key contractor on the F-35 program] $3.7 billion in an interim payment for the production of 50 of the aircraft earmarked for non-U.S. customers, including Ankara."[122] In May, two Members of Congress circulated a letter to other Members expressing concern about Turkey but opposing its exclusion from the F-35 program. According to these two Members

> As of January 2018, Turkey had contributed over $1 billion to the program. This investment would be required to be returned to the Turkish Government if the United States fails to deliver on the contract. Even more significantly, Turkey manufactures critical components of the F-35. Removing them from the program will lead to delays and [cost] overruns to the rest of the partners and allies.[123]

In a July letter to the Senate and House Armed Services Committees, Secretary of Defense Jim Mattis said that he opposed removal of Turkey from the F-35 program "at this time." Secretary Mattis agreed with

---

[121] Senator Thom Tillis, Tillis & Shaheen Secure Bipartisan NDAA Provision Delaying Transfer of F-35s to Turkey, May 24, 2018.

[122] Tuvan Gumrukcu and Ece Toksabay, "U.S. says in talks with Turkey on YPG withdrawal from Syria's Manbij," Reuters, May 30, 2018.

[123] The text of the letter is available at http://dearcolleague.us/2018/05/support-the-f-35-joint-strike-fighter-program/.

congressional concerns about "the authoritarian drift in Turkey and its impact on human rights and rule of law," but said that if "the Turkish supply chain was disrupted today, it would result in an aircraft production break, delaying delivery of 50-75 jets and would take approximately 18-24 months to re-source parts.[124]

Turkey could take a number of measures in response to U.S. actions to end Turkey's involvement with the F-35. Turkish Foreign Minister Mevlut Cavusoglu has said that a U.S. withdrawal from the deal would not be in keeping with the U.S.-Turkey alliance, would trigger Turkish retaliation, and that Turkey could go elsewhere to meet its needs.[125]

Conditioning F-35 Transfer on S-400 Decision (Senate Appropriations)

The Senate version of the FY2019 State, Foreign Operations, and Related Programs Appropriations Act (S. 3108) includes a provision (section 7046(d)(3)) that would withhold funding for the transfer of F-35 aircraft to Turkey until the Secretary of State certifies that Turkey is not purchasing the S-400 from Russia and will not accept delivery of the S-400.

Possible Restrictions against Turkish Officials Entering the United States (Senate Appropriations)

For FY2018, the Senate Appropriations Committee proposed a provision for annual appropriations legislation (section 7046(e) of S. 1780) that would have required the Secretary of State to deny entry into the United States "to any senior official of the Government of Turkey about whom the Secretary has credible information is knowingly responsible for the wrongful or unlawful prolonged detention of citizens or nationals of the

---

[124] Anthony Capaccio and Roxana Tiron, "Mattis Urges Congress Not to Hit Turkey with Lockheed F-35 Ban," Bloomberg, July 19, 2018.

[125] Ibid; Tuvan Gumrukcu, "Turkey says it will retaliate if U.S. halts weapons sales," Reuters, May 6, 2018. One Turkish media source has claimed that Turkey would consider Russian Su-57s as alternatives to the F-35. Dylan Malyasov, "Turkish media: Ankara may switch to buying the Russian Su-57," Defence Blog, May 28, 2018.

United States," subject to a few exceptions or possible waivers on grounds of national interest, international obligation, or changed circumstances.

In March, Senator Jeanne Shaheen said that she and Senator James Lankford had agreed to drop the above provision (which they had originally sponsored) from FY2018 appropriations legislation (P.L. 115-141) to give time for U.S.-Turkey diplomacy to bear fruit on a number of issues, including the status of U.S. citizens and consulate staff imprisoned in Turkey.[126] However, on April 20, the two Senators released a joint statement criticizing President Erdogan for continuing to hold "Pastor Brunson and other innocent Americans behind bars on fabricated charges," and stating that they would pursue targeted sanctions against Turkish officials in FY2019 appropriations legislation.[127] On June 21, 2018, the Senate Appropriations Committee reported the FY2019 Department of State, Foreign Operations, and Related Programs Appropriations Act (S. 3108) which contains a nearly identical provision (section 7046(d)(1)).

Possible U.S. Opposition to Assistance to Turkey from Selected International Financial Institutions (S. 3248)

In July 2018, six Senators introduced the Turkey International Financial Institutions Act (S. 3248), which would direct "the U.S. executive of the World Bank and the European Bank for Reconstruction and Development (EBRD) to oppose future loans, except for humanitarian purposes, to Turkey by the International Finance Corporation (IFC) and EBRD until the administration can certify to Congress that Turkey is 'no longer arbitrarily detaining or denying freedom of movement to United States citizens (including dual citizens) or locally employed staff members of the United States mission to Turkey.'"[128]

---

[126] Amberin Zaman, "US spending bill drops Turkey sanctions," *Al-Monitor Turkey Pulse*, March 22, 2018.

[127] Senator Jeanne Shaheen, Senators Shaheen and Lankford Call for Sanctions on Turkish Officials, April 20, 2018.

[128] U.S. Senate Foreign Relations Committee press release, Senators Introduce Bill Demanding Turkey End Unjust Detention of US Citizens, July 19, 2018.

Syria

Background

Turkey's involvement in Syria's conflict since 2011 has been complicated and costly.[129] Turkey's chief objective has been to thwart the Syrian Kurdish People's Protection Units (YPG, which has links with the PKK) from establishing an autonomous area along the northern Syrian border with Turkey. Turkey appears to view the YPG and its political counterpart, the Democratic Union Party (PYD), as the top threat to its security, given the boost the YPG's military and political success could provide to the PKK's insurgency within Turkey.[130]

Syrian Refugees in Turkey

In addition to its ongoing military activities in Syria, Turkey hosts about 3.4 million registered Syrian refugees—more than any other country. Foreign Minister Mevlut Cavusoglu estimated in November 2017 that Turkey had spent approximately $30 billion on refugee assistance.[131] During Turkey's military operation in Afrin in early 2018, Turkish officials regularly stated their hopes that hundreds of thousands of refugees would return to Syria.[132] A June 2018 media report estimated that about 75,000 have returned.[133]

With the large-scale return of refugees to Syria uncertain, Turkey has focused on how to manage their presence in Turkish society by addressing their legal status,[134] basic needs, employment,[135] education,[136] and impact on local communities. Problems in the Turkish economy may be fueling some negative views of the refugees among Turkish citizens,[137] and some violence between the two groups has been reported.[138]

---

[129] For background, see Burak Kadercan, "Making Sense of Turkey's Syria Strategy: A 'Turkish Tragedy' in the Making," War on the Rocks, August 4, 2017.

[130] Anne Barnard and Ben Hubbard, "Allies or Terrorists: Who Are the Kurdish Fighters in Syria?" *New York Times*, January 25, 2018.

[131] "Turkey spends $30 billion on Syrian refugees: FM," *Hurriyet Daily News*, November 6, 2017.

[132] Dorian Jones, "Turkey Eyes Refugees Returning to Afrin, Syria," Voice of America, March 8, 2018.

[133] "Borders reopened for returning Syrian refugees," *Daily Sabah*, June 27, 2018.

[134] See, e.g., Hosam Al-Jablawi, "Return to Syria Is Less Likely as Syrian Refugees Receive Turkish Citizenship," Atlantic Council SyriaSource, October 13, 2017.

[135] Lauren Frayer, "In Turkey, Syrian Workers Struggle To Obtain Official Employment," NPR, August 14, 2017.

[136] Kinana Qaddour, "Educating Syrian Refugees in Turkey," *Cairo Review of Global Affairs*, December 28, 2017.

[137] See, e.g., Zia Weise, "Syrian refugees in Turkey face calls to return as public mood changes," IRIN, March 27, 2018.

The YPG plays a leading role in the umbrella group known as the Syrian Democratic Forces (SDF), which also includes Arabs and other non-Kurdish elements.

Since 2014, the SDF has been the main U.S. ground force partner against the Islamic State. U.S. support for the SDF has fueled U.S.-Turkey tension because of Turkey's view of the YPG as a threat.[139] As part of SDF operations to expel the Islamic State from Raqqah in 2017, the U.S. government pursued a policy of arming the YPG directly while preventing the use of such arms against Turkey,[140] and Secretary of Defense Jim Mattis announced an end to the direct arming of the YPG near the end of the year.[141] U.S. officials have contrasted their longstanding alliance with Turkey with their current but temporary cooperation with the YPG.[142]

After Turkey moved against IS-held territory in northern Syria as a way to prevent the YPG from consolidating its rule across much of the border area between the two countries (Operation Euphrates Shield, August 2016-March 2017), Turkey launched an offensive directly against the YPG in the Afrin district in January 2018. Some U.S. officials expressed concern during the operation because several YPG units went to help their fellow Kurds in Afrin, causing a manpower drain from the anti-

---

[138] International Crisis Group, "Turkey's Syrian Refugees: Defusing Metropolitan Tensions," January 29, 2018.

[139] U.S. military commanders have generally differentiated between the YPG and the PKK, but in February 2018, U.S. Director of National Intelligence Daniel Coats submitted written testimony to the Senate Select Committee on Intelligence stating that the YPG was the Syrian militia of the PKK. Daniel R. Coats, Director of National Intelligence, Statement for the Record: Worldwide Threat Assessment of the US Intelligence Community, Senate Select Committee on Intelligence hearing, February 13, 2018.

[140] Pentagon statement quoted in Michael R. Gordon and Eric Schmitt, "Trump to Arm Syrian Kurds, Even as Turkey Strongly Objects," *New York Times*, May 9, 2017; Anne Barnard and Patrick Kingsley, "Arming Syrian Kurds Could Come at a Cost," *New York Times*, May 11, 2017.

[141] Lead Inspector General Report to the U.S. Congress, *Overseas Contingency Operations: Operation Inherent Resolve, Operation Pacific Eagle-Philippines*, October 1, 2017-December 31, 2017, p. 25.

[142] Selva Unal, "US determined to keep its word about YPG in Manbij, official says," *Daily Sabah*, March 1, 2018.

IS mission east of the Euphrates.[143] By March, the YPG had abandoned control of the district to Turkish forces and their Syrian rebel allies.[144]

In Afrin and the other areas Turkey has occupied since 2016, Turkey has set up local councils, though questions persist about future governance and Turkey's overarching role.[145] The local councils and security forces reportedly provide public services in these areas with oversight and training from Turkish officials. Some observers, citing signs of a YPG insurgency, predict that the Turkish military may feel compelled to stay for an extended period of time.[146] The U.N. Office of the High Commissioner for Human Rights (OHCHR) published a report in June 2018 alleging possible violations by the de facto authorities of international humanitarian and human rights laws—including actions or omissions that prevent Kurds from returning to their homes.[147]

The town of Manbij, which the SDF seized from the Islamic State in 2016 with U.S. support, is a focal point of U.S.-Turkey tensions in Syria because of a continuing YPG presence there. After concerns grew in early 2018 that Turkish forces could conceivably clash with U.S. Special Operations personnel patrolling Manbij or its vicinity if Turkey advanced on the area, the two countries have sought to deconflict their forces.[148] According to a senior State Department official, on June 4 the two countries endorsed a roadmap which is a broad political framework designed to fulfill the commitment that the United States had made to move the YPG east of the Euphrates and to do so in a way that contributes to security and stability of Manbij and in a fashion that is mutually agreed

---

[143] Eric Schmitt and Rod Nordland, "Amid Turkish Assault, Kurdish Forces Are Drawn Away From U.S. Fight with ISIS," *New York Times*, February 28, 2018.

[144] U.S. officials voiced concerns about possible adverse effects on U.S.-supported anti-IS efforts in eastern Syria. State Department Press Briefing, February 22, 2018.

[145] Khaled al-Khateb, "Turkey backs new opposition governance to mend Afrin," *Al-Monitor Syria Pulse*, April 25, 2018; Haid, "Post-ISIS Governance in Jarablus: A Turkish-led Strategy," Chatham House, September 26, 2017.

[146] Borzou Daragahi, "Turkey Has Made a Quagmire for Itself in Syria," foreignpolicy.com, July 13, 2018.

[147] U.N. OHCHR, "Between a Rock and a Hard Place—Civilians in North-western Syria," Monthly Human Rights Digest, June 2018.

[148] Remarks by Secretary Tillerson, Press Availability with Turkish Foreign Minister Mevlut Cavusoglu, Ankara, Turkey, February 16, 2018; Rebecca Kheel, "US 'deeply concerned' with situation in Syrian city taken by Turkey," thehill.com, March 19, 2018.

between the United States and Turkey in every aspect.[149] According to this official, implementation of the roadmap will be based on developments on the ground,[150] with one major factor being the YPG's willingness to cooperate.[151] Syrian Kurdish leaders have expressed openness to negotiating with any party with whom their interests coincide, including the Syrian government.[152]

Assessment

Turkey's priorities in Syria appear to have evolved during the course of Syria's civil war. While Turkey still officially calls for Syrian President Bashar al Asad to leave power, it has engaged in a mix of coordination and competition with Russia and Iran (Asad's supporters) on some matters since intervening militarily in Syria starting in August 2016. Similar interaction takes place between Turkey and the United States given the U.S. military presence in key areas of northern Syria east of the Euphrates River. Turkey may be seeking to protect its borders, project influence, promote commerce, and counter other actors' regional ambitions.

Turkey is part of the Astana process that it launched with Russia and Iran in January 2017 to seek Syria's post-civil war stability and territorial integrity.[153] In a September 2017 agreement, the three countries identified some specific "de-escalation zones," and Turkey has inserted troops directly into areas of the northern Syrian province of Idlib as part of efforts to establish these zones. Going forward, it is unclear

- to what extent Turkish-supported forces will hold their positions or advance farther into Syrian territory, either with or without U.S. support; and

---

[149] State Department special briefing via teleconference, Senior State Department Officials on the U.S.-Turkish Working Group on Syria, June 5, 2018.
[150] Ibid.
[151] James F. Jeffrey, "Will U.S.-Turkish Progress on Manbij Lead to Wider Cooperation in Syria?" Washington Institute for Near East Policy, June 5, 2018.
[152] Abdel Raheem Said, "U.S.-Kurdish Relations in Syria after the Manbij Roadmap," Washington Institute for Near East Policy, July 5, 2018.
[153] Erin Cunningham, "Iran, Russia and Turkey plan Syria's future as Trump seeks an exit," Washington Post, April 4, 2018.

- how Turkey might administer areas occupied inside Syria and coordinate with local populations and outside actors.

TURKISH FOREIGN POLICY

A number of considerations drive the complicated dynamics behind Turkey's international relationships. Turkey's history as both a regional power and an object of great power aggression translates into wide popularity for nationalistic political actions and discourse. This nationalistic sentiment might make some Turks wary of Turkey's partial reliance on other key countries (for example, the United States for security, European Union countries for trade, and Russia and Iran for energy). Moreover, Turkey's maintenance of cooperative relationships with countries whose respective interests may conflict involves a balancing act. Turkey's vulnerability to threats from Syria and Iraq increases the pressure on it to manage this balance.[154] Involvement in Syria and Iraq by the United States, Russia, and Iran further complicates Turkey's situation. Additionally, grievances that Turkish President Recep Tayyip Erdogan and his supporters espouse against seemingly marginalized domestic foes (the military and secular elite who previously dominated Turkey, the Fethullah Gulen movement, Kurdish nationalists, and liberal activists) extend to the United States and Europe due to apparent suspicions of Western sympathies for these foes.

Turkey's Middle Eastern profile expanded in the 2000s as Erdogan (while serving as prime minister) sought to build economic and political linkages—often emphasizing shared Muslim identity—with Turkey's neighbors. However, efforts to increase Turkey's influence and offer it as a "model" for other regional states appear to have been set back by a number of developments since 2011: (1) conflict and instability that engulfed the region and Turkey's own southern border, (2) Turkey's failed effort to help

---

[154] See, e.g., Shehab Al-Makahleh, "Turkish foreign policy: From defensive to offensive," Al Arabiya, February 3, 2018.

Muslim Brotherhood-aligned groups gain lasting power in Syria and North Africa, and (3) domestic polarization accompanied by government repression.

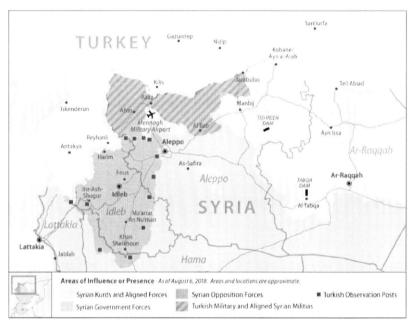

Sources: CRS, based on data from IHS Conflict Monitor, UN OCHA, and Esri. Note: All designations are approximate and subject to change.

Figure 5. Northern Syria: Areas of Control.

Although Turkey shares some interests with traditional Sunni Arab powers Saudi Arabia and Egypt in countering Iran, these countries' leaders regard Turkey suspiciously because of its government's Islamist sympathies and close relationship with Qatar (see "Other International Relationships" below).[155] Turkey maintains relations with Israel, but these have become distant and—at times—contentious during Erdogan's rule.

---

[155] See, e.g., W. Robert Pearson, "Saudi-Turkish ties take a turn for the worse," Middle East Institute, March 8, 2018.

Russia

Turkey-Russia relations appear to have improved significantly since a rapprochement in 2016. Russia had imposed economic sanctions on Turkey and closed Syrian airspace to it after the Turkish military shot down a Russian fighter aircraft near the Turkey-Syria border in November 2015. Since the rapprochement, the two countries have cooperated in a number of areas, most notably

- the possible S-400 air defense deal (see "Possible S-400 Acquisition from Russia" above);
- some military and political coordination in northern Syria (see "Syria" above); and
- energy dealings (see "Energy" above).

Viewpoints vary on the significance of closer Turkey-Russia relations. Some analysts have posited that Erdogan may be seeking closer relations with Russia, possibly at the expense of Turkey's relations with the United States and Europe.[156] Some others view the Turkey-Russia relationship as less of a potential strategic partnership than a "marriage of convenience" as the two nations compartmentalize their relations—alternating between cooperation and competition depending on the specific issue in question.[157] Such a situation, according to one observer, could reflect an effort by Turkey to push for its national interest by "balancing between East and West" without cutting security ties to NATO or economic ties to the EU.[158]

Other observers have explained Turkish policy changes largely by reference to the leverage Russia used with sanctions and airspace closures

---

[156] See, e.g., Aaron Stein, "Ankara's Look East: How Turkey's Warming Ties with Russia Threaten Its Place in the Transatlantic Community," War on the Rocks, December 27, 2017; Suzan Fraser and Ayse Wieting, "Turkey, Russia deepen ties amid troubled relations with West," Chicago Tribune, April 2, 2018.

[157] See, e.g., Mehmet Ogutcu and Dimitar Bechev, "Will Turkey and Russia become 'strategic allies' or sustain a 'marriage of convenience'?" Hurriyet Daily News, February 16, 2018.

[158] Dimitar Bechev, "The Russia-Turkish-Iran Axis: Less Than Meets the Eye," American Interest, April 9, 2018.

after the November 2015 incident.[159] For example, one analyst has argued that Turkish policies favoring Russia are probably due more to Turkey feeling abandoned by the West and intimidated by Russia than to a Turkish preference for Russia over the West.[160] Turkey has a centuries-long history of geopolitical conflict with Russia, and disagreements on various issues persist.[161]

Some U.S. officials have suggested that Russia may be seeking closer ties with Turkey as part of a deliberate strategy to undermine NATO and U.S. strategic relationships more broadly. In written testimony in February 2018, General Joseph Votel, Commander of U.S. Central Command, said that Russia (along with Iran) is trying to "fracture the longstanding U.S.-Turkey strategic partnership."[162] Additionally, in July 2018 U.S. Ambassador to NATO Kay Bailey Hutchison said, "I do think Russia is trying to flip Turkey. They are trying to flip many of our allies."[163]

Iran

While Turkey and Iran are sometimes rivals for regional influence, they also work together on certain regional issues and to ensure Turkish access to Iranian oil and gas. Iranian ties with the Syrian and Iraqi governments and with various Iraqi Kurdish groups provide it with some possible leverage over Turkey.

Turkey and Iran (along with Russia) coordinate their efforts in Syria as part of the Astana process, as mentioned above.[164] However, Turkey "is

---

[159] Aykan Erdemir and Merve Tahiroglu, "Handling Turkey's Erdogan: What Washington can learn from Russia," thehill.com, February 14, 2018.

[160] Soner Cagaptay, "US could stop Turkey, not yet a Moscow ally, from caving to Russia," *The Hill*, May 25, 2018.

[161] See, e.g., "Russia and Turkey in the Black Sea and the South Caucasus," International Crisis Group, June 28, 2018.

[162] Statement of General Joseph L. Votel Before the House Armed Services Committee on the Posture of U.S. Central Command, Terrorism and Iran: Challenges in the Middle East, February 27, 2018.

[163] Ragip Soylu, "Is Russia trying to flip Turkey?" *Daily Sabah*, July 12, 2018.

[164] Raziye Akkoc and Ezzedine Said, "Iran, Russia, Turkey team up to hold sway in Syria," *Times of Israel*, April 2, 2018.

traditionally wary of Tehran's ambitions in its immediate neighborhood."[165] Erdogan and other Turkish officials, who earlier sought the ouster of Iran's key Arab ally, the Asad regime of Syria, have periodically criticized Iran in stark terms, accusing it of destabilizing the region in pursuit of sectarian interests.[166] In a July 2018 column that raised concerns about Turkey's relationships with the United States and a number of regional actors, a senior advisor to Erdogan wrote that Iran is "displaying Persian expansionist policies throughout the Middle East."[167]

President Trump's decision to withdraw from the Iranian nuclear agreement in May 2018 may further complicate both Turkey-Iran and U.S.-Turkey relations. Turkish officials have said that Turkey will not comply with U.S. secondary sanctions that are scheduled to take effect in November, given its dependence on oil and gas imported from Iran.[168] These sanctions will require third-party countries to stop or significantly reduce those imports.[169] The Administration maintains that the United States is unlikely to offer waivers or exceptions from the sanctions for any country, though a State Department official said in July 2018 that "we are prepared to work with countries that are reducing their imports on a case-by-case basis."[170]

Iraq

Turkey's first priority in Iraq appears to be countering threats to Turkey from Kurds based in northern Iraq—primarily the PKK. Another concern—despite generally positive relations between Turkey and Iraq's Kurdistan Regional Government (KRG)—is the possibility that Iraqi

---

[165] Galip Dalay, "Turkey in the Middle East's new battle lines," Brookings Institution, May 20, 2018.

[166] "Iran and Turkey trade barbs over Syria and Iraq," Al Jazeera, February 21, 2017.

[167] Ilnur Cevik, "Turkey is caught between the US and Iran," *Daily Sabah*, July 23, 2018.

[168] Dorian Jones, "Ankara Rules Out Compliance with US Sanctions on Iran," Voice of America, July 24, 2018; Gonul Tol and Engin Polar, "Iran sanctions may see US-Turkey ties get a lot worse," Middle East Institute, August 9, 2018.

[169] See CRS Report RS20871, *Iran Sanctions*, by Kenneth Katzman.

[170] On-The-Record-Briefing Brian Hook, Director of Policy Planning With an Iran Diplomacy Update, U.S. Department of State, July 2, 2018.

Kurdish moves toward independence could spread separatist sentiment among Kurds in Turkey. Turkey also maintains an uneasy relationship with Iraq's central government over concerns that its Shia leaders are unduly influenced by Iran and that Iraq's security forces and Shia militias often mistreat Sunni Arabs and Turkmen. Relations with Baghdad are also strained by Iraqi concerns about the potential impact that Turkish dam construction and water management decisions could have on downstream Iraqi communities.[171] Turkey's military maintains various posts inside northern Iraq and a presence at a base in Bashiqa near Mosul.

Around 2008, Turkey started developing a political and economic partnership with the KRG. As part of this cooperation, in 2013 the KRG began transporting oil through pipelines to Turkish ports for international export. However, Turkey and most other countries strongly opposed the KRG's symbolic 2017 popular referendum on independence. Turkey halted oil exports connected with the KRG pipelines after the referendum. Talks are ongoing between Turkish, Iraqi, and KRG officials over restarting the exports.[172]

Turkey has conducted airstrikes against PKK safe havens in Iraq, with reported intelligence assistance from the United States, since 2007. The KRG—given its own rivalry with the PKK— generally does not object to these strikes, though it remains sensitive to pan-Kurdish sympathies among its population. In June 2018, Turkish forces began moving into KRG territory in preparation for a possible ground operation against the main PKK redoubt in the Qandil Mountains. Partly because of the constraints a Turkish operation would face from the area's harsh terrain and weather conditions, the operation may be more focused on projecting Turkish determination and competence to other stakeholders in northern Iraq than on decisively defeating the PKK.[173]

---

[171] Erika Solomon and Laura Pitel, "Why water is a growing faultline between Turkey and Iraq," *Financial Times*, July 4, 2018.

[172] Galip Dalay, "Evolution of Turkey–Iraqi Kurdistan's Relations," Al Jazeera Centre for Studies, December 20, 2017; Ahmed Rasheed, "Iraq still in talks with Turkey, KRG over resuming Kirkuk oil exports," Reuters, July 2, 2018.

[173] Metin Gurcan, "Turkey takes on Kurds in evolving Qandil operation," *Al-Monitor Turkey Pulse*, June 15, 2018; Necdet Ozcelik, "Understanding Turkey's Qandil Operation," SETA, June 14, 2018.

Israel

Ties between Turkey and Israel, which were close during the 1990s and early 2000s, have deteriorated considerably during Erdogan's rule. This slide has reflected the military's declining role in Turkish society relative to Erdogan and other leaders whose criticisms of Israel resound with domestic public opinion. Despite the countries' differences, trade between the two countries has grown.[174] During Syria's civil war, Turkey has used Israel's port at Haifa as a point of transit for exports to various Arab countries after the conflict cut off overland routes.

After years of downgraded diplomatic ties following the 2010 *Mavi Marmara* (or Gaza flotilla) incident,[175] Turkey and Israel announced the full restoration of diplomatic relations in 2016, in a deal reportedly facilitated by the United States.[176] Nevertheless, the bilateral relationship remains tense. Israelis routinely decry Turkey's ties with Hamas and its refusal to characterize Hamas as a terrorist organization.[177] For their part, Turks bemoan Israel's treatment of Palestinians in the West Bank and especially the Gaza Strip. Additionally, Erdogan has sought to lead regional opposition to the 2017 U.S. recognition of Jerusalem as Israel's capital.[178] Israeli authorities have reportedly been monitoring increased Turkish financial investment and political activism in East Jerusalem, with officials from the Palestinian Authority and Arab states warning Israel of Erdogan's interest in gaining greater influence over the Jerusalem issue.[179] At various points in 2018, President Erdogan and Israeli Prime Minister

---

[174] See, e.g., Menekse Tokyay, "Trade envoy to bolster Turkey's links with Israel," *Arab News*, July 13, 2018.

[175] The incident took place in international waters under disputed circumstances and resulted in the death of nine Turks and an American of Turkish descent.

[176] According to media reports, the rapprochement included Israeli compensation to the families of those killed in the flotilla incident in exchange for an end to legal claims, as well as opportunities for Turkey to assist with humanitarian and infrastructure projects for Palestinian residents in the Gaza Strip.

[177] Seth Frantzman, "The complex, and often toxic, Israel-Turkey relationship," *Jerusalem Post*, May 16, 2018.

[178] Ibid.

[179] Amir Tibon and Yaniv Kubovich, "Jordan, Saudis and Palestinians Warn Israel: Erdogan Operating in East Jerusalem Under Your Nose," *Ha'aretz*, July 1, 2018.

Binyamin Netanyahu have traded public accusations,[180] and in May the two countries temporarily expelled each other's top diplomats in Ankara, Istanbul, and Jerusalem.

Some observers have characterized negative statements by Erdogan and other prominent Turkish voices about Israel, Zionism, and other historical references as anti-Semitic.[181] Erdogan insists that his criticisms of the Israeli government and its policies are not directed to the Jewish people or to Jews in Turkey.

In connection with bilateral tensions, Israel has raised concerns with U.S. officials over Turkey's acquisition of the F-35 and has contemplated measures to limit Turkish influence over holy sites in Jerusalem.[182] Israel also has strengthened security and economic ties with traditional Turkish rivals Greece and Cyprus.[183]

European Union[184]

Turkey has a long history of partnership with the European Union (and its predecessor organizations) and began negotiations to join the EU in 2005. Talks stalled shortly thereafter and Turkey's membership is now seen as unlikely, at least in the near future. Many analysts argue that resistance to Turkish EU accession has been rooted in a fear that Turkey's large Muslim population would fundamentally change the cultural character of the EU and dilute the power of the EU's founding Western

---

[180] "Gaza-Israel violence: Netanyahu and Erdogan in war of words," BBC News, April 1, 2018; Natasha Turak, "Netanyahu and Erdogan trade insults on Twitter over Gaza violence," CNBC, May 16, 2018.

[181] Hannah Lucinda Smith, et al., "Turkey blames 'Jewish lobby' for economic crisis," *Times* (UK), May 30, 2018; Nuray Mert, "Trump's Jerusalem decision must not be a pretext for anti-Semitism," *Hurriyet Daily News*, December 18, 2017.

[182] Amir Tibon and Yaniv Kubovich, "Israel Concerned About F-35 Sale to Turkey, Expects U.S. to Withhold 'Upgrade Capabilities,'" *Ha'aretz*, May 27, 2018; Ben Caspit, "Turkey, Israel battle over Temple Mount," *Al-Monitor Turkey Pulse*, July 11, 2018.

[183] Yaroslav Trofimov, "Turkey's Rise Sparks New Friendship Between Israel and Greece," *Wall Street Journal*, July 21, 2018.

[184] For more information on this subject, see archived CRS Report RS22517, *European Union Enlargement: A Status Report on Turkey's Accession Negotiations*, by Vincent L. Morelli; and CRS Report RS21344, *European Union Enlargement*, by Kristin Archick and Vincent L. Morelli.

European states in particular. Turkey's unwillingness to normalize diplomatic and trade relations with EU member Cyprus presents a major obstacle to its accession prospects. Other EU concerns over Turkey's qualifications for membership center on the treatment of Kurds and religious minorities, media freedoms, women's rights, and the proper and transparent functioning of Turkey's democratic and legal systems.[185]

Turkey-EU Relations in Brief

1959: Turkey applies for associate membership in the then-European Economic Community (EEC)
1963: Turkey is made an associate member of the EEC (Ankara Agreement)
1970: Protocol signed outlining eventual establishment of Customs Union
1982: European Community (EC, successor to the EEC and forerunner of the EU) freezes relations with Turkey in response to 1980 coup; relations resume 4 years later
1987: Turkey applies to join the EC as a full member
1996: Customs Union between Turkey and the EU takes effect
1999: EU recognizes Turkey as a candidate for membership
2005: Accession negotiations begin
2016: In a symbolic vote, the European Parliament passes a resolution urging that accession talks with Turkey be halted

---

Debate regarding the extent to which Turkey meets EU standards has intensified in recent years in light of domestic controversies since 2013 and President Erdogan's consolidation of power. Erdogan has used anti-European rhetoric to gain support both at home and among the substantial Turkish diaspora communities in Europe. Turkish domestic expectations of full accession to the EU have apparently been in decline for several years, though support for joining the EU remains according to some polls.[186] In its Turkey 2018 report, the European Commission noted a number of membership criteria in which there has been "serious backsliding," including the judiciary and freedom of expression. Despite the lack of significant progress in accession negotiations, the EU provides Turkey hundreds of millions of euros in annual pre-accession financial and technical assistance (separate from the support for refugees addressed

---

[185] European Commission, Turkey 2018 Report, op. cit.
[186] "Turkish citizens' support for EU membership on the rise: Poll," *Hurriyet Daily News*, January 9, 2018.

below).[187] Since 2011, nearly four million refugees or migrants from Syria and other countries have come to Turkey, posing significant humanitarian, socioeconomic, and security challenges. Turkey and the European Union (EU) reached an arrangement in March 2016 providing for the return from Greece to Turkey of "irregular migrants or asylum seekers whose applications have been declared inadmissible."[188] In exchange, the EU agreed to resettle one Syrian refugee for every Syrian readmitted to Turkey and provide Turkey with six billion euros to be used to support refugees, among other incentives.[189] The deterrent effect of the arrangement appears to have contributed to a dramatic reduction in the number of people crossing from Turkey to the Greek islands, leading one U.N. official to characterize the deal's impact as "huge."[190] Ongoing Turkey-EU disputes and questions about the deal's compatibility with international legal and human rights standards, however, call its long-term viability into question.[191]

Armenia

From 1915 to 1923, hundreds of thousands of Armenians died as a result of actions of the Ottoman Empire (Turkey's predecessor state). U.S. and international characterizations of these events influence Turkey's domestic and foreign policy, and are in turn influenced by developments in Turkey-Armenia relations. Turkey and Armenia initially agreed in 2009 on a set of joint protocols to normalize relations, but the process stalled

---

[187] For further information, see http://publications.europa.eu/webpub/eca/special-reports/turkey-7-2018/en/.

[188] European Commission Fact Sheet, "Implementing the EU-Turkey Statement—Questions and Answers," June 15, 2016, available at http://europa.eu/rapid/press-release_MEMO-16-1664_en.htm.

[189] As part of the agreement, the EU also promised to grant visa-free travel to Turkish citizens if Turkey meets certain requirements, and "re-energize" Turkey's EU accession process. Ibid.

[190] "UN agency praises 'huge impact' of EU-Turkey refugee deal," *Hurriyet Daily News*, April 18, 2018.

[191] See, e.g., Paivi Leino and Daniel Wyatt, "No public interest in whether the EU-Turkey refugee deal respects EU treaties and international human rights?" *European Law Blog*, February 28, 2018.

Turkey   265

shortly thereafter and there has been little or no momentum toward restarting it.[192]

Congress has considered how to characterize the events of 1915-1923 on a number of occasions. In 1975 (H.J.Res. 148) and 1984 (H.J.Res. 247), the House passed proposed joint resolutions that referred to "victims of genocide" of Armenian ancestry from 1915 and 1915-1923, respectively.[193] Neither proposed joint resolution came to a vote in the Senate. A number of other proposed resolutions characterizing these World War I-era events as genocide have been reported by various congressional committees (see Appendix C for a list). In the 115th Congress, resolutions have been introduced in both the House (H.Res. 220) and Senate (S.Res. 136) that would characterize the events as genocide.

All U.S. Presidents since Jimmy Carter have made public statements memorializing the events, with President Ronald Reagan referring to a "genocide of the Armenians" during a Holocaust Remembrance Day speech in 1981.[194] In an April 2018 statement, the second of his presidency, President Trump (echoing statements made by President Obama) said that the events were "one of the worst atrocities of the 20th century" and that "one and a half million Armenians were deported, massacred or marched to their deaths."[195] In addition to past statements or actions by U.S. policymakers, the website of the Armenian National

---

[192] Another source of tension between Turkey and Armenia, beyond the 1915-1923 events, is the dispute between Armenia and Azerbaijan (which is closely linked with Turkey through ethnolinguistic ties) over the Armenian-occupied region of Nagorno-Karabakh within Azerbaijan's internationally recognized borders.

[193] Unlike most proposed resolutions on the matter in recent years, neither H.J.Res. 148 nor H.J.Res. 247 explicitly identified the Ottoman Empire or its authorities as perpetrators of the purported genocide. H.J.Res. 247 stated that "one and one-half million people of Armenian ancestry" were "the victims of the genocide perpetrated in Turkey."

[194] Additionally, in a May 1951 written statement to the International Court of Justice, the Truman Administration cited "Turkish massacres of Armenians" as one of three "outstanding examples of the crime of genocide" (along with Roman persecution of Christians and Nazi extermination of Jews and Poles). International Court of Justice, *Reservations on the Convention of the Prevention and Punishment of the Crime of Genocide: Advisory Opinion of May 28, 1951: Pleadings, Arguments, Documents*, p. 25.

[195] See, e.g., White House, Statement by the President on Armenian Remembrance Day, April 24, 2018. Beginning with President Obama in 2009, annual White House statements (including those from President Trump) have continuously referenced the "Meds Yeghern," an Armenian phrase that translates roughly to "great crime." Vartan Matiossian, "The 'Exact Translation': How 'Medz Yeghern' Means Genocide," *Armenian Weekly*, May 15, 2013.

Institute, a U.S.-based organization, asserts that at least 25 other countries (not counting the United States or Armenia) have characterized the events as genocide in some way, including 15 of the 28 EU member states.[196]

Cyprus and Greece[197]

Since Cyprus became independent of the United Kingdom in 1960, Turkey has viewed itself as the protector of the island's ethnic Turkish-Cypriot minority from potential mistreatment by the ethnic Greek-Cypriot majority.[198] Responding to Greek and Greek-Cypriot political developments that raised concerns about a possible Greek annexation of Cyprus, Turkey's military intervened in 1974 and established control over the northern third of the island. This prompted an almost total ethnic and de facto political division along geographical lines that persists today.[199] The ethnic Greek-Cypriot-ruled Republic of Cyprus is internationally recognized as having jurisdiction over the entire island, while the de facto

---

[196] The EU states listed as having recognized a genocide are Austria, Belgium, Cyprus, the Czech Republic, Denmark, France, Germany, Greece, Italy, Lithuania, Luxembourg, the Netherlands, Poland, Slovakia, and Sweden. The European Parliament has also referred to the deaths as genocide. The non-EU states are Argentina, Bolivia, Brazil, Canada, Chile, Lebanon, Paraguay, Russia, Switzerland, Vatican City, Venezuela, and Uruguay. In April 2015, the Republic of Cyprus's ethnic Greek parliament passed a resolution making it a crime to deny that the events constituted genocide. In 2007, Switzerland criminally fined an ethnic Turkish politician for denying that the events constituted genocide, and in 2012 France passed a law making it a crime to deny that the events constituted genocide—though the law was subsequently invalidated by the French Constitutional Council. Long-standing Turkish law criminalizes characterization of the events as genocide.

[197] For more information on this subject, see CRS Report R41136, *Cyprus: Reunification Proving Elusive*, by Vincent L. Morelli.

[198] Turkey views its protective role as justified given its status as one of the three guaranteeing powers of the 1960 Treaty of Guarantee that was signed at the time Cyprus gained its independence. The United Kingdom and Greece are the other two guarantors.

[199] Turkey retains between 30,000 and 40,000 troops on the island (supplemented by several thousand Turkish Cypriot soldiers). This is countered by a Greek Cypriot force of approximately 12,000 with reported access to 50,000 reserves. "Cyprus - Army," *IHS Jane's World Armies*, June 5, 2018. The United Nations maintains a peacekeeping mission (UNFICYP) of approximately 900 personnel within a buffer zone headquartered in Cyprus's divided capital of Nicosia (known as Lefkosa in Turkish). Since the mission's inception in 1964, UNFICYP has suffered 186 fatalities. The United Kingdom maintains approximately 3,000 personnel at two sovereign military bases on the southern portion of the island at Akrotiri and Dhekelia.

Turkish Republic of Northern Cyprus (in the northern third) has only Turkish recognition.

The Republic of Cyprus's accession to the EU in 2004 and Turkey's refusal to normalize political and commercial relations with it are seen as major obstacles to Turkey's EU membership aspirations. Moreover, EU accession may have reduced incentives for Cyprus's Greek population to make concessions toward a reunification deal.[200] Turkey and Turkish Cypriots have opposed efforts by the Republic of Cyprus to explore and develop offshore energy deposits without a solution to the question of the island's unification.[201]

Turkey's relations with Greece are also fraught. The two countries joined NATO in 1952, but intercommunal tensions, the Cyprus question, and border disputes "ensured that war between the two allies remained a real risk well into the 1990s."[202] Despite more regular diplomatic relations in the following two decades, Turkish relations with Greece have again deteriorated in recent years, with the number of Turkish violations of Greek territory and airspace spiking in early 2018.[203] While the two nations agreed in July 2018 to focus on reducing tensions in the Aegean, the area could remain a flashpoint going forward.

Other International Relationships

Turkey seeks to use political and economic influence to strengthen relationships with non-Western countries. Through political involvement, increased trade and investment, and humanitarian and development projects, Turkey has curried favor with foreign countries not only in the greater Middle East, but also in the Balkans,[204] the Caucasus and Central

---

[200] The Greek Cypriots rejected by referendum a United Nations reunification plan (called the Annan plan after then Secretary-General Kofi Annan) in 2004 that the Turkish Cypriot population accepted.

[201] For more information, see CRS Report R44591, *Natural Gas Discoveries in the Eastern Mediterranean*, by Michael Ratner.

[202] "Why Turkey and Greece cannot reconcile," *Economist*, December 14, 2017.

[203] Patrick Kingsley, "Tiny Islands Make for Big Tensions Between Greece and Turkey," *New York Times*, April 21, 2018.

[204] Zia Weise, "Turkey's Balkan Comeback," *Politico*, May 15, 2018.

Asia,[205] and sub-Saharan Africa.[206] Gulen movement-affiliated organizations had spearheaded some of these ties with other countries before Turkey's government classified the movement as a terrorist organization. Questions persist about how these ties will develop in response to changes in Turkey.

Over the past year, Turkey established a military base in Somalia and announced a number of economic initiatives with countries near the Horn of Africa.[207] Prospects of greater Turkish influence in this area, especially considering Turkey's close relationship with Qatar, have sparked concern from a number of Arab countries for whom the Horn has important strategic value.[208] Since 2015, Turkey has deployed troops to Qatar, and has supported it politically and economically during its tensions with other Gulf Arab states.[209]

APPENDIX A. PROFILES OF KEY FIGURES IN TURKEY

Recep Tayyip Erdogan—President (pronounced *air-doe-wan*).

Born in 1954, Erdogan was raised in Istanbul and in his familial hometown of Rize on the Black Sea coast. He attended a religious *imam*

---

[205] Sinem Cengiz, "Turkey carves out a new role for itself in Central Asia," *Arab News*, May 4, 2018.
[206] Jan Philipp Wilhelm, "Turkey's Erdogan seeks more influence in Africa," Deutsche Welle, March 2, 2018.
[207] Mustafa Gurbuz, "Turkey's Challenge to Arab Interests in the Horn of Africa," Arab Center Washington DC, February 22, 2018.
[208] Ibid.
[209] Yunus Paksoy, "Turkish Military in Qatar: Bonds of mutual trust," *Daily Sabah*, June 12, 2018.

hatip secondary school in Istanbul. In the 1970s, Erdogan studied business at what is today Marmara University, became a business consultant and executive, and became politically active with the different Turkish Islamist parties led by eventual prime minister Necmettin Erbakan.

Erdogan was elected mayor of Istanbul in 1994 but was removed from office, imprisoned for six months, and banned from parliamentary politics for religious incitement after publicly reciting a poem drawing from Islamic imagery. After Erbakan's government resigned under military pressure in 1997 and his Welfare Party was disbanded, Erdogan became the founding chairman of the AKP in 2001. The AKP won a decisive electoral victory in 2002, and has led the government ever since. After the election, a legal change allowed Erdogan to run for parliament in a 2003 special election, and after he won, Erdogan replaced Abdullah Gul as prime minister. Erdogan and his personal popularity and charisma have been at the center of much of the domestic and foreign policy change that has occurred in Turkey since he came to power. Erdogan became Turkey's first popularly elected president in August 2014 and won reelection to a newly empowered presidency in June 2018. Many observers believe that he primarily seeks to consolidate power and to avoid the reopening of corruption cases that could implicate him and close family members or associates. Erdogan is married and has two sons and two daughters. He is widely believed to be positioning his son-in-law Berat Albayrak (currently treasury and finance minister) as a possible successor. Erdogan does not speak English.

Kemal Kilicdaroglu — Leader of Republican People's Party (CHP) (*kill-itch-dar-oh-loo*)

Born in 1948 in Tunceli province in eastern Turkey to an Alevi background, Kilicdaroglu is the leader of the CHP, which is the main opposition party and traditional political outlet of the Turkish nationalist secular elite. In recent years, the party has also attracted various liberal and social democratic constituencies.

After receiving an economics degree from what is now Gazi University in Ankara, Kilicdaroglu had a civil service career—first with the Finance Ministry, then as the director-general of the Social Security Organization. After retiring from the civil service, Kilicdaroglu became politically active with the CHP and was elected to parliament from Istanbul in 2002. He gained national prominence for his efforts to root out corruption among AKP officials and the AKP-affiliated mayor of Ankara. Kilicdaroglu was elected as party leader in 2010 but has since faced criticism for the CHP's failure to make electoral gains. The party's 2018 presidential nominee, Muharrem Ince, may be a potential rival to Kilicdaroglu going forward.

Kilicdaroglu is married with a son and two daughters. He speaks fluent French.

Devlet Bahceli — Leader of Nationalist Action Party (MHP) (*bah-cheh-lee*)

Born in 1948 in Osmaniye province in southern Turkey, Bahceli is the leader of the MHP, which is the traditional Turkish nationalist party of Turkey that is known for opposing political accommodation with the Kurds.

Bahceli moved to Istanbul for his secondary education, and received his higher education, including a doctorate, from what is now Gazi

University in Ankara. After a career as an economics lecturer at Gazi University, he entered a political career as a leader in what would become the MHP. He became the chairman of the MHP in 1997 and served as a deputy prime minister during a 1999-2002 coalition government. He was initially elected to parliament in 2007.

Bahceli has allied with Erdogan, providing support for the 2017 constitutional referendum and for Erdogan's 2018 presidential bid.

Bahceli speaks fluent English.

Meral Aksener — Founder and Leader of the Good (*Iyi*) Party (*awk-sheh-nar*)

Born in 1956 in Izmit in western Turkey to Muslims who had resettled in Turkey from Greece, Aksener is the founder and leader of the Good Party. She founded the party in 2017 as an alternative for nationalists and other Turks who oppose the MHP's alliance with Erdogan.

Aksener studied at Istanbul University and received a doctorate in history from Marmara University, becoming a university lecturer before entering politics. She was first elected to parliament in 1995 with the True Path Party, and served as interior minister in the coalition government that was ultimately forced from office in 1997 by a memorandum from Turkey's military. She served in parliament with the MHP from 2007 to 2015 and served for most of that time as deputy speaker.

Aksener became a forceful opponent of Erdogan after the MHP agreed in 2016 to provide him the necessary parliamentary support for a constitutional referendum establishing a presidential system of government. She left the party and campaigned vigorously against the proposed changes, which won adoption in 2017 despite the controversy that attended the vote. After founding the Good Party, she ran as its presidential candidate in the 2018 elections.

Selahattin Demirtas — Former Co-Leader and 2018 Presidential Candidate of Peoples' Democratic Party (HDP) (*day-meer-tosh*)

Born in 1973 to an ethnic Kurdish family, Demirtas is the most prominent member of the HDP, which has a Kurdish nationalist base but has also reached out to a number of non-Kurdish constituencies, particularly liberals and minorities. The constituency of the party and its various predecessors overlaps with that of the PKK, but the party professes a nonviolent stance and claims an independent identity.

Demirtas was raised in Elazig in eastern Turkey. He attended universities in both Izmir and Ankara and received his law degree from Ankara University. He became a human rights activist leader in Diyarbakir and was elected to parliament for the first time in 2007, becoming co-leader of the HDP's immediate predecessor party in 2010. His national visibility increased after he ran as one of two candidates opposing Erdogan for the presidency in 2014. His personal popularity and charisma are generally seen as major reasons for the HDP becoming the first pro-Kurdish party to pass the electoral threshold of 10% in June and November 2015 parliamentary elections.

Demirtas was arrested in November 2016 on terrorism-related charges and remains in custody. He stepped down from party leadership in January 2018 but ran for president in 2018 from prison, garnering about 8.5% of the vote; the HDP won about 12% of the nationwide parliamentary vote, however, and will be the third largest party in parliament.

Demirtas is married with two daughters.

Abdullah Ocalan — Founder of the PKK (*oh-juh-lawn*)

Born in or around 1949 in southeastern Turkey (near Sanliurfa), Ocalan is the founding leader of the PKK.

After attending vocational high school in Ankara, Ocalan served in civil service posts in Diyarbakir and Istanbul until enrolling at Ankara University in 1971. As his interest developed in socialism and Kurdish nationalism, Ocalan was jailed for seven months in 1972 for participating in an illegal student demonstration. His time in prison with other activists helped inspire his political ambitions, and he became increasingly politically active upon his release.

Ocalan founded the Marxist-Leninist-influenced PKK in 1978 and launched a separatist militant campaign against Turkish security forces—while also attacking the traditional Kurdish chieftain class—in 1984. He used Syrian territory as his safe haven, with the group also using Lebanese territory for training and Iraqi territory for operations. Syria forced Ocalan to leave in 1998 after Turkey threatened war for harboring him.

After traveling to several different countries, Ocalan was captured in February 1999 in Kenya—possibly with U.S. help—and was turned over to Turkish authorities. The PKK declared a cease-fire shortly thereafter. Ocalan was sentenced to death, in a trial later ruled unfair by the European Court of Human Rights, but when Turkey abolished the death penalty in

2002, the sentence was commuted to life imprisonment. He resides in a maximum-security prison on the island of Imrali in the Sea of Marmara, and was in solitary confinement until 2009.

Although other PKK leaders such as Cemil Bayik and Murat Karayilan have exercised direct control over PKK operations during Ocalan's imprisonment, some observers believe that Ocalan still ultimately controls the PKK through proxies. PKK violence resumed in 2003 and has since continued off-and-on, with the most recent cease-fire ending in July 2015.

APPENDIX B. SIGNIFICANT U.S.-ORIGIN ARMS TRANSFERS OR POSSIBLE ARMS TRANSFERS TO TURKEY (CONGRESSIONAL NOTIFICATIONS SINCE 2009)

Amount/Description	FMS or DCS	Year			Primary Contractor(s)	Estimated Cost
		Cong. Notice	Contract	Delivery		
400 RIM-162 Ship-air missiles (ESSM)	DCS	2009	Signed	2011-2016 (346 estimated)	Raytheon	$300 million
72 PATRIOT Advanced Capability Missiles (PAC-3), 197 PATRIOT Guidance Enhanced Missiles, and associated equipment	FMS	2009			Raytheon and Lockheed Martin	$4 billion
14 CH-47F CHINOOK Helicopters	FMS	2009	2011 (for 6)	2016 (6)	Boeing	$1.2 billion ($400 million for 6)
3 AH-1W SUPER COBRA Attack Helicopters	FMS	2011	Signed	2012	N/A (from U.S. Marine Corps inventory)	$111 million
117 AIM-9X-2 SIDEWINDER Block II Air-air missiles (SRAAM) and associated equipment	FMS	2012	2014	2015-2016	Raytheon	$140 million
48 MK-48 Mod 6	FMS	2014			Raytheon and	$170 million

Amount/Description	FMS or DCS	Year			Primary Contractor(s)	Estimated Cost
		Cong. Notice	Contract	Delivery		
Advanced Technology					Lockheed	
All-Up-Round (AUR)					Martin	
Warshot torpedoes and associated equipment						
Amount/Description	FMS or DCS	Year			Primary Contractor(s)	Estimated Cost
		Cong. Notice	Contract	Delivery		
145 AIM-120C-7 Air-air missiles (AMRAAM)	FMS	2014	Signed	2016-2017 (72 estimated)	Raytheon	$320 million
21 MK-15 Phalanx Block 1B Baseline 2 Close-in weapons systems (CIWS) (sale/upgrade)	FMS	2015	2015 (for 6)	2017 (4 estimated)	Raytheon	$310 million
Joint Direct Attack Munitions (JDAM) and associated equipment	FMS	2015	Signed (for 1000)	2017 (250 estimated)	Boeing	$70 million

Sources: Defense Security Cooperation Agency, Stockholm International Peace Research Institute Arms Transfer Database, *Defense News*, *Hurriyet Daily News*, Global Security.

Notes: All figures and dates are approximate; blank entries indicate that data is unknown or not applicable. FMS refers to "Foreign Military Sales" contemplated between the U.S. government and Turkey, while DCS refers to "Direct Commercial Sales" contemplated between private U.S. companies and Turkey.

APPENDIX C. CONGRESSIONAL COMMITTEE REPORTS OF RESOLUTIONS USING THE WORD "GENOCIDE" IN RELATION TO EVENTS REGARDING ARMENIANS IN THE OTTOMAN EMPIRE FROM 1915 TO 1923

Date Reported or of Vote for Report	Proposed Resolution(s)	Committee
April 5, 1984	S.J.Res. 87	Senate Judiciary
September 28, 1984	S.Res. 241	Senate Foreign Relations
July 9, 1985	H.J.Res. 192	House Post Office and Civil Service
July 23, 1987	H.J.Res. 132	House Post Office and Civil Service
August 3, 1987	H.Res. 238	House Rules
October 18, 1989	S.J.Res. 212	Senate Judiciary
October 11, 2000	H.Res. 596 and H.Res. 625	House Rules

Appendix C. (Continued)

Date Reported or of Vote for Report	Proposed Resolution(s)	Committee
May 22, 2003	H.Res. 193	House Judiciary
September 15, 2005	H.Res. 316 and H.Con.Res. 195	House International Relations
March 29, 2007	S.Res. 65	Senate Foreign Relations
October 10, 2007	H.Res. 106	House Foreign Affairs
March 4, 2010	H.Res. 252	House Foreign Affairs
April 10, 2014	S.Res. 410	Senate Foreign Relations

In: The Middle East
Editor: Doyle Keller

ISBN: 978-1-53616-191-5
© 2019 Nova Science Publishers, Inc.

Chapter 7

IRAN: U.S. ECONOMIC SANCTIONS AND THE AUTHORITY TO LIFT RESTRICTIONS (UPDATED)*

Dianne E. Rennack

ABSTRACT

On May 8, 2018, President Donald Trump signed National Security Presidential Memorandum 11, "ceasing U.S. participation in the JCPOA [Joint Comprehensive Plan of Action] and taking additional action to counter Iran's malign influence and deny Iran all paths to a nuclear weapon." The action sets in motion a reestablishment of U.S. unilateral economic sanctions that will affect U.S. businesses and include secondary sanctions that target the commerce originating in other countries that engage in trade with and investment in Iran.

Prior to this juncture, the United States had led the international community in imposing economic sanctions on Iran in an effort to change the government of that country's support of acts of international terrorism, poor human rights record, weapons and missile development

---

* This is an edited, reformatted and augmented version of Congressional Research Service, Publication No. R43311, dated May 10, 2018.

and acquisition, role in regional instability, and development of a nuclear program. The United States' abrogation of its participation in the JCPOA, at least in the near-term, sets the United States apart from its allies and partners in what has been for more than a decade a unified, multilateral approach to Iran's malign activities.

This chapter identifies the basis in U.S. law for sanctions imposed on Iran, and the nature of the authority to waive or lift those restrictions. It comprises four tables that present legislation and executive orders that are specific to Iran and its objectionable activities in the areas of terrorism, human rights, and weapons proliferation.

On July 14, 2015, the United States, China, France, Germany, the Russian Federation, the United Kingdom, European Union, and Iran agreed to a Joint Comprehensive Plan of Action to "ensure that Iran's nuclear programme will be exclusively peaceful.... " In turn, the negotiating parties and United Nations would "produce the comprehensive lifting of all U.N. Security Council sanctions as well as multilateral and national sanctions related to Iran's nuclear programme, including steps on access in areas of trade, technology, finance, and energy."

On January 16, 2016, the International Atomic Energy Agency verified that Iran had implemented the measures enumerated in the JCPOA to disable and end its nuclear-related capabilities. Secretary of State Kerry confirmed the arrival of Implementation Day (defined in Annex V of the JCPOA). President Obama, the State Department, and the Department of the Treasury's Office of Foreign Assets Control initiated steps for the United States to meet its obligations under the JCPOA (Annexes II and V)—revoking a number of executive orders, delisting individuals and entities designated as Specially Designated Nationals, issuing general licenses to authorize the resumption of some trade, and exercising waivers for non-U.S. persons as allowable by various laws. President Trump's May 8 announcement indicates that the United States will, over the next three to six months, reconstruct the U.S. sanctions regime.

RECENT EVENTS

On May 8, 2018, President Donald Trump announced that the United States was ending its participation in the Joint Comprehensive Plan of

Action (JCPOA).[1] The JCPOA is an agreement signed on July 14, 2015, by the United States, Russia, China, France, Britain (all permanent members of the U.N. Security Council), Germany (P5+1),[2] and Iran, to require Iran to limit its nuclear program and, in exchange, require the United States and others to ease economic sanctions affecting Iran's access to some of its hard currency held abroad (see text box, below).[3] The President's decision sets in motion a restoring of U.S. unilateral economic sanctions that will affect U.S. businesses and include secondary sanctions that target commerce originating in other countries that engage in trade with and investment in Iran. The Secretaries of the Treasury and State are required to take appropriate steps to reimpose as quickly as possible, but not later than 180 days, the U.S. sanctions that were waived or lifted in implementing the United States' part of the JCPOA. In addition, the Secretary of Defense is tasked with preparing "to meet, swiftly and decisively, all possible modes of Iranian aggression against the United States, our allies, and our partners. The Department of Defense shall ensure that the United States develops and retains the means to stop Iran from developing or acquiring a nuclear weapon and related delivery systems."[4]

---

[1] White House press release. "NSPM-11—Ceasing U.S. Participation in the JCPOA and Taking Additional Action to Counter Iran's Malign Influence and Deny Iran All Paths to a Nuclear Weapon," May 8, 2018.

[2] Also referred to as the E3/EU+3.

[3] Implementing interim versions of the 2015 agreement—primarily the *Joint Plan of Action Reached on November 24, 2013*, and related extensions—generated sanctions guidance including U.S. Department of the Treasury. Office of Foreign Assets Control. *Guidance Relating to the Provision of Certain Temporary Sanctions Relief In Order To Implement the Joint Plan of Action Reached on November 24, 2013, Between the P5+1 and the Islamic Republic of Iran*, January 20, 2014. 79 F.R. 5025; January 30, 2014. See also: U.S. Department of the Treasury. Office of Foreign Assets Control. *Publication of Guidance Relating to the Provision of Certain Temporary Sanctions Relief, as Extended, July 21, 2014*. 79 F.R. 45233; August 4, 2014; and *Guidance Relating to the Provision of Certain Temporary Sanctions Relief in Order to Implement the Joint Plan of Action Reached on November 24, 2013, Between the P5+1 and the Islamic Republic of Iran, as Extended Through June 30, 2015*. 79 F.R. 73141; December 8, 2014. See, also: Department of the Treasury. *Frequently Asked Questions Relating to the Temporary Sanctions Relief To Implement the Joint Plan of Action Between the P5+1 and the Islamic Republic of Iran*, January 20, 2014. OFAC has also issued a number of General Licenses related to sanctions relief, all available at http://www.treasury.gov/ofac. See also Iranian Transactions and Sanctions Regulations, at 31 *Code of Federal Regulations* (CFR) Part 560.

[4] NSPM-11, section 4.

To explain how the United States will reestablish the sanctions regime, the Department of the Treasury's Office of Foreign Assets Control (OFAC) issued a new set of *Frequently Asked Questions* shortly after the President's announcement.[5] The State Department also reported to Congress a set of waiver revocations, determinations, certifications, and findings to establish, in effect, a timeline for the reimposition of sanctions on certain Iranians and those who engage in business with and investment in Iran.[6]

Going forward, the sequence of what may happen next, based on OFAC's FAQs and State Department's reports, includes the following:

- Treasury establishes two wind-down periods—90 days (August 6, 2018) or 180 days (November 4, 2018)—for those involved in certain commercial or financial activities with Iran to complete those transactions and withdraw.

- On or after August 6, 2018, OFAC will reimpose sanctions affecting the government of Iran's ability to purchase or acquire U.S. dollars; trade in gold, precious metals, graphite, raw or semi-finished metals, including aluminum and steel, coal, and software; trade in or purchase of the *rial*; maintenance of accounts outside of Iran denominated in *rial*; trade in Iran's sovereign debt; and trade in Iran's automotive sector.

- On or after August 6, 2018, OFAC will revoke licenses that allow importation into the United States of Iranian carpets and foodstuffs; and specific licenses that allow export or reexport of commercial aircraft and related parts and services.[7]

---

[5] Department of the Treasury. Office of Foreign Assets Control. Frequently Asked Questions Regarding the Re-Imposition of Sanctions Pursuant to the May 8, 2018 National Security Presidential Memorandum Relating to the Joint Comprehensive Plan of Action (JCPOA). https://www.treasury.gov/resource-center/sanctions/Programs/Documents/jcpoa_winddown_faqs.pdf.

[6] Department of State. *Report to Congress: Waiver of Certain Sanctions to Provide for a Wind-Down Period for Sanctions Relief Previously Provided Consistent with the Joint Comprehensive Plan of Action*; and *Waiver Revocations, Determinations, Certifications, and Findings*. May 8, 2018.

[7] OFAC has issued three Statements of Licensing Policy (SLP) that serve as guidance for issuing specific licenses, all in support of Treasury regulations stated at 31 CFR Part 560 (Iranian

Iran   281

- On or after November 4, 2018, OFAC will reimpose sanctions relating to ports, shipping, shipbuilding; petroleum- and petrochemical-related transactions; transactions between foreign financial institutions and the Central Bank of Iran (CBI) or other Iranian financial institutions; certain specialized financial messaging services; underwriting services, insurance or reinsurance; and Iran's energy sector.

- On or after August 6 or November 4, depending on how it relates to sectors and other factors described above, the President is expected to reimpose the relevant provisions of several executive orders that were revoked to implement the United States' part of the JCPOA. The President could issue a new executive order, or amend the Executive Order 13716 of January 16, 2016,[8] which revoked the original order (in effect, unrevoking the original language).[9]

- Effective November 5, 2018, OFAC will revoke previously issued authorizations that were permitted under General License H of January 16, 2016—relating to foreign entities owned or controlled by a U.S. person.[10]

- No later than November 5, 2018, those individuals and entities removed from the OFAC's Specially Designated Nationals (SDN)

Transaction Regulations): *Support of Democracy and Human Rights in Iran and Academic and Cultural Exchange Programs*, July 17, 2006; *Support of Human Rights-, Humanitarian-, and Democracy-Related Activities with Respect to Iran* (undated); and *Activities Related to the Export or Re-export to Iran of Commercial Passenger Aircraft and Related Parts and Services*, January 16, 2016.

[8] 81 F.R. 3693.

[9] OFAC cites the revoked sections of Executive Orders 13574, 13590, 13622, 13628, and 13645. These orders expanded the original national emergency issued in Executive Order 12957 of March 15, 1995. The original order draws on authorities stated in the National Emergencies Act (NEA; 50 U.S.C. 1601 *et seq.*) and the International Emergency Economic Powers Act (IEEPA; 50 U.S.C. 1701 et seq.); the subsequent orders, while based on NEA and IEEPA authorities, also drew on the body of law that forms the Iran sanctions regime.

[10] OFAC has issued some dozen General Licenses (GL) to allow for limited transactions with Iranian persons and entities ranging across engagement with international organizations, civil aircraft safety, educational services, sports activities, nongovernmental organizations activities in Iran, personal communications, trade in food and medicine, commercial use of the Internet, and the transportation of human remains. Full list is available at https://www.treasury.gov/resource-center/sanctions/Programs/Pages/iran.aspx.

list[11] to effectuate the JCPOA will be redesignated, "as appropriate."[12]

- No later than November 5, 2018, those identified pursuant to Executive Order 13599, relating to trade with Iran's energy and petrochemical sectors, will be moved to the SDN list. They will, however, also have "additional sanctions information—subject to secondary sanctions" attached to their SDN designation.[13]

Of particular interest to other countries that purchase oil from Iran is how, or if, the United States will implement secondary sanctions on foreign financial institutions to deter such purchases, as provided for in the National Defense Authorization Act for Fiscal Year 2012.[14] The law requires the President to assess the world petroleum market and whether foreign countries have reduced their consumption of Iran-origin petroleum over the previous six months. If they have not, the United States may deny access to the U.S. financial system. Foreign countries may, however, seek exception. OFAC provides that

[t]he State Department will evaluate and make determinations with respect to significant reduction exceptions provided for in section 1245(d)(4)(D) of the NDAA at the end of the 180-day wind-down period. Countries seeking such exception are advised to reduce their volume of crude oil purchases from Iran during this wind-down period. Consistent with past practice, the Secretary of State, in consultation with the Secretary of the Treasury, the Secretary of Energy, and the Director of National Intelligence, would make such determinations following a process of rigorous due diligence. For the initial set of such

---

[11] When the President or Secretary of the Treasury (or his delegate) determines that an individual or entity meets the criteria of objectionable activities stated in law relating to U.S. foreign policy and the application of economic sanctions, OFAC designates the person or entity as a Specially Designated National (SDN). Depending on the statute violated, the SDN may be subject to property under U.S. jurisdiction being blocked, assets frozen, and U.S. persons may be prohibited from engaging in transactions with the SDN, the SDN's property, or interests in property. OFAC maintains a consolidated SDN database comprising all the multitude of U.S. sanctions regimes, at https://sanctionssearch.ofac.treas.gov/.

[12] *FAQ* 1.3, May 8, 2018.

[13] *FAQ* 3, May 8, 2018.

[14] Section 1245(d)(4), P.L. 112-81 (22 U.S.C. 8513a), as amended.

determinations, the State Department intends to consider relevant evidence in assessing each country's efforts to reduce the volume of crude oil important from Iran during the 180-day wind-down period, including the quantity and percentage of the reduction in purchases of Iranian crude oil, the termination of contracts for future delivery of Iranian crude oil, and other actions that demonstrate a commitment to decrease substantially such purchase. The State Department expects to engage in consultations with countries currently purchasing Iranian crude oil during the 180-day wind-down period.[15]

Based on determinations to waive the application of section 1245 from 2012 to 2015, when the JCPOA entered into effect, countries that are possibly facing renewed pressure to reduce their Iranian petroleum consumption include China, India, Japan, Malaysia, Singapore, South Africa, South Korea, Sri Lanka, Taiwan, and Turkey.[16] Countries that benefited from exemptions during that period include Belgium, the Czech Republic, France, Germany, Greece, Italy, Netherlands, Poland, Spain, and the United Kingdom.[17]

The regime of economic sanctions against Iran, at its height beginning in 2012, was arguably the most complex the United States and the international community have ever imposed on a rogue state. Iran's economy was once integrated into world trade, markets, and banking. As relations deteriorated, for the United States dating back to Iran's 1979 revolution and hostage-taking at the U.S. embassy, and for the larger international community over more recent human rights, regional stability, and nuclear and missile proliferation concerns, this complete economic integration offered seemingly limitless opportunities to impose economic restrictions and create points where pressure could be applied to bring Iran back into conformity with international norms.

---

[15] *FAQ* 5.2, May 8, 2018.
[16] For example, State Department Public Notice 8610 of January 22, 2014 (79 F.R. 4522).
[17] For example, State Department Public Notice 8678 of March 25, 2014 (79 F.R. 18382).

Joint Comprehensive Plan of Action, Vienna, July 14, 2015

On July 14, 2015, the E3/EU+3 and Iran reached agreement on a Joint Comprehensive Plan of Action (JCPOA) in which "Iran reaffirms that under no circumstances will Iran ever seek, develop or acquire any nuclear weapons." The Agreement also stated, "This JCPOA will produce the comprehensive lifting of all U.N. Security Council sanctions as well as multilateral and national sanctions related to Iran's nuclear programme, including steps on access in areas of trade, technology, finance and energy." (JCPOA, *Preamble and General Provisions*, paras. iii and v.)

A 37-point main text and five annexes comprise the JCPOA. Annex II and its multiple attachments that identify "persons, entities and bodies set out in Annex II" define "Sanctions-related commitments." Annex V, the "Implementation Plan," establishes the timeline for each party to implement its responsibilities.

The U.S. government summarizes the key markers relating to sanctions as follows:

- The U.N. Security Council resolution endorsing the JCPOA will terminate all the provisions of the previous
- U.N. Security Council resolutions on the Iranian nuclear issue simultaneously with the International Atomic Energy Agency (IAEA)-verified implementation of agreed nuclear-related measures by Iran and will establish specific restrictions.
- The EU will terminate all provisions of the EU Regulation, as subsequently amended, implementing all the nuclear related economic and financial sanctions, including related designations, simultaneously with IAEAverified implementation of agreed nuclear-related measures by Iran as specified in Annex V.
- The United States will cease the application, and will continue to do so, in accordance with the JCPOA, of the sanctions specified in Annex II, to take effect simultaneously with the IAEA-verified implementation of the agreed upon related measures by Iran as specified in Appendix V. (Note: U.S. statutory sanctions focused on Iran's support for terrorism, human rights abuses, and missile activities will remain in effect and continue to be enforced.)
- Eight years after Adoption Day or when the IAEA has reached the Broader Conclusion that all the nuclear material in Iran remains in peaceful activities, whichever is earlier, the United States will seek such legislative action as may be appropriate to terminate or modify to effectuate the termination of sanctions specified in Annex II.

Text of the JCPOA is available at http://eeas.europa.eu/top_stories/2015/150714_iran_ nuclear_deal_en.htm. Text of the U.S. Government's "Key Excerpts of the JCPOA" is available at https://www.whitehouse.gov/sites/default/files/docs/jcpoa_key_excerpts.pdf.

The Role of Congress

Congress remains seized of the matter of Iran's illicit activities, particularly monitoring Iran's reported activities related to military power, international terrorism, terrorism financing, illicit cyber activities, and ballistic missile research and development. Substantive reports required of the administration include the following:

- In the National Defense Authorization Act for Fiscal Year 2010 (P.L. 111-84; October 28, 2009; §1245; 10 U.S.C. 113 note), as amended, Congress requires the Secretary of Defense to provide a wide-sweeping annual report on the current and future strategy, capabilities, and composition of Iran's military force.
- In the Intelligence Authorization Act, FY2016 (Division M, Consolidated Appropriations Act for 2016; P.L. 114-113; December 18, 2015; §514 [22 U.S.C. 8701 note]), Congress requires the Director of National Intelligence, in consultation with the Secretary of the Treasury, to report regularly to Congress on the monetary value of sanctions relief Iran has received and if it has made use of the funds to support international terrorism, the regime of Bashar al Assad in Syria, nuclear weapons or ballistic missiles development at home or elsewhere, human rights abuses, or personal wealth of any senior government official.
- In the National Defense Authorization Act for Fiscal Year 2017 (P.L. 114-328; December 23, 2016, §1226), as amended, Congress requires the Secretaries of State and the Treasury, quarterly through 2022, to report on unilateral and multilateral efforts to impose sanctions on entities or individuals connected with Iran's ballistic missile launches.[18]
- In the Countering Iran's Destabilizing Activities Act of 2017 (P.L. 115-44, Title I; §103, 22 U.S.C. 9402), Congress requires the

---

[18] Section 7041(b)(3)(B) of the Department of State, Foreign Operations and Related Programs Appropriations Act, 2018 (Division K, P.L. 115-141) requires nearly the same report, but as a one-time delivery, no later than late September 2018.

Secretaries of State, Defense, the Treasury, and the Director of National Intelligence to report within 180 days and biennially thereafter a "strategy for deterring conventional and asymmetric Iranian activities and threats that directly threaten the United States and key allies in the Middle East, North Africa, and beyond."

- In the Countering Iran's Destabilizing Activities Act of 2017 (P.L. 115-44, Title I; §104(e), 22 U.S.C. 9403), Congress requires the President to report to Congress within 180 days and every 180 days thereafter on those who contribute to Iran's ballistic missile program.
- In the Countering Iran's Destabilizing Activities Act of 2017 (P.L. 115-44, Title I; §109, 22 U.S.C. 9408), Congress requires the President to report to Congress within 180 days and every 180 days thereafter on the designation for sanctions made by the European Union related to Iran's ballistic missile program, terrorism, or human rights abuses.

AUTHORITY TO WAIVE OR LIFT ECONOMIC SANCTIONS

The ability to impose or ease economic sanctions with some nimbleness and responsiveness to changing events is key to effective use of the tool in furtherance of national security or foreign policy objectives. Historically, both the President and Congress have recognized this essential requirement and have worked together to provide the President substantial flexibility. In the collection of laws that are the statutory basis for the U.S. economic sanctions regime on Iran, the President retains, in varying degrees, the authority to tighten and relax restrictions.

The President has the authority to impose a wide range of economic sanctions under the National Emergencies Act (NEA) and the International Emergency Economic Powers Act (IEEPA)—the authority on which sanctions-initiating executive orders are most often based.[19] Using these

---

[19] National Emergencies Act, P.L. 94-412; 50 U.S.C. 1601 *et seq.*; and International Emergency Economic Powers Act, P.L. 95-223; 50 U.S.C. 1701 *et seq.*

Iran 287

statutes, the President maintains that Iran poses an "unusual and extraordinary threat, which has its source in whole or substantial part outside the United States, to the national security, foreign policy, or economy of the United States...."[20] On March 15, 1995, President William Clinton declared that Iran's proliferation activities posed a threat to the United States that constituted a national emergency; this declaration has been renewed annually since 1995, as required by statute, and is the basis for subsequent executive orders that have expanded restrictions on economic relations with Iran.[21] If or when President Trump restores the provisions of the executive orders that President Obama had revoked to implement the U.S. responsibilities under the JCPOA (see Table 4), he is likely to cite the 1995 national emergency as the legal basis for his actions.

In the Comprehensive Iran Sanctions, Accountability, and Divestment Act of 2010 (CISADA; P.L. 111-195, as amended; 22 U.S.C. 8501 et seq.),[22] Congress grants to the President the authority to terminate most of the sanctions imposed on Iran in that act as well as those provided for in the Iran Threat Reduction and Syria Human Rights Act of 2012 (P.L. 112-158; 22 U.S.C. 8701 et seq.), and Iran Freedom and Counter-proliferation Act of 2012 (P.L. 112-239; 22 U.S.C. 8801 et seq.). Before terminating these sanctions, however, the President must certify that the government of Iran has ceased its engagement in the two critical areas of terrorism and weapons, as set forth in Section 401 of CISADA—

SEC. 401 [22 U.S.C. 8551]. GENERAL PROVISIONS.

(a) SUNSET.—The provisions of this Act (other than sections 105 and 305 and the amendments made by sections 102, 107, 109, and 205) shall terminate, and section 13(c)(1)(B) of the Investment Company Act of 1940, as added by section 203(a), shall cease to be effective, on the date

---

[20] IEEPA, §292(a); 50 U.S.C. 1701(a).

[21] Executive Order 12957; March 15, 1995; 60 F.R. 14615. An earlier order, relating to the taking of hostages at the American Embassy in Tehran in 1979, also remains active and is based on a separate announcement that a national emergency exists. Executive Order 12170; November 14, 1979; 44 F.R. 65729.

[22] Section 401(a) and (b)(1) of the Comprehensive Iran Sanctions, Accountability, and Divestment Act of 2010 (CISADA; P.L. 111-195; 22 U.S.C. 8551), as amended. Table 1 shows the sanctions for which Section 401 waiver authority is applicable.

that is 30 days after the date on which the President certifies to Congress that—

(1) the Government of Iran has ceased providing support for acts of international terrorism and no longer satisfies the requirements for designation as a state sponsor of terrorism (as defined in section 301) under—

section 6(j)(1)(A) of the Export Administration Act of 1979 (50 U.S.C. App. 2405(j)(1)(A)) (or any successor thereto);

section 40(d) of the Arms Export Control Act (22 U.S.C. 2780(d)); or

section 620A(a) of the Foreign Assistance Act of 1961 (22 U.S.C. 2371(a)); and

(2) Iran has ceased the pursuit, acquisition, and development of, and verifiably dismantled its, nuclear, biological, and chemical weapons and ballistic missiles and ballistic missile launch technology.

(b) PRESIDENTIAL WAIVERS.—

(1) IN GENERAL.—The President may waive the application of sanctions under section 103(b), the requirement to impose or maintain sanctions with respect to a person under section 105(a), 105A(a), 105B(a), or 105C(a) the requirement to include a person on the list required by section 105(b), 105A(b), 105B(b), or 105C(b), the application of the prohibition under section 106(a), or the imposition of the licensing requirement under section 303(c) with respect to a country designated as a Destination of Diversion Concern under section 303(a), if the President determines that such a waiver is in the national interest of the United States.

International Terrorism Determination

To lift the majority of the economic sanctions imposed by CISADA, the President must determine and certify that the government of Iran no longer supports acts of international terrorism. The government of Iran is designated as a state sponsor of acts of international terrorism, effective January 1984, pursuant to the Secretary of State's authorities and responsibilities under Section 6(j) of the Export Administration Act of

1979. Various statutes impede or prohibit foreign aid, financing, and trade because of that designation. Three laws (§620A, Foreign Assistance Act of 1961 [22 U.S.C. 2371]; §40, Arms Export Control Act [22 U.S.C. 2780]; and §6(j), Export Administration Act of 1979 [50 U.S.C. app. 2405(j)]) form the "terrorist list."[23] Because these statutes are not Iran-specific, they are not included in Table 1.

The President holds the authority to remove the designation of any country from the terrorist list. Though each of the three laws provides slightly different procedures, the authority to delist Iran resides with the President, and generally requires him to find that

- there has been a fundamental change in the leadership and policies of the government;
- the government is not supporting acts of international terrorism; and
- the government has assured that it will not support terrorism in the future.

Alternatively, the President may notify Congress that the terrorism designation will be rescinded in 45 days, and that the rescission is justified on the basis that

- the government has not supported an act of terrorism in the preceding six months; and
- the government has assured that it will not support terrorism in the future.

---

[23] Section 40A, Arms Export Control Act (22 U.S.C. 2780) also prohibits trade in defense articles and defense services to any country the President finds "is not cooperating fully with United States antiterrorism efforts." The President may waive the prohibition if he finds it "important to the national interests" to do so. This provision requires the President to annually identify uncooperative states; Iran has been listed since the provision's enactment in 1996 (first list was issued in 1997; authority to make certifications is currently delegated to the Secretary of State). On May 1, 2017, the Secretary of State issued the latest list, which continues to designate Iran. Department of State Public Notice 10006. 82 *Federal Register* 24424 (May 26, 2017). See also: CRS Report R43835, *State Sponsors of Acts of International Terrorism— Legislative Parameters: In Brief*, by Dianne E. Rennack.

In the case of foreign aid, the President also is authorized to provide aid despite the terrorism designation if he finds that "national security interests or humanitarian reasons justify" doing so and so notifies Congress 15 days in advance. In practical terms, the process of removing a state from the list of sponsors of international terrorism is studied and argued throughout the entire executive branch interagency, with those departments that are tasked with administering the restrictions—primarily State, Commerce, Treasury, Justice, and Defense—each weighing in. For a state to be delisted—which has occurred, most recently, to North Korea and Libya—the Secretary of State publishes a public notice that the respective government no longer supports acts of international terrorism; that starts the 45-day countdown required by legislation. After 45 days (or later), both the President and the Secretary of State issue determinations and announcements, which is followed by a rewriting of each department's regulations governing exports, arms sales, transactions, and other related matters. The requirement that the foreign government has not supported terrorist acts for six months may be retrospective.

LEGISLATION AND EXECUTIVE ORDERS

The first two tables presented in this chapter identify the legislative bases for sanctions imposed on Iran, and the nature of the authority to waive or lift those restrictions. Table 1 presents legislation, and Table 2 shows executive orders that are specific to Iran and its objectionable activities in the areas of terrorism, human rights, and weapons proliferation.

The latter two tables identify legislative and executive authorities that have been exercised to meet the requirements agreed to in the JCPOA on Implementation Day. Table 3 presents legislation, and Table 4 shows executive orders that have been waived, revoked, or altered to provide sanctions relief, based on Executive Order 13716 of January 16, 2016, and Departments of the Treasury and State *Guidance Relating to the Lifting of Certain U.S. Sanctions Pursuant to the Joint Comprehensive Plan of Action on*

Implementation Day, also issued on January 16. It is the authorities summarized in these latter two tables that will be the focus of the reestablishing of economic sanctions to implement President Trump's May 8 announcement.

Public laws that are not specific to the objectionable activities of the government of Iran but have been invoked to impede transactions or other economic or diplomatic relations are not included here. Failure to achieve human rights standards as a condition for foreign aid (e.g., the Foreign Assistance Act of 1961, International Religious Freedom Act of 1998, Trafficking Victims Protection Act of 2000, and related annual appropriations), or refusal to comply with international nonproliferation norms (e.g., Chemical and Biological Weapons Control and Warfare Elimination Act of 1991), for example, can trigger a range of economic sanctions. These and other authorities have been applied to Iran. It is unlikely that these statutes would be amended if and when they no longer apply to Iran. Sanctions authorized by these statutes are applied, and lifted, by executive branch decision.

On the other hand, because the President holds sole authority to renew, alter, and revoke executive orders he issues pursuant to the National Emergencies Act (NEA) and the International Emergency Economic Powers Act (IEEPA), Table 2 includes actions taken that are specific to Iran and also actions taken that are not specific to Iran (e.g., Executive Order 13224 and 13382 target terrorists and proliferators, respectively) but have been applied to that country. The authorities in these orders have been exercised to affect Iran in a significant way. Executive orders are subject to their underlying statutory authorities: economic sanctions are most often based on the President's authorities established in IEEPA. These are applied and lifted by the President; often their implementation and administration are delegated to the Secretary of the Treasury, who in turn assigns the task to Treasury's Office of Foreign Assets Control. Many of the Iran-specific sanctions in statute cite the President's authority to curtail transactions under IEEPA. In some instances, Congress has enacted restrictions on the President's unilateral authority to revoke an order, and the economic restrictions therein, until specific conditions are met.

Table 1. Iran—Economic Sanctions Currently Imposed in Furtherance of U.S. Foreign Policy or National Security Objectives (generally in order of enactment)

Statutory Basis	Rationale	Restriction	Authority To Impose	Authority To Lift or Waive
FOREIGN AID: AUTHORIZATION AND APPROPRIATIONS				
Sec. 307, **Foreign Assistance Act of 1961** (P.L. 87-195; 22 U.S.C. 2227; asamended)	General foreign policy reasons	Limits proportionate share of foreign aid to international organizations which, in turn, expend funds in Iran.	Statutory requirement	No waiver; exemption for certain UNICEF and IAEA programs. Secretary of State may block funds if he determines that IAEA programs are "inconsistent with U.S. nonproliferation and safety goals, will provide Iran with training or expertise ... , or are being used as a cover for the acquisition of sensitive nuclear technology" and notifies Congress.
Sec. 7007, **Foreign Operations Appropriations** (Div. K, P.L. 115-141)	General foreign policy reasons	Prohibits direct funding to the Government of Iran, including Export-Import Bank funds.	Statutory requirement	No waiver, though "notwithstanding" clauses elsewhere in appropriations and authorization statutes could result in aid being made available.
Sec. 7015(f), **Foreign Operations Appropriations** (Div. K, P.L. 115-141)	General foreign policy reasons	Prohibits most foreign aid to Iran, "except as provided through the regular notification procedures of the Committees on Appropriations."	Statutory requirement	President may waive or lift by exercising notification procedures of the Committee on Appropriations.

Statutory Basis	Rationale	Restriction	Authority To Impose	Authority To Lift or Waive
Sec. 7041(b), **Foreign Operations Appropriations** (Div. K, P.L. 115-141)	Nuclear nonproliferation	Prohibits U.S. Export-Import Bank from providing financing "to any person that is subject to sanctions under" Sec. 5(a)(2) or (3) of the Iran Sanctions Act of 1996—those under sanctions for engaging in production or export to Iran of refined petroleum products.	Statutory requirement	No waiver, though those sanctioned under Sec. 5(a)(2) and (3), Iran Sanctions Act of 1996, is subject to change. See below.
IRAQ SANCTIONS ACT OF 1990				
(P.L. 101-513; 50 U.S.C. 1701 note; extended to apply to Iran by Sec. 1603 of the Iran-Iraq Arms Non-proliferation Act of 1992; see below)				
Sec. 586G	Nonproliferatio	Prohibits —Sales under the Arms Export Control Act (foreign military sales); —Export licenses for commercial arms sales for any USML item; —Export of Commerce Control List items; and —export of nuclear equipment, materials, or technology:	Statutory requirement	President may waive if he finds it "essential to the national interest" to do so and notifies the Armed Services, Foreign Affairs/Relations Committees 15 days in advance (Sec. 1606, IIANA).
RAN-IRAQ ARMS NON-PROLIFERATION ACT OF 1992 (IIANA)				
(Title XVI of P.L. 102-484 (National Defense Authorization Act for Fiscal Year 1993); 50 U.S.C. 1701 note; as amended)				
Sec. 1603	Nonproliferation	Makes selected sanctions in Sec. 586G, Iran Sanctions Act of 1990, applicable for Iran (see above).		President may waive; see Sec. 586G, Iran Sanctions Act of 1990, above.

Table 1. (Continued)

Statutory Basis	Rationale	Restriction	Authority To Impose	Authority To Lift or Waive
Sec. 1604	Nonproliferation	For a period of 2 years, for any **person** who "transfers goods or technology so as to contribute knowingly and materially" to Iran's efforts "to acquire chemical, biological, or nuclear weapons or to acquire destabilizing numbers and types of advanced conventional weapons": —prohibits USG procurement contracts; and —prohibits U.S. export licenses.	Statutory requirement	President may waive if he finds it "essential to the national interest" to do so and notifies the Armed Services, Foreign Affairs/Relations Committees 15 days in advance (Sec. 1606, IIANA).
Sec. 1605	Nonproliferation	For any **foreign government** that "transfers or retransfers goods or technology so as to contribute knowingly and materially" to Iran's efforts "to acquire chemical, biological, or nuclear weapons or to acquire destabilizing numbers and types of advanced conventional weapons": —Suspends foreign aid for one year; —Requires U.S. opposition and "no" votes in international financial institutions for one year; —Suspends weapons codevelopment and coproduction agreements for one year;	Statutory requirement	President may waive if he finds it "essential to the national interest" to do so and notifies the Armed Services, Foreign Affairs/Relations Committees 15 days in advance (Sec. 1606, IIANA).

Statutory Basis	Rationale	Restriction	Authority To Impose	Authority To Lift or Waive
		—Suspends exchange agreements and related exports pertaining to military and dual-use technology for one year (unless such activities contribute to U.S. security); and —Prohibits the export of USML items for one year.		
Sec. 1605(c)	Nonproliferation	The President may exercise IEEPA authorities, excluding instances of "urgent humanitarian assistance," toward the foreign country. (See IEEPA authorities, below.)	At the President's discretion	At the President's discretion, following IEEPA authorities (see below)
IRAN SANCTIONS ACT OF 1996 (ISA 1996)[a] (P.L. 104-172; 50 U.S.C. 1701 note; as amended; Act sunsets effective December 31, 2026 (Sec. 13(b))				
Sec. 5(a), Sec. 6	Nonproliferation Anti-terrorism	Sec. 5(a) identifies developing Iran's energy sector as behavior to be investigated and cause for sanctions: —investing in Iran's petroleum resources; —providing to Iran goods, services, technology, information, or support relating to production of refined petroleum products; —trades in, facilitates, or finances Iran's refined petroleum products;	President imposes, based on investigation (Sec. 4(e)). Generally, imposed for a period of 2 years (Sec. 9(b)).	*Waivers issued pursuant to Sec. 4(c)(1)(A) are revoked, effective May 8, 2018. Sanctions imposed under Sec. 5(a) are reimposed but subject to a 90-day wind-down waiver, effective May 8, 2018.* The President may waive, case-by-case, for 6 months and for further 6-12 months depending on circumstances, for a foreign national if he finds it "vital to the national security interests" and notifies the Committees on Finance, Banking, Foreign Relations. Foreign Affairs, Ways and Means, Financial Services, 30 days in advance (Sec. 4(c)).

Table 1. (Continued)

Statutory Basis	Rationale	Restriction	Authority To Impose	Authority To Lift or Waive
		—joint ventures with the Government of Iran to develop refined petroleum resources; —supporting Iran's development of petroleum products; —supporting Iran's development of petrochemical products; —transporting crude oil from Iran; and —concealing Iran origin of petroleum products in the course of transporting such products. President may choose among the following penalties, and is required to impose at least five (Sec. 6): —deny Export-Import Bank program funds; —deny export licenses; —prohibit loans from U.S. financial institutions; —prohibit targeted financial institutions being designated as a primary dealer or a repository of government funds; —deny U.S. government procurement contracts;	President may Delay imposition of sanctions for up to 90 days in order to initiate consultations with foreign government of jurisdiction (Sec. 9(a)).	The President may waive for 12 months if the targeted person is subject to a government cooperating with U.S. in multilateral nonproliferation efforts relating to Iran, it is vital to national security interests, and he notifies Congress 30 days in advance. The President may cancel an investigation (precursor to imposing sanctions) if he determines the person is no longer engaged in objectionable behavior and has credible assurances such behavior will not occur in the future (Sec. 4(e)). The President may not apply sanctions if transaction: —meets an existing contract requirement; —is completed by a sole source supplier; or —is "essential to the national security under defense coproduction agreements"; —is specifically designated under certain trade laws; —complies with existing contracts and pertains to spare parts, component parts, servicing and maintenance, or information and technology relating to essential U.S. products, or medicine, medical supplies or humanitarian items (Sec. 5(f)).

Statutory Basis	Rationale	Restriction	Authority To Impose	Authority To Lift or Waive
		—limit or prohibit foreign exchange transactions; —limit or prohibit transactions with banks under U.S. jurisdiction; —prohibit transactions related to U.S.-based property; —prohibit investments in equity of a targeted entity; —deny visas to, or expel, any person who holds a position or controlling interest in a targeted entity; —impose any of the above on a targeted entity's principal executive officers; and —economic restrictions drawing from IEEPA authorities (see below). All U.S. government agencies are required to certify any prospective contractor as not being subject to sanctions under this section (Sec. 6(b)).		The requirement to impose sanctions under Sec. 5(a) has no force or effect if the President determines Iran: —has ceased programs relating to nuclear weapons, chemical and biological weapons, ballistic missiles; —is no longer designated as a state supporter of acts of international terrorism; and —"poses no significant threat to United States national security, interests, or allies." (Sec. 8). President may lift sanctions if he determines behavior has changed (Sec. 9(b)(2)). President may waive sanctions if he determines it is "essential to national security interests" to do so (Sec. 9(c)). President may delay imposition of sanctions expanded by amendments in the Comprehensive Iran Sanctions, Accountability, and Divestment Act (CISADA), relating to development and export of refined petroleum products, for up to 180 days, and in additional 180-day increments, if President certifies objectionable activities are being curtailed (CISADA, Sec. 102(h)). President may waive contractor certification requirement, case-bycase, if he finds it "essential to national security interests" to do so (Sec. 6(b)(5))

Table 1. (Continued)

Statutory Basis	Rationale	Restriction	Authority To Impose	Authority To Lift or Waive
Sec. 5(b), Sec. 6	Nonproliferation Anti-terrorism	Sec. 5(b) identifies developing Iran's WMD or other military capabilities as cause for sanctions: —exports, transfers, and transshipments of military/weapons goods, services, or technology; and —joint ventures relating to uranium mining, production, or transportation. President may choose among the following penalties, and is required to impose at least five (Sec. 6): —deny Export-Import Bank program funds; —deny export licenses; —prohibit loans from U.S. financial institutions; —prohibit targeted financial institutions being designated as a primary dealer or a repository of government funds; —deny U.S. government procurement contracts; —limit or prohibit foreign exchange transactions; —limit or prohibit transactions with banks under U.S. jurisdiction;	Statutory requirement; generally imposed for a period of 2 years (Sec. 9(b)). President may delay imposition of sanctions for up to 90 days in order to initiate consultations with foreign government of jurisdiction (Sec. 9(a)).	The President may not apply sanctions if: —in the case of joint venture, is terminated within 180 days; —President determines the government of jurisdiction did not know person was engaged in activity, or has taken steps to prevent recurrence; —case-by-case, President determines approval of activity is "vital to national security interests of the United States" and notifies Congress; or The President may not apply sanctions if transaction: —meets an existing contract requirement; —is completed by a sole source supplier; or —is "essential to the national security under defense coproduction agreements"; —is specifically designated under certain trade laws; —complies with existing contracts and pertains to spare parts, component parts, servicing and maintenance, or information and technology relating to essential U.S. products, or medicine, medical supplies or humanitarian items (Sec. 5(f)).

Statutory Basis	Rationale	Restriction	Authority To Impose	Authority To Lift or Waive
		—prohibit transactions related to U.S.-based property; —prohibit investments in equity of a targeted entity; —deny visas to, or expel, any person who holds a position or controlling interest in a targeted entity; —impose any of the above on a targeted entity's principal executive officers; and —economic restrictions drawing from IEEPA authorities (see below). All U.S. government agencies are required to certify any prospective contractor as not being subject to sanctions under this section (Sec. 6(b)).		President may waive contractor certification requirement, case-bycase, if he finds it "essential to national security interests" to do so (Sec. 6(b)(5)). President may lift sanctions if he determines behavior has changed (Sec. 9(b)(2)). President may waive sanctions if he determines it is "essential to national security interests" to do so (Sec. 9(c)).
IRAN, NORTH KOREA, AND SYRIA NONPROLIFERATION ACT (INKSA) (P.L. 106-178; 50 U.S.C. 1701 note; as amended)				
Sec. 3	Nonproliferation	Foreign persons identified by President as having transferred to or acquired from Iran goods, services, or technology related to weapons or missile proliferation may, at the President's discretion, be: —denied entering into procurement contracts with the U.S. government;	At the President's discretion	President may choose to not impose sanctions, but must justify to Committees on Foreign Affairs and Foreign Relations (Sec. 4). President may choose to not impose sanctions if he finds: —targeted person did not *knowingly* engage in objectionable transaction;

Table 1. (Continued)

Statutory Basis	Rationale	Restriction	Authority To Impose	Authority To Lift or Waive
		—prohibited transactions relating to import into the United States; —prohibited arms sales from the United States of USML articles and services; —denied export licenses for items controlled under the Export Administration Act of 1979 or Export Administration Regulations.		—transaction did not *materially* contribute to proliferation; —government of jurisdiction adheres to relevant nonproliferation regime; or —government of jurisdiction "has imposed meaningful penalties" (Sec. 5(a)).
TRADE SANCTIONS REFORM AND EXPORT ENHANCEMENT ACT OF 2000 (TSRA) (Title IX of P.L. 106-387 (Agriculture, Rural Development, Food and Drug Administration, and Related Agencies Appropriations Act, 2001); 22 U.S.C. 7201 *et seq.;* as amended)				
Sec. 906 (22 U.S.C. 7205)	Anti-terrorism	Requires export licenses for agricultural commodities, medicines, medical devices to any government designated as a state sponsor of acts of international terrorism.	Statutory requirement	No waiver; the executive branch (primarily Departments of Commerce, for exportation, and Treasury for related transactions) may issue export licenses limited to a 12-month duration but there is no limit on the number or nature of licenses generally.
Sec. 908 (22 U.S.C. 7207)	Anti-terrorism	Prohibits U.S. assistance—foreign aid, export assistance, credits, guarantees— for commercial exports to Iran.	Statutory requirement	President may waive if "it is in the national security interest of the United States to do so, or for humanitarian reasons."

Statutory Basis	Rationale	Restriction	Authority To Impose	Authority To Lift or Waive
IRAN NUCLEAR PROLIFERATION PREVENTION ACT OF 2002 (INPPA)				
(Subtitle D of title XIII of P.L. 107-228 (Foreign Relations Authorization Act for Fiscal Year 2003))				
Sec. 1343(b) (22 U.S.C. 2027(b))	Nonproliferation	Requires the U.S. representative to the IAEA to oppose programs that are "inconsistent with nuclear nonproliferation and safety goals of the United States."	Discretionary, based on findings of the Secretary of State	No waiver; however, "nay" votes are based on the Secretary of State's annual review of IAEA programs and determinations.
IRAN FREEDOM SUPPORT ACT (IFSA)				
(P.L. 109-293; 50 U.S.C. 1701 note)				
Sec. 101	Democracy promotion General foreign policy reasons	Makes permanent the restrictions the President imposed under IEEPA/NEA authorities in Executive Order 12957, which: —prohibits any U.S. person from entering into a contract or financing or guaranteeing performance under a contract relating to petroleum resource development in Iran; and Executive Order 12959, which: —prohibits any U.S. person from investing in Iran; and Executive Order 13059, which: —prohibits any U.S. person from exporting where the end-user is Iran or the Government of Iran; —prohibits any U.S. person from investing in Iran;	Statutory requirement	President may terminate the sanctions if he notifies Congress 15 days in advance, unless "exigent circumstances" warrant terminating the restrictions without notice, in which case Congress shall be notified within 3 days after termination.

Table 1. (Continued)

Statutory Basis	Rationale	Restriction	Authority To Impose	Authority To Lift or Waive
		—prohibits any U.S. person from engaging in transactions or financing related to Iran-origin goods or services		
COMPREHENSIVE IRAN SANCTIONS, ACCOUNTABILITY, AND DIVESTMENT ACT OF 2010 (CISADA) (P.L. 111-195; 22 U.S.C. 8501 *et seq.;* as amended)				
Sec. 103(b)(1) and (2) (22 U.S.C. 8512)	Nonproliferation Human rights Anti-terrorism	Prohibits most imports into the United States of goods of Iranian origin. Prohibits a U.S. person from exporting most U.S.-origin goods, services, or technology to Iran.	Statutory requirement	Allows imports, exports, food, medicine, and humanitarian aid as covered by IEEPA and TSRA. President may allow exports if he determines to do so is in the national interest. Most of CISADA, including sanctions under this section, ceases to be effective when President removes Iran's designation as a sponsor of acts of international terrorism and that country has ceased its pursuit of weapons of mass destruction (WMD) (Sec. 401; 22 U.S.C. 8551). President may waive if he finds it "in the national interest" to do so (Sec. 401(b)).
Sec. 103(b)(3) (22 U.S.C. 8512)	Nonproliferation Human rights Anti-terrorism	Freezes assets of individual, family member, or associates acting on behalf of individual, in compliance with IEEPA authorities.	President determines	President's discretion. Most of CISADA, including sanctions under this section, ceases to be effective when President removes Iran's designation as a sponsor of acts of international terrorism and that country has ceased its pursuit of WMD (Sec. 401; 22 U.S.C. 8551). President may waive if he finds it "in the national interest" to do so (Sec. 401(b)).

Statutory Basis	Rationale	Restriction	Authority To Impose	Authority To Lift or Waive
Sec. 104(c) (22 U.S.C. 8513(c))	Anti-money laundering Anti-terrorism (financing) Nonproliferation	Imposes IEEPA-authorized economic restrictions, to be issued by Secretary of the Treasury in new regulations and prohibits U.S. banks opening or maintaining correspondent or payable-through accounts for any foreign financial institution that —facilitates Iran's acquisition of WMD; —facilitates Iran's support of foreign terrorist organizations (FTO); —facilitates activities of persons subject to U.N. Security Council sanctions —engages in money laundering; —facilitates Iran's Central Bank or other financial institution in objectionable activities; or —facilitates transactions of IRGC or others under IEEPA sanctions.	Statutory requirement	*Sec. 104(c)(2)(E)(ii)(I) no longer applicable to transactions or services for specifically identified Iranian financial institutions. "Statutory sanctions authorities will no longer apply ... " to the extent an SDN has been delisted.* Secretary of the Treasury may waive if he finds it "necessary to the national interest" to do so (subsec. (f)). Most of CISADA, including sanctions under this section, ceases to be effective when President removes Iran's designation as a sponsor of acts of international terrorism and that country has ceased its pursuit of WMD (Sec. 401; 22 U.S.C. 8551).
Sec. 104(c)(4) (22 U.S.C. 8513(c)(4))	Anti-money laundering Anti-terrorism (financing) Nonproliferation	Subjects National Iranian Oil Company (NIOC) and National Iranian Tanker Company (NITC) to IEEPA-authorized economic restrictions, promulgated by the Secretary of the Treasury under Sec. 104(c) (above) if found to be affiliated with the Iranian Revolutionary Guard Corps (IRGC)	Requires Secretary of the Treasury determination	Secretary of the Treasury may waive if he finds it "necessary to the national interest" to do so (subsec. (f)). If the country of primary jurisdiction is exempted under Sec. 1245, National Defense Authorization Act, 2012 (NDAA'12), that exemption extends to financial entities engaged in transactions with NIOC and NITC (Sec. 104(c)(4)(C)).

Table 1. (Continued)

Statutory Basis	Rationale	Restriction	Authority To Impose	Authority To Lift or Waive
				Most of CISADA, including sanctions under this section, ceases to be effective when President removes Iran's designation as a sponsor of acts of international terrorism and that country has ceased its pursuit of WMD (Sec. 401; 22 U.S.C. 8551).
Sec. 104A (22 U.S.C. 8513A)	Anti-money laundering Anti-terrorism (financing) Nonproliferation	Expands restriction established in Sec. 104 (above) to also apply to any foreign financial institution that facilitates, participates, or assists in activities identified in Sec. 104(c).	Requires Secretary of the Treasury to issue new regulations	Secretary of the Treasury may waive if he finds it "necessary to the national interest" to do so (sec. 104(f)). Most of CISADA, including sanctions under this section, ceases to be effective when President removes Iran's designation as a sponsor of acts of international terrorism and that country has ceased its pursuit of WMD (Sec. 401; 22 U.S.C. 8551).
Sec. 105 (22 U.S.C. 8514)	Human rights	Imposes sanctions on individuals the President identifies as responsible for or complicit in the human rights crackdown around the 2009 national election. Sanctions include visa ineligibility and IEEPArelated economic restrictions.	Statutory requirement of the President	President may terminate sanctions when he determines and certifies that the government of Iran has released political prisoners detained around the June 2009 election; ceased related objectionable activities; investigated related killings, arrests, and abuses; and made public commitment to establishing an independent judiciary and upholding international human rights standards.

Statutory Basis	Rationale	Restriction	Authority To Impose	Authority To Lift or Waive
				Most of CISADA, including sanctions under this section, ceases to be effective when President removes Iran's designation as a sponsor of acts of international terrorism and that country has ceased its pursuit of WMD (Sec. 401; 22 U.S.C. 8551). President may waive if he finds it "in the national interest" to do so (Sec. 401(b)).
Sec. 105A (22 U.S.C. 8514A)	Human rights	Imposes sanctions on any individual the President identifies as providing goods or technology to the government of Iran to facilitate human rights abuses, including "sensitive technology." Includes making such materials available to the IRGC. Sanctions include visa ineligibility and IEEPA related economic restrictions.	Statutory requirement of the President	President may terminate sanctions when he determines an individual has taken steps toward stopping objectionable activity, and will not reengage. Most of CISADA, including sanctions under this section, ceases to be effective when President removes Iran's designation as a sponsor of acts of international terrorism and that country has ceased its pursuit of WMD (Sec. 401; 22 U.S.C. 8551). President may waive if he finds it "in the national interest" to do so (Sec. 401(b)).
Sec. 105B (22 U.S.C. 8514B)	Human rights (freedom of expression and assembly)	Imposes sanctions on any individual the President identifies as engaging in censorship or limiting the freedom of assembly. Sanctions include visa ineligibility and IEEPA related economic restrictions.	Statutory requirement of the President	Most of CISADA, including sanctions under this section, ceases to be effective when President removes Iran's designation as a sponsor of acts of international terrorism and that country has ceased its pursuit of WMD (Sec. 401; 22 U.S.C. 8551).

Table 1. (Continued)

Statutory Basis	Rationale	Restriction	Authority To Impose	Authority To Lift or Waive
				President may waive if he finds it "in the national interest" to do so (Sec. 401(b)).
Sec. 105C (22 U.S.C. 8514C)	Human rights (diversion of food and medicine)	Imposes sanctions on any individual the President identifies as diverting food and medicine from reaching the Iranian people. Sanctions include visa ineligibility and IEEPArelated economic restrictions	Statutory requirement of the President	Most of CISADA, including sanctions under this section, ceases to be effective when President removes Iran's designation as a sponsor of acts of international terrorism and that country has ceased its pursuit of WMD (Sec. 401; 22 U.S.C. 8551). President may waive if he finds it "in the national interest" to do so (Sec. 401(b)).
Sec. 106 (22 U.S.C. 8515)	Human rights (freedom of expression and assembly)	Prohibits entering into procurement contracts with any individual the President identifies as exporting sensitive technology to Iran. Sec. 412, Iran Threat Reduction and Syria Human Rights Act (ITRSHRA), further defines "sensitive technology."	Statutory requirement of the President	President may exempt some products defined in specific trade laws and IEEPA. Most of CISADA, including sanctions under this section, ceases to be effective when President removes Iran's designation as a sponsor of acts of international terrorism and that country has ceased its pursuit of WMD (Sec. 401; 22 U.S.C. 8551). President may waive if he finds it "in the national interest" to do so (Sec. 401(b)).
Sec. 108 (22 U.S.C. 8516)	International obligations	President may issue any regulations to comply with U.N. Security Council resolutions.	Discretion of the President	Discretion of the President. Most of CISADA, including sanctions under this section, ceases to be effective when President removes Iran's designation as a sponsor of acts of international

Statutory Basis	Rationale	Restriction	Authority To Impose	Authority To Lift or Waive
Sec. 303 (22 U.S.C. 8543)	Export controls (nonproliferation; anti-terrorism)	President may identify and designate a country as a "Destination of Division Concern" if he finds it diverts export-controlled goods and technology to Iran that would materially contribute to that state's development of WMD, delivery systems, and international terrorism. President may delay or deny export licenses.	Discretion of the President	President terminates designation—and ensuing trade restrictions—on determining that country "has adequately strengthened the export control system." Most of CISADA, including sanctions under this section, ceases to be effective when President removes Iran's designation as a sponsor of acts of international terrorism and that country has ceased its pursuit of WMD (Sec. 401; 22 U.S.C. 8551).
NATIONAL DEFENSE AUTHORIZATION ACT FOR FISCAL YEAR 2012 (NDAA 2012) (Sec. 1245 of P.L. 112-81; 22 U.S.C. 8513a; as amended)				
Sec. 1245	Anti-money laundering	Designates Iran's financial sector, including its Central Bank, as a "primary money laundering concern." —Requires the President to block and prohibit all transactions of any Iranian financial institution under U.S. jurisdiction. —Requires the President to prohibit opening of correspondent and payable-through accounts for any institution that conducts transactions for the Central Bank of Iran. —Authorizes the President to impose IEEPA-based sanctions.	Statutory requirement	*Waivers issued pursuant to Sec. 1245(d)(5) are revoked, effective May 8, 2018. Sanctions imposed under Sec. 1245(d)(1) are reimposed but subject to a 90-day wind-down waiver, effective May 8, 2018.* President may delay imposition of sanctions if government of primary jurisdiction reduces its crude oil purchases from Iran. Renewable every 180 days. *Most recently waived, through May 12, 2018, in Presidential Determination No. 2018-1 of November 15, 2017 (82 Federal Register 59503).* President may waive imposition if he finds it "in the national security interest of the United States" to do so.

Table 1. (Continued)

Statutory Basis	Rationale	Restriction	Authority To Impose	Authority To Lift or Waive
				Sanctions under this section cease to be effective 30 days after President certifies and removes Iran's designation as a sponsor of acts of international terrorism and that country has ceased its pursuit of WMD (Sec. 401, CISADA; 22 U.S.C. 8551) (Sec. 605; 22 U.S.C. 8785) (Sec. 1245(i)).
IRAN THREAT REDUCTION AND SYRIA HUMAN RIGHTS ACT OF 2012 (ITRSHRA) (P.L. 112-158; 22 U.S.C. 8701 et seq.)				
Sec. 211 (22 U.S.C. 8721)	Nonproliferation Anti-terrorism	President imposes IEEPAbased sanctions on any person he determines has engaged in transactions relating to providing a vessel or insuring a shipping service that materially contributes to the government of Iran's proliferation activities.	Statutory requirement	President may waive imposition if he finds it "vital to the national security interests of the United States" to do so. Most of ITR, including sanctions under this section, ceases to be effective when President removes Iran's designation as a sponsor of acts of international terrorism and that country has ceased its pursuit of WMD (Sec. 401, CISADA; 22 U.S.C. 8551) (Sec. 605; 22 U.S.C. 8785).
Sec. 212 (22 U.S.C. 8722)	Nonproliferation Anti-terrorism	President imposes IEEPA-and Iran Sanctions Act-(ISA) based sanctions (see above) on any person he determines has provided underwriting services or insurance for NIOC or NITC.	Statutory requirement	*Waivers issued pursuant to Sec. 212(d)(1) are revoked, effective May 8, 2018. Sanctions imposed under Sec. 212(a) are reimposed but subject to a 90-day wind-down waiver, effective May 8, 2018.*

Statutory Basis	Rationale	Restriction	Authority To Impose	Authority To Lift or Waive
				President may terminate if objectionable activity has ceased. Most of ITR, including sanctions under this section, ceases to be effective when President removes Iran's designation as a sponsor of acts of international terrorism and that country has ceased its
Sec. 213 (22 U.S.C. 8723)	Nonproliferation Anti-terrorism	President imposes IEEPA-and ISA-based sanctions (see above) on any person he determines has engaged in transactions relating to Iran's sovereign debt.	Statutory requirement	*Waivers issued pursuant to Sec. 213(b)(1) are revoked, effective May 8, 2018.* *Sanctions imposed under Sec. 213(a) are reimposed but subject to a 90-day wind-down waiver, effective May 8, 2018.* Most of ITR, including sanctions under this section, ceases to be effective when President removes Iran's designation as a sponsor of acts of international terrorism and that country has ceased its pursuit of WMD (Sec. 401, CISADA; 22 U.S.C. 8551) (Sec. 605; 22 U.S.C. 8785).
Sec. 217 (22 U.S.C. 8724)	Nonproliferation Anti-terrorism	Requires President to certify that the Central Bank of Iran is not engaging in activities related to WMD or terrorism before he lifts IEEPA-based sanctions imposed pursuant to E.O. 13599 (see Table 2). Requires President to certify that sanctions evaders are engaged in activities related to WMD or terrorism before he lifts IEEPA-based sanctions imposed pursuant to E.O. 13608 (see Table 2).	Statutory requirement	President may still lift sanctions, but is slowed in doing so and must certify on new conditions relating to terrorism and proliferation.

Table 1. (Continued)

Statutory Basis	Rationale	Restriction	Authority To Impose	Authority To Lift or Waive
Sec. 218 (22 U.S.C. 8725)	Nonproliferation Anti-terrorism	Extends IEEPA-based sanctions imposed on parent companies to their foreign subsidiaries, to prohibit transactions with the government of Iran.	Statutory requirement	Most of ITR, including sanctions under this section, ceases to be effective when President removes Iran's designation as a sponsor of acts of international terrorism and that country has ceased its pursuit of WMD (Sec. 401, CISADA; 22 U.S.C. 8551) (Sec. 605; 22 U.S.C. 8785).
Sec. 220(c) (22 U.S.C. 8726(c))	Nonproliferation Anti-terrorism	President may impose IEEPA-based sanctions on financial messaging services that facilitate transactions for the Central Bank of Iran or other restricted financial institutions.	At the President's discretion	*Committed to refrain from imposing discretionary sanctions blocking access to property or assets.* President's discretion. Most of ITR, including sanctions under this section, ceases to be effective when President removes Iran's designation as a sponsor of acts of international terrorism and that country has ceased its pursuit of WMD (Sec. 401, CISADA; 22 U.S.C. 8551) (Sec. 605; 22 U.S.C. 8785)
Sec. 221 (22 U.S.C. 8727)	Nonproliferation Anti-terrorism Human rights	Requires the President to identify senior Iranian government officials involved in proliferation, support of terrorism, or human rights violations. Requires the Secretaries of State and Homeland Security to, respectively, deny identified persons and their family members visas and entry into the United States.	Statutory requirement	President may waive if he finds it "essential to the national interests of the United States" and notifies Congress in advance. Most of ITR, including sanctions under this section, ceases to be effective when President removes Iran's designation as a sponsor of acts of international terrorism and that country has ceased its pursuit of WMD (Sec. 401, CISADA; 22 U.S.C. 8551) (Sec. 605; 22 U.S.C. 8785).

Statutory Basis	Rationale	Restriction	Authority To Impose	Authority To Lift or Waive
Sec. 301 (22 U.S.C. 8741)	National security Nonproliferation	Requires the President to identify members, agents, and affiliates of the IRGC and impose IEEPA-based sanctions. Requires the Secretaries of State and Homeland Security to, respectively, deny identified persons and their family members visas and entry into the United States	Statutory requirement	President may waive if he finds it "vital to the national security interests of the United States to do so." Most of ITR, including sanctions under this section, ceases to be effective when President removes Iran's designation as a sponsor of acts of international terrorism and that country has ceased its pursuit of WMD (Sec. 401, CISADA; 22 U.S.C. 8551) (Sec. 605; 22 U.S.C. 8785
Sec. 302 (22 U.S.C. 8742)	National security Nonproliferation	Requires the President to identify those who materially engage in support or transactions with the IRGC or related entities subject to IEEPAbased sanctions. Further requires the President to impose ISA-based sanctions on and additional IEEPA based sanctions on those he identifies. President is not required to publicly identify such individual if "doing so would cause damage to the national security of the United States."	Statutory requirement	President may terminate when he determines objectionable activities have ceased. President may waive if activities have ceased or if "it is essential to the national security interests of the United States to do so." President may forego imposing sanctions if similar exception has been made under Sec. 104(c) of CISADA (see above). Most of ITR, including sanctions under this section, ceases to be effective when President removes Iran's designation as a sponsor of acts of international terrorism and that country has ceased its pursuit of WMD (Sec. 401, CISADA; 22 U.S.C. 8551) (Sec. 605; 22 U.S.C. 8785). See also: State Department Public Notice 8610 of January 22, 2014 (79 F.R. 4522) Guidance of January 20, 2014) Guidance of July 21, 2014 (79 F.R. 45233) Guidance of November 25, 2014 (79 F.R. 73141)

Table 1. (Continued)

Statutory Basis	Rationale	Restriction	Authority To Impose	Authority To Lift or Waive
Sec. 303 (22 U.S.C. 8743)	Nonproliferation United Nations compliance	President is required to identify any agency of a foreign country that materially assists or engages in transactions with IRGC or any entity subject to U.N. Security Council sanctions. President may cut off most foreign aid, deny arms sales and transfers, deny export licenses, require opposition to loans to that foreign country in the international financial institutions, deny USG financial assistance, or impose other IEEPA-based sanctions.	Statutory requirement; however, President Selects specific actions	President may terminate if objectionable activities have ceased, or if "it is essential to the national security interests of the United States to terminate such measures." President may waive imposition of any measure if he explains his decision to Congress (and justification may be subsequent to action taken). Most of ITR, including sanctions under this section, ceases to be effective when President removes Iran's designation as a sponsor of acts of international terrorism and that country has ceased its pursuit of WMD (Sec. 401, CISADA; 22 U.S.C. 8551) (Sec. 605; 22 U.S.C. 8785).
Sec. 411 (22 U.S.C. 8751)	Human rights Nonproliferation Anti-terrorism	Requires the President to maintain IEEPA-based sanctions pursuant to E.O. 13606 (see Table 2) until he certifies Iran has ceased its support of international terrorism and pursuit of weapons proliferation, under Sec. 401, CISADA (see above).	Statutory requirement	President's determination
Sec. 501 (22 U.S.C. 8771)	Nonproliferation	Requires the Secretaries of State and Homeland Security to, respectively, deny visas and entry into the United States to Iranian citizens who seek education in the United States related to energy, nuclear science, or nuclear engineering.	Statutory requirement	Most of ITR, including sanctions under this section, ceases to be effective when President removes Iran's designation as a sponsor of acts of international terrorism and that country has ceased its pursuit of WMD (Sec. 401, CISADA; 22 U.S.C.

Statutory Basis	Rationale	Restriction	Authority To Impose	Authority To Lift or Waive
IRAN FREEDOM AND COUNTER-PROLIFERATION ACT OF 2012 (IFCA)				
(Title XII, subtitle D, of National Defense Authorization Act for Fiscal Year 2013; **NDAA 2013**; P.L. 112-239; 22 U.S.C. 8801 *et seq.*)				
Sec. 1244 (22 U.S.C. 8803)	Nonproliferation	*The President, in sec. 3 of E.O. 13716 of January 16, 2016, authorizes the Secretary of the Treasury, in consultation with the Secretary of State, to block property and interests in property of those "providing significant financial, material, technological, support, or goods or services to transactions related to the energy, shipping, and shipbuilding sectors of Iran. E.O. 13716 of January 16, 2016, at sec. 3(b), further authorizes the Secretaries to block loans above $10 million in any 12-month period; prohibit foreign exchange, transfers or credits through U.S. financial institutions; block property, investments under U.S. jurisdiction; block U.S. persons from investing in debt of a sanctioned person; prohibit imports; and extend restrictions to officers of sanctioned entity.* *E.O. 13716 of January 16, 2016, at sec. 3(c), further authorizes the Secretaries to block property of any individual who is found to engage in diversion of food and medicine intended for the people of Iran; misappropriation of resources; transactions with a sanctioned person; or owned or controlled by a sanctioned person.*	Statutory requirement	*Waivers issued pursuant to Sec. 1244(i) are revoked, effective May 8, 2018.* *Sanctions imposed under Sec. 1244(c)(1) are reimposed but subject to a 90-day wind-down waiver, effective May 8, 2018.* *Statement of Licensing Policy (SLP) for transactions related to providing Iran commercial passenger aircraft, and related spare parts and services, for exclusively civil aviation end use will be revoked in 90 days, effective May 8, 2018.* *Sanctions imposed under Sec. 1244(d)(1), (d)(2), (h)(2), are reimposed but subject to a 90-day winddown waiver, effective May 8, 2018.* Humanitarian-related transactions are exempted. President may exempt transactions related to Afghanistan reconstruction and development, if he determines it in the national interest to do so. President may exempt application to those countries exempted from NDAA'12 requirements (see above). Some aspects of trade in natural gas are exempted.

Table 1. (Continued)

Statutory Basis	Rationale	Restriction	Authority To Impose	Authority To Lift or Waive
		Designates entities that operate Iran's ports, and entities in energy, shipping, and shipbuilding, including NITC, IRISL, and NIOC, and their affiliates, as "entities of proliferation concern." Requires the President to block transactions and interests in property under U.S. jurisdiction of such entities. Requires the President to impose ISA-based sanctions on any person who knowingly engages in trade related to energy, shipping, or shipbuilding sectors of Iran.		President may waive for 180 days if he finds it "vital to the national security of the United States" to do so.
Sec. 1245 (22 U.S.C. 8804)	Nonproliferation	Requires the President to impose ISA-based sanctions on any person who knowingly engages in trade related to precious metal, or material used in energy, shipping, or shipbuilding, if controlled by IRGC or other sanctioned entity	Statutory requirement	*Waivers issued pursuant to Sec. 1245(g) are revoked, effective May 8, 2018. Sanctions imposed under Sec. 1245(a)(1), (c), relating to correspondent or payable-through accounts, are reimposed but subject to a 90-day wind-down waiver, effective May 8, 2018.* President may exempt those he determines are exercising "due diligence" to comply with restrictions. President may waive for 180 days, and may renew that waiver in 6-month increments, if he finds it "vital to the national security of the United States" to do so.

Statutory Basis	Rationale	Restriction	Authority To Impose	Authority To Lift or Waive
Sec. 1246 (22 U.S.C. 8805)	Nonproliferation	Requires the President to impose ISA-based sanctions on any person who knowingly provides underwriting or insurance services to any sanctioned entity with respect to Iran	Statutory requirement	*Waivers issued pursuant to Sec. 1246(e) are revoked, effective May 8, 2018.* *Sanctions imposed under Sec. 1246(a), relating to SDN designations and underwriting, insurance, or reinsurance, are reimposed but subject to a 90-day wind-down waiver, effective May 8, 2018.* Humanitarian-related transactions are exempted. President may exempt those he determines are exercising "due diligence" to comply with restrictions. President may waive for 180 days, and may renew that waiver in 6-month increments, if he finds it "vital to the national security of the United States" to do so.
Sec. 1247 (22 U.S.C. 8806)	Nonproliferation	Requires the President to prohibit any correspondent or payable-through account by a foreign financial institution that is found to facilitate a "significant financial transaction" on behalf of any Iranian Specially Designated National (SDN).	Statutory requirement	*Waivers issued pursuant to Sec. 1247(f) are revoked, effective May 8, 2018.* *Sanctions imposed under Sec. 1247(a), relating to SDN designations and foreign financial institutions, are reimposed but subject to a 90-day wind-down waiver, effective May 8, 2018.* Humanitarian-related transactions are exempted. President may exempt application to those countries exempted from NDAA'12 requirements (see above). President may waive for 180 days, and may renew that waiver in 6-month increments, if he finds it "vital to the national security of the United States" to do so.

Table 1. (Continued)

Statutory Basis	Rationale	Restriction	Authority To Impose	Authority To Lift or Waive
Sec. 1248 (22 U.S.C. 8807)	Human rights	Requires the President to apply Sec. 105(c), CISADAbased sanctions (see above) to the Islamic Republic of Iran Broadcasting and the President of that entity, and to add this entity and individual to the SDN list.	Statutory requirement	President may waive if he finds it "in the national interest" to do so (Sec. 401(b), CISADA). President may terminate sanctions when he determines and certifies that the government of Iran has released political prisoners detained around the June 2009 election; ceased related objectionable activities; investigated related killings, arrests, and abuses; and made public commitment to establishing an independent judiciary and upholding international human rights standards (Sec. 105(d), CISADA).
COUNTERING IRAN'S DESTABILIZING ACTIVITIES ACT OF 2017 (Title I of the Countering America's Adversaries Through Sanctions Act (CAATSA); P.L. 115-44; 22 U.S.C. 9401 *et seq.*)				
Sec. 104 (22 U.S.C. 9403)	Nonproliferation (ballistic missiles)	Requires President to impose IEEPA-based sanctions and deny visas for those who engage in activities that materially contribute to Iran's ballistic missile program.	Statutory requirement	Sec. 112 provides the President the authority to waive for 180 days, case-by-case, if he finds it vital to U.S. national security interests to do so. Determination may be renewed in additional 180-day increments with congressional notification. Also constructed in context of E.O. 13382 (see Table 2).

Statutory Basis	Rationale	Restriction	Authority To Impose	Authority To Lift or Waive
Sec. 105 (22 U.S.C. 9404)	Terrorism	Requires President to impose IEEPA-based sanctions with respect to IRGC and foreign affiliates	Statutory requirement	Sec. 112 provides the President the authority to waive for 180 days, case-by-case, if he finds it vital to U.S. national security interests to do so. Determination may be renewed in additional 180-day increments with congressional notification. Also constructed in context of E.O. 13224 (see Table 2).
Sec. 106 (22 U.S.C. 9405)	Human rights	Authorizes the President to impose IEEPA-based sanctions on those identified by the Secretary of State as "responsible for extrajudicial killings, torture, or other gross violations of internationally recognized human rights" against Iranians who are whistleblowers against state corruption, human rights violations, or civil liberties violations.	Discretion of the President	Sec. 112 provides the President the authority to waive for 180 days, case-by-case, if he finds it vital to U.S. national security interests to do so. Determination may be renewed in additional 180-day increments with congressional notification.
Sec. 107 (22 U.S.C. 9406)	Nonproliferation	Requires the President to impose IEEPA-based sanctions on those he finds to engage in arms trade with Iran.	Statutory requirement	Sec. 107(d) authorizes the President to waive if in U.S. national security interest; Iran is no longer a national security threat; and Iran no longer "satisfies the requirements for designation as a state sponsor of terrorism." In addition, sec. 112 provides the President the authority to waive for 180 days, case-bycase, if he finds it vital to U.S. national security interests to do so. Determination may be renewed in additional 180-day increments with congressional notification.

Table 1. (Continued)

Statutory Basis	Rationale	Restriction	Authority To Impose	Authority To Lift or Waive
				Sec. 112 provides the President the authority to waive for 180 days, case-by-case, if he finds it vital to U.S. national security interests to do so. Determination may be renewed in additional 180-day increments with congressional notification
Sec. 108 (22 U.S.C. 9407)	Nonproliferation Terrorism	Requires the President to review, 5 years after enactment, all Iran-related SDN to determine their role in ballistic missile proliferation or terrorism.	Statutory requirement	Sec. 112 provides the President the authority to waive for 180 days, case-by-case, if he finds it vital to U.S. national security interests to do so. Determination may be renewed in additional 180-day increments with congressional notification.

Notes: AECA = Arms Export Control Act; CISADA = Comprehensive Iran Sanctions, Accountability, and Divestment Act of 2010; DNI = Director of National Intelligence; E.O. = Executive Order; FTO = Foreign Terrorist Organization; IAEA = International Atomic Energy Agency; IEEPA = International Emergency Economic Powers Act; IFI = International Financial Institution; IFSA = Iran Freedom Support Act; IIANA = Iran-Iraq Arms Non-Proliferation Act of 1992; INA = Immigration and Nationality Act of 1952; INKSA = Iran, North Korea, Syria Nonproliferation Act; IRGC = Iranian Revolutionary Guard Corps; ISA = Iran Sanctions Act of 1996; ITRSHRA = Iran Threat Reduction and Syria Human Rights Act of 2012; NDAA = National Defense Authorization Act; NEA = National Emergencies Act; NICO = Naftiran Intertrade Company; NIOC = National Iranian Oil Company; NITC = National Iranian Tanker Company; SDN = Specially Designated National; TSRA = Trade Sanctions Reform Act of 2000; UNICEF = U.N. Children's Fund; UNPA = United Nations Participation Act of 1945; UNSC = United Nations Security Council; USC = United States Code; USML = United States Munitions List; USTR = U.S. Trade Representative; WMD = Weapons of Mass Destruction.

[a.] The State Department published a current and complete list of 16 entities subject to sanctions under the ISA 1996 as of March 4, 2015. See Department of State Public Notice 9061 of March 4, 2015 (80 *Federal Register* 12544; March 9, 2015).

Table 2. Executive Orders Issued to Meet Statutory Requirements to Impose Economic Sanctions on Iran

Executive Order	Underlying Statute	Restriction	Authority To Lift or Waive
E.O. 12170 (November 14, 1979)	IEEPA/NEA	Declares a national emergency exists relating to 1979 events in Iran; blocks Iranian government property subject to U.S. jurisdiction. Secretary of the Treasury administers.	President The President most recently continued the national emergency declared in E.O. 12170 in a notice of November 6, 2017 (82 F.R. 51969).
E.O. 12938 (November 14, 1994)	IEEPA/NEA AECA (also invoked in Sec. 3(b)(1), INKSA)	Declares a national emergency exists relating to the proliferation of weapons of mass destruction and the means of delivery. Succeeds and replaces similar authorities of 1990 and 1994. Establishes export controls, sanctions affecting foreign aid, procurement, imports, on proliferators. Establishes sanctions—affecting foreign aid, IFI support, credits, arms sales, exports, imports, landing rights—targeting foreign countries that produce or use chemical or biological weapons. Secretaries of State, Commerce, Defense, and the Treasury administer.	President
E.O. 12957 (March 15, 1995)	IEEPA/NEA	*The President, in sec. 4 and 5 of E.O. 13716 of January 16, 2016, prohibits donations for the benefit of any blocked person under this or related Orders. E.O. 13716 of January 16, 2016, at sec. 6, further prohibits entry into the United States of any person blocked under sec. 3(a)(i) or 3(c)(i) (see IFCA, sec. 1244).*	President Sec. 101(a), IFSA, codifies this EO. The President must notify Congress 15 days in advance of its termination, unless exigent circumstances justify acting first. The President most recently continued the national emergency declared in E.O. 12957 in a notice of March 12, 2018 (83 F.R. 11393).

Table 2. (Continued)

Executive Order	Underlying Statute	Restriction	Authority To Lift or Waive
		Declares a national emergency exists relating to Iran's proliferation activities; prohibits persons under U.S. jurisdiction from entering into certain transactions with respect to Iranian petroleum resources. Secretaries of the Treasury and State administer	
E.O. 12959 (May 6, 1995)	IEEPA/NEA ISDC '85	Expands national emergency set forth in E.O. 12957; prohibits entering into new investment. Secretaries of the Treasury and State administer.	President Sec. 101(a), IFSA, codifies this EO. The President must notify Congress 15 days in advance of its termination, unless exigent circumstances justify acting first.
E.O. 13059 (August 19, 1997	IEEPA/NEA ISDC '85	Clarifies steps taken in E.O. 12957 and E.O. 12959; prohibits most imports from Iran, exports to Iran, new investment, transactions relating to Iran-origin goods regardless of their location Secretaries of the Treasury and State administer.	President Sec. 101(a), IFSA, codifies this EO. The President must notify Congress 15 days in advance of its termination, unless exigent circumstances justify acting first.
E.O. 13224 (September 23, 2001)	IEEPA/NEA UNPA'45 (also invoked in Sec. 211, ITRSHRA)	Declares a national emergency exists relating to international terrorism, in the aftermath of events of September 11, 2001; blocks property and prohibits transactions with persons who commit, threaten to commit, or support terrorism. Generates a list of designated individuals who are incorporated into the Specially Designated Nationals (SDN) list. Secretaries of the Treasury, State, Homeland Security, and the Attorney General administer	President

Executive Order	Underlying Statute	Restriction	Authority To Lift or Waive
E.O. 13382 (June 28, 2005)	IEEPA/NEA (also invoked in Sec. 211, ITRSHRA)	Expands national emergency set forth in E.O. 12938; blocks property of WMD proliferators and their supporters. Secretaries of State, the Treasury, and the Attorney General administer.	President See also Guidance of January 20, 2014 (79 F.R. 5025) Guidance of July 21, 2014 (79 F.R. 45233) Guidance of November 25, 2014 (79 F.R. 73141)
E.O. 13553 (September 28, 2010)	IEEPA/NEA CISADA	Expands national emergency set forth in E.O. 12957; blocks property of certain persons with respect to human rights abuses by the government of Iran. Generates a list of designated individuals for whom property under U.S. jurisdiction is blocked. Imposes sanctions on those who enter into transactions with designated individuals. This is the initial implementation of requirements under CISADA. Secretaries of the Treasury and State administer	President
E.O. 13574 (May 23, 2011)	Revoked. See Table 4.		
E.O. 13590 (November 20, 2011)	Revoked. See Table 4.		
E.O. 13599 (February 5, 2012)	IEEPA/NEA NDAA'12	Expands national emergency set forth in E.O. 12957; blocks property of the government of Iran and Iranian financial institutions, including the Central Bank of Iran. Secretaries of the Treasury, State, and Energy, and DNI administer.	President Sec. 217, ITRSHRA, requires the President notify Congress 90 days in advance of termination of this E.O., and certify a number of objectionable activities have ceased.

Table 2. (Continued)

Executive Order	Underlying Statute	Restriction	Authority To Lift or Waive
E.O. 13606 (April 22, 2012)	IEEPA/NEA	Expands, in the case of Iran, national emergency set forth in E.O. 12957; blocks the property and suspends entry into the United States of persons found to commit human rights abuses by the governments of Iran and Syria, facilitated misuse of information technology. Generates new list of SDN. Secretaries of the Treasury and State administer.	President Sec. 411, ITRSHRA, requires the President notify Congress 30 days in advance of termination of this E.O., and certify a number of objectionable activities have ceased pursuant to Sec. 401, CISADA.
E.O. 13608 (May 1, 2012)	IEEPA/NEA	Expands, in the case of Iran, national emergency set forth in E.O. 12957; prohibits transactions with and suspends entry into the United States of foreign sanctions evaders. Generates new list of SDN. Secretaries of the Treasury and State administer	President Sec. 217, ITRSHRA, requires the President notify Congress 30 days in advance of termination of this E.O., and certify a number of objectionable activities have ceased pursuant to Sec. 401, CISADA.
E.O. 13622 (July 30, 2012)		Revoked. See Table 4.	
E.O. 13628 (October 9, 2012)	IEEPA/NEA ISA '96 CISADA ITRSHRA INA	Partially revoked; see Table 4. Expands national emergency set forth in E.O. 12957; primarily implements ITRSHRA. Further prohibits U.S. financial institutions from making loans or credits, foreign exchange transactions, and transfers or credits between financial institutions. Blocks property of those who deal in equity or debt instruments of a sanctioned person. Prohibits imports, exports. Extends sanctions to other officers of sanctioned entities. Blocks property affiliated with human rights abusers, including those who limit freedom of expression.	President

Executive Order	Underlying Statute	Restriction	Authority To Lift or Waive
		Blocks entry into the United States of those who engage in certain human rights abuses The President, and Secretaries of the Treasury, State, and Commerce, the USTR, Chairman of Federal Reserve Board, and President of Ex-Im Bank, administer	
E.O. 13645 (June 3, 2013)		Revoked. See Table 4.	
E.O. 13694 (April 1, 2015) as amended by E.O. 13757 (December 28, 2016)	IEEPA/NEA	Authorizes the Secretary of the Treasury, in consultation with the Attorney General and the Secretary of State, to block property and interests in property of those found to have engaged in "cyber-enabled activities originating from ... outside the United States" that have affected a critical infrastructure sector, computers or networks, financial information, trade secrets, personal identifiers, or election processes, among other targets.	President.
E.O. 13716 (January 16, 2016)	IEEPA/NEA ISA'96 CISADA ITRSHRA IFCA'12 INA	Revokes several other E.O. (see Table 4). At sec. 3(a), authorizes the Secretary of the Treasury, in consultation with the Secretary of State, to block property and interests in property of those "providing significant financial, material, technological, support, or goods or services to transactions related to the energy, shipping, and shipbuilding sectors of Iran." At sec. 3(b), further authorizes the Secretaries to block loans above $10 million in any 12-month period; prohibit foreign exchange, transfers or credits through U.S. financial institutions; block property, investments under U.S. jurisdiction; block U.S. persons from investing in debt of a sanctioned person; prohibit imports; and extend restrictions to officers of sanctioned entity.	President.

Executive Order	Underlying Statute	Restriction	Authority To Lift or Waive
		At sec. 3(c), further authorizes the Secretaries to block property of any individual who is found to engage in diversion of food and medicine intended for the people of Iran; misappropriation of resources; transactions with a sanctioned person; or owned or controlled by a sanctioned person.	
Presidential Proclamation 9645 (September 24, 2017)	INA	Suspends entry into the United States of persons from a number of foreign countries, including Iran. [Based on E.O. 13780, March 6, 2017]	Currently facing a challenge in the U.S. Supreme Court. Commissioner, U.S. Customs and Border Protection may issue visas on a case-by-case basis. Secretary of Homeland Security, in consultation with Secretary of State, may devise "a process to assess whether any suspensions and limitations should be continued, terminated, modified, or supplemented."

Notes: AECA = Arms Export Control Act; CISADA = Comprehensive Iran Sanctions, Accountability, and Divestment Act of 2010; DNI = Director of National Intelligence; E.O. = Executive Order; IEEPA = International Emergency Economic Powers Act; IFI = International Financial Institution; IFCA = Iran Freedom and Counterproliferation Act of 2012; IFSA = Iran Freedom Support Act; INA = Immigration and Nationality Act of 1952; INKSA = Iran, North Korea, Syria Nonproliferation Act; ISA = Iran Sanctions Act of 1996; ITRSHRA = Iran Threat Reduction and Syria Human Rights Act of 2012; NDAA = National Defense Authorization Act; NEA = National Emergencies Act; NICO = Naftiran Intertrade Company; NIOC = National Iranian Oil Company; SDN = Specially Designated National; UNPA = United Nations Participation Act of 1945; USTR = U.S. Trade Representative.

[a.] Presidential Proclamation 9645, restricting entry into the United States from certain countries, is currently being challenged in the U.S. Supreme Court. See CRS Legal Sidebar LSB10017, Overview of "Travel Ban" Litigation and Recent Developments, by Hillel R. Smith and Ben Harrington.

Table 3. Legislation Made Inapplicable on Implementation Day to Meet Requirements of the JCPOA

Effective January 16, 2016; Reestablished pending 90-day (August 6) or 180-day (November 4) wind-down periods, pursuant to President's announcement of May 8, 2018, unless otherwise noted

Section Affected	Target	No Longer Applied	Waiver or Revocation: Rationale
IRAN SANCTIONS ACT OF 1996 (ISA 1996)[a] (P.L. 104-172; 50 U.S.C. 1701 note; as amended; Act sunsets effective December 31, 2026 (Sec. 13(b)))			
Sec. 5(a)	Non-U.S. persons who: —make investments above specified thresholds that could directly and significantly contribute to the maintenance or enhancement of Iran's ability to develop petroleum resources; —knowingly sell, lease, or provide to Iran goods, services, technology, information, or support that could directly and significantly facilitate the maintenance or enhancement of Iran's domestic production of refined petroleum products; —sell or provide to Iran refined petroleum products or sell, lease, or provide to Iran goods, services, technology, information, or support that could directly and significantly contribute to the enhancement of Iran's ability to import refined petroleum products;	Sanctions drawn from ISA'96 and IEEPA authorities	*Waivers issued pursuant to Sec. 4(c)(1)(A) are revoked, effective May 8, 2018. Sanctions imposed under Sec. 5(a) are reimposed but subject to a 90-day winddown waiver, effective May 8, 2018. See Table 1.*

Table 3. (Continued)

Section Affected	Target	No Longer Applied	Waiver or Revocation: Rationale
	—knowingly participate in certain joint ventures for the development of petroleum resources outside of Iran; —knowingly sell, lease, or provide to Iran goods, services, technology, information, or support that could directly and significantly contribute to the maintenance or enhancement of Iran's ability to develop petroleum resources located in Iran or domestic production of refined petrochemical products; —knowingly sell, lease, or provide to Iran goods, services, technology, or support that could directly and significantly contribute to the maintenance or expansion of Iran's domestic production of petrochemical products; —own, operate, or control, or insure a vessel used to transport crude oil from Iran to another country; —own, operate, or control a vessel used in a manner that conceals the Iranian origin of crude oil or refined petroleum products transported on the vesse		

Section Affected	Target	No Longer Applied	Waiver or Revocation: Rationale
COMPREHENSIVE IRAN SANCTIONS, ACCOUNTABILITY, AND DIVESTMENT ACT OF 2010 (CISADA)			
(P.L. 111-195; 22 U.S.C. 8501 *et seq.*; as amended)			
Sec. 104(c)(2)(E)(ii)(I) (22 U.S.C. 8513(c)(2)(E)(ii)(I))	Foreign financial institutions that knowingly facilitate a significant transaction or provide significant financial services for a person whose property or interests in property are blocked in connection with Iran's proliferation of WMD or their means of delivery	Correspondent or payable-through account sanctions	No longer applicable to transactions or services for specifically identified Iranian financial institutions "Statutory sanctions authorities will no longer apply.... " to the extent an SDN has been delisted.
NATIONAL DEFENSE AUTHORIZATION ACT FOR FISCAL YEAR 2012 (NDAA 2012)			
(Sec. 1245 of P.L. 112-81; 22 U.S.C. 8513a; as amended)			
Sec. 1245(d), (d)(1)	Significant financial transactions by foreign financial institutions, including transactions with the Central Bank of Iran	Correspondent or payable-through account sanctions	*Waivers issued pursuant to Sec. 1245(d)(5) are revoked, effective May 8, 2018. Sanctions imposed under Sec. 1245(d)(1) are reimposed but subject to a 90-day wind-down waiver, effective May 8, 2018.* See Table 1. *Most recently waived, through May 12, 2018, in Presidential Determination No. 2018-1 of November 15, 2017 (82 Federal Register 59503).*

Table 3. (Continued)

Section Affected	Target	No Longer Applied	Waiver or Revocation: Rationale
IRAN THREAT REDUCTION AND SYRIA HUMAN RIGHTS ACT OF 2012 (ITRSHRA) (P.L. 112-158; 22 U.S.C. 8701 et seq.)			
Sec. 212(a) (22 U.S.C. 8722(a))	Non-U.S. persons who knowingly provide underwriting services or insurance or reinsurance for NIOC, NITC, or a successor entity to either company, in cases where the transactions are for activities described in sections 4.2.1, 4.3, and 4.4 of Annex II of the JCPOA	Sanctions drawn from ISA'96 and IEEPA authorities	*Waivers issued pursuant to Sec. 212(d)(1) are revoked, effective May 8, 2018. Sanctions imposed under Sec. 212(a) are reimposed but subject to a 90-day wind-down waiver, effective May 8, 2018.* See Table 1
Sec. 213(a) (22 U.S.C. 8723(a))	Non-U.S. persons who purchase, subscribe to, or facilitate the issuance of sovereign debt of the Government of Iran, including governmental bonds	Sanctions drawn from ISA'96 and IEEPA authorities	*Waivers issued pursuant to Sec. 212(d)(1) are revoked, effective May 8, 2018. Sanctions imposed under Sec. 212(a) are reimposed but subject to a 90-day wind-down waiver, effective May 8, 2018.* See Table 1
Sec. 220(c) (22 U.S.C. 8726(c))	Non-U.S. persons who knowingly provide specialized financial messaging services that facilitate transactions for the Central Bank of Iran or other financial institutions not designated as an SDN	Blocking access to property or assets	Committed to refrain from imposing discretionary sanctions.

Section Affected	Target	No Longer Applied	Waiver or Revocation: Rationale
IRAN FREEDOM AND COUNTER-PROLIFERATION ACT OF 2012 (IFCA)			
(Title XII, subtitle D, of National Defense Authorization Act for Fiscal Year 2013; NDAA 2013; P.L. 112-239; 22 U.S.C. 8801 *et seq.*)			
Sec. 1244(c), (c)(1) (22 U.S.C. 8803(c), (c)(1))	Non-U.S. persons who knowingly provide significant financial, material, technological, or other support to, or goods or services to a person who is part of the energy, shipping, or shipbuilding sectors, or a port operator, or Iranian individuals or entities identified in the JCPOA (Annex II, Attachment 3) for delisting	Blocking access to property or assets	*Waivers issued pursuant to Sec. 1244(i) are revoked, effective May 8, 2018. Sanctions imposed under Sec. 1244(c)(1) are reimposed but subject to a 90-day wind-down waiver, effective May 8, 2018. Statement of Licensing Policy (SLP) for transactions related to providing Iran commercial passenger aircraft, and related spare parts and services, for exclusively civil aviation end use will be revoked in 90 days, effective May 8, 2018.* See Table 1.
Sec. 1244(d)(1) (22 U.S.C. 8803(d)(1))	Non-U.S. persons who knowingly sell, supply, or transfer to or from Iran significant goods or services used in connection with the energy, shipping, or shipbuilding sectors of Iran, including NIOC, NITC, and IRISL	Sanctions drawn from ISA'96 authorities	*Waivers issued pursuant to Sec. 1244(i) are revoked, effective May 8, 2018. Sanctions imposed under Sec. 1244(d)(1) are reimposed but subject to a 90-day wind-down waiver, effective May 8, 2018.* See Table 1.
Sec. 1244(d)(2) (22 U.S.C. 8803(d)(2))	Significant financial transactions by foreign financial institutions for the sale, supply, or transfer to or from Iran of significant goods or services used in connection with the energy, shipping, or shipbuilding sectors, including NIOC, NITC, IRISL	Correspondent or payable-through account sanctions	*Waivers issued pursuant to Sec. 1244(i) are revoked, effective May 8, 2018. Sanctions imposed under Sec. 1244(d)(2) are reimposed but subject to a 90-day wind-down waiver, effective May 8, 2018.* See Table 1.

Table 3. (Contineud)

Section Affected	Target	No Longer Applied	Waiver or Revocation: Rationale
Sec. 1244(h)(2) (22 U.S.C. 8803(h)(2))	Financial transactions by foreign financial institutions for the sale, supply, or transfer to or from Iran of natural gas	Correspondent or payable-through account sanctions	*Waivers issued pursuant to Sec. 1244(i) are revoked, effective May 8, 2018. Sanctions imposed under Sec. 1244(h)(2) are reimposed but subject to a 90-day wind-down waiver, effective May 8, 2018.* See Table 1.
Sec. 1245(a)(1), (a)(1)(A), (a)(1)(B), (a)(1)(C)(i)(II), (a)(1)(C)(ii)(II) (22 U.S.C. 8804)	Non-U.S. persons who sell, supply, or transfer to or from Iran precious metals or specified materials (graphite, raw or semi-finished metals), subject to certain limitations	Sanctions drawn from ISA'96 authorities	*Waivers issued pursuant to Sec. 1245(g) are revoked, effective May 8, 2018. Sanctions imposed under Sec. 1245(a)(1), relating to correspondent or payablethrough accounts, are reimposed but subject to a 90-day wind-down waiver, effective May 8, 2018.* See Table 1.
Sec. 1245(c) (22 U.S.C. 8804(c))	Significant financial transactions by foreign financial institutions for the sale, supply, or transfer to or from Iran of precious metals or specified materials (graphite, raw or semifinished metals) that are within the scope of waivers under sec. 1245(a)(1)	Correspondent or payable-through account sanctions	*Waivers issued pursuant to Sec. 1245(g) are revoked, effective May 8, 2018. Sanctions imposed under Sec. 1245(c), relating to correspondent or payablethrough accounts, are reimposed but subject to a 90-day wind-down waiver, effective May 8, 2018.* See Table 1.

Section Affected	Target	No Longer Applied	Waiver or Revocation: Rationale
Sec. 1246(a) (22 U.S.C. 8805(a))	Non-U.S. persons who provide underwriting services, insurance, or reinsurance in connection with activities involving Iran that are described in sections 17.1 to 17.2 and 17.5 of Annex V of the JCPOA, or to or for any individual or entity whose property and interests in property are blocked solely pursuant to E.O. 13599.	Sanctions drawn from ISA'96 authorities	*Waivers issued pursuant to Sec. 1246(e) are revoked, effective May 8, 2018. Sanctions imposed under Sec. 1246(a), relating to SDN designations and underwriting, insurance, or reinsurance, are reimposed but subject to a 90-day wind-down waiver, effective May 8, 2018.* See Table 1
Sec. 1246(a)(1)(B)(i), (a)(1)(B)(ii), (a)(1)(B)(iii)(I), (a)(1)(C) (22 U.S.C. 8805(a))	Persons who knowingly provide underwriting services or insurance or reinsurance to or for any person designated for the imposition of sanctions in connection with Iran's proliferation of WMD or their means of delivery.	Sanctions drawn from ISA'96 authorities	*Waivers issued pursuant to Sec. 1246(e) are revoked, effective May 8, 2018. Sanctions imposed under Sec. 1246(a), relating to SDN designations and underwriting, insurance, or reinsurance, are reimposed but subject to a 90-day wind-down waiver, effective May 8, 2018.* See Table 1.

Source: U.S. Department of the Treasury. U.S. Department of State. Guidance Relating to the Lifting of Certain U.S. Sanctions Pursuant to the Joint Comprehensive Plan of Action on Implementation Day. January 16, 2016 (Guidance of January 16, 2016); Department of State. Report to Congress: Waiver of Certain Sanctions to Provide for a Wind-Down Period for Sanctions Relief Previously Provided Consistent with the Joint Comprehensive Plan of Action; and Waiver Revocations, Determinations, Certifications, and Findings. May 8, 2018.

Notes: The Guidance of January 16, 2016 notes that "This document is explanatory only and does not have the force of law. Please see particularly the legally binding provisions cited ... governing the sanctions. This document does not supplement or modify the statutory authorities, Executive orders, or regulations."

Table 4. Executive Orders Revoked or Amended on Implementation Day to Meet Requirements of the JCPOA

Effective pursuant to Executive Order 13716 of January 16, 2016

Executive Order	Underlying Statute	Restriction	Authority to Lift or Waive
E.O. 13574 (May 23, 2011)	IEEPA / NEA ISA '96 CISADA	*Revoked.* Expanded national emergency set forth in E.O. 12957; implemented new sanctions added to ISA. Prohibited U.S. financial institutions from making loans or credits, or engaging in foreign exchange transactions. Prohibited imports from, and blocks property of, a sanctioned person. The President, and Secretaries of the Treasury and State, administered.	President
E.O. 13590 (November 20, 2011)	IEEPA/NEA	*Revoked.* Expanded national emergency set forth in E.O. 12957; blocked property of those who trade in goods, services, technology, or support for Iran's energy and petrochemical sectors. Prohibited Ex-Im Bank from entering into transactions with sanctioned person. Required Federal Reserve to deny goods and services. Prohibited U.S. financial institutions from making most loans or credits. Secretaries of State, the Treasury, and Commerce, the U.S. Trade Representative (USTR), Chairman of Federal Reserve Board, and President of Ex-Im Bank, administered.	President
E.O. 13622 (July 30, 2012)	IEEPA / NEA NDAA '12	*Revoked.* Expanded national emergency set forth in E.O. 12957; authorized sanctions on foreign financial institutions that finance activities with NIOC, NICO. Prohibited correspondent and payable through accounts. Prohibited Ex-Im financing, designation as a primary dealer of U.S. debt instruments, access to U.S. financial institutions. Blocked property; denied imports and exports. The President, and Secretaries of the Treasury, State, and Commerce, the USTR, Chairman of Federal Reserve Board, and President of Ex-Im Bank, administered.	President See also: Guidance of January 20, 2014 (79 F.R. 5025) Guidance of July 21, 2014 (79 F.R. 45233) Guidance of November 25, 2014 (79 F.R. 73141)

Executive Order	Underlying Statute	Restriction	Authority to Lift or Waive
E.O. 13628 (October 9, 2012)	IEEPA/NEA ISA '96 CISADA ITRSHRA INA	*Partially revoked. See Table 2.* Denied access to certain financing tools, property, and imports, if one engaged in expansion of Iran's refined petroleum sector.	President
E.O. 13645 (June 3, 2013)	IEEPA/NEA CISADA IFCA INA	*Revoked.* Expanded national emergency set forth in E.O. 12957; imposed restrictions on foreign financial institutions engaged in transactions relating to, or maintaining accounts dominated by, Iran's currency (*rial*). Prohibited opening or maintaining U.S.-based payable-through correspondent accounts. Blocked property under U.S. jurisdiction. Imposed restrictions on those, including foreign financial institutions, found to be materially assisting in any way an Iran-related SDN. Imposed restrictions on those found to engage in transactions related to Iran's petroleum or related products. Required the Secretary of State to impose restrictions on financing (Federal Reserve, Ex-Im Bank, commercial banks) on those found to engage in significant transactions related to Iran's automotive sector. Blocked property of those found to have engage in diversion of goods and services intended for the people of Iran The President, and Secretaries of the Treasury, State, Homeland Security, and Commerce, the USTR, Chairman of Federal Reserve Board, and President of Ex-Im Bank, administered.	President See also Guidance of January 20, 2014 (79 F.R. 5025) Guidance of July 21, 2014 (79 F.R. 45233) Guidance of November 25, 2014 (79 F.R. 73141)

Source: Executive Order 13716 of January 16, 2016 (81 F.R. 3693-3698).

Appendix. Key U.S. Legal Authorities That Remain in Place After Implementation Day

U.S. Department of the Treasury U.S. Department of State Guidance Relating to the Lifting of Certain U.S. Sanctions Pursuant to the Joint Comprehensive Plan of Action on Implementation Day

Key U.S. Legal Authorities That Remain in Place After Implementation Day

A number of U.S. legal authorities that are outside the scope of the JCPOA and are directed toward, or have been used to address, U.S. concerns with respect to, Iran remain in place after Implementation Day. A non-exhaustive list of such authorities is set out below:

Trade Sanctions

Trade Embargo

The U.S. domestic trade embargo imposed on Iran under the national emergency declared in E.O. 12957, as implemented through the ITSR, also referred to as U.S. primary sanctions, remains in place following Implementation Day. Pursuant to the ITSR and with limited exceptions,[24] U.S. persons, as defined in section 560.314 of the ITSR, continue to be broadly prohibited from engaging in transactions or dealings directly or indirectly with Iran or its government. In addition, non-U.S. persons continue to be prohibited from knowingly engaging in conduct that seeks to evade U.S. restrictions on transactions or dealings with Iran or that causes the export of goods or services from the United States to Iran.

---

[24] These exceptions include the three categories of activity the United States has committed to license pursuant to section 5 of Annex II of the JCPOA, as well as activities that are exempt from regulation or authorized under the ITSR. See section IV above and sections J, K, and L of the JCPOA FAQs for further details.

Please note that, under the ITSR, the clearing of transactions involving Iran through the U.S. financial system, including foreign branches of U.S. financial institutions continues to be prohibited.

Export Controls

U.S. controls on the exportation or reexportation of goods, technology, and services to Iran imposed pursuant to the ITSR, including sections 560.204 and 560.205, as well as the Export Administration Regulations, 15 C.F.R. parts 730-774 (EAR), and the International Traffic in Arms Regulations, 22 CFR parts 120-130 (ITAR), remain in place. Pursuant to these authorities and unless exempt from regulation or authorized under the relevant regulations, the exportation or reexportation by a U.S. person or from the United States to Iran or the Government of Iran, as well as the reexportation by non-U.S. persons of items that contain 10 percent or more U.S.-controlled content with knowledge or reason to know that the reexportation is intended specifically to Iran or the Government of Iran, generally requires a license.

Designation Authorities and Blocking Sanctions

In addition, the United States retains a number of authorities that are directed toward, or have been used to address, U.S. concerns with respect to Iran. Generally, these authorities provide for the imposition of blocking sanctions on persons meeting certain criteria or engaging in specified conduct, as well as their support networks.

Designation Authorities

The activities targeted by these authorities include the following:

1. *Support for terrorism*: E.O. 13224 (blocking property and prohibiting transactions with persons who commit, threaten to commit, or support terrorism);
2. *Iran's human rights abuses*:

- E.O.s 13553 and 13628 (implementing sections 105, 105A, and 105B of CISADA (related to persons who are responsible for or complicit in human rights abuses committed against the citizens of Iran; transfers of goods or technologies to Iran that are likely to be used to commit serious human rights abuses against the people of Iran; and persons who engage in censorship or similar activities with respect to Iran)); and
- E.O. 13606 (relating to the provision of information technology used to further serious human rights abuses);

3. *Proliferation of WMD and their means of delivery, including ballistic missiles*: E.O.s 12938 and 13382;

4. *Support for persons involved in human rights abuses in Syria or for the Government of Syria*: E.O.s 13572 and 13582;

5. *Support for persons threatening the peace, security, or stability of Yemen*: E.O. 13611;

6. *Transactions or activities described in section 1244(c)(1)(A) of IFCA if the transaction involves any person on the SDN list (other than an Iranian financial institution whose property and interests in property are blocked solely pursuant to E.O. 13599)*: Section 1244(c)(1) of IFCA;

7. *Diversion of goods intended for the people of Iran*: CISADA 105C, as added by section 1249 of IFCA (relating to the diversion of goods, including agricultural commodities, food, medicine, and medical devices, intended for the people of Iran, or the misappropriation of proceeds from the sale or resale of such goods);

8. *Knowingly and directly providing specialized financial messaging services to, or knowingly enabling or facilitating direct or indirect access to such messaging services for a financial, institution whose property or interests in property are blocked in connection with Iran's proliferation of WMD or their means of delivery, or Iran's*

support for international terrorism: Section 220 of the TRA [ITRSHRA];[25]

9. *Officials, agents, and affiliates of the IRGC*: Section 301 of the TRA[26] (providing for the designation of officials, agents, or affiliates of the IRGC); and

10. *Foreign sanctions evaders*: E.O. 13608 (authorizing the imposition of prohibitions on transactions or dealings by U.S. persons involving persons determined to have: (i) violated, attempted to violate, conspired to violate, or caused a violation of U.S. sanctions with respect to Iran or Syria (including sanctions imposed under counter-proliferation or counter-terrorism authorities); or (ii) facilitated deceptive transactions for or on behalf of any person subject to U.S. sanctions concerning Iran or Syria).[27]

Blocking Authorities

The persons targeted by these authorities include the following:

1. *The Government of Iran and Iranian Financial Institutions*: E.O. 13599, section 217(a) of the TRA, section 560.211 of the ITSR; and

2. *Islamic Republic of Iran Broadcasting and its president under section 105(c) of CISADA*: Section 1248 of IFCA.

Correspondent and Payable-through Account Sanctions

After Implementation Day, FFIs may be subject to correspondent or payable-through account secondary sanctions for:

---

[25] The United States has committed not to apply the sanctions under section 220 of the TRA with respect to the CBI or any financial institution listed in Attachment 3 to Annex II of the JCPOA

[26] Section 302(b)(2) of the TRA further provides for discretionary blocking of persons determined to meet the criteria set out in section 302(a). See section VII.D.1 below.

[27] E.O. 13608 is not a blocking authority. However, U.S. persons are prohibited from engaging in transactions or dealings with persons sanctioned under this authority.

1. Knowingly facilitating a significant financial transaction with designated Iranian financial institutions that remain or are placed on the SDN List (section 1245(d) of NDAA 2012);
2. Knowingly facilitating a significant financial transaction on behalf of any Iranian persons that remain or are placed on the SDN List (section 1247(a) of IFCA);
3. Knowingly facilitating a significant financial transaction or providing significant financial services for any other person on the SDN List with the "[IFSR]" identifying tag (i.e., the Islamic Revolutionary Guard Corps (IRGC) and any of its designated officials, agents, or affiliates; individuals and entities designated pursuant to E.O. 13382 in connection with Iran's proliferation of WMD or their means of delivery; and individuals and entities designated pursuant to E.O. 13224 in connection with Iran's support for international terrorism) (section 104(c)(2)(E) of CISADA);
4. Knowingly facilitating a significant financial transaction for the sale, supply, or transfer to or from Iran of significant goods and services used in connection with the energy, shipping, or shipbuilding sectors of Iran where the transactions involve persons who remain or are placed on the SDN List (section 1244(d)(2) of IFCA); or
5. Knowingly conducting or facilitating a significant financial transaction for the sale, supply, or transfer to or from Iran of graphite, raw or semi-finished metals such as aluminum and steel, coal, and software for integrating industrial processes that have been determined pursuant to section 1245(e)(3) of IFCA to be used as described in that section if the transactions involve (i) persons on the SDN List; (ii) the sale, supply, or transfer of materials described in section 1245(d) of IFCA that have not been approved by the procurement channel established pursuant to paragraph 16 of UNSCR 2231 and section 6 of Annex IV of the JCPOA, in cases in which the procurement channel applies; or (iii) the sale, supply, or transfer of materials described in section 1245(d) of

IFCA if the material is sold, supplied, or transferred, or resold, retransferred, or otherwise supplied directly or indirectly, for use in connection with the military or ballistic missile program of Iran (section 1245(c) of IFCA).

Menu-Based Sanctions

After Implementation Day, menu-based secondary sanctions continue to attach to:

1. Persons who materially assist, sponsor, or provide financial, material, or technological support for, or goods or services in support of: the IRGC or any of its officials, agents, or affiliates blocked pursuant to IEEPA; persons that engage in significant transactions with (i) any of the foregoing or (ii) persons subject to financial sanctions pursuant to the UNSCRs that impose sanctions with respect to Iran, or a person acting for or on behalf of, or owned or controlled by, such person (section 302(a) of the TRA);

2. Non-U.S. persons who engage in transactions or activities described in sections 1244(d)(1) and 1246(a) of IFCA if the transactions involve persons on the SDN List; and

3. Non-U.S. persons who sell, supply, or transfer directly or indirectly to or from Iran graphite, raw or semi-finished metals such as aluminum and steel, coal, and software for integrating industrial processes that have been determined pursuant to section 1245(e)(3) of IFCA to be used as described in that section if the transactions involve (i) persons on the SDN List; (ii) the sale, supply, or transfer of materials described in section 1245(d) of IFCA that have not been approved by the procurement channel established pursuant to paragraph 16 of UNSCR 2231 and section 6 of Annex IV of the JCPOA, in cases in which the procurement channel applies; or (iii) the sale, supply, or transfer of materials described in section 1245(d) of IFCA if the material is sold,

supplied, or transferred, or resold, retransferred, or otherwise supplied directly or indirectly, for use in connection with the military or ballistic missile program of Iran (section 1245(a) of IFCA).

Non-Proliferation Sanctions

On Transition Day, the United States will seek such legislative action as may be appropriate to terminate, or modify to effectuate the termination of, the nuclear proliferation-related statutory sanctions set forth in paragraph 4.9 of Annex II of the JCPOA, including sanctions under the Iran, North Korea and Syria Nonproliferation Act on the acquisition of nuclear-related commodities and services for nuclear activities contemplated in the JCPOA, to be consistent with the U.S. approach to other non-nuclear weapon states under the Treaty on the Non-Proliferation of Nuclear Weapons. The JCPOA does not address the application of a number of generally- applicable nonproliferation statutes related to transfers of proliferation-sensitive equipment and technology, or statutes that provide for sanctions for activities that would be outside the scope of the JCPOA.

Terrorism List Sanctions

Iran remains designated as a state sponsor of terrorism under relevant laws (section 6(j) of the Export Administration Act; section 40 of the Arms Export Control Act; and section 620A of the Foreign Assistance Act), and the JCPOA does not alter that designation. A number of different sanctions laws and restrictions are keyed to this designation, including restrictions on foreign assistance (22 U.S.C. § 2371), a ban on defense exports and sales (22 U.S.C. § 2780), controls on exports of certain sensitive technology and dual-use items (50 U.S.C. App. § 2405), and various financial and other restrictions.

INDEX

A

access, xvi, 24, 37, 57, 58, 73, 76, 85, 132, 141, 153, 173, 183, 185, 186, 202, 212, 234, 235, 239, 242, 258, 266, 278, 279, 282, 284, 310, 328, 329, 332, 333, 336

activism, 11, 23, 51, 63, 84, 261

Afghanistan, 153, 235, 313

age, viii, 2, 4, 5, 13, 19, 24, 80, 92, 130, 190, 192

agencies, 24, 40, 69, 70, 71, 91, 156, 297, 299

Air Force, 35, 36, 67, 68, 73, 152, 182, 238, 240

airports, 104

al Abadi, Prime Minister Haider, x, 88, 89, 93, 95

al Mahdi, Adel Abd, x, 88, 89, 97, 99, 123

Al Qaeda, 3, 6, 27, 29, 32, 40, 55, 71, 76, 77, 83, 165, 173, 178

Al Saud family, vii, ix, 1, 2, 10, 13, 14, 29, 30, 64, 65, 79, 80

ambassadors, 59, 142

appointments, viii, 2, 132, 222

appropriations, 33, 34, 77, 110, 111, 115, 116, 119, 152, 153, 201, 205, 206, 207, 245, 249, 250, 291, 292

Appropriations Act, xv, 34, 72, 111, 114, 116, 151, 155, 206, 214, 249, 250, 285, 300

Appropriations Committee, 33, 34, 249, 250

Arab countries, 261, 268

Arabian Peninsula, 27, 28, 30, 54, 64, 65

armed conflict, 37, 38, 55, 164, 229

armed forces, 34, 131, 155, 205, 207

armed groups, xiii, 53, 59, 102, 103, 121, 122, 158, 174, 204

Armenia, 264, 265, 266

Armenians, 134, 264, 265, 275

arms sales, viii, ix, 1, 3, 6, 34, 35, 52, 56, 58, 60, 65, 73, 84, 86, 152, 216, 233, 241, 245, 290, 293, 300, 312, 319

Atomic Energy Agency, xvi, 45, 48, 83, 278, 284, 318

authorities, x, 7, 12, 20, 21, 22, 23, 24, 25, 26, 32, 36, 38, 42, 47, 48, 53, 60, 61, 62, 69, 80, 81, 83, 84, 87, 91, 93, 104, 107, 109, 110, 112, 113, 118, 123, 141, 153, 154, 159, 175, 184, 193, 194, 228, 230, 242, 243, 244, 253, 261, 265, 273, 281,

288, 290, 291,295, 297, 299, 301, 302, 303, 319, 325, 327, 328, 329, 330, 331, 334, 335, 337

Azerbaijan, 226, 265

B

background information, xiv, 158

Bahrain, 8, 19, 59, 60, 138

ballistic missiles, 76, 84, 122, 239, 285, 288, 297, 316, 336

bilateral, ix, xii, xv, 3, 9, 22, 35, 38, 39, 43, 47, 48, 49, 51, 60, 63, 64, 79, 83, 85, 113, 128, 139, 142, 148, 151, 203, 212, 214, 215, 233, 241, 242, 261, 262

bilateral relationship, 9, 22, 64, 212, 261

bilateral ties, ix, 3, 79

bin Abd al Aziz, King Salman, viii, 2, 4, 14, 50, 61, 80

bin Salman, Crown Prince Mohammed, viii, 2, 4, 9, 10, 13, 15, 16, 44, 49, 50, 64, 80, 82

biological weapons, 297, 319

border control, 104, 204

border crossing, 76, 84, 122, 139, 176, 212

border security, 4, 37, 111, 152, 153, 154, 155, 201, 204, 205, 206, 207

Brunson case, xiv, 213

Brunson, Andrew, xiv, 213, 215, 225, 242, 244

business environment, 136

businesses, xvi, 60, 219, 223, 277, 279

C

cabinet members, 98

candidates, 24, 97, 99, 187, 272

China, xvi, 41, 45, 46, 48, 85, 220, 223, 227, 241, 278, 279, 283

Christian, xii, 92, 134, 138, 139, 157, 159, 160, 161, 166, 167, 168, 170, 172, 175, 191, 217, 231, 232, 244

Christianity, 231

Christians, xiii, 139, 157, 160, 231, 265

citizens, x, xiii, xv, 16, 18, 19, 20, 26, 32, 81, 87, 88, 89, 90, 95, 96, 100, 133, 135, 138, 143, 158, 197, 198, 214, 243, 244, 248, 249, 250, 251, 263, 264, 312, 336

civil liberties, 32, 220, 317

civil servants, 219

civil service, 10, 135, 270, 273

civil society, 194

civil war, xiii, xiv, 54, 76, 138, 152, 157, 161, 163, 182, 191, 213, 254, 261

commercial, 10, 36, 47, 56, 63, 73, 74, 120, 267, 280, 281, 293, 300, 313, 329, 333

competition, x, 13, 15, 42, 88, 90, 254, 257

conference, 33, 75, 109, 111, 114, 120, 123, 198

conflict, vii, xii, xiii, xiv, 1, 27, 37, 39, 50, 53, 55, 56, 57, 58, 61, 65, 77, 84, 89, 102, 107, 122, 142, 155, 157, 158, 161, 164, 172, 173, 176, 178, 179, 180, 181, 188, 189, 190, 197, 200, 201, 204, 207, 212, 251, 255, 258, 261

confrontation, 59, 60, 62, 102, 165, 169, 170, 186, 230, 245

Congress, iv, v, vii, viii, ix, xi, xiv, xv, 2, 3, 6, 7, 8, 27, 33, 34, 35, 36, 37, 39, 47, 48, 51, 56, 58, 64, 71, 72, 73, 74, 77, 80, 82, 83, 84, 85, 87, 88, 93, 99, 101, 110, 111, 112, 113, 114, 115, 118, 119, 120, 124, 127, 129, 147, 151, 152, 153, 154, 164, 200, 204, 205, 208, 211, 214, 215, 230, 231, 233, 234, 239, 244, 245, 246, 247, 248, 249, 250, 252, 265, 280, 285, 286, 287, 288, 289, 290, 291, 292, 296, 298, 301, 310, 312, 319, 320, 321, 322, 331

consolidation, xv, 4, 11, 14, 17, 63, 64, 214, 220, 263

constitutional amendment, 137, 221

Index

construction, 45, 46, 47, 83, 138, 147, 191, 197, 226, 227, 260

consumption, 42, 43, 44, 45, 282, 283

controversial, xi, 24, 83, 88, 90, 100, 171, 177, 216, 220

cooperation, viii, ix, xi, xiv, 2, 3, 7, 9, 20, 31, 33, 34, 35, 36, 39, 43, 45, 46, 47, 48, 49, 50, 51, 52, 54, 60, 63, 64, 79, 83, 84, 86, 103, 113, 114, 127, 151, 153, 165, 205, 213, 227, 235, 238, 241, 252, 257, 260

coordination, 63, 86, 114, 115, 165, 254, 257

corruption, ix, x, 2, 7, 10, 15, 64, 87, 90, 96, 106, 110, 135, 218, 269, 270, 317

cost, 33, 34, 55, 110, 115, 116, 151, 196, 235, 239, 248

Council of Representatives (COR), x, 88, 89

counterterrorism, viii, ix, 2, 4, 7, 20, 26, 27, 31, 32, 34, 37, 39, 40, 63, 75, 77, 79, 83, 102, 111, 113, 152, 153, 165, 205

critical infrastructure, 39, 40, 63, 323

criticism, 25, 32, 57, 58, 81, 90, 124, 175, 232, 243, 270

crude oil, 18, 41, 282, 296, 307, 326

currency, xiv, 213, 215, 216, 224, 333

D

deaths, 6, 39, 57, 175, 178, 181, 265, 266

democracy, 132, 149, 200, 222, 248

Democratic Party, 96, 272

demographic change, 160

Department of Defense, 33, 37, 38, 56, 114, 115, 147, 148, 154, 155, 180, 235, 236, 279

Department of Energy, 47

Department of the Treasury, xvii, 278, 279, 280

detainees, 23, 24, 25, 80, 175, 219

detection, 150

detention, 23, 24, 107, 215, 242, 244, 249

domestic agenda, 81

domestic policy, 7, 9

domestic resources, 49

E

economic assistance, 91, 149, 151, 200

economic crisis, 262

economic development, 229

economic growth, 18, 135, 166, 200, 202, 223

economic integration, 283

economic landscape, 7

economic performance, 11

economic reform, 137, 212

economic relations, 287

economic resources, xi, 128, 129

economic transformation, 11, 16, 43

economics, 270, 271

education, 7, 11, 19, 64, 118, 135, 149, 166, 190, 193, 251, 312

educational exchanges, 19

educational services, 281

Egypt, 8, 29, 50, 59, 60, 155, 165, 194, 199, 205, 207, 208, 220, 226, 256

election, x, 19, 88, 90, 95, 96, 97, 101, 103, 123, 124, 132, 167, 172, 188, 218, 220, 223, 269, 304, 316, 323

electricity, xii, 44, 45, 47, 96, 118, 124, 128, 133, 137, 197

energy, ix, xvi, 3, 16, 18, 40, 42, 43, 44, 46, 47, 49, 50, 79, 83, 85, 110, 111, 199, 224, 225, 226, 241, 255, 257, 267, 278, 281, 282, 284, 295, 312, 313, 314, 323, 329, 332, 338

energy consumption, 43

energy prices, 42

energy security, 111

344 *Index*

equipment, xiv, 36, 64, 74, 114, 116, 124, 153, 154, 175, 201, 203, 206, 213, 240, 274, 275, 293, 340

Europe, xiv, 213, 218, 223, 225, 226, 228, 232, 238, 241, 244, 255, 257, 263

European Commission, 220, 263, 264

European Community, 263

European Investment Bank, 198

European Parliament, 263, 266

European Union, xvi, 145, 211, 220, 228, 242, 255, 262, 264, 278, 286

executive branch, viii, 2, 33, 36, 38, 68, 75, 117, 119, 201, 290, 291, 300

Executive Order, 120, 242, 281, 282, 287, 290, 291, 301, 318, 319, 320, 321, 322, 323, 324, 332, 333

executive power, 131

exports, 41, 43, 47, 85, 106, 107, 225, 242, 243, 260, 261, 290, 295, 298, 300, 302, 319, 320, 322, 332, 340

extremists, 27, 31, 173

F

faith, vii, ix, 1, 58, 76, 79

families, 25, 132, 177, 178, 195, 261

family members, ix, 2, 10, 13, 15, 64, 269, 310, 311

Federal Register, 289, 307, 318, 327

Federal Reserve, 323, 332, 333

Federal Reserve Board, 323, 332, 333

financial, xv, 16, 18, 30, 31, 32, 65, 70, 80, 82, 91, 104, 107, 121, 135, 138, 145, 196, 198, 202, 207, 208, 210, 211, 214, 216, 224, 261, 263, 280, 281, 282, 284, 296, 298, 303, 304, 307, 310, 312, 313, 315, 321, 322, 323, 327, 328, 329, 330, 332, 333, 335, 336, 337, 338, 339, 340

financial crisis, 135, 224

financial distress, 216

financial institutions, 208, 210, 211, 281, 282, 296, 298, 303, 310, 313, 315, 321, 322, 323, 327, 328, 329, 330, 332, 333, 335, 338

financial sector, 307

financial support, 16, 18, 30, 31, 32

financial system, 198, 282, 335

fiscal deficit, 116

fiscal surpluses, 11

food, 57, 76, 85, 135, 141, 156, 281, 302, 306, 313, 324, 336

foreign affairs, 246

foreign aid, xi, 88, 93, 289, 290, 291, 292, 294, 300, 312, 319

foreign assistance, xii, 34, 74, 110, 114, 123, 128, 148, 340

foreign exchange, 297, 298, 313, 322, 323, 332

foreign investment, 135, 197

foreign person, 121, 210

foreign policy, viii, ix, 1, 4, 15, 59, 79, 85, 233, 241, 255, 264, 269, 282, 286, 287

France, xii, xvi, 45, 46, 157, 159, 160, 181, 185, 198, 199, 222, 266, 278, 279, 283

freedom, viii, 2, 7, 19, 26, 100, 107, 117, 186, 219, 231, 248, 250, 263, 305, 306, 322

funding, 8, 19, 31, 32, 33, 71, 74, 93, 109, 110, 111, 112, 114, 116, 118, 119, 147, 152, 153, 156, 180, 197, 198, 201, 205, 249, 292

fundraising, 32, 173, 210

funds, xi, 6, 31, 32, 33, 56, 72, 74, 75, 77, 88, 93, 107, 109, 111, 112, 114, 116, 119, 145, 147, 150, 153, 154, 155, 200, 204, 205, 206, 207, 212, 237, 245, 285, 292, 296, 298

G

Germany, xvi, 50, 145, 266, 278, 279, 283

Index

global economy, 224
global markets, ix, 79
goods and services, 332, 333, 338
governance, ix, 3, 10, 13, 53, 65, 89, 111, 219, 253
government budget, 5
government funds, 296, 298
government procurement, 296, 298
government repression, 256
government spending, 17, 121, 166, 202
governments, 9, 22, 39, 48, 58, 76, 97, 131, 139, 142, 170, 187, 218, 228, 258, 322
grants, 91, 109, 149, 152, 198, 203, 237, 287
Greece, 231, 242, 262, 264, 266, 267, 271, 283

H

Hezbollah, xiii, 28, 54, 102, 120, 122, 124, 158, 161, 162, 163, 164, 165, 166, 169, 170, 172, 173, 174, 175, 176, 177, 178, 179, 180, 181, 182, 183, 184, 185, 186, 187, 188, 189, 190, 197, 198, 200, 203, 204, 207, 208, 209, 210, 211, 212
high school, 273
higher education, 8, 19, 231, 270
history, xv, 160, 215, 232, 255, 258, 262, 271
House of Representatives, 38, 129, 215
human, viii, ix, xvi, 2, 7, 8, 19, 20, 21, 22, 23, 32, 79, 80, 82, 117, 129, 175, 219, 228, 249, 253, 264, 272, 277, 278, 281, 283, 284, 285, 286, 290, 291, 304, 305, 310, 316, 317, 321, 322, 323, 335, 336
human remains, 281
human resources, ix, 79
human rights, viii, xvi, 2, 7, 8, 19, 20, 21, 22, 23, 24, 26, 32, 57, 80, 82, 117, 129, 163, 174, 175, 179, 190, 193, 195, 219, 220, 228, 242, 249, 253, 264, 272, 273,

277, 278, 281, 283, 284, 285, 286, 287, 290, 291, 302, 304, 305, 306, 310, 312, 316, 317, 318, 321, 322, 323, 324, 335, 336
humanitarian aid, 114, 165, 302
humanitarian crises, 37
humanitarian organizations, 212

I

identity, x, 88, 90, 160, 196, 228, 255, 272
imports, 41, 215, 225, 226, 243, 259, 302, 313, 319, 320, 322, 323, 332, 333
Incirlik air base, xiv, 213, 234, 235, 246
income tax, 136
independence, xi, 88, 90, 102, 103, 104, 108, 114, 132, 160, 181, 225, 260, 266
individuals, x, xvii, 19, 20, 21, 22, 25, 26, 30, 31, 32, 64, 69, 70, 71, 80, 88, 90, 95, 108, 112, 207, 278, 281, 285, 304, 320, 321, 329, 338
industry, 18, 35, 47, 48, 50, 237
information technology, 322, 336
infrastructure, xiii, 6, 11, 36, 39, 40, 55, 58, 76, 83, 109, 110, 116, 158, 163, 181, 190, 198, 202, 224, 229, 261
institutions, x, 55, 88, 89, 165, 166, 202, 208, 211, 219, 220, 230, 231, 281, 322, 332, 333
insurgency, 38, 94, 189, 228, 251, 253
insurgent attacks, vii, ix, 87, 89
intelligence, viii, 2, 37, 56, 69, 70, 73, 93, 101, 152, 219, 234, 238, 240, 260
interference, 22, 37, 117, 172
internally displaced, x, 87, 91, 107
internally displaced persons (IDPs), x, 87, 91, 92, 107, 108, 118
International Atomic Energy Agency, xvi, 45, 48, 83, 278, 284, 318
international financial institutions, xv, 142, 214, 294, 312

346 *Index*

international law, 57, 61
International Military Education and Training (IMET), xii, 33, 34, 117, 128, 147, 149, 156, 204, 237
International Monetary Fund (IMF), xii, 16, 17, 18, 106, 128, 133, 136, 137, 217, 224
International Narcotics Control, 31, 117, 204
international relations, xv, 215, 255
international terrorism, xvi, 277, 285, 288, 289, 290, 297, 300, 302, 303, 304, 305, 306, 307, 308, 309, 310, 311, 312, 320, 337, 338
intervention, 55, 63, 138, 176, 179, 224, 234, 246
investment, xi, xvi, 63, 81, 88, 91, 109, 110, 220, 224, 248, 261, 267, 277, 279, 280, 320
Iran, v, vii, x, xiii, xiv, xvi, 3, 8, 9, 25, 28, 35, 42, 49, 50, 51, 52, 53, 54, 59, 60, 62, 63, 77, 84, 85, 88, 90, 95, 96, 97, 100, 102, 103, 112, 119, 120, 121, 122, 123, 158, 161, 164, 169, 179, 180, 182, 189, 197, 207, 208, 209, 212, 214, 220, 225, 228, 242, 243, 254, 255, 256, 257, 258, 259, 260, 277, 278, 279, 280, 281, 282, 283, 284, 285, 286, 287, 288, 289, 290, 291, 292, 293, 294, 295, 296, 297, 298, 299, 300, 301, 302, 303, 304, 305, 306, 307, 308, 309, 310, 311, 312, 313, 314, 315, 316, 317, 318, 319, 320, 321, 322, 323, 324, 325, 326, 327, 328, 329, 330, 331, 332, 333, 334, 335, 336, 337, 338, 339, 340
Iran Sanctions Act, 293, 308, 318, 324
Iraq, v, vii, ix, x, xi, xii, 3, 8, 9, 27, 29, 42, 51, 52, 84, 87, 88, 89, 90, 91, 92, 93, 94, 95, 96, 97, 99, 100, 101, 102, 103, 104, 105, 106, 107, 108, 109, 110, 111, 112, 113, 114, 115, 116, 117, 118, 119, 120, 121, 122, 123, 124, 125, 127, 128, 129, 133,139, 141, 153, 154, 155, 173, 178,

194, 205, 228, 234, 235, 255, 259, 260, 293, 318
Iraqi politicians, x, 88, 90
Iraqi security forces, xi, 88, 90, 93, 95, 100, 102, 103, 104, 111, 113
Iraqis, vii, ix, 29, 87, 88, 89, 90, 91, 100, 106, 107, 109, 110, 114, 125
IS fighters, vii, ix, 87, 89, 94, 102, 178
ISIL, vii, ix, xi, 3, 27, 87, 89, 107, 115, 127, 153, 216
ISIS, vii, ix, xi, 3, 27, 30, 31, 87, 89, 95, 101, 102, 118, 127, 129, 143, 153, 155, 174, 203, 216, 253
Islam, 22, 26, 29, 30, 32, 54, 179, 232
Islamic faith, vii, ix, 1, 79
Islamic law, 10, 24, 26
Islamic State, vii, ix, xi, 3, 6, 7, 26, 27, 28, 29, 30, 32, 50, 53, 55, 57, 60, 63, 74, 76, 77, 83, 87, 88, 89, 90, 91, 93, 94, 95, 100, 102, 104, 106, 108, 109, 112, 113, 116, 119, 120, 124, 127, 129, 139, 153, 155, 164, 165, 173, 174, 175, 177, 178, 200, 216, 235, 252, 253
Israel, xii, xiv, 8, 34, 40, 54, 60, 61, 62, 85, 128, 129, 130, 133, 138, 142, 143, 145, 146, 147, 158, 159, 161, 163, 164, 173, 178, 179, 180, 181, 182, 183, 184, 185, 188, 189, 190, 199, 200, 209, 212, 213, 226, 231, 242, 256, 258, 261, 262
Israeli-Palestinian peace, xi, 127, 146
issues, vii, xi, xiv, 3, 7, 15, 20, 21, 23, 24, 50, 58, 63, 69, 86, 88, 89, 90, 100, 106, 107, 116, 124, 127, 129, 143, 158, 171, 176, 181, 184, 188, 212, 213, 214, 216, 241, 250, 258, 291
Italy, 31, 184, 185, 199, 226, 266, 283

J

Japan, 41, 145, 227, 283

JCPOA, xvi, 8, 51, 52, 277, 278, 279, 280, 281, 282, 283, 284, 287, 290, 325, 328, 329, 331, 332, 334, 337, 338, 339, 340

Jews, 29, 54, 159, 231, 262, 265

jihad, 30

jihadist, 27, 200

joint ventures, 296, 298, 326

Jordan, v, xi, xii, 127, 128, 129, 130, 132, 133, 134, 135, 136, 137, 138, 139, 140, 141, 142, 143, 144, 145, 146, 147, 148, 149, 150, 151, 152, 153, 154, 155, 156, 165, 191, 194, 205, 207, 235, 261

Jordanian politics, vii, xi, 127, 137

journalists, 80, 220

judiciary, 132, 218, 263, 304, 316

jurisdiction, 36, 72, 204, 242, 266, 282, 296, 297, 298, 300, 303, 307, 313, 314, 319, 320, 321, 323, 333

justification, 75, 100, 312

K

Kurdish forces, xi, 88, 90, 104, 124, 253

Kurdish militants, xiv, 214, 244

Kurdish security forces, xi, 88, 90

Kurdistan Region, x, 88, 89, 90, 93, 103, 104, 107, 108, 112, 113, 114, 123, 228, 259

Kurdistan Regional Government (KRG), x, 88, 89, 90, 93, 97, 104, 106, 107, 108, 114, 117, 123, 124, 228, 259, 260

Kurds, xiv, 90, 104, 106, 120, 123, 124, 214, 216, 217, 221, 227, 228, 229, 230, 232, 233, 252, 253, 259, 260, 263, 270

Kuwait, 28, 109, 123, 137, 162, 165

L

labor market, 192

law enforcement, 69, 70, 111

laws, xvii, 20, 22, 24, 76, 131, 132, 137, 142, 253, 278, 286, 289, 291, 296, 298, 306, 340

leadership, ix, 2, 3, 4, 8, 10, 13, 15, 16, 35, 40, 52, 54, 55, 63, 65, 81, 123, 180, 198, 232, 272, 289

Lebanese Armed Forces (LAF), xiii, 158, 162, 164, 165, 170, 173, 174, 175, 176, 177, 178, 180, 183, 184, 194, 201, 202, 203, 204, 205, 206

Lebanese leaders, xii, 157, 160, 188, 195, 209, 212

Lebanon, v, vii, xii, xiii, xiv, 51, 52, 84, 155, 157, 158, 159, 160, 161, 162, 163, 164, 165, 166, 167, 168, 169, 170, 171, 172, 173, 174, 175, 176, 177, 178, 179, 180, 181, 182, 183, 184, 185, 187, 188, 190, 191, 192, 193, 194, 195, 196, 197, 198, 199, 200, 201, 202, 203, 204, 205, 206, 207, 208, 209, 210, 211, 212, 266

legal issues, 10

legislation, xiv, xv, xvi, 6, 33, 34, 48, 56, 58, 72, 74, 93, 110, 115, 120, 131, 158, 169, 208, 209, 211, 214, 216, 233, 244, 245, 249, 250, 278, 290

legislative proposals, 34, 56, 58, 246

loans, 109, 154, 198, 237, 250, 296, 298, 312, 313, 322, 323, 332

M

majority, 15, 90, 95, 117, 130, 131, 160, 167, 174, 188, 218, 221, 222, 233, 266, 288

management, 15, 91, 110, 111, 149, 209, 260

materials, 46, 184, 293, 305, 330, 338, 339

media, xv, 20, 21, 23, 24, 29, 31, 46, 69, 173, 178, 182, 184, 214, 219, 220, 223, 235, 236, 243, 249, 251, 261, 263

348 *Index*

medical, 22, 47, 76, 192, 244, 296, 298, 300, 336

medical reason, 22, 245

medicine, 47, 57, 76, 281, 296, 298, 302, 306, 313, 324, 336

Mediterranean, 146, 184, 199, 200, 226, 267

membership, 24, 60, 193, 209, 262, 263, 267

Middle East, vii, xi, xiv, 1, 7, 8, 9, 23, 35, 40, 41, 45, 49, 51, 52, 84, 101, 103, 118, 127, 133, 135, 136, 138, 153, 154, 165, 174, 187, 213, 218, 225, 239, 241, 255, 256, 258, 259, 267, 286

military, vii, viii, ix, xi, xii, xiii, xiv, 2, 4, 6, 7, 8, 29, 32, 33, 34, 35, 36, 37, 39, 50, 52, 53, 54, 55, 56, 57, 58, 59, 60, 63, 64, 65, 71, 73, 76, 84, 87, 88, 89, 91, 93, 101, 102, 103, 106, 108, 111, 113, 115, 116, 120, 121, 123, 124, 128, 129, 130, 131,132, 139, 147, 148, 151, 152, 153, 156, 158, 161, 162, 164, 165, 172, 173, 175, 180, 189, 196, 197, 199, 200, 201, 203, 205, 213, 214, 216, 218, 219, 228, 234, 235, 236, 237, 238, 246, 247, 251, 252, 253, 254, 255, 257, 260, 261, 266, 268, 269, 271, 285, 293, 295, 298, 339, 340

military aid, xii, 85, 128, 148, 152, 201

military exercises, 203

military occupation, 180

military pressure, 269

military-to-military, 33

money laundering, 208, 209, 303, 307

Muslims, 29, 30, 32, 51, 54, 142, 174, 232, 233, 271

N

National Defense Authorization Act (NDAA), xv, 6, 38, 39, 58, 72, 74, 75, 111, 113, 120, 152, 153, 180, 205, 207, 214, 216, 246, 247, 248, 282, 285, 293, 303, 307, 313, 315, 318, 321, 324, 327, 329, 332, 338

national emergency, 281, 287, 319, 320, 321, 322, 332, 333, 334

national identity, xii, 157, 196

national interests, 289, 310

national security, ix, x, xiv, 2, 4, 7, 12, 27, 34, 52, 58, 68, 75, 79, 80, 88, 89, 95, 101, 102, 111, 114, 121, 122, 124, 152, 211, 213, 220, 240, 243, 286, 287, 290, 295, 296, 297, 298, 299, 300, 307, 308, 311, 312, 314, 315, 316, 317, 318

nationalism, 273

nationalists, 255, 271

nationality, 194

nuclear program, xvi, 3, 49, 50, 242, 278, 279, 284

Nuclear Regulatory Commission, 47

nuclear weapons, 45, 220, 284, 285, 294, 297

O

Obama Administration, 3, 6, 33, 34, 35, 36, 55, 71, 72, 73, 74, 84, 113, 151, 180

Obama, President Barack, xvii, 6, 8, 50, 61, 69, 72, 152, 265, 278, 287

oil, vii, viii, ix, 1, 2, 3, 11, 16, 17, 18, 25, 41, 42, 43, 44, 45, 63, 65, 79, 81, 86, 90, 104, 106, 107, 135, 199, 225, 242, 258, 259, 260, 282, 283

oil production, 18, 41, 86, 106

oil reserves, vii, ix, 1, 41, 44, 79

oil revenues, 11

operations, viii, xi, xiii, 2, 4, 6, 7, 18, 26, 29, 37, 39, 40, 53, 55, 56, 57, 58, 70, 74, 75, 76, 77, 85, 88, 93, 94, 101, 102, 108, 111, 113, 115, 116, 119, 129, 145, 152, 153, 158, 165, 173, 174, 175, 177, 183,

184, 188, 206, 216, 227, 234, 235, 252, 273, 274

opportunities, 8, 10, 33, 45, 63, 66, 102, 110, 122, 135, 225, 261, 283

oversight, viii, 2, 10, 56, 64, 73, 102, 103, 111, 233, 253

P

Palestinian Authority, 62, 143, 145, 146, 147, 261

parallel, viii, 2, 8, 23, 40, 42, 50, 60, 80, 118, 174

paramilitary forces, x, 88, 89

Pastor Brunson, xv, 214, 225, 242, 243, 244, 247, 250

peace, xi, 61, 113, 121, 127, 142, 143, 146, 161, 183, 184, 266, 336

personal autonomy, 23

personal communication, 281

petroleum, 40, 41, 281, 282, 283, 293, 295, 296, 297, 301, 320, 325, 326, 333

policy, ix, xiv, 2, 31, 49, 50, 57, 59, 60, 63, 64, 80, 119, 124, 158, 169, 173, 190, 195, 202, 221, 252, 257, 292, 301

policy initiative, ix, 80

policy issues, 64

policy options, 124

policymakers, xiii, 16, 158

political crisis, 163, 196

political disputes, xiii, 157

political force, xiii, 89, 123, 158, 188

political leaders, 102, 172

political participation, 10

political power, 218, 219

political system, 137, 166, 170

political uncertainty, 216

politics, vii, x, xi, xv, 4, 12, 58, 88, 90, 99, 101, 125, 127, 137, 160, 162, 188, 214, 220, 222, 269, 271

Popular Mobilization Forces (PMF), x, 88, 90, 95, 100, 101, 102, 103, 124

popular support, 187

population, xii, xiii, 8, 10, 11, 19, 60, 94, 107, 108, 130, 133, 140, 143, 144, 145, 157, 158, 160, 163, 175, 176, 190, 191, 194, 218, 227, 229, 260, 262, 267

presidency, xv, 160, 197, 214, 222, 265, 269, 272

primary sector, 196

private sector, 16, 18, 81, 110, 130, 136

private sector investment, 110

procurement, 110, 152, 237, 238, 294, 299, 306, 319, 338, 339

project, 145, 146, 147, 198, 226, 241, 254

proliferation, xvi, 154, 278, 283, 287, 290, 293, 299, 300, 308, 309, 310, 312, 314, 318, 319, 320, 327, 331, 336, 337, 338, 340

protection, ix, 39, 40, 77, 79, 160, 195, 232

protective role, 266

public concerns, 20

public debt, xii, 128, 133, 136, 166, 196, 198, 202

public education, 202

public figures, 21

public finance, 106

public health, 193

public interest, 264

public life, 24

public officials, 132

public opinion, 261

public schools, 149

public sector, 11, 18, 135, 202

public service, 166, 197, 202, 253

public-private partnerships, 198

purchasing power, 217

purchasing power parity, 217

350 *Index*

R

recognition, 60, 62, 130, 181, 261, 267
recommendations, iv, 16, 185
reconciliation, 60, 109
reconstruction, x, 26, 87, 89, 91, 109, 110, 121, 123, 195, 313
recovery, vii, x, 36, 87, 89, 112, 196
reelection, x, xv, 88, 89, 214, 269
refugee camps, 145, 175, 176, 179, 191
refugees, xiii, 61, 62, 130, 133, 135, 139, 140, 141, 144, 150, 158, 159, 161, 164, 165, 175, 176, 188, 190, 191, 192, 193, 194, 195, 196, 202, 251, 263, 264
regional instability, xvi, 135, 278
regulations, 24, 32, 192, 208, 209, 280, 290, 303, 304, 306, 331, 335
reinsurance, 281, 315, 328, 331
relief, xi, 52, 62, 81, 88, 93, 100, 116, 122, 279, 285, 290
religion, 19, 26, 230
religious sects, xiii, 157, 159
requirement, 38, 75, 76, 231, 286, 288, 290, 292, 293, 294, 296, 297, 298, 299, 300, 301, 302, 303, 304, 305, 306, 307, 308, 309, 310, 311, 312, 313, 314, 315, 316, 317, 318
reserves, vii, ix, 1, 5, 11, 18, 41, 44, 59, 79, 92, 198, 217, 266
resolution, 7, 61, 74, 75, 114, 119, 185, 187, 212, 230, 245, 263, 265, 266, 284
resources, ix, 16, 49, 50, 65, 79, 83, 107, 109, 135, 145, 153, 188, 199, 295, 296, 313, 320, 324, 325, 326
response, 8, 18, 20, 22, 43, 54, 74, 82, 97, 107, 109, 118, 137, 138, 163, 170, 180, 190, 219, 234, 244, 245, 246, 249, 263, 268
restrictions, vii, viii, xvi, 2, 19, 21, 23, 24, 32, 73, 75, 107, 131, 186, 192, 193, 206, 278, 283, 284, 286, 287, 290, 291, 297,

299, 301, 303, 304, 305, 306, 307, 313, 314, 315, 323, 333, 334, 340
revenue, 16, 18, 43, 45, 81, 106, 107, 136, 196, 220
rights, iv, viii, 2, 19, 20, 21, 23, 24, 50, 62, 80, 82, 85, 133, 143, 193, 199, 228, 230, 231, 263, 302, 304, 305, 306, 310, 312, 316, 317, 319, 322, 336
risk, ix, 2, 37, 39, 56, 58, 76, 80, 112, 119, 163, 175, 194, 212, 267
rule of law, 216, 220, 225, 248, 249
rules, 23, 24, 39, 72, 77, 82, 133, 216
rural areas, 94, 135
Russia, xiv, 42, 43, 45, 46, 48, 85, 86, 138, 139, 183, 189, 196, 199, 213, 214, 216, 220, 223, 225, 226, 227, 237, 238, 239, 240, 241, 246, 247, 248, 249, 254, 255, 257, 258, 266, 279

S

Safadi, Ayman, xii, 128, 148
safe haven, 94, 172, 173, 201, 206, 228, 260, 273
Salih, Barham, x, 88, 89, 97, 123
sanctions, vii, xiv, xv, xvi, xvii, 26, 31, 42, 43, 51, 82, 112, 120, 121, 122, 170, 207, 208, 209, 210, 211, 213, 214, 215, 216, 224, 233, 240, 242, 243, 245, 246, 250, 257, 259, 277, 278, 279, 280, 281, 282, 283, 284, 285, 286, 287, 288, 290, 291, 293, 295, 296, 297, 298, 299, 301, 302, 303, 304, 305, 306, 307, 308, 309, 310, 311, 312, 314, 315, 316, 317, 318, 319, 321, 322, 327, 328, 329, 330, 331, 332, 334, 335, 337, 339, 340
Saudi Arabia, v, vii, viii, ix, xii, 1, 2, 3, 5, 6, 7, 8, 9, 10, 12, 14, 15, 16, 17, 18, 19, 20, 21, 22, 23, 24, 25, 26, 27, 28, 29, 30, 31, 32, 33, 34, 35, 36, 37, 38, 39, 40, 41, 42, 43, 44, 45, 46, 47, 48, 49, 50, 51, 52, 53,

54, 55, 56, 57, 59, 60, 61, 62, 63, 64,65, 66, 68, 69, 71, 72, 73, 74, 76, 77, 79, 81, 84, 85, 122, 128, 129, 137, 164, 169, 179, 189, 197, 198, 203, 256

Saudi military, viii, 2, 6, 35, 37, 55, 56

savings, 33, 225

school, 9, 138, 145, 187, 190, 219, 269

scope, ix, 3, 16, 54, 80, 110, 185, 330, 334, 340

secondary education, 270

Secretary of Defense, 38, 77, 152, 153, 154, 207, 246, 247, 248, 252, 279, 285

Secretary of Homeland Security, 324

Secretary of the Treasury, 170, 282, 285, 291, 303, 304, 313, 319, 323

secularism, 230, 232

security, viii, ix, x, xi, xiii, xv, 2, 3, 7, 8, 9, 11, 16, 20, 21, 25, 26, 27, 28, 29, 32, 33, 34, 39, 40, 49, 50, 52, 53, 55, 58, 61, 63, 64, 65, 73, 79, 80, 83, 87, 88, 89, 90, 93, 94, 96, 102, 103, 104, 106, 107, 110, 111, 112, 113, 114, 116, 117, 120, 122, 124, 125, 129, 132, 139, 148, 153, 155, 158, 165, 172, 173, 175, 176, 179, 181, 182, 183, 184, 187, 188, 194, 200, 201, 202, 204, 205, 207, 214, 219, 228, 229, 236, 237, 245, 251, 253, 255, 257, 260, 262, 264, 273, 274, 295, 311, 317, 336

security assistance, xi, 52, 73, 88, 93, 111, 116, 120, 122, 148, 184, 200, 202, 205

security forces, viii, xi, 2, 7, 11, 20, 25, 26, 63, 67, 80, 88, 90, 93, 95, 96, 102, 103, 104, 107, 111, 113, 114, 139, 152, 154, 174, 205, 219, 253, 260, 273

security guard, 245

security services, 173

security threats, 11, 29, 50

Senate, 7, 33, 34, 37, 38, 47, 48, 49, 56, 69, 71, 72, 74, 75, 77, 85, 111, 112, 116, 129, 165, 205, 206, 210, 235, 245, 247, 248, 249, 250, 252, 265, 275, 276

Senate Foreign Relations Committee, 37, 47, 48, 49, 56, 71, 73, 74, 75, 77, 235, 250

services, iv, viii, 2, 24, 37, 38, 49, 74, 118, 135, 166, 187, 193, 196, 197, 208, 211, 246, 280, 281, 289, 295, 298, 299, 300, 302, 303, 308, 310, 313, 315, 323, 325, 326, 327, 328, 329, 331, 332, 334, 335, 336, 338, 339, 340

Shia Muslim, xii, 25, 51, 157, 161, 174

social change, ix, 2, 82

social contract, 135

social policy, 83

social services, 193, 209

socialism, 273

society, 15, 19, 20, 130, 162, 172, 173, 251, 261

solution, 6, 56, 61, 62, 85, 133, 143, 144, 176, 196, 267

state control, 102

state of emergency, 222, 223, 229

strategic cooperation, vii, 1, 216, 233

strategic position, 237

suicide, 7, 28, 174, 175

suicide attacks, 174

suicide bombers, 175

Sunni Islamist extremist terrorism, vii, 1

Sunni Muslim, xii, 29, 54, 134, 157, 160, 161, 218, 233

Syria, xi, xii, xiii, xiv, 3, 8, 9, 25, 27, 28, 29, 32, 50, 51, 52, 53, 59, 63, 84, 86, 94, 95, 104, 113, 116, 127, 128, 129, 133, 138, 139, 140, 141, 143, 145, 150, 153, 154, 155, 158, 159, 160, 161, 162, 164, 165, 172, 173, 174, 175, 176, 177, 178, 179, 180, 181, 182, 183, 188, 189, 190, 192, 194, 195, 196, 197, 199, 200, 204, 205, 207, 212, 213, 214, 216, 228, 229, 233, 235, 241, 248, 251, 252, 253, 254, 255, 256, 257, 258, 259, 261, 264, 273, 285, 287, 306, 318, 322, 324, 336, 337, 340

352 *Index*

Syria conflict, xiv, 158, 172, 173, 178, 179, 197, 201

T

technology, ix, xvi, 6, 36, 40, 56, 73, 74, 79, 224, 237, 239, 241, 248, 278, 284, 288, 292, 293, 294, 295, 296, 298, 299, 302, 305, 306, 307, 325, 326, 332, 335, 340
technology transfer, 40, 239
telecommunications, 163, 188
tensions, xi, xiv, 3, 26, 88, 90, 93, 212, 213, 216, 228, 234, 235, 243, 246, 247, 253, 262, 267, 268
territorial, 104, 113, 117, 181, 232, 239, 254
territorial control, 104
territory, x, 48, 55, 87, 89, 113, 130, 142, 177, 181, 211, 228, 233, 234, 235, 236, 252, 254, 260, 267, 273
terrorism, vii, xvi, 1, 11, 19, 20, 24, 30, 31, 32, 34, 59, 60, 62, 65, 68, 70, 83, 85, 164, 176, 201, 206, 210, 215, 228, 272, 278, 284, 285, 286, 287, 288, 289, 290, 295, 298, 300, 302, 303, 304, 307, 308, 309, 310, 312, 317, 318, 320, 335, 337, 340
terrorist activities, 211
terrorist acts, 290
terrorist attack, 7, 25, 26, 31, 40, 139, 141, 229
terrorist groups, 7, 31, 32, 63, 70, 102, 165, 172, 194, 201, 206, 207, 244
terrorist organization, 23, 27, 32, 102, 112, 116, 120, 205, 211, 261, 268, 303
threats, ix, xi, 2, 3, 11, 27, 29, 31, 37, 52, 53, 54, 55, 57, 60, 79, 97, 107, 113, 127, 154, 164, 202, 204, 231, 255, 259, 286
Tillerson, Rex W., xii, 128, 148
Title I, 285, 286, 300, 316
trade, xvi, xvii, 41, 133, 135, 139, 212, 225, 242, 255, 259, 261, 262, 263, 267, 277, 278, 279, 280, 281, 282, 283, 284, 289, 296, 298, 306, 307, 313, 314, 317, 323, 332, 334
training, xi, 3, 10, 33, 34, 35, 36, 56, 63, 65, 73, 88, 93, 110, 111, 113, 114, 152, 153, 154, 173, 175, 179, 189, 203, 206, 211, 239, 247, 253, 273, 292
transactions, 31, 208, 240, 280, 281, 282, 290, 291, 297, 298, 299, 300, 302, 303, 307, 308, 309, 310, 311, 312, 313, 314, 315, 320, 321, 322, 323, 324, 327, 328, 329, 330, 332, 333, 334, 335, 337, 338, 339
transformation, ix, 2, 65, 82, 99, 218
Treasury, 179, 180, 242, 243, 279, 280, 285, 286, 290, 291, 300, 303, 304, 319, 320, 321, 322, 323, 332, 333
Trump Administration, viii, ix, xi, xv, 1, 2, 3, 6, 9, 47, 48, 51, 53, 62, 73, 74, 79, 82, 83, 84, 85, 88, 90, 93, 97, 109, 110, 112, 113, 114, 115, 118, 119, 133, 143, 146, 165, 214, 215, 234
Trump, President Donald, xii, xvi, 3, 6, 9, 27, 33, 35, 36, 37, 50, 51, 59, 61, 74, 85, 111, 128, 129, 143, 149, 201, 240, 242, 243, 244, 259, 265, 277, 278, 287, 291
Turkey, v, vii, xiv, xv, 82, 104, 107, 145, 154, 165, 191, 194, 213, 214, 215, 216, 217, 218, 219, 220, 221, 222, 223, 224, 225, 226, 227, 228, 229, 230, 231, 232, 233, 234, 235, 236, 237, 238, 239, 240, 241, 242, 243, 244, 245, 246, 247, 248, 249, 250, 251, 252, 253, 254, 255, 256, 257, 258, 259, 260, 261, 262, 263, 264, 265, 266, 267, 268, 269, 270, 271, 272, 273, 274, 275, 283
Turkey-Israel tensions, xiv, 213
Turkey-Russia cooperation, xiv, 213
Turks, 217, 219, 225, 228, 229, 232, 233, 241, 243, 244, 255, 261, 271

U

U.N. High Commissioner for Refugees (UNHCR), xiii, 140, 158, 190, 191, 192, 195, 196

U.N. Security Council, xvi, 52, 53, 55, 84, 161, 163, 182, 184, 185, 187, 201, 278, 279, 284, 303, 306, 312

U.S. arms sales, viii, 1, 34, 73, 84, 237

U.S. assistance, xiii, xiv, 34, 58, 112, 114, 124, 129, 149, 155, 158, 164, 200, 202, 204, 300

U.S. Department of Commerce, 40

U.S. Department of the Treasury, 207, 228, 279, 331, 334

U.S. Export-Import Bank, 293

U.S. Geological Survey, 199

U.S. history, 65

U.S. military forces, xi, 56, 88, 91

U.S. policy, xiii, xvi, 8, 23, 50, 63, 103, 129, 133, 158, 164, 165, 174, 210, 265, 278

U.S. sanctions, xiv, xvii, 42, 43, 120, 122, 209, 213, 216, 224, 245, 278, 279, 282, 290, 331, 334, 337

U.S. Treasury, 208

U.S.-Jordanian relations, vii, xi, 127, 133

U.S.-Turkey relations, xiv, 213, 215, 216, 225, 233, 241, 242, 246, 259

United Kingdom, xvi, 266, 278, 283

United Nations, xvi, 37, 57, 60, 84, 90, 91, 105, 109, 134, 140, 141, 161, 162, 175, 181, 183, 184, 185, 190, 206, 220, 266, 267, 278, 312, 318, 324

United States, vii, viii, ix, x, xi, xii, xiii, xiv, xv, xvi, xvii, 2, 3, 5, 8, 9, 19, 26, 27, 29, 31, 35, 37, 41, 45, 47, 48, 49, 50, 51, 52, 55, 56, 58, 60, 61, 63, 70, 71, 75, 76, 79, 82, 88, 90, 91, 93, 95, 96, 97, 101, 103, 104, 112, 113, 114, 115, 116, 118, 119, 123, 124, 127, 128, 129, 130, 133, 138, 143, 147, 148, 149, 151, 152, 154, 156, 158, 161, 162, 164, 165, 170, 184, 185, 194, 198, 200, 202, 203, 208, 212, 213, 214, 215, 216, 218, 222, 230, 233, 234, 235, 236, 237, 240, 241, 242, 243, 244, 246, 247, 248, 249, 250, 253, 254, 255, 257, 259, 260, 261, 266, 277, 278, 280, 281, 282, 283, 284, 286, 287, 288, 289, 297, 298, 300, 301, 302, 307, 308, 310, 311, 312, 314, 315, 318, 319, 322, 323, 324, 334, 335, 337, 340

urban, 132, 135, 140, 145, 191, 223, 227

urban areas, 132, 140, 191

V

Vice President, 117, 143, 144, 245

violence, xiii, 25, 26, 55, 103, 117, 121, 157, 163, 165, 192, 198, 229, 230, 231, 233, 242, 245, 251, 262, 274

violent crime, 245

violent extremist, 50, 116

vote, 24, 34, 72, 106, 167, 170, 185, 188, 220, 231, 234, 263, 265, 272, 273

voters, 24, 95, 104

voting, 97, 104, 170, 197, 215

W

waiver, 7, 26, 34, 121, 193, 208, 211, 240, 280, 287, 288, 292, 293, 295, 300, 301, 307, 308, 309, 313, 314, 315, 325, 327, 328, 329, 330, 331

war, xiii, 7, 37, 51, 52, 56, 57, 62, 84, 110, 131, 138, 158, 159, 161, 162, 163, 173, 180, 181, 182, 183, 189, 190, 197, 234, 262, 267, 273

water, 44, 46, 57, 96, 118, 124, 135, 142, 145, 146, 147, 149, 150, 197, 202, 260

weapons, viii, xvi, 2, 35, 36, 41, 55, 56, 63, 77, 132, 152, 153, 173, 179, 182, 183,

185, 188, 189, 204, 238, 249, 275, 277, 278, 287, 288, 290, 294, 298, 299, 302, 312, 319

weapons and missile development, xvi, 277

weapons of mass destruction, 152, 153, 302, 319

Western countries, 230, 267

Western Europe, 263

Western orientation, 241

White House, 38, 61, 72, 97, 129, 146, 243, 244, 265, 279

World Bank, 137, 196, 197, 198, 209, 217, 223, 250

Y

Yemen, viii, 2, 3, 4, 6, 7, 8, 9, 27, 28, 29, 34, 35, 37, 38, 39, 50, 51, 52, 53, 54, 55, 56, 57, 58, 59, 63, 72, 73, 74, 75, 76, 77, 84, 336

Related Nova Publications

QATAR: POLITICAL, ECONOMIC AND SOCIAL ISSUES

EDITOR: Haitham M. Alkhateeb, PhD

SERIES: Politics and Economics of the Middle East

BOOK DESCRIPTION: *Qatar: Political, Economic and Social Issues* is organized into three main themes – political, economic and social issues – that are suitable as a reference work for advanced undergraduate and postgraduate students and scholars actively researching in this area.

HARDCOVER ISBN: 978-1-53615-221-0
RETAIL PRICE: $230

IRAN: ECONOMIC, POLITICAL AND NUCLEAR POLICIES

EDITOR: Everett Fowler

SERIES: Politics and Economics of the Middle East

BOOK DESCRIPTION: Since the Islamic Revolution in Iran in 1979, the United States and Iran have been estranged and at odds. During the 1980s and 1990s, U.S. officials identified Iran's support for militant Middle East groups as the primary threat posed by Iran to U.S. interests and allies.

HARDCOVER ISBN: 978-1-53614-827-5
RETAIL PRICE: $230

To see a complete list of Nova publications, please visit our website at www.novapublishers.com

Related Nova Publications

THE AFGHAN WAR OF 1879-80

AUTHOR: Howard Hensman

SERIES: Politics and Economics of the Middle East

BOOK DESCRIPTION: This book, originally published in 1882, is comprised of a series of letters written from the field of the Second Anglo-Afghan War. The author was a correspondent of the Pioneer (the second oldest English language newspaper in India) and the only journalist to accompany the Anglo-Indian field forces on their march through Afghanistan. The letters offer a firsthand account of the war from a British perspective.

HARDCOVER ISBN: 978-1-53613-686-9
RETAIL PRICE: $310

YEMEN: ISSUES AND CHALLENGES OF THE 21ST CENTURY

EDITOR: Tobias Steinar

SERIES: Politics and Economics of the Middle East

BOOK DESCRIPTION: The authors aim to illustrate the vicious circle of poverty and make some recommendations that could play a role in breaking the cycle of poverty by equity and efficiency of the Islamic inspiration.

SOFTCOVER ISBN: 978-1-53613-658-6
RETAIL PRICE: $82

To see a complete list of Nova publications, please visit our website at www.novapublishers.com

Related Nova Publications

INTERNAL CONFLICT REGIONS IN THE MIDDLE EAST: IRAQ AND SYRIA

EDITOR: Dana V. Gray

SERIES: Politics and Economics of the Middle East

BOOK DESCRIPTION: This book discusses the political, and internal conflicts of both Iraq and Syria. It provides information on the politics, governance, and human rights in Iraq; an overview of armed conflict in Syria, as well as the United States response; and an overview of the humanitarian response in Syria as well.

HARDCOVER ISBN: 978-1-63321-259-6
RETAIL PRICE: $140

ECONOMIC AND SOCIAL ISSUES IN THE MIDDLE EAST AND NORTH AFRICAN COUNTRIES

EDITOR: Nilgün Cil Yavuz, MD

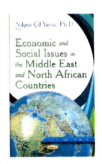

SERIES: Politics and Economics of the Middle East

BOOK DESCRIPTION: The main aim of this book is to shed light on the main economic, social and political problems and characteristics of MENA economies by considering the latest in the global and regional turmoil.

HARDCOVER ISBN: 978-1-62948-152-4
RETAIL PRICE: $179

To see a complete list of Nova publications, please visit our website at www.novapublishers.com